The Special Branch

The British Spy Novel, 1890-1980

LeRoy L. Panek

Bowling Green University Popular Press
Bowling Green, Ohio 43403

124680

FOR ALEX

CONTENTS

Preface

MOST OF US have never met a real spy; as far as I know I have not. Yet for the past eighty years a large group of us has read a mountain of fiction about spies. Popular from its inception in the late 1890s, the spy novel has, in recent years, enjoyed unrivaled popularity. Individual spy novels sell appreciably better than individual detective books, or love romances, or gothics, or science fiction books. Scarcely a week goes by without at least one spy title appearing in the best seller lists, and people who would be hard pressed to name an individual detective story writer know all about books by Ludlum or LeCarré.

In spite of this wide popularity, neither the critical nor the academic community has expressed much interest in the evolution or the craft of the spy novel. I can tick off on one hand the books which deal, even tangentially, with spy fiction. While we are going through something of a boom in the study of detective fiction, the spy novel, obscurred in the catch-all category of "mystery fiction," has remained an unknown country. In part this neglect of the spy story comes from outright snobbery in academic and critical circles which see any kind of adventure fiction as inferior, and praise the somewhat dubious claims of the detective story to intellectual respectability. Partly, though, our ignorance of spy fiction comes from more concrete causes. First of all, no one knows much about where the spy novel came from or how it developed. Although spy fiction does not have a seminal figure like Poe to whom people can point and say "The spy novel begins with this respected literary figure," it does have a separate literary development as well as its own set of changing conventions, which, once known, will open avenues for further exploration and generate critical handles for other spy writers. Equally formidable, the spy novel is an intimidating subject simply because it is so huge an area. There are many unclassified and undiscussed spy books and spy writers. But what does one do when faced with writers like Oppenheim, LeQueux and Horler, each of whom literally wrote hundreds of novels, most of which are nauseatingly bad, but some of which are historically important? We simply cannot dismiss them out of hand, but even people interested in popular fiction should not be condemned to read the millions of words written by these mealy-mouthed incompetents. Finally, the spy novel causes apoplexy in literary purists, because it is so often a mixed form. While spy novels do remain distinct from other popular genres in that they deal with international intrigue, they often slide over into the territory of the detective story, or the love romance, or the gangster book, or the treasure hunt tale.

As you can imagine, these are the straw men which I intend to knock down, or at least cause to wobble, in what follows. Skipping over Cooper's *The Spy*, which has no real impact on modern spy fiction, I am going to provide a peek at the spy novel as it has been written from the 1890s to the present. To do this I have had to make countless compromises. First, while acknowledging that the spy story exists in other forms and in other countries, I have decided to tackle only spy novels written by British authors. Also, I have left out discussion of Conrad's and Maugham's spy books: *The Secret Agent, Under Western Eyes* and *Ashenden* are certainly important books, but there exists plenty of competent criticism of them for readers to look at and I wish to pay attention to lesser known writers. I have, further, left out any number of important British spy writers from detailed consideration—Val Williams, William Haggard, Ken Follett and Ted Allbeury, to name only a few. I am not quite writing a tight literary history and have had to draw lines somewhere. In what follows I discuss seventeen of the most important or representative British spy novelists. With these men, I have attempted to present some basic literary analysis and criticism, trying both to place them in historical perspective and to describe and analyze the content and form of their fiction. While I have no wish to daze readers with recondite and abstruse literary approaches, I did not write the following as simply an *aficionado*'s handbook. There will be few plot summaries, and no hero-worshiping biographies of fictional characters. Now, all of this sounds foreboding, but I did not write this book as a joyless experience, either for myself or for readers. The spy novel as a medium is not often entirely purposeful and serious. Many spy books came from writers who wrote either to amuse themselves or to make money or both, and it is at least partly mistaken to treat them altogether seriously. I have tried to take the spy novel as I found it— as a half-serious, half-diversionary medium. Further, although I have tried to cover the same basic information about all seventeen writers, I have allowed myself some leeway in organizing the chapters. With Greene, for instance, I have organized by book instead of by idea, and have concentrated on Greene's use of detective conventions in his spy books, because this seemed to be a more fruitful approach than that which I have taken to more popular writers.

I have taken up the subject of the spy novel for several reasons. First, I stumbled across it in writing my book on the detective story between the wars. In this connection, I found that one cannot begin to understand modern detective fiction without trying to unravel the tangle of "thrillers" written in the teens and twenties. Separating out the spy novel is a first step in this direction. Secondly, I discovered that the spy novel provides hours of diverting, amusing and even interesting reading, and that it occasionally has something important to say about the human estate. I would like others to realize this, too. I have taken up the subject of the spy novel also out of the conviction that serious, or studious people ought to pay at least a bit of attention to popular literature. *Greenmantle* may not be as important a book or as good a book as *To the Lighthouse*, but it has been read by infinitely more people than Woolf's novel, and it does attempt to show them literary craftsmanship and to touch their lives. We ought to recognize and understand this. Finally, I have written this book because it has, like the spy novel itself, been amusing and diverting to do so. This book aside, I think that we would be a lot better off if more writers were amused and diverted by their endeavors.

I would like to extend my thanks to the National Endowment for the Humanities which provided me with a Summer Stipend to work on parts of this project. Thanks, too, to Barton Whaley who gave me some helpful leads. I owe much to the tireless and ingenious help of Carol Quinn, Reference Librarian at Western Maryland College, and to Crystal Bellinger who carped about some things until I got them right and who typed portions of the manuscript. Finally, for my wife, who does not especially like to allow spy books in the house, I will do the next one for you.

Westminster, Maryland
June, 1981

Chapter 1
William LeQueux
(1864-1927)

TODAY IT TAKES a determined will and a high tolerance for unrefined and unmitigated twaddle to get through many books by William LeQueux or E. Phillips Oppenheim. If we hope to understand the British spy novel, to say nothing of the love romance or the detective novel, however, we have to plough through their writing. They were the first British writers to begin to explore the form of the detective novel (as opposed to the detective short story), and they were the first writers to write consistently about espionage. Without LeQueux or Oppenheim to react against and remake we never would have had Conrad's spy novels, to say nothing of the spy novels of John Buchan and his followers. But today they seem silly, inept and warped.

Both Oppenheim and LeQueux were rooted in the 1890s: actually Oppy began writing in the 80s with *Expiation* (1887), but he did not hit stride until the 90s, while LeQueux began his career with *Guilty Bonds* in 1891. Together they flogged out a monstrous amount of fiction, well over one hundred novels apiece, with Oppenheim writing five novels a year, and with LeQueux cranking out eight novels in his good years. Neither man wrote spy novels exclusively or even primarily. They turned out mysteries, love romances, finance romances, political novels and gangster stories *a la* Edgar Wallace, as well as spy books. LeQueux and Oppenheim carried to extinction certain trends in late Victorian fiction. They inherited and passed on many motifs from the "Sensation Novelists," Wilkie Collins, Charles Reade, Mrs. Henry Wood and Sheridan LeFanu. The gothic and occult atmosphere, the grotesque villainy and the emotion-blocked secrets of the Sensation Novelists come in to both writers. LeQueux's handling of mysteries brought Wilkie Collins to the minds of contemporary reviewers,[1] and Oppenheim's *A Daughter of Astrea* (1998) is patently a copy of *The Moonstone* by a less competent writer. Both LeQueux and Oppenheim pointed their fiction at the new, large lower-middle class female audience developed by the newly-invented circulating libraries, and by writers of the love romance like Charlotte Yonge, Rhoda Broughton and Ouida. Lady typists were one of Oppenheim's favorite character types. LeQueux repeatedly takes his readers into lush drawing rooms and off to fancy foreign resorts to show them the worlds which they would never see in person. As the heroine of LeQueux's *The Bond of Black* (1899) puts it: "I used to be envious when you wrote telling me of the sunshine and flowers you had on the Riviera. It must be a perfect Paradise. I should like to go there and spend a winter."[2] Later in the same novel, the hero points out the central fantasy with which LeQueux hopes to hook his readers:

"Are you happy in that low-class drapery place, where you are compelled to dance attendance on the wives of city clerks, and are treated with contempt by them because they think it a sign of good breeding to show capriciousness, and give you all the unnecessary trouble possible? In their eyes—in the eyes of those around you—you are only a 'shop girl,' but in mine, Muriel ... you are a queen—a woman fitted to be my wife."[3]

The appeal to the shop girl or the typist, the obsession with depicting the High Life, and the stereotyped characters of the self-sacrificing woman, the cad and the spotless hero which we find so often in LeQueux and Oppenheim all come from the Victorian love romance.

From Conan Doyle both writers got the impulse toward the detective novel. His inventor, although he tried four times, could never successfully extend Sherlock Holmes over the course of a novel: the real detective novel did not begin until after the First World War. LeQueux and Oppenheim, however, made numerous stabs at writing detective novels without achieving much. When LeQueux creates detective figures, as in *The Red Room* (1909), they look very much like Sherlock Holmes, but have none of his efficiency and lack his remarkable eccentricities.

Both writers pad out obvious detective problems with sentimental claptrap. Their combinations of bits of detective stories with gobs from the love story and the Sensation Novel, however, sold, and LeQueux and Oppenheim turned out their pseudo-detective novels with such ease and unconcern for probity that younger writers' reactions against their hopelessly slipshod books did much to produce the "Golden Age" of the detective story after the First World War. Indeed, LeQueux's incessant bunging in of "unknown poisons" whenever he needed to patch up a plot is, in itself, enough to convince the most pedestrian of readers that they can do much better in the line of detective writing than LeQueux could.

These elements contribute to LeQueux's and Oppenheim's spy

figures, but they hardly created them. For the elements which organize and prompt these writers to try spy fiction we need to look elsewhere. Both LeQueux and Oppenheim felt the paranoia of Empire at its apogee. The French and the Germans in Africa, the Boers in South Africa, the Russians sniffing around in Afghanistan: everyone was sniping away at the Empire, and no one in government seemed to be doing much about it. In response, Oppenheim and, even more LeQueux, turned to a new sort of fiction which appeared in the 1870s and 1880s. George Chesney's *The Battle of Dorking* (1871) introduced the war prophecy novel. These war prophecy books fueled national paranoia by depicting future contests in which modern, mechanized armies and navies crushed the ill-prepared defenders of Albion. These war prophecy novels, of course, argued for practical military reform in England, but they also introduced elements (the secret weapon, the role of the spy, etc.) necessary for the evolution of the spy novel.

The Franco-Prussian War, so argues I.F. Clarke in *Voices Prophesying War,* gave birth to the war prophecy movement, but it also added another event necessary for the start of the spy novel in Oppenheim and LeQueux—the Dreyfus case. In December 1894 a court martial convicted Alfred Dreyfus of spying against France for the Germans. The international furor over this verdict culminated in Zola's "J'Accuse" early in 1898, as well as the novelist's flight to England. Dreyfus added just what LeQueux and Oppenheim needed to bring them to the spy novel: a hot public issue and a figure of great sentimental potential. The connection of the Dreyfus case and the spy novel was not lost on contemporary reviewers. Thus, in reviews of one of LeQueux's novels we get critics saying that "the subject of international espionage and the possibilities of secret service have been suggested to novelists by the Dreyfus case."[4] and that "the Dreyfus case has probably inspired the author."[5] Responding to this particular issue, therefore, the writers scraped up some material from the Dreyfus case and tossed it together with some old motifs, and with *The Mysterious Mr. Sabin* (1898) and *The Day of Temptation* (1899) they concocted the spy novel—of sorts.

If we are to believe LeQueux's vapid "Official Biography" by Norman Sladen, *The Real LeQueux* (1938), the author was a sort of latter-day Jos Sedley, collecting tin-pot royalty from the nether regions of Europe and scooping up decorations from them to pin on his formal clothes. Sladen boasts that LeQueux was a genuine, bottled-in-bond spy himself; but that his missions were too dreadfully hush-hush for detailed publication. Whatever the truth of LeQueux's life—and Sladen gives virtually no insight into it—the real LeQueux was an industrious, but hardly talented, newspaper writer and a tireless inventor of extremely tiresome fictions. Steinbrunner and Penzler tell us that LeQueux "...wrote ... espionage stories and novels that anticipated every development in that form until the works of Eric Ambler."[6] Poppycock: if he invents things it is usually by accident and not design, and the inventions lose their force because they are embedded in such sentimental drivel and are communicated with little skill. If LeQueux is significant for the spy novel, it is because he, with Oppenheim, made the form popular and because writers as diverse as Graham Greene and Peter Cheyney allude to him as an example of the fake, old-fashioned spy yarn.

After an initial foray into the novel of political intrigue with *Guilty Bonds* (1891), LeQueux took up the war prophecy book, a genre admirably described in I.F. Clark's book cited above. LeQueux's *The Great War in England in 1897* (1893) appeared in serial form in *Answers*, and twenty years after *The Daily Mail* spent a great deal of time and money promoting the serial version of his *The Invasion of 1910*. These pseudo-histories are much like the numerous war prophecy books which appeared in the 1890s, in which Russia, France, Germany or combinations of the same invade Britain, only to be repulsed at the last moment by some god out of the machine. Looking back toward Chesney's *The Battle of Dorking*, LeQueux's prophecy novels include all the standard features. They are, first of all, arguments for military preparedness—Lord Roberts wrote an introduction for the book version of *The Great War* and seconded its political message. They turn on the absence of the British fleet, they draw readers by local, geographic references (the *Daily Mail* printed maps for the serial version of *The Invasion of 1910* so that readers could gage the fictional enemy's approaches to their homes), and they include two other elements vital for the development of spy fiction. Like his fellow prophets (H.G. Wells in *The War of the Worlds* is the ultimate example), LeQueux works the secret weapon into his books. In *The Great War* the Russians threaten to destroy Edinburgh with a terrible new weapon—bombs dropped from a gas-filled balloon—but they are thwarted by the pneumatic dynamite gun invented by an independent Scots mechanic. More important, in *The Great War* LeQueux introduces, amid the over-riding concerns of fake military history, a small espionage plot in which a naive young Englishman shows a draft treaty to a Russian spy and in which the author draws a brief history of the spy, Count von Beilstein, whom the Russians have blackmailed into acting as their agent. Neither of these things ıeceives much attention in *The Great War*: the secret weapon occupies only one of the many episodes, and LeQueux mishandles and truncates the spy business. They did, however, provide him with elements to expand upon and he uses them, especially the tragic personal history of the spy, once the Dreyfus case made espionage a hot topic for popular fiction.

No one in his right mind would want to drag through the course of all of LeQueux's novels, or even his spy novels. They bog down too often in the worst brand of Victorian sentiment, and they spin mysteries out of airy nothings. Two are sufficient to give readers a taste of the real LeQueux, one from early in the writer's career and one from late in it.

Behind the Throne (1905) gives us a representative example of early LeQueux. First of all, the title hints that this book will give us secret, inside information: many of LeQueux's books, like *Society Intrigues I Have Known* (1920), in fact, try to attract the reader solely interested in juicy gossip. The issues in *Behind the Throne* involve political hanky-panky in Italy, thereby implying by the foreign setting (which he also uses in *The Day of Temptation*) that British governments can never be charged with this sort of corruption. The story line follows the fortunes of Camillo Morini, the Italian Minister of War. Through the conniving of his crooked assistant, Angelo Borselli, as well as because of the impossible financial demands of his office, Morini becomes involved in peculation, skimming bribes from War Office contracts. With the help of Jules Dubard, a millionaire French playboy and secret agent, the sinister Borselli plans with the socialists in Italy's parliament to unseat Morini and assume the War Ministry himself. But there are complications. First, Dubard falls in love with the Minister's daughter, Mary, and she promises to marry him if Dubard saves her father's position. Then there is George MacBean, the secretary of aristocratic background who has been forced to take a position with a particularly boorish, *nouveau riche* British M.P.; MacBean's pulses throb for Mary Morini who, likewise, vibrates in his presence. Amid all this, LeQueux introduces Captain Solaro, an Italian officer jailed for ostensibly selling the secret plans of Italy's frontier defenses to France. Finally, he seeds throughout the novel the mystery of General Sazarac's death: people literally stammer and quiver whenever anyone mentions the Sazarac affair, but we do not find out anything about it until the very end of the book.

If you find this summary tiresome, it represents only the skeleton without the messy viscera and flabby skin found in the novel itself. Typical LeQueux elements abound in *Behind the*

Throne. Everyone, it seems, has a dreadful secret to withhold from others: Morini has his peculation, Mary has her selfless promise of marriage, Dubard and Broselli have their shenanigans with the French and Italian governments, MacBean knows something about the Sazarac business, and so does Solaro. No one, though, wants to cough up the truth until the final chapter when Solaro descends out of the blue, released from prison by an amnesty, and unravels the truth about Dubard and Borselli having killed General Sazarac and sold the plans for Italy's defenses to France. Once this key secret comes out, all the other secrets pop open, the Minister retires with honor, and George and Mary fall into each other's arms. Thus, we have the secret, the mystery organization revealing the facts only at the end, and the *deus ex machina* so beloved by LeQueux in both his detective novels and his spy novels. We also have the tempter-temptee relationship of which he was very fond. In *In White Raiment* (1900), which is not a spy book, the narrator identifies one of the characters only as "The Tempter." There is, of course, LeQueux's earlier spy book, *The Day of Temptation,* and he includes a chapter in *Behind the Throne,* entitled "The Path of the Tempter," in which Dubard lures Mary to sacrifice herself to gain her father's safety. Dwelling upon the tempter theme, which we can follow through LeQueux's novels from the 1890s through the 1920s, not only suits the books' general background in the love romance, but, in the same line of literary development, indicates the secularized religious overtones which appear throughout the books. This last item we can see not only in the tempter theme and in the fact that *The Bond of Black* (1899) revolves around thwarting a cult of satanists, but we also find religious echoes in many of LeQueux's titles like *Whoso Findeth A Wife* (1897), *If Sinners Entice Thee* (1898) or *As We Forgave Them* (1904). This, too, LeQueux inserted in his novels because he expected his readers to be the same group that read the love romance.

In *Behind the Throne* LeQueux summons up his main impetus toward the spy novel, the Dreyfus case. Here Captain Solaro is unjustly convicted of passing military secrets to the enemy, he is shipped off to an island penal colony to do his time, and he is finally vindicated at the end, exposing along the way chicanery in high places. If this general parallel is not enough, LeQueux has Mary Morini drive it home by saying, "It is a vile, despicable conspiracy which has sent to prison in disgrace an innocent man—a second case of Dreyfus."[7]

What espionage that exists in *Behind the Throne* exists to provide the basis for the mystery, which resolves the characters' problems which stem largely from human and not political situations, and, as such, is only of technical interest. LeQueux does, however, pay a bit of attention to the mechanics of spying through the minor character of Filomena. Filomena does Borselli's dirty work of framing Solaro and searching the British M.P.'s house for secret papers. Here we have an instance of an agent working in ignorance of her control's sinister motives. Thus, when Filomena becomes inquisitive, Borselli shuts her up by telling her that, "If you render secret service to the Ministry you must never reason as to the why or the wherefore. Always rest assured that we are acting solely for the benefit and safety of Italy."[8] LeQueux, generally, in the early novels sees foreign secret agents as pawns of evil ministers—as Filomena serves Borselli or as Gemma Fanetti serves Montelupo in *The Day of Temptation*—while secret servants of the British Crown, like Kershaw Kirk in *The Red Room* (1911) serve a government which runs exclusively upon proper principles. Also LeQueux tries to give his audience information about the nature of secret agents and the organizations in which they operate. In the early novels there are two types of secret agents, both of which we can find in *The Day of Temptation*. First, there is the super spy who saves his country from disaster. Thus Dr. Malvano is "...a fearless man of marvelous resource and activity—a man who has, in the past, obtained knowledge of secrets which has passed credence."[9] The second type is the unwilling agent who acts as a spy because of some sort of blackmail or other duplicity. In *The Day of Temptation,* Gemma Fanetti fills this role:

"You became a spy?"
"Yes," she answered hoarsely. "I became a mean, despicable traitor, a wretched, soul tortured woman, whose denunciations caused the arrest and imprisonment of the most dangerous members of the gang...."[10]

There are also a few straightforward agents like Filomena, and the German agent in *The Red Room*, but, by and large LeQueux underplays these types as they have, for him, little emotional potential.

On the prophecy level, LeQueux tries to inform the British public about secret services in the rest of the world. Thus, in *Behind the Throne* Borselli gives Filomena this bit of gratuitous information:

"Most of the men in the French secret service are recruited from the army or the detective police.... But I intend that Italy, like Russia, shall in the future rely upon the shrewdness of clever women like yourself."[11]

Not only does he describe the secret services of other countries but LeQueux also causes MacBean to read his clergyman uncle a lesson on the need for national preparedness in England and, by implication, for a vital system of intelligence:

We English hold the foreigner in too great contempt. We are apt to forget that there are other Powers constantly conspiring to undermine our strength and to overthrow our sovereignty. The rural stay-at-home entertains a belief in England's security that is really childish in its simplicity, and if we have not a wise King, a strong Cabinet, and shrewd men in our diplomatic service, the mine must explode some day, depend upon't."[12]

Behind the Throne, though, has little to do with war prophecy and its attendant practical politics. LeQueux's novels exist to wrench hearts, to jerk tears, to trip palpitations and to teach demeanor.

Perhaps the most surprising element of *Behind the Throne* to readers conditioned by more recent spy stories is that its hero is such a complete chump, and that LeQueux's other early heroes are equally chumps. MacBean really does nothing in the novel, and this sheds an unenviable light upon him since the book details manifold threats to his beloved. The same sort of thing happens with Charles Armytage in *The Day of Temptation*, and to other male leads in LeQueux's early novels. Now, we can view this from a couple of perspectives. We can build on Steinbrunner and Penzler and make LeQueux's heroes into forerunners of Ambler's heroes, being men trapped in the middle by powers greater than themselves. This is the false approach. We need to see LeQueux's early heroes as the creations of a writer who ignores (or does not know) the active tradition of the school-boy story for the conventions of the love romance. Later male spy writers would include love romance motifs coming from *The Sheik*, focusing on the notion that all women want to be raped. LeQueux, however, comes from the older tradition of the love romance, centering on the idea that what women really want from a man is understanding and patience. Under his hand, however, this picture of the ideal man degenerates from patience to passivity and LeQueux winds up making heroes into chumps.

A good deal changed in the world between 1905 and 1925 when *Hidden Hands* was raised up. LeQueux, though, learned very little about writing in the intervening twenty years, even if in his later books he portrays a different aspect of espionage. *Hidden Hands* falls into two parts. In the first of these, Seton Darville tracks down a German spy ring which intends to blow up the Forth bridge, thereby blocking the British fleet in its base. The plot possesses a touch of war prophecy business, as the demolition of the Forth bridge will wave the starting flag for the German invasion of England. The second part of the novel shows Darville winning, losing and winning again the heart of the heroine, Edris Temperly. Both plots of the novel ooze with unadulterated bilge. Darville, for instance, tracks the German saboteurs from Corfu to Edinburgh, LeQueux never doubting that his readers will overlook the patent absurdity of planning to blow up a bridge in Scotland while staying in the Aegean. In the second half of the book one wonders why even a silly young twit like Edris would go for an old goat like Darville. But, of course, LeQueux did not look at it that way. Corfu, like the ski resort in the second part of the novel, has to be there because it gives readers the vitally important atmosphere of High Life for which they probably bought the novel. Darville, rather than being a nasty old goat to LeQueux, contained a spiritual significance, and also holds LeQueux's own fantasy portrait of himself. Darville, you see, is a world-renowned novelist. We can, therefore, learn something about LeQueux by looking at his description of the fictional creator of best sellers:

He placed before him the blank sheets of ruled manuscript paper, which bore a red line from top to bottom, and with a sigh took up his fountain pen, and began to work in that uneven, scribbly hand, specimens of which were ever and anon reproduced among the handwritings of popular authors. His writing was characteristic of a man of erratic temperament who scribbled swiftly, as indeed he did. His pen flew over the paper, for his thoughts always arose quicker than his pen could register them. He declared that he wrote mechanically, and that he only conjured up his characters for the moment, and the next second all rememberance of them left him. During the hours of the morning when he wrote, he lived with his characters and experienced within himself all their loves, their hatreds, their sympathies, and their bitter regrets. But as soon as he rose from his table all knowledge of the romance he was weaving left him, and he again became just an ordinary being, a careless cosmopolitan without a single thought in the world.[13]

The final clause about gets it right. Here we go from the unnecessary detail about Darville's writing impedimenta, to stress on the emotional side of his characters (and note that the range of emotions fits the love romance and not the adventure story), to the legitimizing of his pose as a cosmopolitan by denying any lasting attachment to his creations.

But wait. Here is no simple, careless cosmopolitan or successful romancer. Seton Darville is the head of the British Secret Service. LeQueux lets the cat which has been mewing for sixty-odd pages out of the bag here:

Upon the polished dining-room table lay a pile of secret documents dealing with the inner most juggling of European diplomacy, secrets concerning the intrigues of foreign statesmen and financiers, which would have horrified them had they but known that they were in the hands of the ubiquitous Seton Darville, the head of the great, outspread, octopus-like organization which, with its secret headquarters, was the eyes and ears of Britain throughout the world—the Secret Service.[14]

Okay, LeQueux was the first writer of spy novels to appreciate the linkage of industrial and financial machinations to international politics—he shows this, for example, in *The Red Room* with industrial espionage, and he shows it here with the mention of financiers. The rest of the passage above is so much hooey. For LeQueux, though, Darville runs the whole Secret Service show decisively, competently, and without concern for his own comfort. The secret headquarters is not much, but officers of the Special Branch do drop everything for him, and Ministers clear their calendars whenever he rings up. LeQueux draws for us a fairly up-to-date Secret Service with mail searches and illegal break-ins in order to keep Britain safe from a) Germans, b) Bolshies, and c) others intent on doing her the dirty. LeQueux, moreover, cannot let Darville have only occupational interest for readers. To be interesting spies need special attributes. Thus, to raise Darville above the level of the grotty little spy, LeQueux tells us that he does his job without pay. We get this hot and heavy in the following colloquy between Darville and the Prime Minister:

"You pay me a direct compliment, Darville," declared the Prime Minister. "Without your constant vigilance all over the face of Europe I dont know where we should be. If it were not for you, I fear we should cut a very sorry figure sometimes. And yet you are unpaid! You do arduous, brilliant work for the country year after year, often risking your liberty, and without asking for any other reward than the joy of serving your country. Recollect that a baronetcy is due you. Why have you twice refused it?"
. . .
"And, if I did [accept payment], I should be just a paid spy and a servant of the state, Lord Heverbridge," Darville replied quietly. "No, I would rather pay my own expenses and be free. Then nobody can point to me in scorn"[15]

Money, then, makes the sole distinction between lover and whore. Darville shows himself a patriot by protecting his country without emoluments or fees. This attitude comes pretty directly from the snobby, anti-police bias in the detective story where the private detective, like Holmes, is in every way superior to the paid agents of the state. LeQueux wants Darville to be a High Class patriot, but this does not really show when we consider the love plot.

From the start LeQueux grounded his fictions in the love

romance and his late books are no exceptions. In the twenties, however, LeQueux and other popular writers had to distance themselves from D.H. Lawrence and other "sex novelists." Therefore, in the first paragraph of *Double Nought* (1927), Lionel Hipwell announces that

At least, I am not one who slops about in the oozy slime of the sex problem.[16]

The "sex problem" for LeQueux no doubt meant that portrayal of uppity women and men emasculated by intellect. Granted, he does not show these, but LeQueux continues to treat the subject of love. In fact, compared to the early novels, *Hidden Hands* is much more insistent on the conventional roles for lovers. Thus, Darville lives for half of the novel with a secret passion for Edris Temperley, who is half his age. In the middle of the novel they discover their mutual passion and pledge themselves to one another. Edris, then falls victim to the temptations and blandishments of a younger man, Karl Weiss, and fools around with him behind Darville's back. Darville, however, uses the offices of the Secret Service to open her mail and to tail her to her assignations; he is about to pull a David-Uriah the Hittite move by sending Weiss off spying to the Soviet Union, when Edris comes to her senses, confesses her weakness, and collapses into Darville's arms. It never occurs to LeQueux that this is monstrously irregular, and that Darville violates law and public trust left and right. He simply wants to render emotion in his characters, and to draw the secularized conversion so common to the love romance. It seems to him that Darville is as masterful as a lover as he is in protecting his country.

It is a sad truth that not many writers of fiction have much impact on events or on public morality. We can, therefore, only see irony in the fact that William LeQueux was one of the few writers who did. Now, LeQueux had virtually no talent as a writer of spy novels, detective novels, love romances, or anything else. His plotting is execrable, his characters are buffoons, and his style is tedious to the extreme. Yet he has had broad impact on the twentieth century. As I have noted, spy writers as different as Greene and Cheyney look back on LeQueux as the founder of the form. But his influence goes far beyond this. Clarke finds that LeQueux had a hand in the making of the First World War:

There can be no doubt that the authors of many tales of future warfare shared in the responsibility for the catastrophe that overtook Europe. Men like Danrit, LeQueux, and August Nieman helped to raise the temperature of international disputes.[17]

If this judgment is a bit overblown, LeQueux is certainly responsible for a more lasting danger to civilization. By howling for the need for an unbridled secret service, and by developing the spy as a character with extraordinary emotional and moral qualities, LeQueux threatened the fundamentals of democracy. Greene knew all about this when he made Rowe in *The Ministry of Fear* cry out in his nightmare:

"The world has been remade by William LeQueux."[18]

NOTES

[1]"Since the day of Wilkie Collins, there has not been a writer able to keep up a mystery so cleverly as Mr. LeQueux." *The Bond of Black* (London: White, 1899), endpapers.

[2]*The Bond of Black,* p. 123.

[3]*The Bond of Black*, pp. 186-7.

[4]*The Bond of Black,* endpapers.

[5]*The Bond of Black,* endpapers.

[6]C. Steinbrunner and O. Penzler, *Encyclopedia of Mystery and Detection* (New York: McGraw, Hill, 1976), p. 243.

[7]*Behind the Throne* (London: Methuen, 1905), p. 98.

[8]*Behind the Throne*, p. 78.

[9]*The Day of Temptation* (New York: Dillingham, 1899), pp. 179-80.

[10]*The Day of Temptation*, p. 291.

[11]*Behind the Throne*, p. 79.

[12]*Behind the Throne*, pp. 27-8.

[13]*Hidden Hands* (London: Hodder and Stoughton, 1925), pp. 34-5.

[14]*Hidden Hands,* p. 63.

[15]*Hidden Hands,* pp. 119-120.

[16]*Double Nought* (London: Hodder and Stoughton, n.d.), p. 16.

[17]I.F. Clarke, *Voices Prophesying War 1763-1984* (Oxford: Oxford University Press, 1966), p. 135.

[18]*The Ministry of Fear* (New York: Bantam, 1963), p. 57.

Chapter 2
E. Phillips Oppenheim
(1866-1946)

His publishers called him "The Prince of Storytellers," and John Buchan said that "E. Phillips Oppenheim is the greatest Jewish writer since Isaiah." Buchan, I think, was being ironic, but Oppy's publishers had sales figures to back up their title. He was hot stuff, but Oppenheim was scarcely a great or even a good writer. He wrote lousy plots, wooden characters, cliched dialogue, and bogus description. Any other age would have immediately relegated him to the dusty storerooms of libraries and musty used book shops—our age certainly has. Fortunately for Oppenheim, he began to write at a time when the British reading public expanded and the American reading public thirsted for snobby English novels, when enterprising merchants pushed popular literature by means of commercial lending libraries, and when readers had not yet seen the potential of the action/adventure spy novel. Having the faculties of writing quickly, of joining popular forms together, and of merging fantasy and fact, Oppenheim made enough money to deserve at least the first part of the "Prince of Storytellers" tag.

Oppenheim spread his limited talents to most of the forms of the novel popular in the nineties and afterward. He wrote romances about love, like *A Daughter of Marionis* (1895), which dwell on the various exercises of the passions. He wrote finance romances, like *The Millionaire of Yesterday* (1900), or *The Lighted Way* (1912), which tell of the trials and glories of having and losing money. He also wrote what reviewers of the period called "novels of social political life" like *A Prince of Sinners* (1903) or *A Lost Leader* (1906). Further, Oppy cranked out mystery novels of every shape: there are action detective stories like *The Black Box* (1915), revenge stories like *The Avenger* (1907), and in the thirties there are puzzle concoctions like *General Besserley's Puzzle Box* (1935), and *General Besserley's Second Puzzle Box* (1939). Most of these mystery stories are pretty transparent and, in fact, exist as containers for Oppenheim's other interests. He wrote some reasonably unadorned adventure yarns like *The Daughter of Astrea* (1898), but most importantly for us, Oppy wrote a whole cartload of spy novels. He is, indeed, one of the first practitioners of the form.

Oppy's spy novels present numerous problems to anyone attempting to survey the history of the form. The primary problem is that they are bad novels, bad technically, stylistically, and bad morally. Reading much Oppenheim tests the resolve of any analyst. About the best thing I can say about them is that they are not quite as bad as LeQueux's. Few people really mind reading a couple of rotten novels for the cause, but Oppenheim, by Hubin's list, wrote one hundred and sixteen novels. That is a lot for the cause. I will begin, therefore, with the admission that I have not read all of Oppenheim's novels: I have, though, read some seventy of them, and this is more than enough to give authority to my discussion. The second problem with Oppenheim is that he wrote over a considerable period—*Expiation* appeared in 1887 and *Mr. Mirakel* came out in 1943. What I am going to do, rather than trying to survey all of the books, is to discuss three representative novels from the beginning, middle and end of Oppenheim's career.

Oppenheim's first spy novel, *The Mysterious Mr. Sabin* (1898), uses the war prophecy formula: it is a prediction of an averted war instead of an actual one, and it thereby takes the predictive war story and channels it into the course which would be expanded by Childers in 1903 and lots of others later on. He is also somewhat in advance of his contemporaries in the selection of England's enemy. In *Voices Prophesying War* Clark notes that France and Russia were England's main antagonists in early fictional contests of the future, but here, five years before *The Riddle of the Sands,* Oppenheim factors Germany into the equation. In spite of these exceptions, *The Mysterious Mr. Sabin* does introduce motifs common to the predictive war story. Oppenheim mentions the weakness of the fleet, the feebleness of England's coastal defenses, the precariousness of defending the Empire, and the devastating effect of secret weapons (Mr. Sabin has invented electric mines in Addison's laboratories in America). Later in *The Great Impersonation* (1920) Oppenheim dedicated a novel to Lord Roberts, the patron of LeQueux's predictive story *The Great War in England in 1897* (1894). He does not in *The Mysterious Mr. Sabin* or any of his other novels make war prophecy motifs into political propaganda, but uses them merely as details of the plot. Instead he bases the plot of *The Mysterious Mr. Sabin* on historical events. Oppy builds this plot on the Boulangist risings in France in 1888-9 (with Boulanger flirting with the Bourbons and the Bonapartes, only to give up his chance for power for Marguerite de Bonnemains) just as he inclines to build his wartime plots on actual events. He adapts the historical material into Mr. Sabin's plot to restore the Princess Helene of Bourbon and Prince Henri of Ortens to the French throne which fails partly because Helene gives up her ambition for the man she loves. This theme of restoring monarchies becomes one of Oppenheim's standards, only he shifted his ground to Russia, predicting the ouster of the communists in favor of a new Czar in *Gabriel Samara Peacemaker* (1925) and *The Dumb Gods Speak* (1937). Indeed, Oppy's bias in government is toward monarchy, and he usually expresses this by centering his spy novels on the one great man who moves, shapes, or prevents events. This continues even in his last novel, *Mr. Mirakel,* which is really the story of a king in mufti.

The projected French revolution in *The Mysterious Mr. Sabin,* though, does not involve revolutionaries: monarchists, being what they are, can have no truck with grimy revolutionaries, and in all of Oppy's fiction the portrait of the revolutionary is one of a wretched reptile. If they cannot use internal rising, the monarchists have to depend upon external force to seat them on the throne of their ancestors. Mr. Sabin markets for a suitable external force in *The Mysterious Mr. Sabin,* but first he must secure payment for other states monkeying with the internal affairs of France, and the payment which he decides on is England. Sabin plans to sell England's liberty to her jealous neighbors. Now, colonial friction rubbed particularly hot in the 1880s and the 1890s. Britain and Russia collided over Afghanistan and Persia, and Oppenheim does show a Russian spy trying to sneak a peek at the plans of England's defense, but, we are assured in the novel, Russia is fairly honorable and will not sell its republican ally, France, down the river regardless of its love for monarchy. Who will? The Germans. Thus the German Ambassador, Baron von Knignstein, gives Sabin this diatribe:

It is the ties of kindred . . . which breed irritability, not kindliness! I tell you, my friend, that there is a great storm gathering. It is not for nothing that the great hosts of my country are ruled by a war lord! I tell you that we are arming to the teeth, silently, swiftly, and with a purpose. It may seem to you a small thing; but let me tell you this—we are a jealous nation! And we have cause for jealousy. In whatever part of the world we put down our foot, it is trodden on by our ubiquitous cousins! Wherever we turn to colonize, we are too late; England has already secured the finest territory, the most fruitful of the land. We must either take her leavings or go abegging. Wherever we develop, we are held back by the commercial and colonizing genius—it amounts to that of this wonderful country. There is no room for a growing England and a growing Germany! So! one must give way, and Germany is beginning to mutter that it shall not always be her sons who go to the wall. You say that France is our natural enemy. I deny it! France is our historical enemy—nothing else! In military circles to-day a war with England would be wildly, hysterically popular; and sooner or later a war with England is as certain to come as the rising of the sun and the waning of the moon: I can tell you even now where the first blow will be struck! It is fixed! It is to come! So![1]

After a few more exclamation points and cliches we learn that Germany intends to provoke England into war over colonial issues in Africa, and Oppenheim brings the novel to the brink of war between England and Germany: the Kaiser blusters and the Prime Minister reacts coolly. But there is no war. Sabin cannot deliver England up to her foes.

England's danger and deliverance rest on papers. *The Mysterious Mr. Sabin* is a paper chase novel without much chase— perhaps paper possession would be a better term. Oppenheim centers lots of his spy books on papers: take *A Maker of History* (1905) or *Miss Brown of the XYO* (1927) for instance. This motif is not only a way of introducing lady typists, one of Oppy's character types, but more importantly it shows the evolution of the spy novel from the Victorian detective novel. Blackmail forms the basis for many Victorian detective stories—probably because of the fetish for outward propriety. It is a short step from threatening an individual with exposure of his secrets to threatening a nation with exposure of its weaknesses and secrets. Mr. Sabin fills both roles: he blackmails Lady Deringham with her old love letters which expose her momentary weakness, and he steals papers which threaten to expose the strategic and tactical debility of Britain. In *The Mysterious Mr. Sabin* England's safety depends on the scantily guarded work of the half-mad Lord Deringham who is preparing the definitive study of Britain's naval preparedness and defense. Swallowing this, however, is the same as believing the fact that the naval defense plans pilfered in *The Thirty Nine Steps* cannot be remade or altered. It is unlikely that knowledge of flaws in ship design or the orientation of coastal defenses would absolutely insure the victory of an invader, yet these form the base for the political haggling in *The Mysterious Mr. Sabin* and innumerable later spy books by Oppy and his successors.

But this is not simply a novel of international politics, it is a spy book. For Oppenheim there is spying and there is spying. Mr. Sabin does a lot of underhanded things in this novel: he blackmails Lady Deringham, coshes Wolfenden and assorted servants, employs thieves, lies and steals. Yet he refuses to consider himself a spy and the readers are not supposed to do so either. Thus when Felix reveals his mission to Sabin, we get

"So you are a lacquey after all, then?" he remarked—"a common spy."[2]

Spies do things for money and do not formulate policy. An even baser example of spying is among the Germans. One particular branch of German agents are the "Doomschen," people who

...have committed a crime punishable by death,—that...are on parole only so long as...[they] remain in the service of the Secret Police.[3]

If you formulate policy and do your work for nothing, though, you are not a spy but a patriot or a diplomatist. This class attracts Oppy's attention and admiration, as it does LeQueux, and there are innumerable examples of the diplomatist-spy in his novels. In fact, Oppenheim distorts the structure of *The Mysterious Mr. Sabin* in order to make the point that his heroes are people of larger being than those limited by political events. Thus the novel shows the salvation of England and the frustration of Sabin's plans fully eighty pages before the end of the book. The last eighty pages show us that Sabin is suave, witty, and courageous; he escapes from nasty Germans and also atones for having been a rake. Look, Oppy says, you may not like this man's politics, but he is as noble as all get out. Further, the stereotype about spies and police agents causes one of the gargantuan flaws in the plot. Sabin does not fail because he does not have the goods or the will to use them. His plot fails because a mysterious representative of an even more mysterious underground organization plummets out of the heavens and tells him that the High Council has decided that he should stop fooling around with the balance of power in the world, and he drops his plans at once. Oppenheim has recourse to this *deus ex machina* because he does not want to sully his young aristocratic romantic lead (Wolfenden) with action. Thus, all that Wolfenden does is get the girl and stand around looking, to eyes conditioned by action heroes, like a ninny.

For Oppenheim, characters are to serve one, settled, unchangeable role. Wolfenden is the romantic lead, Sabin is the Byronic hero (complete with club foot), Helene is the female lead, Blanche Merton is the fallen woman, and Lord Deringham is the mad genius. Each has his or her own cliche. The only development which Oppy allows is with secrets that people hold about themselves but eventually release. Thus, Lady Deringham eventually confesses her indiscretion with Sabin, Helene reveals her real name and her heart after Wolfenden pursues them for a couple of hundred pages, and we find out that Sabin is the Duc de Souspenier, who aspires to be the Richelieu to the new French monarchy. No one surprises or acts out of character. The readers know them, Oppenheim intends them to appeal to specific romantic fantasies, and the readers will meet them again and again in Oppy's later novels.

Mr. Sabin ends up in New England quietly playing golf (one of Oppenheim's passions, many of his heroes are scratch golfers) until an international secret society kidnaps his wife and sets him running again in *The Yellow Ribbon* (1903). Most of Oppenheim's books, moreover, have an American connection, and the reason is obvious. A best selling writer can make a fair living from the British public, but if he aspires to yachts, to fancy motor cars, to the opulent life of his own fictions, then he must sell more books. Where? In the United States. Thus, fairly early in his career Oppenheim looked toward American markets, and his books came out first from Little, Brown and Company in Boston. To appeal to this market Oppenheim combines romance and high life of the Old World (the sloe-eyed woman and the aristocrat's son) with the technology, wealth, and spunk of the New World (the energetic, rich inventor) and evolves a formula where the two worlds meet. All of this becomes more acute in the books written before America's entry into World War I, where Oppy adds out and out flattery in order to move public opinion in the U.S. toward the camp of the Allies. Thus, in *The Pawns Count* (1918) we find that American women are prettier:

Pamela was beautiful and unusual. She had the long, slim body of the New York girl, the complexion and eyes of a Southerner, the savoir faire of a French woman. She was extraordinarily cosmopolitan, and yet extraordinarily American.[4]

and Washington D.C., is the new Rome:

The stateliness of the city, its sedate and quiescent air after the turmoil of New York, impressed him profoundly. Everywhere its diplomatic associations made themselves felt. Congress was in session, and the faces of the men whom he met in the hotels and restaurants seemed to him some index of the world power which flung its far-reaching arms from beneath the Capitol dome.[5]

This transparent flattery of the U.S., though, does not in itself make Oppenheim's war-time spy novels different from his early books (in many ways they are quite similar), but in some ways his books of the second phase do present a slightly different face of diplomacy and espionage.

For one thing, Oppenheim shifts the focus of his heroes. In the early books he generally segregates the romantic hero from the action and adventure: indeed, action and adventure generally get little attention in Oppy's novels from first to last, carrying out the diplomatist-spy distinction. During the war, however, his heroes act more. Francis Newgate runs about to expose German plotting in *The Double Traitor* (1915), Thomson in *The Kingdom of the Blind* (1916) runs about a good bit to discover German spies in London, and John Lutchester is energetically ubiquitous in *The Pawns Count*. Mind you, Oppenheim never gives us the details of the action—we never find out in *The Pawns Count*, for instance, just how Lutchester appears at exactly the right moment to save Pamela from the Japanese agent—but there is plenty of action in these books, almost too much. Instead of being passive heroes like Wolfenden or like Wrayson in *The Avenger* (1907), these men act. Lutchester, for example, works some sort of oriental system of self-defense on Nikasti, the Japanese Secret Service man, and he also bests a Bowery assassin on the streets of New York. But Oppenheim joins this action with romantic suavity, financial genius, and political adroitness. Thus Lutchester shows the virtues of Oppenheim's wartime agents, but he also highlights the writer's difficulty in dealing with a new sort of popular hero. Lutchester is, as I have indicated, active, intelligent, and efficient. He thwarts the secret weapon plot, and unravels the Germany, America, Japan triangle in the novel. He saves the reputation of one woman, wins another for his wife, and makes a bundle on the stock market without even trying. He knows how to dress, how to order dinner, and how to play golf. Further, he is related to the Duke of Worcester: "one of the oldest families in England." Yet Lutchester is not Oppy's ideal hero: he is Oppenheim's attempt to portray the droll sportsman who plays the game with ease and wit. He cops the secret formula without wrinkling his suit, he belittles his accomplishments with Oppenheim reduction, making fun of the melodramatic potential in his acts. This passage comes after rescuing Graham from his captors:

"I had pictured for myself a dramatic entrance...a quiet turning of the key, a soft approach—owing to my shoes...a cough, perhaps or a breath...discovery, me with a revolver in my hand pointed at the arch villain— 'If you stir you're a dead man!'... Natural collapse of the villain. With my left hand I slash the bonds holding Graham, with my right I cover the miscreants. One of them, perhaps, might creep behind me, and I hesitate. If I move my revolver the other two will get the drop on me—I think that is the correct expression? A wonderful moment, that, Miss Van Teyl!"[6]

This kind of hero, however, discomfited Oppenheim. His real heroes connect to nineteenth century concepts of style, versus the newer concepts of self-consciousness and action. In *The Pawns Count* Oppenheim's themes, particularly the contrast of the lackadasical game player opposed to the machine-like troglodytes of Germany, moved him to the new hero who would inhabit the detective and spy novels of the twenties and the thirties. But he never did like this hero, and he switched quickly back to the sober hero, as Dominey in *The Great Impersonation* shows. Oppy did, though, keep the stress on action, which was new in his war time novels.

Another quiver (it is scarcely a movement) resides in Oppenheim's treatment of women. In his earlier books, women's main role lies in defying authority and marrying for love. This happens in *The Mysterious Mr. Sabin* as well as in romances like *Jeanne of the Marshes* (1909): it happens all over the lot. Whether Oppenheim altered his diagnosis of the reading public and its tastes, or whether the activity of American women changed it, or whether women's new roles in war time Britain changed it, Oppenheim's women change during and after the war. In *The Pawns Count* we meet Pamela Van Teyl who runs at a pretty fast pace during the first part of the novel: she participates in dangerous situations, has physical confrontations with evil men (made especially more threatening in that one is a Turk, one a Black, and one a Japanese), and she acts the part of a secret agent for the American government with muscular patriotism. She involves herself in danger, moreover, as she puts it, because "I love adventures." In the middle of the book, however, Lutchester takes over the important action roles and additionally shows that Pamela never really played an essential role in the spy business but was unwitting bait to draw out the enemy. At this she falls into the hero's arms to become his wife and return to England to do some suitably feminine war work. Perhaps the purest statement of this theme comes in *Miss Brown of the XYO* (1927) where Miss Brown tells the Great Man:

There is nothing I should like so much in the world as to be your secretary, and go on with the work.[7]

This is a real leap for Oppy's women, but hardly a step for womankind.

Oppenheim's novels during the war ostensibly serve as lessons in security consciousness. *The Kingdom of the Blind* overtly teaches that "loose lips sink ships" with sailors blabbing away in front of a

German spy and with a young woman prying into her man's war work. *The Pawns Count* likewise begins with a buoyant young engineer recklessly gassing about his new explosive and later being killed as a sort of just dessert. The war books get a bit more specific about secret weapons than *The Mysterious Mr. Sabin* does. We find underwater telescopes, trawling nets for subs, new explosives, green rays, etc., but Oppenheim uses these as subsidiary motifs much as he did in the earlier spy books. The war rearranges international conspiracies; they form the basis of the political plots, not because of their nature but because they rest on written documents. In *The Pawns Count,* for instance, Germany offers its aid to Japan if she decides to attack America (an idea repeated in *The Wrath to Come,* 1924), and also offers its aid to the United States in case of Japanese attack. And the Germans are stupid enough to put all of this down on papers which they let float around in the States. Likewise, the war simply rearranged Oppy's use of real events as organizers in his spy books. Thus, *The Kingdom of the Blind* culminates in the April, 1915 zeppelin raids on London, and *The Pawns Count* is an apology for the Battle of Jutland.

The use of the Battle of Jutland brings up another theme which increases in volume as we head toward the thirties: the ineptness of British governments. *The Pawns Count* points out that any sane government would have called Jutland a great victory, but that the British government is so limp wristed that its first announcement makes the battle sound like a German victory. Perhaps the peak of Oppy's frankness about governments comes in *Miss Brown of the XYO* where we get this: "This country, since the war, has been governed by a nursery full of nincompoops."[8] When we probe through Oppenheim's rhetoric, though, we find that his political opposition does not rest on any international platform, but that he simply abhors any government which uses an income tax. And if they do not have income taxes he prefers monarchies or dictatorships.

The Pawns Count is in many ways representative of all of Oppy's books in that it intends to appeal to readers on a number of levels. The war does shape some of the concerns in the book, but others remain the same as in Oppenheim's first novels. For one thing, he wants to capture readers through their fascination with wealth and the prospect of getting rich quick. In his finance novels he concentrates on this, superficially showing that money alone will not buy happiness, but really proving that it is pretty good to be rolling in dough. This motive seeps into *The Pawns Count,* too. Here we find that German-Americans use their money to subvert British interests in the States, and Fischer tries to buy a U.S. Senator as well as a wife for himself, but money does not work this way. Instead, we find that Lutchester makes a bundle on the stock market because he has faith in his country, because he needs it to humiliate his German competitor, and because it proves his competence. We will see more of this later. Another popular taste which Oppenheim appeals to is that engendered in the British by Edgar Wallace, the taste for the gangster story. In *The Pawns Count* the main German agent goes to Hell's Kitchen in New York where he not only sees the denizens of a gangster saloon, but he also hires a bruiser to murder Lutchester. In fact Fischer hires all of the gangsters to sabotage American munitions plants. Another fad which we see Oppy exploiting in *The Pawns Count* is that of orientalism. Oppenheim early on appreciated the public's interest in the Orient—shortly after the Russo-Japanese War (1905) he features the Japanese aristocrat, Prince Maiyo, in *The Illustrious Prince* (1910). He continues this in *The Pawns Count* with Prince Nikasti, the agent of Japan who receives the Kaiser's mendacious offer. Ironic in the light of the screaming bigotry expressed toward other non-Europeans (particularly Blacks), Oppenheim lambastes the ignorant racism of the floor valet at the hotel toward Nikasti, and presents him as an admirable exotic, disciplined, anxious to avoid Western mental and moral flab, and awake to delicate beauty (he has a bowl of roses in his room). Other races should have had wars with Russia, as it did alter stereotypes—in Oppenheim at least. Later Oppenheim shifted the same attitudes and roles to Chinese characters, as in *The Dumb Gods Speak*. Also in *The Pawns Count* Oppy carries over his favorite blackmail-spying connection. Fischer, the German agent, lures Pamela's brother into embezzling from his stock broking firm, and then uses this fact as a lever to try to get the secret papers. Finally, in this novel we see Oppy flirting with low-class spying, what with gangsters going around blowing up munitions plants, but the main action of the book concentrates on Fischer and Lutchester, who are not spies but diplomatists, high on the social scale and high in the councils of their governments. This shows best in Oppy's final view of Fischer. He does not treat him as a contemptuous thug but as a patriot, and at the close of *The Pawns Count* Fischer sails for Germany with almost the same mix of pathos and admiration that Oppenheim gives to Mr. Sabin when he departs for the New World.

Up the Ladder of Gold (1931) marks Oppenheim's last phase, the phase of the Great Man. He had been working toward this for a long time, but here we find novels definitely centered on the Great

Man's manipulation of history. This last phase shows, indeed magnifies, the defects in Oppy's workmanship. *Up the Ladder of Gold* reeks of dictation: throughout the characters refer to each other by their full names ("do you mean Warren Rand" or "John Glynde can you") as if the author were working from a list of characters while he wove his story. Wove is not, however, a good term, since the plot of *Up the Ladder of Gold* incompetently joins three separate stories. First, Oppy recounts Rand's attempt to coerce the governments of the world into peace. Then he tells the love story of Tellesom and Rand's daughter. Finally he narrates the taming of Stanley Erdish—a woman who aspires to a man's job but then realizes that she cannot cut it. He does not have enough material or imagination to flesh out any of these strands into a full novel, so Oppy joins them together hoping that the German spy, Behrling, will serve as a bridge. He does not. Oppenheim's essential problem here as elsewhere is that his conception of character is so limited and routine that he cannot find many resources in people to exploit or explore.

The political part of *Up the Ladder of Gold* rests on Warren Rand. Rand is the latest incarnation of the Great Man in Oppenheim's books. Here the Great Man combines several motifs. First he is, like Humberstone in *The Dumb Gods Speak*, rich, but Rand is not just rich, mind you; he is "the world's richest man." Attendant upon this, he possesses the organizational drive, the channeled vision, and the daring enterprise which all of Oppy's rich men have. This part of his personality, the tunnel vision which creates the money-mad usurer, however, Oppenheim uses another way. Rand transfers his financial genius to international diplomacy and tries to force the nations of the world to buy peace as they can be forced to buy arms or oil or enriched uranium. In Oppy's world, though, organizational drive, vision and energy are not enough to make the quintessential millionaire. Rand comes from America and he has the habits and situational morality of elite gangsterism which Oppy and much of Europe half-admired and half-feared. The Great Man has created revolutions where it has suited him, has ordered cement shoes for his enemies, and is not in the least fastidious about shedding blood himself. Indeed, in *Up the Ladder of Gold* he kills a hired thug and blows up two new French warships in order to preserve himself and his plans. Finally, Rand has the other desideratum of the Great Man—he owns the press. Money without influence tinkles like a cymbal, but backed by most of the newspapers in the world it resounds like a bass drum.

In many ways Rand repeats the cliches of Mr. Sabin. His

Byronic loneliness, his single-minded vision, his insistence on ends over means all match the first incarnation of the Great Man. Coming also from the 1890s, *Up the Ladder of Gold* is an optimistic picture of the naturalists' and muckrakers' world. Like Frank Norris, Oppenheim shows his hero cornering the world market of a precious commodity—here it is gold and not wheat. Oppy describes the externals of Rand's blackmail, extortion, murder, etc. All this, however, gets laundered by Rand's political intent. By fair means or foul Rand brings the world to disarmament and peace. The other ingredients, the focusing lenses, in the Great Man's character come from Oppenheim's liking for biography. Rand presents a pretty clear version of Lord Northcliffe, the press lord, in his manipulation and forming of public opinion through the press. He is also an updating of Henry Ford and his sponsorship of the "peace ship" *Oscar II* in 1915 to end the European war. Here, though, farce turns into victory.

Although Oppenheim always felt that the British government consisted of a bunch of incompetent bunglers, his conviction grew after the war. In Italy and Germany he saw fascism doing things, and he came to the belief that individuals always represent the will of the nation better than cabinets or parliaments. *Up the Ladder of Gold* is a new version of *l'etat c'est moi*. Warren Rand acts like a government. He corners the gold market and through his financial lever forces states, because of their poverty, to agree to peace. He runs his own secret service which provides better information than the intelligence organs of governments. He praises more lavishly (in money) and blames more scathingly (with bullets) than the weak-kneed governments can or will. Quite the same thing happens in *The Dumb Gods Speak* and by negative implication in *Mr. Mirakel*, where the Great Man gives up on the world and creates his own kingdom aloof from the unreason and untidiness of World War II.

The major sub-plot of *Up the Ladder of Gold* involves Rand's secret service ace, Tellesom, and Sarah Hincks, Rand's daughter, who has taken on her divorced mother's name. Tellesom, for all his chin and chest, does not do a lot in the espionage line—anonymous agents or one-shot characters (like Phillipson who has spent five years spying and sabatoging in the Soviet Union) do the real spying. Further, Rand knows more than his chief security man and protects himself pretty well without Tellesom's aid. Tellesom simply hangs around doing an odd job here and there, like watching the German, British and Italian statesmen who collude to thwart the peace treaty which Rand is boosting. His prowess exists largely on paper and, like Wolfenden in *The Mysterious Mr. Sabin,* his role is mostly that of lover. He fills two species of this genus: he is the man (who exists only in fiction) who has never really thought about women, and he is the older man who cannot believe that a young woman could possibly fall in love with him. His woman, Sarah Hincks, points out for the experienced reader the first irony of the novel. Oppenheim has a persistent prejudice against fast, gay young people. We constantly find his purposeful folks censuring insouciant, witty wastrels. Oppy does not like Noel Coward, or Wimsey, or Campion, or Bertie, or any of their kin. In *Up the Ladder of Gold,* Sarah Hinks travels with fun-seeking young people who spend most of their time dancing, drinking, blathering and otherwise kicking up their heels. She rejects these clotpolls for the serious, reserved Tellesom. So, where is the irony? Oppy dedicated *Up the Ladder of Gold* to P.G. Wodehouse, founder of the Drones, lover of the cross-talk act, and the onlie begettor of Bertie and Jeeves. As much as admitting his failure to integrate Tellesom in the main action, Oppy gives him some very local and limited detective action where he pulls rabbits out of hats to destroy Behrling's plot to frame him for murder.

The other sub-plot in the novel is one of those in which Oppenheim almost makes a reasonable statement but then retreats. Rand is a doctrinaire misogynist who believes that women's places are in the typing pool. Because of her androgynous name, Stanley Erdish, through correspondence, gets the job of being Rand's English press agent. She does an impeccable job of keeping his name out of the papers, and she blackmails Rand into keeping her in the position in spite of her sex. In practice she not only does her own job,

"...but she is the most valuable stenographer I have ever known in my life. She took Madame deRiga's telephone message from Paris—a woman who speaks like a hurricane—without a mistake. She also listened in to the Prime Minister's conversation the last time you were with him and transcribed it faultlessly. We must be served, Warren Rand. Our work demands the finest service in the world. Miss Stanley Erdish gives it to us."[9]

Well, Stanley Erdish longs for a spot of adventure in her life and she inveigles John Glynde (who has a weakness for her) into sending her on a mission—to abstract a treaty from a swinish Afghan potentate who is bargaining with the Soviets. She does get the treaty, but she also bungles the job and has the police on her trail when Tellesom, who is handy, saves her bacon. After this she hares it back to London, marries John Glynde and sinks into the bliss of being a banker's wife. There is a place for everything and everything in its place.

On the whole, *Up the Ladder of Gold* fits into Oppenheim's general habit of adapting the predictive war book. Indeed, many of his post-war spy books hinge on predictions of the future; *Gabriel Samara Peacemaker*, for instance, takes place in the 1940s when the Russian people have kicked out the Soviets. *Up the Ladder of Gold* makes the requisite warning, in this case about the ineptness of governments and the impotence of the League of Nations to really do good work. He works in passing reference to the secret weapon (in this case, for once, a grimly accurate prediction of cluster bombs) just as he works ray weapons into *The Dumb Gods Speak*. But Oppy does not really care about any of this: the predictive story or the adventure story is simply something to hang characters on.

Oppy's characters, however, never acquire flesh—none of them ever existed or could exist in life. They are creatures of snobbish sentiment. Snobbish sentiment is the constant burden of all of Oppenheim's novels. They all, for instance, open at some posh spot inhabited by high society people. His heroes all possess high minds and fancy titles. Ordinary people, well, they do not count. Norgate's valet in *The Double Traitor* is incinerated by a German bomb, and the hero barely mentions that his valet died in his stead. The same sort of thing happens in *Up the Ladder of Gold*. Oppy's people are above considerations of regular folks; they want to shape policy. This diplomatic connection robs his heroes of the redeeming quality of being he-men. They are, consequently, a collection of boobs, just as his heroines are a gallery of brainless twits. In terms of theme, Oppenheim does little better. He returns again and again to the virtues of monarchy, the putrid state of government, and to invective against the Soviet Union—usually this boils down to portraying Soviet leaders as dissolute, maniacal deviants. He never deals with the issues of man's aggression as a cause for war in *Up the Ladder of Gold* even though he brings it up, and his only response to the Hitler War takes the beautiful people out of the world's conflict to a perfume-scented bower. As a stylist Oppy ranks near the bottom, and his sense of description is unbalanced and stultifying.

Still, unfortunately, Oppenheim is one of the first important spy writers. He adapted the popular form of the predictive war story and came up with novels which center on secret and clandestine diplomacy. The problem is that he did not create a spy hero. We can probably attribute this failure to Oppy's writing for a mostly female audience. He comes from the sensation novel of the last century and from the love romance to the spy book and he writes it in that direction. For creation of the tradition of British espionage novels (leaving out Childers and Conrad) we have to wait for the materials of the boy's adventure tale to be bent to the service of espionage. We have to wait for the Great War and for John Buchan.

NOTES

[1] *The Mysterious Mr. Sabin* in *The Oppenheim Secret Service Omnibus* (Boston: Little, Brown, 1946), p. 111.

[2] *The Mysterious Mr. Sabin*, p. 235.

[3] *The Mysterious Mr. Sabin*, p. 310.

[4] *The Pawns Count* (Boston: Little, Brown, 1918), pp. 4-5.

[5] *The Pawns Count*, p. 269.

[6] *The Pawns Count*, p. 44.

[7] *Miss Brown of the X.Y.O.* (Boston: Little, Brown, 1927), p. 161.

[8] *Miss Brown of the X.Y.O.*, p. 280.

[9] *Up the Ladder of Gold* (New York: Grosset & Dunlap, 1931), p. 158.

Chapter 3
Erskine Childers
(1870-1922)

In 1903 *The Riddle of the Sands: A Record of Secret Service* stood out more clearly as an original work than it does today. Given the facts that only Oppenheim and LeQueux infested the genre of the spy novel and that the subject as fiction was only a few years old, Childers' work stands as a beacon amidst so much unrelieved bilge. Today, though, the novel seems flawed and tedious: its structure breaks down, its dependence on maps betrays considerable narrative weakness, and surely even sailors find that all of the messing about in the *Dulcibella* is a bit much. Nevertheless, Childers remains the first espionage writer to favor fact over romance (in all its forms), he is the first writer to successfully shape the war prophecy story into a spy novel, and he is the first writer who joins the schoolboy story to the elements of espionage in order to unify his fiction and make it mean something beyond the transitory warning that the Germans are coming.

Childers lays the keel of *The Riddle of the Sands* on the traditional concepts of cold baths and hard work coming from the public school and the schoolboy story. His subtitle reads "A Record of the Secret Service." This does not mean *the* Secret Service, for writers had not yet invented it; it means secret service to one's country by the devoted individual, and this is what the public school and the schoolboy story tried to fix in the minds of the privileged youth of Great Britain. Not only do we get this message about duty from the book, but we also see, as in the schoolboy story, the maturation of the hero in his move from pampered idleness to rugged responsibility. "Carruthers" (Childers tells us that he uses pseudonyms in order to convince us that actual reputations are at stake and, of course, to add realism), the main character, enters the novel as a bored, frivolous functionary of the Foreign Office. At the start of the action he lolls around London in September while everyone else in his circle has decamped to the country to slaughter game or make divots and generally whoop it up at other people's country estates. Carruthers, "... a young man of condition and fashion, who knows the right people, belongs to the right clubs, [and] has a safe, possibly a brilliant, future in the Foreign Office..."[1] has pulled desk duty and cannot have his vacation during the prime season. Believing himself a martyr, Carruthers sulks until he receives a note from an old school acquaintance, Arthur Davies, inviting him to Germany for a spot of sailing. With his white flannels, his blazer, and other natty togs, Carruthers travels to Flensburg, on the northwest coast of Germany. Here Davies takes him to his "yacht" *Dulcibella*, a tiny but doughty craft with no crew, no creature comforts and not even enough room to stow Carruthers' yachting kit. Carruthers first becomes miffed at this, having expected a jolly, pleasant, soft, upper middle class holiday on the foam. However,

Whether it was somthing pathetic in the look I had last seen on his [Davies'] face..., whether it was one of those instants of clear vision in which our separate selves seem divided, the baser from the better, and I saw my silly egotism in contrast with a simple generous nature; whether it was an impalpable air of mystery which pervaded the whole enterprise...; whether it was only the stars and the cool air rousing atrophied instincts of youth and spirits [both men are in their twenties]; probably, indeed, it was all of these influences, cemented into strength by a ruthless sense of humour which whispered that I was in danger of making a mere commonplace fool of myself in spite of all my laboured calculations; but whatever it was, in a flash my mood changed.[2]

The rude conditions on the *Dulcibella*, the hard work, the fresh air and Davies' companionship convert Carruthers: they make him the sort of fellow who would be the pride of Gordonstoun school.

Carruthers changes because if he is really to become a man, he must change. This comes from the traditions of the schoolboy story. He also changes because of the ideological basis of *The Riddle of the Sands*. Carruthers begins as an indolent member of the incompetent bureaucracy of a slumbering government. Childers shows him awakening to the harsh, dangerous, exciting world of reality, just as the novel argues the government should do. The hero does not appreciate the international importance of his acts until near the end of the novel. For Childers to have motivated Carruthers with patriotic duty throughout the book would have not only vitiated the mystery plot, but it would also have probably added an element of priggishness to the main character which the author wished to avoid. Consequently, in the middle of the book, before the hero realizes that the Germans pose a threat to England's security, Carruthers acts not out of duty but because he has caught the fever of the hunt:

Close in the train of Humour came Romance, veiling her face, but I knew it was the
rustle of her robes that I heard in the foam beneath me; I knew that it was she who
handed me the cup of sparkling wine and bade me drink and be merry.... It was the
purest of her pure vintages, instilling the ancient inspiration which, under many
guises, quickens better brains than mine, but whose essence is always the same; the
gay pursuit of a perilous quest.[3]

The term "quest" reverberates throughout the novel from the
Preface to the Epilogue. The danger of the sea as opposed to the
apathy of Whitehall in September, and the search for clues coupled
with its attendant role-playing to avoid detection by the enemy,
transform Carruthers and make him into a man who can warn his
country and save it from invasion.

Davies, the other major character in *The Riddle of the Sands,*
serves in several ways as a contrast to Carruthers. He is, by and
large, a failure—he fails to get a commission in the Navy, he fails to
keep the secret of his love from Carruthers, and he fails as a
detective and as a plotter. He is, however, a crackerjack sailor able to
pilot his teak-hulled cockle-shell through and over almost any
stretch of coastline. Before Carruthers joins him, Davies in his
puttering around in the *Dulcibella* gets a bit too near an area where
Germany is readying its secret invasion of England. To stop what
seems to be snooping, Dollman, the English traitor in German
employ, tries to kill Davies by luring him and his boat into
dangerous waters. Sensing that he is on to something, Davies sends
for Carruthers, but he, himself, never knows what the Germans are
cooking up in the rivers, channels and canals of Friesland. Childers
portrays Davies part comically and part sentimentally. The author,
through the narrator, insists that comedy mixes with adventure in
The Riddle of the Sands. The comedy appears first in the defeat of
Carruthers' expectations of a soft yachting holiday, but mostly it
centers around Davies and his obsession with his boat. His
continual tossing of unneeded material overboard to lighten ship
may be good seamanship, but Childers puts it in because of its comic
potential. Davies is also Childers' small concession to the element of
love romance which LeQueux and Oppenheim made a part of the
early spy novel. Part of his motive for the adventure, and a part
which he keeps secret from Carruthers, rests on Davies' love for
Clara Dollman. Unlike his predecessors, however, Childers pretty
rigorously subordinates the love romance and the comedy to the
demands of the adventure plot and the political significance of the

novel.

With one element of Davies' character, though, Childers lets his enthusiasm outrun his aesthetic judgment. In Davies Childers centers the considerable nautical interest of *The Riddle of the Sands*. Here is a brief example of the mass of technical sailing material in the novel:

Note the spot marked "second rest" (approximately correct, Davies says) and the course of the channel from that point westward. You will see it broadening and deepening to the dimensions of a great river, and finally merging in the estuary of the Ems. Note, too, that its northern boundary, the edge of the now uncovered Nordland Sand, leads, with one interruption (marked A), direct to Memmert, and is boomed throughout. You will understand why Davies made so light of the rest of his problem. Compared with the feats he had performed, it was child's play, for he always had that visible margin to keep touch with if he chose, or to return to in case of doubt.[4]

The Riddle of the Sands contains page after page of this sort of material, and it ruins the book as a novel. Few readers want uninterrupted material about sailing or about the north coast of Germany. Now, Childers included this material because he was a devoted small boat sailor, but he had other purposes too. The technical data, and Davies' skill as a sailor cut down and, to a degree, replace the sentiment which LeQueux and Oppenheim use as filler between the problem and the solution. Childers sensed that male readers would be more interested in the sailing material than in the sentiment of earlier spy romances. He also used the sailing data out of political considerations which have largely disappeared. Early espionage tales like Oppenheim's *The Mysterious Mr. Sabin* (1898) center their problems on Britain's naval defense because this had been and still was the key to the country's survival. With all of the naval material in *The Riddle of the Sands* Childers makes the sea not only the strategic problem of the book but also the subject of his novel.

Davies also functions as the mouthpiece for the political points of the novel. Britons were becoming edgy at the turn of the century about the extent and jurisdiction of their Empire: we get Kipling's "Recessional" (1897) boosting the moral mission of Imperial England, and Conrad's *Heart of Darkness* (1899) probing the morality of another imperial state. In spy fiction writers worried not only about attacks on the fringes of the Empire (Buchan's *The Half-Hearted [1901]* and Kipling's *Kim* [1901] both use the possibility of a Russian invasion of India as the political problem in their plots) they also sensed what was in fact true—other nations wanted Empires too, and when the map was all colored in the world would compete with Britain in India or in Africa. In *The Riddle of the Sands* Germany replaces Russia as the great imperial and economic competitor. Davies grasps the situation when Carruthers gives him the Foreign Office *precis* of Germany:

He used to listen rapt while I described her [Germany's] marvellous awakening in the last generation, under the strength and wisdom of her rulers; her intense patriotic ardour; her seething industrial activity, and, most potent of all, the forces that were moulding Europe, her dream of a colonial empire, entailing her transformation from a land-power to a sea power. Impregnably based on vast territorial resources which we cannot molest...she grows and strengthens, and waits, an ever more formidable factor in the future of our delicate network of empire....
    "And we aren't ready for her," Davies would say.[5]

The Riddle of the Sands is, of course, a war prophecy book and Clarke treats it as such. Like LeQueux's *The Great War in England in 1897*, it argues for certain specific shifts in British military practice and policy: the need for a North Sea base and naval squadron, and the need to establish a naval reserve force. Childers frames the novel with these points, and, in fact, the novel is a hypothetical argument for them. As he suggests in the Preface, Childers is taking the case to the public so that it will influence pending government action. The Postscript tells us that the government has now acted on some of these points by establishing a North Sea base on the Forth and is studying the idea of a volunteer naval reserve force, but Childers ends by suggesting that governments frequently do not perform their promises, and he leaves the readers with the question: "Is it not becoming patent that the time has come for training all Englishmen systematically either for the sea or the rifle?"[6] These arguments and their fictional presentation fall squarely in the realm of the conventional war prophecy story from *The Battle of Dorking* to LeQueux's prophecies. Childers, though, does add a new element to the genre. The trouble with war prophecy books as fictions lies in the fact that they usually attempt to cover an entire war. In *The Great War* LeQueux chronicles everything from the first to the last shot; Wells, in *War of the Worlds* (1898) covers the time between the beginning of the invasion to the defeat of the Martians. This immense scope vitiates many parts of successful fiction: it leaves little time for character development, and it ties the structure too closely to geography rather than allowing any sort of organic development. What *The Riddle of the Sands* does is to cut the war prophecy plot down to size and deal with only one, manageable part of the invasion—the planning for the hypothetical invasion.

Childers takes the cut-down war prophecy plot, and he unifies it by using detective story elements. He wrote *The Riddle of the Sands* almost two decades before the advent of the genuine detective novel which makes an enigma and its solution the central concern of the plot. Here Childers, like the detective writers of the twenties, conceives of his plot as a riddle to which Davies and Carruthers (not the readers) seek an answer. He also calls the motivating problem a "puzzle," the standard detective story term. The puzzle (it is not really a riddle at all) in the novel is what are the Germans up to along the coast of East Friesland? We get very little inkling and Davies and Carruthers have virtually no clues until the last third of the book when Carruthers sneaks up on the German plotters and overhears snatches of their plans. Even then the hero does not fathom what the Germans are cooking up. In spite of his jaunt through Friesland in disguise, Carruthers does not put all of the pieces together until, in the last thirty pages, he stows away on a tug which is taking a troop barge on a trial run for the invasion of England. Childers handles this portion of the novel with some skill, balancing information with adventure suspense. Unifying the war prophecy plot with the detective structure makes Childers a real innovator in the world of spy fiction. It does not, however, atone for the dreariness of the navigational material, and it cannot overcome the fact that Childers is stuck in the sentimental cliches of character coming from LeQueux and Oppenheim.

Only Carruthers, built on the school boy adventure pattern, stands out from the other characters in *The Riddle of the Sands*. The rest adhere to one sentimental trap or another. Among the Germans who set up the invasion plot is Dollman, who goes off to England to spy at Chatham during the middle portion of the novel. This is the fellow who tried to wreck Davies in the *Dulcibella* before Carruthers arrived on the scene. In spite of his perfect German, though, Dollman is an Englishman (Lieutenant X) in German hire. Childers leads us to expect to hear all about Dollman's past—Carruthers intends to go to England to research him but cancels this in favor of his trip through Friesland—but we never do. He remains the melancholy figure of the exile, with his past obscured to keep him that way until he commits suicide by dropping over the side of the *Dulcibella* into the North Sea on the trip back to England. Even more sentimental than Dollman is his daughter, Clara. Like the women in LeQueuex or Oppenheim, Clara is caught between powerful, opposing forces. She has, first of all, her father's treachery to live with, and she also has the fact of her love for Davies. Both of these she must keep secret, since confessing will lose her one or the other of her loved ones. She, then, needs to exist struggling with her explosive packet of passion. Clara's and, in turn, Davies' emotional predicament, what Childers calls "the warm human envelope" of the story in the Preface, causes Carruthers to add the rescue of the Dollmans to his political quest, and this, in the author's view, was supposed to humanize the whole business.

Regardless of its defects, *The Riddle of the Sands* stands out among the pioneering forays into the territory of the spy novel. Childers hampers it with sentiment, with obsessional seamanship, and with a transitory political message, but, to damn with faint praise, he is not as bad in this as Oppenheim or LeQueux, and he did introduce significant structural innovations. He adapts the war prophecy book into a usable form, he uses the schoolboy pattern rather than depending on the effete gentlemen of LeQueux and Oppenheim, and he uses a focused detective interest to run his plot. None of these things saves *The Riddle of the Sands* from its weaknesses, but they do provide the basis for later writers, especially Buchan, to make something out of the fledgling spy story.

NOTES

[1] *The Riddle of the Sands* (London: Nelson, n.d.), p. 15.
[2] *The Riddle of the Sands*, pp. 37-8.
[3] *The Riddle of the Sands*, pp. 116-7.
[4] *The Riddle of the Sands*, p. 264.
[5] *The Riddle of the Sands*, p. 382.

Chapter 4
John Buchan
(1875-1940)

If John Buchan had not existed he would have had to have been invented. The modern novel of espionage simply would not have developed along the same lines without him. This is not true of his predecessors: Oppenheim, Wallace, LeQueux, and Childers all pale in significance when compared to Buchan. They suffer in terms of popularity (Buchan remains in print and readily available in libraries while one must fossick around to find the others) and they pale in terms of their impact on subsequent writers. Their turgid prose, awkward manners, and vague backgrounds are dead and embalmed for us while Buchan's books can still capture readers. One simply cannot understand the development of the spy novel, or the detective novel for that matter, without a grounding in Buchan.

John Buchan, 1st Baron Tweedsmuir of Elsfield, P.C., G.C.M.G., G.C.V.O., C.H., ended up as Governor General of Canada. He was, in that wonderful Edwardian term, a terrific swell. The son of a Glasgow minister, Buchan worked his way up the social ladder. Lawyer, publisher, editor, M.P. for the Scottish Universities, Buchan knew almost everybody who was anybody in British society, from Lloyd George to Robert Graves, from Henry James to Churchill, from Asquith to T.E. Lawrence. Like many other middle-class men who rose to social prominence at the time, Buchan needed extra money to support himself in a day when public men were expected to be independently wealthy. He did this by writing. Throughout his career Buchan produced a number of kinds of books: he wrote short stories and essays which appeared serially and then in book form, from *Scholar Gypsies* (1896) to *The Runagates Club* (1928); he wrote a number of studies of historical and literary figures, like *The Marquis of Montrose* (1913), *Sir Walter Scott* (1932), and *Oliver Cromwell* (1934); and he wrote twenty-odd novels. Buchan's novels fall into four classes. First, there are historical novels like *Witchwood* (1927), which is set in seventeenth-century Scotland. There are also idea books like *The Gap in the Curtain*

(1932), which explores foreknowledge and predestination, and *Sick Heart River* (1941), which articulates the doctrine of work. Buchan also wrote a number of straight adventure novels like *The Dancing Floor* (1926), in which a lovely woman is saved from berserk Greek islanders on an atavistic rampage, and *John MacNab* (1925), in which three sportsmen relish the adventure of poaching other people's game. This all sifts down, leaving twelve novels which deal with espionage.

Buchan entered the field early with *The Half-Hearted* (1900), which he later called "a stupid book, written during a period of violent prejudice at Oxford."[1] Here Lewis keeps the Russians from invading India just as the Spartans plug up Thermopylae against the Persians (Buchan had the Spartan bee in his bonnet, referring to Thermopylae in the early short story "The Lemnian," frequently alluding to the boy and the fox story, and having Sandy say "I'm going to try the Thermopylae stunt" in *The Courts of Morning*). Written for the boys' magazine, *Captain*, *Prester John* (1910) shows boys ardent for some desperate glory how David Crafurd saves South Africa from black revolution and finds his fortune while doing it. In 1913, on a cruise to the Azores, Buchan composed his first real thriller, *The Power-House,* in order to "amuse myself...[and as] a tribute at the shrine of my master in fiction—E. Phillips Oppenheim—the greatest Jewish writer since Isaiah."[2] Here Edward Leithen uncovers and thwarts Andrew Lumley's plans to loose anarchy on the world. It is really pretty shoddy stuff, but this all changed with the next spy-thriller, *The Thirty Nine Steps* (1915). When Buchan sent this novel to George Blackwood he wrote that "I have amused myself in bed [he was recuperating from chronic ulcer trouble] writing a shocker of the style of *The Power-House*. It has amused me to write, but whether it will amuse you to read is another matter."[3] This shows the weakness of self-deprecation: although *The Thirty Nine Steps* shares some of the flaws of *The Power-House* (the vagueness of the villains and their plans as well as the swashbuckling neglect of details in the plot), it brings new inspiration and impetus to Buchan's spy novels and to the genre as a whole.

The Thirty Nine Steps introduces Richard Hannay, who here uncovers a plot to pilfer Britain's naval defense plans. Buchan was so taken with Hannay, as was the public, that he used him in four subsequent novels. In *Greenmantle* (1916), Hannay, Blenkiron, Sandy Arbuthnot and Peter Pienaar thwart a German-inspired *jihad* and assist the Russian capture of Erzerum. The same group, minus Sandy and plus Mary Lamington (later Hannay), crack a

German spy ring, uncover a German plot to spread anthrax, and take part in the Battle of Arras in *Mr. Standfast* (1919). *The Three Hostages* (1924) brings back the *Power-House* motif of the Master Villain trying to wreck civilization and Hannay, Mary, Sandy and Archie Roylance spike his guns. Finally, Hannay appears in *The Island of Sheep* (1936), which is not a spy book but a crime thriller turning on extortion on a grand scale. *The Courts of Morning* (1929) introduces Hannay only in the Prologue, but it deals with the old gang—Archie, Sandy, Blenkiron, and Geordie Hamilton. Blenkiron and Sandy stir up a revolution in a copper-rich South American country, Olifa, in order to squelch a shadowy anti-American plot, to convert the Master Mind, Castor, from his antiseptic and theoretical inhumanity, and to shake the complacent, middle-class government.

Jumping backward, in 1922 Buchan introduced his other series character who gets mixed up in spy stuff, Dickson McCunn. Dickson, in *Huntingtower* (1922), teams up with a scruffy bunch of Glasgow slum kids, the Gorbals Die-Hards, and a wandering poet-paper maker in order to do a bunch of bolshies in the eye and to save the Princess Saskia and the Romanov jewels. The tone is even lighter in the second Dickson McCunn novel, *Castle Gay* (1930), which shows two of the grown-up Die-Hards, Jaikie Galt and Dougal Crombie, rescuing Thomas Carlyle Craw from conflicting groups of Evallonian politicos. In the last of these books, *The House of the Four Winds* (1935), the action shifts from Britain to ruritanian Evallonia where Jaikie, Randal Glynde and Dickson fight communists and help to restore Prince John to the throne of his ancestors.

Buchan's only other espionage novel, *A Prince of the Captivity* (1933), is not part of a series and, to a larger degree than any of the other books, fuses espionage material with the idea book. It begins and ends in espionage, with Adam Melfort serving Britain behind enemy lines in the early portions and saving Loeffler and Creevey from fascist and communist thugs at the end. The espionage at the start of the book is about as real as Buchan gets, with a recognition of the anonymous, unglamorous, fragmented, and tragic side of espionage—perhaps due to Maugham's *Ashenden,* or to the realistic accounts of the war published by Graves and Sassoon. But this is hardly enough to make a difference to the overall gist of espionage in *The Prince of the Captivity* since it finishes with romantic derring-do. The notable part of the novel, however, is the middle, which encompasses Melfort's search for a leader who can pull the world out of its political and moral slough. This is not a successful novel, but it shows Buchan's desire to make the spy novel something more than a simple adventure entertainment.

After this breathless run-through, we, of course, need to stop to consider what Buchan's novels aim to accomplish and why he is important. The answer to both of these questions lies in the fact that his novels, unlike those of his early contemporaries, transmit the art of the traditional novel, and they present certain important nineteenth-century ideas without the mawkishness and the clutter which we find in lesser Edwardian writers. Buchan's spy novels, and his straight adventure tales, come from several well-known, obvious, and acknowledged sources. There is, first, the tradition of Walter Scott, to whom there are copious allusions in almost all of Buchan's books, and Robert Louis Stevenson. Janet Smith discusses these influences in her exemplary literary biography of Buchan, and I really do not want to belabor them here. It is, perhaps, enough to say that Buchan saw Scott and Stevenson as writers who restored the traditions of the romance to the development of the novel rather than exclusively following the path of character analysis which began to preoccupy eighteenth-century writers. Thus, in *Sir Walter Scott,* Buchan notes that when Scott began to write

What was needed was a writer who could unite both strains, for in the medieval world the two were inseparable, the mystery and the fact, credulity and incredulity, the love of the marvellous and the descent into jovial common sense; who could make credible beauty and terror in their strangest forms by showing them as the natural outcome of the clash of human character; who could satisfy a secular, popular craving with fare in which the most delicate palate could also delight.[4]

Buchan saw his own writing as serving a similar purpose, combining adventure and realism and hitting readers who had a taste for fiction which was neither rarified and consumptive nor brutish and inane. At least some of this can be seen in *Mr. Standfast,* where Buchan builds in a contrast between the aesthetes who fawn over the Russian novel, *Leprous Souls,* and Hannay's attraction to English classics. Buchan, in conformity to his view of Scott and the development of the novel, wished also to refocus on the primacy of the art and satisfaction of story telling. Therefore one word, yarn, surfaces again and again in virtually all of his novels, and, to counterbalance the fabulous side of story telling he often bases his books on real events or people. *Greenmantle* culminates in an actual, historical battle which took place recently, as does *Mr. Standfast. Prester John* echoes several African revolts (perhaps, as Shepperson suggests, it is based on Bambata's revolt in Natal in

1906)[5] and *Greenmantle* surely echoes Gordon at Khartoum. There are real people, too: Buchan based Hannay in part on "Tiny" Ironside, he put Aubrey Herbert and T.E. Lawrence into Sandy, and Leithen has some pretty clear similarities to Buchan himself. Indeed, a number of real people enter the novels, from the Kaiser in *Greenmantle* to General Haig in *Mr. Standfast.* Over the years Buchan strove to create a consistent and developed group of realistic people—Hannay, Blenkiron, Sandy, Archie, Leithen, Lamancha, Palliser-Yeats, etc.—who would participate in the yarns and give the stable, realistic grounding to the wild and improbable action.

Another tradition which informs Buchan's novels is that of the public school and the schoolboy novel. But we must be careful here; the part which these things play in Buchan has been grossly distorted and oversimplified by writers who see Buchan as simply an advocate of cold baths and priggish morality. Before one makes too many snap judgments, it must be recalled that Buchan himself was not a public schoolboy and that, although he was politically a Tory, Buchan supported many of the progressive issues of his times: he wrote in favor of women's suffrage, voted for the recognition of the Soviet Union, and appealed for the release of conscientious objectors after the First World War. The clearest *caveat* in this respect comes in *The Island of Sheep,* when Hannay describes his boy, Peter John:

He was never meant for any kind of schoolboy, for the talk of "playing the game" and the "team spirit" and "the honour of the Old House" simply made him sick. He was pretty bad at his books, though he learned to slog along at them, but he was a hopeless duffer at games, which indeed he refused to learn. He detested his preparatory school, and twice ran away from it.[6]

Yet Peter John is not a sullen, ignorant weasel. He goes a long way toward saving the day in this novel. Buchan was not an apostle of pig-headed heartiness. He accepted some of the motifs and ideals of public school life, but he strained them through a finer sensibility.

Writing popular fiction when he did, though, Buchan could not avoid some things which came from the public school tradition. The Victorian age saw numerous changes and attempted changes in the field of education. There was a real and concerted drive to make public school education more meaningful and fulfilling for boys. Corresponding with this, a movement began to provide moral and absorbing literature for boys: the schoolboy novel, like *Tom Brown's School Days,* and the schoolboy magazine. Buchan's novel *Prester John* brings the whole issue to bear, for it was written for and published in the schoolboy magazine *Captain. Prester John* carried the marks of the typical schoolboy story. It mixes exotic high adventure, the thwarting of John Laputa's black rebellion, with moral examples showing the curse of drink and the rewards of hard work, and to these adds a lesson in homage to the British Empire—David uses some of his treasure to set up a school for Africans which in turn leads to their economic well-being and happiness.

Although Buchan has certain fixed public school images, like his constant allusions to Spartans, none of his subsequent books is so blatantly schoolboyish as *Prester John*. There is, moreover, almost a graphable development in Buchan's attachment to the form and spirit of the schoolboy novel. *Prester John, The Power-House,* and *The Thirty Nine Steps* have a number of similarities. They are short, fast-paced books which end with the hero saving the world and enriching his character with adventure. *Greenmantle, Mr. Standfast, The Three Hostages,* and *The Courts of Morning* are much longer books which, although they deal with the same ideas and character points, deal with them on an increasingly more complex level and move away from fantasy into a realer world. The Dickson McCunn novels return to the schoolboy ambience in their lighter tone, their adolescent heroes, and their fantasy settings. Finally, in *A Prince of the Captivity,* Buchan moves much further, from the schoolboy world and combines the spy-adventure material with the material of the idea book.

The most prominent schoolboy motif which carries through all of Buchan's spy novels is the preoccupation with converting and improving character. Tom Brown, because of his stay at Rugby and the forming influence of Thomas Arnold, becomes a good young man. The same kind of thing can be seen in any number of places in Buchan's novels. Particularly with Hannay, the hero becomes his best self because of the models of his friends. Thus Peter's image intrudes again and again into Hannay's mind in *Mr. Standfast.* More significant that this, however, are the novels which have conversion as their main theme. In both *The Courts of Morning* and *A Prince of the Captivity* the heroes, Sandy and Melfort, kidnap great but evil men, Castor and Creevey, put them in different surroundings, and confront them with new people and new ideas in order to convert them to active goodness. On a more mundane level this whole idea persists in most of Buchan's novels in the theme of friendship. The utility and value of friendship forms the backbone of any number of schoolboy novels, and it forms the spine of many of Buchan's novels, too. While schoolboy books usually portray friendship through benevolent and enlightened fagging, and while this percolated into the fiction of Rider Haggard and Conan Doyle,

Buchan shows a more humane and equal friendship shared between men. One can see the place of friendship as early as *The Thirty Nine Steps,* where Hannay is so stale living in London because "I had no real pal to go about with."[7] The progress through the Hannay novels is in a real sense the accumulation and exploration of friends. Adding Peter, Sandy, Blenkiron, and later Archie makes it easier for Buchan to fill out the adventure plots, but describing Hannay's friends in *Greenmantle, Mr. Standfast, The Three Hostages* and *The Courts of Morning* has a value all of its own. Buchan shows his hero's pleasure in different kinds of people, from the high-strung, romantic Sandy Arbuthnot to the homey simplicity of Peter Pienaar and Andrew Amos, to the callow bumptiousness of Archie Roylance, to the commercial bustle of John S. Blenkiron. Each has a sphere of competence which Hannay admits and respects, and each provides compassion and solace for his fellows in his own way. Their friendship is genuine—so genuine that Buchan feels no need to explain it beyond showing it in action. It is, further, action which cements the bond of friendship in the books.

Another congruent feature of the schoolboy story which is frequently traced to Buchan is the absence of believable, complete female characters. Victorian and Edwardian popular fiction in general has little place for women. When they appear, as in Oppenheim, they are either mysterious noblewomen or working gals on the make for a husband. Buchan participates in some of this. No significant women appear in the early thrillers, *Prester John, The Power-House* or *The Thirty Nine Steps,* and they play only minimal roles in the late books, *A Prince of the Captivity* and *Sick Heart River.* Buchan saw these as male books. He was not, however, totally out of sympathy with women. He knew that creation of women characters was his weak point. In this connection he wrote to his sister, commenting on one of the characters in her novel, *The Seatons,* that "in Elizabeth you draw a wonderful picture of a woman (a thing I could about as much do as fly to the moon)."[8] Consciousness counts for something. Moreover Buchan did try to create females whose functions in their world went beyond waiting at home or lolling around dispensing unworldly beauty. His heroines are not frail beings who are put in the plot to be kidnapped or to inspire and reward the heroes. They, of course, do these things, but they do more. Mary Lamington in *Mr. Standfast* and *The Three Hostages,* Janet Roylance and Barbara Dasent in *The Courts of Morning,* and Alison Westwater in *Castle Gay* and *The House of the Four Winds* may be tomboyish, but they function the same way that the heroes' male friends do—acting and thinking. The only difference is that they, not by design, mind you, send the heroes off into occasional flights of pastoral fantasy and bouts of being tongue-tied. Mary, Janet, Babs and Alison bind themselves to the same values and tasks which the men do and do not see themselves in any different light than the men view themselves. Barbara's relationship with Sandy has a bit of the Orient in it, but Hilda von Einem in *Greenmantle* certainly tilts the bubble the other way. The only consciously separate motive for action on the part of women comes in *The Three Hostages,* when Mary is seized by militant motherhood in her confrontation with Medina over the return of little Davie's consciousness. One can be put off by the athletic heartiness of Buchan's women, but one certainly should not equate his treatment of them with the treatment of women in the schoolboy novel.

Women and friendship, important in slightly different ways to the schoolboy story and to Buchan, are really a secondary concern. School fiction taught moral lessons which would aid the reader in his adult life and allow him to mature as an asset to his community. Boys' books sermon on the whole cultural baggage of Victorian masculinity—honesty, manliness, reverence, good sportsmanship, etc. Buchan does not have too much truck with these; he assumes them. His major text is the book of work. "Job" and "work" pepper Buchan's novels. Hannay and the other heroes always take on monstrously difficult jobs. Indeed, one cannot understand much about Buchan without understanding the Victorian doctrine of work, a doctrine which Buchan not only wrote about but also lived. Going back to Carlyle (remembering that Mr. Craw in *Castle Gay* is Thomas Carlyle Craw) we can find maxims on work which can be used as keys to Buchan. In *Sartor Resartus* we find these classifications and admonitions:

Our works are the mirror wherein the spirit first sees its natural lineaments.

Do the Duty which lies nearest thee; which thou knowest to be a duty! The second Duty will have already have become clearer.[9]

Now look at Buchan. Many of his books begin with a bored hero who just lolls around. *The Power-House* starts with Leithen tired of his routine work; *The Thirty Nine Steps* opens with Hannay sunk in ennui in London; *Greenmantle* begins with Hannay and Sandy bored by their convalescence; *The Courts of Morning* starts with Sandy rusting away, unused. Buchan even alludes to the arch boredom-work poem, *Ulysses.* Boredom as the opening state for the hero smacks us in the eye in *John MacNab,* where the first chapter is "IN WHICH THREE GENTLEMEN CONFESS THEIR ENNUI." Then, some outside force comes in and gives the hero a mission which is real enough but which is also largely undefined. Thus, how is Hannay to find Scudder's murderer and avert the impending catastrophe—whatever it is? How are Hannay and his pals to confound the Greenmantle plot, to track down Ivery, to checkmate Medina? How are Dickson and the Die-Hards going to protect the Princess, or Mr. Craw or regain Prince John's throne? Never do the heroes have a thorough, preconceived plan. They succeed by starting (doing the nearest duty) and the rest comes as the action proceeds (the second duty becomes clearer). Further, it is in doing the job that Buchan sees worth revealed. At rest in the city or at Fosse, Hannay is just a beefy colonial, Sandy is a neurotic, Archie is an innocent, Peter is a disreputable old man, and the Die-Hards are a gang of snotty slum hooligans. But give them a job to do and they become their real selves. Buchan devoted his last novel, *Sick Heart River,* to this message, showing Leithen getting out of his death bed to save a man's life and sanity, and finally sacrificing his own life pushing a tribe of Canadian Indians to work to save themselves from want and disease.

During the war years the link between duty and work was easy and clear for Buchan: the hero fights for his country against Germany. Thus in *The Thirty Nine Steps, Greenmantle,* and *Mr. Standfast,* the heroes strive to defeat German plans. After the war Buchan went through a process of refocusing the objects of duty. In the Dickson McCunn books, anti-Bolshevism, which becomes less political and more localized in one character as the books proceed, forms the duty and the work of the heroes. Also, here Buchan adds some manufactured duty to the country of Evallonia in the last two novels, *Castle Gay* and *The House of the Four Winds.* He attaches more importance, however, to personal values in the Dickson McCunn books, and Dickson's duty to his romantic consciousness and Jaikie's duty to individual people overshadow the fuzzy political duties implied by the never-never land which they inhabit. The same holds true for *The Three Hostages* and *The Courts of Morning:* duty to self and duty to other individuals pull the heroes in a milieu in which no real patriotic duty exists. As the political and economic situation in Europe ground down, however, Buchan became increasingly conscious of the need for impassioned belief, hard work, and political leadership. This lies at the center of Archie's political conversion in *John MacNab,* which is largely forgotten by *The Courts of Morning.* Later Buchan expanded on this political duty in *A Prince of the Captivity,* where Melfort's duty during the war is spying for his country, his next duty is saving an adventurer who has been lost in the Arctic waste, and his final duty is to find and protect a leader who will revive England and Europe. During the middle of the novel he follows the careers of three who fail—a labor leader, a priest and a politician—but he does find Loeffler, the German leader, and Creevey, who may have the grit to save the world from going down the drain. Thus Melfort pursues increasingly abstract duties but through attention, care, and perseverance makes them concrete and real.

Which takes us smack up against the issue of providence. Although it does not obtrude too heavily into Buchan's spy novels, providence clearly plays an important role in the articulation of character and plot. Plot first. Coincidence plays a large part in what happens in every one of Buchan's spy novels. Let us just take a look at the ways in which the hero first meets the villain. David Crawfurd, in *Prester John,* meets John Laputa, the black leader of a revolt in South Africa, on a beach in Scotland where the former goes while skipping kirk service and where the latter goes to practice strange rituals. In *The Power-House,* Leithen's car breaks down in the country and he meets Lumley at the first house he reaches. Hannay stumbles on the Blackstone gang while running from pursuit in the Scottish borders. In *Greenmantle,* Hannay blunders into Hilda von Einem's estate after he and Peter get lost in a fog. The crucial meeting with Ivery in *Mr. Standfast* occurs in a crowded tube station during an air-raid on London. Significantly, Dickson meets the villains in *Huntingtower* as the result of flipping a coin. Only in *The Three Hostages, The Courts of Morning,* and *A Prince of the Captivity* do the meetings lack an air of coincidence—partly, at least, because there are no real villains in the last two books. One can safely say, in fact, that coincidence is the main principle of plotting in most of Buchan's novels. Take a look at *Greenmantle,* with its multitudinous coincidences: Hannay's meeting with Peter in Lisbon, the fact that Stumm takes charge of Hannay, the snowstorm in the forest, the peasant's hut, the engineer's death, Peter's reappearance on the Danube, the reappearance of Rasta, the advent of the Companions of the Rosy Hours, Greenmantle's death, Stumm's reappearance, the theft of the plans, the cossack attack. I could probably add a bunch of others, or go through the other novels, but it would not purpose much. The point is that the accidents are no accidents. They are providence working in concert with the hero's efforts so that the right will prevail. And Buchan acknowledges this. He is more sophisticated than to give prayerful thanks at every providential juncture, but he nonetheless acknowledges them. Usually this comes with strategically placed use of the word "luck," as in this instance from *The Three Hostages:*

My thoughts were always on the Blind Spinner, and there I could not advance one single inch. Macgillivray's watchers had nothing to report. It was no use my paying another visit to Madame Breda, and going through the same rigmarole. I could only stick to Medina and pray for luck.[10]

This, naturally, precurses the necessary discovery. Buchan also uses the words "fate" and "providence" for the same purpose but not as prominently, as they are a bit out of character with his heroes. Perhaps the novel in which providence gets most open acknowledgment is *Greenmantle,* where there are numerous references to *kismet* due to the setting in Constantinople. Providence, however, comes into all of the novels as a mover of the action and as an accepted part of the heroes' faiths. The equation, then, is work, duty, providence.

Providence, though, works as more than being simply a part of the heroes' conscious philosophy. Buchan makes his characters self-conscious only up to a point: they go beneath the surface but are no motive-mongers or self-seekers beyond finding what is necessary to sustain them in their worlds. Thus they really never bother thinking an awful lot about why things happen or why they succeed. They accept providence and its acts through them. Principally providence acts through them in the form of instinct. Frequently Buchan's heroes do reckless, impulsive things. Especially toward the end of *Greenmantle,* Hannay throws caution out and rushes into action, finding afterward that he has done the right thing. This is providence all right, but as Buchan sees it, it is not simply fortune protecting the mentally deficient. His heroes do things out of instinct. Thus when Hannay approaches the German letter drop in *Mr. Standfast,* he says

But that dark mountain mass changed my outlook. I began to have a queer instinct that that was the place, that something might be concealed there, something pretty damnable.[11]

And he is right. Buchan's heroes are not fortune's fools but have instinct as a built-in compass to show them the directions of providence for the successful completion of their jobs.

The final place where providence operates most is with the disposal of the villains. We need to recognize that Buchan's novels are not very violent and, to my recollection, no Buchan hero ever kills an individual—as distinct from shooting at a crowd. No one dies in several books, and where villains die at the end, they either die by accident, as Medina does in *The Three Hostages,* or they die at the hands of their own people. The case of Ivery in *Mr. Standfast* is significant: he dies as he rushes across no man's land, killed accidentally by his own people. Or rather he does not die accidentally; he is disposed of by providence and not by human causes.

But all of this about work and providence has been in the way of showing Buchan's tie to the boy's story and his elaboration of some of its tenets until they transcend the source. Not quite the same thing happened with Buchan's use of detective story traditions. When Buchan went into the thriller business, (and make no mistake, his popular book a year was not only recreation but also business,) there was no such thing as the detective novel as we know it: the modern detective novel began with E.C. Bentley's *Trent's Last Case* (1914), which, incidentally, Buchan discovered and published. There were, admittedly, detective short stories written by Conan Doyle and his imitators, but there were no detective novels which focused on the solution of one reasonably domestic crime. Sayers, Christie and the rest wrote them in reaction to Buchan, not *vice versa*. In 1910 the chameleon books of Wallace and Oppenheim, which combine crime, puzzle, espionage, romance and veneration of the high-life, were the only brand of detective novel available. Buchan locked onto this pattern in the Hannay novels. In each of the Hannay books, the hero must solve an enigmatic verbal puzzle before the big evil can be confronted. This part of the Hannay books becomes increasingly important until in *The Three Hostages* it is one of the major organizing ideas of the novel. Buchan located the detective puzzle of *The Thirty Nine Steps* in the decoding of Scudder's ciphered notes. Rather than showing readers how Hannay does this, Buchan merely tells us that, while staying at the literary innkeeper's hostelry, he does it. With *Greenmantle,* Buchan gives more attention to the subject and lets readers follow along from Harry Bullivant's cryptic "Kasredin, cancer, V.I." to Hannay's rumination on the clues. We, for all the good it does, have a good chance of doping out "V.I." before Hannay does. We get a chance of seeing Hannay, Blenkiron and Mary struggle with the snatches of incomprehensible German overheard by Hannay in *Mr. Standfast*. Finally there comes the poetic challenge in *The Three Hostages* which Buchan uses to organize this peacetime spy book. Now Buchan may use the detective puzzle for structure in a casual sort of way, but in no way does it form an essential part of the plot.

The answers to the puzzles in the books do not come from patient research or careful reasoning. They arrive as a result of inspiration which would be anathema to the new detective novelists of the twenties. Further, we never see the actual working out of the problem. Some of this happens off stage, or we get an answer as a *fiat*, as with Blenkiron's pinning down of "celsius" in *Mr. Standfast*. In terms of plot, the solution to the conundrum does relatively little: it simply makes the villain and his plans known but it does not solve this problem. The problem of evil must still be won through action, work, inspiration, providence and all the rest. Included as it is with many other elements of fiction, the detective puzzle is only one strand of Buchan's plots. But significantly it is only in the Hannay books that Buchan weaves in the puzzle. This is because Buchan wanted to counteract some of the non-intellectual parts of Hannay with cerebration, which is not the case with Leithen, Sandy or Dickson McCunn.

Before we get to Hannay, though, there are some other pieces of business which need to be transacted. Buchan paid some tongue-in-cheek homage to Oppenheim as his inspiration in thriller writing, but to find his real master we need to look to a far older and far better writer than Oppenheim. One simply cannot read Buchan without noticing the multitudinous allusions to *Pilgrim's Progress*. Even without *Mr. Standfast*, a novel stretched on the frame of Bunyan, one can scarcely miss the citations of *Pilgrim's Progress* which appear in virtually every novel. Why are they there? Well, the surface answer is that *Pilgrim's Progress* forms part of the Scottish, Calvinistic heritage into which Buchan was born. Bunyan, however, is more important to Buchan as a thriller writer than simply being part of his cultural equipage. *Pilgrim's Progress* is a pretty pure and clear model for the thriller writer to follow. For those who don't remember the book, it roughly goes like this. Christian, feeling the weight of his sins, leaves his home and family in the City of Destruction, and sets out for a better place. On his travels he meets various people who hinder him and others who help him—it being difficult to discern the nature of the former but not the latter. He also confronts people who clearly embody gigantic evil, whom he manages to elude. Further, Christian passes through a landscape which tempts and tries him physically and morally as well as gives him solace and strength. Finally, he crosses the river and ascends Mount Zion. Of course, in Bunyan a detailed theological allegory attends these things, but when *Pilgrim's Progress* is reduced to its essential story it has all the elements which we find in Buchan's thrillers. There is the loose terminal date (Christian's race with time to gain salvation before death), the journey through a landscape which tries and proves physical and moral strength, the antagonists who are difficult to discern, not because they are disguised but because the hero does not have the perspective to recognize them, as well as the big, blatant angatonists, the stalwart friends and the reward of success at the end. We find this in all the spy novels and I could have made the last sentence even more difficult by adding parenthetical examples. *Mr. Standfast* serves as a laboratory-pure case of Buchan following Bunyan. Hannay acts the part of Christian, whom Ivery and Greeson roundly deceive during his journey during the first part of the novel. Hannay makes several journeys through desperate landscapes in order to stop the Wild Birds before their return to Germany. The book also contains various helpful companions, Blenkiron, Mary, Wake and Peter, who vie for the various allegorical labels in Bunyan. Although Bunyan propels *Mr. Standfast*, he is clearly important to the technique of all the other spy novels. An illustration of the persistence of one motif will, perhaps, serve to stand for the rest. In Bunyan one of Christian's early obstacles is the Hill of Difficulty, which he must laboriously ascend in order to prove his faith. Now consider climbing and mountains in Buchan. Lewis defeats the bad guys in a mountain pass just as Melfort does in *A Prince of the Captivity*. David must ascend a rock chimney in *Prester John*; Hannay, half goofy with asphyxiation, climbs a dove cote in *The Thirty Nine Steps*; and Stumm traps the adventurers on a hill in *Greenmantle*. In *Mr. Standfast* Hannay and Wade climb the Alps to get in at the finish, Hannay and Medina have it out on Scottish crags in *The Three Hostages* and Sandy scampers up a mountain in *The Courts of Morning* in order to block the pass with a landslide. Enough? I could add more. At any rate there is a lot of climbing. Some of this can be traced to Buchan's concern with Thermopolyae, but there is more. Few of these acrobatics are necessary and some are downright anti-climactic—in *Mr. Standfast* Wade and Hannay rush over the Alps only to discover Blenkiron sitting on the Wild Birds. The point is that Buchan *via* Bunyan saw climbing as a means of showing character and that one could not accept the final reward without having been pitted against the physical and psychological stress of climbing.

Just as Christian leaves the City of Destruction for the perils of the wild world which threatens danger and promises redemption, so do Buchan's heroes leave the city for wild country. This is the case in all his spy books except *The Power-House*, which largely develops in and around London with only a bit of reported action from wild

places. Even the city-bound hero of *The Power-House*, Edward
Leithen, leaves for the wilds in three of the four subsequent novels
(*John MacNab, The Dancing Floor* and *Sick Heart River*). The pull
of rough country, as symbolically important as it may be, really lies
at the center of Buchan's achievement and accounts for much of his
attraction for readers. This he did not get from Oppenheim and only
got it in a general way from Bunyan. Buchan's use of rough country,
I think, can be best seen through an examination of Buchan's
contemporary, Robert Baden-Powell, for Buchan represents,
directly or indirectly, the fictional jelling of many of the things for
which Baden-Powell stood.

General Sir Robert Baden-Powell served in most of Britain's
imperial wars in the last part of the nineteenth century. He started
his military career at the tail end of the Afghan War, served in the
Ashanti War and the Matabele War (cf. Peter Pienaar), and gained
immense fame for his leadership at Mafeking during the Boer War.
During peaceful periods he acted as a military spy in Dalmatia,
Turkey, Germany, Austria and Russia, collecting information on
fortifications, troop dispositions and armaments. Like Buchan, he
was a man of moderate means, and he supplemented his army pay
by writing books. Some of the more significant of these are *Aids to
Scouting* (1899), *Sport in War* (1900) and *My Adventures as a Spy*
(1915). He also founded the Boy Scouts and published a number of
volumes connected with this project, including *Scouting for Boys*
(1908), *Scouting Games* (1910) and *Yarns for Boys* (1910). As a
writer, Baden-Powell fused any number of Victorian ideas into one
body of work of which the Boy Scouts were the logical outcome. First
of all, Baden-Powell learned a military lesson from guerilla wars in
India and Africa, and wrote on the necessity of armies knowing and
using the landscape rather than blundering about with large bodies
of troops. This is what *Aids to Scouting* was all about—military
scouting (i.e. spying). Here he discusses how to use cover, how to use
disguise, etc. In addition to stressing how the scout or spy can
master and blend into his environment, Baden-Powell stressed the
importance of strict and accurate observation and deduction. This
can be seen in a letter of 1906 to William Smith, where Baden-Powell
outlines how the principles of military scouting can be inculcated in
boys:

The instructor should read to the would-be scouts a detective tale from Gaboriau or
Conan Doyle (Sherlock Holmes), laying special stress on the clues to the crime, and
deductions therefrom. He should examine the boys to see that they have grasped the
idea of drawing conclusions from small signs.[12]

He again combines spying and detection in this passage from *My Adventures as a Spy*: "One of the attractive features of the life of a spy is that he has, on occasion, to be a veritable Sherlock Holmes."[13] As important as this, B-P insists over and over again that warfare, particularly scouting, is fun—it is a game. We can see this in the title of his book of 1900, *Sport in War,* and again in a chapter entitled "The Sport of Spying," in *My Adventures as a Spy.* The chapter begins with this passage, "Undoubtedly spying would be an intensely interesting sport even if no great results were obtainable from it. There is a fascination which gets hold of anyone who has tried the art."[14] This outlook colors his attitudes toward the men who engage in espionage—even during World War I: "A good spy—no matter which country he serves—is *of necessity* a brave and valuable fellow."[15] Added to this there is B-P's affection for what he explicitly calls "yarns." His adult books are full of recountings of his own adventures as a scout or as a spy, and his Boy Scout books, like *Yarns for Boy Scouts* (1910), obviously place a high value on the yarn.

Much of what we find in Baden-Powell is traceable to general trends in the culture, like the Victorian interest in health, the growing prominence of games at schools, the practical response to the Boer War, etc. But direct or indirect, we can trace all of these things in Buchan's spy novels; indeed, we can trace some of the most attractive features of Buchan's spy novels to them. Buchan, like Baden-Powell, combined military scouting with detection, and saw the whole construct as a game in which the opposite side, no matter how loathsome its dogma or personal habits, must be appreciated and honored as men with conviction—and as sportsmen.

First, let us start with scouting in Buchan, for here there are a number of concrete points of contact with Baden-Powell. To start with, Buchan knows about Boy Scouts and uses them in his works. In *Huntingtower*, a group of slum urchins aspire to become a Boy Scout troop, but lacking the means they form their own troop and christen themselves the Gorbals Die-Hards. When they come into contact with the sinister bolshies who are after the Romanov jewels they demonstrate their pluck through superior organization, wit, spying, woodcraft and stamina. *Huntingtower* could almost be one of the Chief Scout's yarns for Boy Scouts. This novel, though, deals with scouting for boys, while Buchan was very much absorbed with scouting for men. Scouting plays a sustained and significant role in the Hannay novels. In *The Thirty Nine Steps* Hannay's impromptu acting and using the land to avoid pursuit easily parallel B-P's advice on the same in *Aids to Scouting*, a book, it should be remembered, which was considered so important that it was issued to troops in the Great War. Buchan abstracted this part of Hannay, the disguising and scouting part, and developed it more fully in the character of Peter Pienaar (who is mentioned in *The Thirty Nine Steps* and *The Island of Sleep* and who appears in *Greenmantle* and *Mr. Standfast*). Peter has been not only a big game hunter and minor con-man, but from his first mention is "the best scout I ever knew."[16] Practically the whole justification for introducing Peter in *Greenmantle*—other than being Hannay's pal, which is certainly important—is his crawl from the Turkish lines to the Russian trenches which precipitates the fall of Erzerum. Otherwise he is a fifth wheel, contributing nothing to the forwarding of the plot. Practically the same is true of *Mr. Standfast*. Peter, of course, stands for self-sacrifice to goad on the other characters, but Archie and the whole Air Corps admire him for his application of the principles of terrestrial scouting to aerial warfare. Peter uniquely contributes skill as a scout and scouting performs a vital part of Buchan's fictions. Indeed, some of Buchan's best narrative passages come when Peter or Hannay uses the landscape to stalk or to escape the enemy, perceiving not only the tip and roll of the countryside but also appreciating its color, texture, sound and smell.

As in Baden-Powell, Buchan combines the danger and thrill of adventure, the emotional exhilaration of spying, with detective elements traceable to Gaboriau or Conon Doyle,the rational satisfaction of spying. Further, he, like Baden-Powell, finds that the whole construct of spying provides the same satisfaction and uses the same values as those found in games. Baden-Powell makes the connection between playing and spying perfectly clear in *My Adventures as a Spy*: "The game of Hide-and-Seek is really one of the best games for a boy, and can be elaborated until it becomes scouting in the field. It teaches you a lot."[17] Although Buchan could not read this statement before he wrote *The Thirty Nine Steps*, the whole novel can really be seen as an extended game of hide-and-seek, and this applies to many of the other novels too. Buchan's hero (and his readers) gets, in turn, to play both roles in the game. First he hides from his pursuers using environmental cover and disguise, and then he seeks the enemy who has either hidden in disguise or hidden by putting space between himself and the hero—or both. The verve of the game is of immense importance for Buchan's appeal, but for Buchan and for Baden-Powell the real importance was didactic: "it teaches you a lot."

All of this game business in Buchan and Baden-Powell carried over from games in school, where it was not supposed to matter whether a boy won or lost, but how his character was molded. In this sense, Buchan repeats the terms "game," "sport" and "sportsman" as frequently as he invokes "job," "work" and "duty." Whether they were ever real or not, Buchan brings the values of sport to the spy novel. This accounts for the fact that his heroes are amateurs instead of professionals. Reflecting the snobbish public school bias against professional sportsmen, Buchan's heroes, by remaining amateur spies, have broader personalities and concerns than the narrow professional, and they also bring wider-ranging intelligence to bear, as Bullivant makes clear to Hannay in *Greenmantle*. The fact that there are comic scenes in *The Thirty Nine Steps, Greenmantle* and *Mr. Standfast* reinforces that at least one facet of spying is happy play, just as others are earnest struggle, which is also part of play. Perhaps the most telling games attitude in Buchan comes in regard to the villains. Just as in games one is a cad if he traduces the loser and forgets the loser's effort and value as a human being, so Hannay always feels sympathy for his opponents. Even in *Greenmantle*, where Hannay thrashes Stumm, who is a bully and to Hannay's mind a closet queen, he feels that "My anger had completely gone and I had no particular ill-will left against Stumm. He was a man of remarkable qualities."[18] Buchan intends no irony. His heroes were to be good sports who are determined to persevere when they are losing and are humble and magnanimous in victory. This holds true for all his spy novels. It is the reason that Buchan opens *Castle Gay* with an international rugby match which Wee Jaikie wins for Scotland. Adventure is sport, and each shows a man's character.

Which brings us to Buchan's heroes, for in spite of the moral significance of the action or the crispness of the adventure, it is the image of the characters which remains with readers. Although Leithen was probably Buchan's favorite character, employed both in thrillers and idea books as well as in Buchan's last testament, *Sick Heart River*, Richard Hannay is more important for Buchan's spy novels and for his fiction (as opposed to his convictions).

Hannay looks about the way I do—or you do, for that matter. Never mind the deductions which we can draw about his appearance by scouring the books for details or by comparing him to other characters. He looks like us. This is one of the effects of the first person narration which Buchan uses in the Hannay novels. Some critics would have it that Hannay is a snob and that he appeals to snobbery in his readers, but this is only a half-truth. Buchan goes to some pains to draw Hannay as a character who combines romantic features with the attributes of the average man.

The romantic features in Hannay's character are relatively easy to pick out. First of all he is an exile, with all the benefits but none of the drawbacks of this traditional literary figure. Hannay is a stranger in Britain, having been raised since childhood in South Africa, and, particularly at the start of *The Thirty Nine Steps,* he is alone and alienated in a foreign capital. In part of his consciousness, Hannay clings to scenes and people from his past in a far off, exotic land. None of this, however, gets out of hand. Hannay may be a colonial but he is also a Scotsman returning home, and his affection for the British countryside soon almost effaces his reveries of Rhodesia and South Africa. Indeed, in *Mr. Standfast,* Hannay becomes a passionate devotee not of Scottish or African but English countryside.

In that moment I had a kind of revelation. I had a vision of what I had been fighting for, what we all were fighting for. It was peace, deep and holy and ancient, peace older than the oldest wars... It was more; for in that hour England first took hold of me. Before my country had been South Africa, and when I thought of home, it had been the wide sun-steeped spaces of the veld or some scented glen of the Berg. But now I realized that I had a new home. I understood what a precious thing this little England was, how old and kindly and comforting, how wholly worth striving for.[19]

This, after a sensory feast of British nature. Like Archie Roylance, who is a passionate bird-watcher, the hero appreciates the surface beauty and the inner worth of the land. One other romantic feature of Buchan's hero lies in his astronomical success, not only in terms of winning but in worldly terms too. But this, also, is modified. Hannay may win, but in every case he wins with the help of his friends—even in *Thirty Nine Steps,* Hannay's recollection of Peter's scouting swings the pendulum of success. Yes, he is successful in worldly terms, but Buchan moderates this. Hannay has made his pile in Rhodesia, but "it is not one of the big ones but good enough for me." He is comfortably, not opulently, off. Granted, he gets to be a brigadier general pretty quickly, but he is not all that important. Haig does not ask his advice, and he obeys lots of orders. I suspect that Buchan would have only created him a colonel, that standard rank in the spy story, if he had not been created a colonel himself.

Most of Buchan's efforts in making Hannay, however, are to show him as the average man—not statistically average but ideally average. One principal way of doing this shows through in Hannay's dependent independence. Naturally, since the books focus on him and since he acts as the adventure hero, Hannay must win the day. He must bluff the Blackstone gang, face Stumm, and meet Medina alone on the crags. He gets plenty of help, though. Even in the first novel where Hannay is much alone, the recollection of Peter's advice about acting enables him to succeed. After *The Thirty Nine Steps* he becomes more dependent on others for success. He does do his bit, but Sandy really dismantles the jihad and Peter delivers the goods in *Greenmantle,* Blenkiron gets the drop on Ivery and Peter clears the skies in *Mr. Steadfast,* and Mary faces down Medina in *The Three Hostages.* Hannay does his bit, but he is no superhuman figure who can do it all alone, and he realizes it. Significantly, he does not seek the assignments and adventures in the books, but, as in the case of *The Thirty Nine Steps,* they are foisted on him or, as in the later books, he volunteers because it is his duty to his country or society; he even refuses an adventure for the easy life in *The Courts of Morning.*

Another average side of Hannay is his immersion in his physical self. No part-time lounge lizard, part-time he-man this. Dick Hannay works with his hands and is used to hard work. He has been a working mining engineer, used to frontier life, and physical exertion exhilarates him just as stuffy cities depress him. With all this stress on the physical, though, Hannay is no mental or cultural troglodyte. This is one of the purposes of the puzzles which Buchan inserts in these books: they show that Hannay has a mind, not one of lightning comprehension, but a good, sturdy, work-a-day mind. Further, Hannay has substantial culture. He works at educating himself, going through a course of reading English classics with delight and enthusiasm in *Mr. Standfast.* Also in the same novel, Buchan expands his hero's cultural horizons by bringing him into contact with Lancelot Wake, the intellectual conscientious objector, whom Hannay learns to respect even though he can neither accept his values nor convert him. In *The Island of Sheep,* he can even accept and rejoice in the fact that his son is not very much like him. Withal, Buchan never intended to make his hero either a pea-brained he-man or a wise, highly cultured man. He wanted to make Hannay into an average man who knows his own limitations and who respects the worth and honesty of others.

Hannay's position also shows through in his attitudes toward class. To bar misunderstanding, however, one must again remember that Hannay is not the middle class average but the ideal average man. Indeed Hannay views with contempt the middle class commuter who lives an easy, unexamined life in the suburbs. Thus he cannot stand the idea of the frivolous citizens of Biggleswick in *Mr. Standfast,* and he has the same prejudice against Lombard, who has settled for the soft life in *The Island of Sheep*. When it comes to practical experience, though, Hannay rather likes most of the Biggleswickeans, and Lombard ultimately plays a part which belies his middle-class cushion. Hannay makes himself at home with all people of good will, and he especially cottons to those who are direct, truthful and hard-working. On one level this appears in his affection and partnership with Peter, Andrew Amos (who appears in *Mr. Standfast* and *The Three Hostages)*, and George Hamilton (who appears in *Mr. Standfast* and *The Courts of Morning)*. These men are simple, honest but shrewd doers, who wear their class as a scutcheon as proud as any aristocratic family. The same holds true of Hannay's attitudes toward peasants, shopkeepers, roadmenders and Cabinet members. Yes, he may be a shade politer to Sir Walter Bullivant than he is to a German peasant, but just a shade. Hannay is, in fact, devoted to Buchan's muscular toryism, which involves recognition of the value and worth of all who contribute.

The trouble with many people's views of Buchan is that they are Hannay-obsessed and find his work-oriented, hearty values to be repellent. This view colors Richard Osborne's admittedly nostalgic view as well as that of Jonathan Gathorne-Hardy.[20] We do, though, need to recall that Hannay is not Buchan, but a character who was purposely drawn, purposely drawn when England was at war; we need to consider Dickson McCunn, who acts in some ways as an antidote to some of the things which Buchan developed in the Hannay books. For one thing, Buchan once more liberated comedy with the first Dickson McCunn novel, *Huntingtower*. Liberated? Yes. When Buchan began the Hannay books with *The Thirty Nine Steps*, he broke away from the earnest tone which he inherited from Oppenheim and wove comedy and adventure together as Scott does in *Ivanhoe*. He attempts to predict the readers' response to the book in showing Bullivant's reaction to Hannay's tale: "he laughed" at the part about Sir Harry, "grew merry" upon hearing of Jopley, "grew solemn" and became "solemnised" when hearing about the murder of Scudder and the entrance of the bald archeologist. Although he throws in bits of slap-stick, like the cinema-making scene in *Mr. Standfast*, Buchan made the subsequent Hannay books more totally serious until *The Three Hostages*, where there is little comedy. He grew to see the times and the issues involved in the Hannay novels as too important to join with humor; in fact, he never saw the copper-bottomed Hannay as basically funny, even though he occasionally gets caught in comedy of situation. In the Dickson McCunn books, Buchan's comic field expands. Here there is more comedy, and there is not only comedy of situation of a zanier order, but also comedy of character. Perhaps the craziest situation comes in *The House of the Four Winds*, when Randal Glynde steps into Jaikie's second floor room from the back of an elephant. In terms of comedy of character, we find peripheral antics, like Wee Jaikie in *Huntingtower* chanting communist anthems, ignorant of their meaning:

> Proley Tarians, arise!
> Wave the Red flag to the skies,
> Heed nae mair the Fat Man's lees,
> Slap them doun his throat![21]

They include, moreover, comic portraits of the major characters. These comic characters are treated lovingly but ironically, and they are a corrective for too much Hannay.

Obviously I have been working toward a discussion of Dickson McCunn. Buchan acknowledges in Dickson the level of fantasy which lies under the spy/adventure story. Dickson is not much like Dick Hannay: he is a solidly middle-class Scot, who sells his prosperous Glasgow grocery business to United Supply Stores, Ltd., takes to the road, and, when he gets mixed up in adventure, is proud of bringing his business acumen to the aid of the friends he has met on the road. In some ways he is the antithesis of Hannay. Far from being the brawny hero, Dickson is in his mid-fifties in the first novel, he never mixes it up with the villains, and he does not go off on spontaneous rampages the way Hannay does. Certainly providence plays a role in his adventures, but not in the specific ways that it does in the Hannay books. Rather than blatantly working to make things turn out right, providence operates to teach people things. Sure, it arranges events so that the meek and the good win the world from powerful and energetic nasties, but it works hard at converting people. Providence liberates Dickson from his work-a-day middle class prison and his mundane point of view. At the start of *Huntingtower*, Dickson sets out to fulfill his pastoral illusions about freedom from trade, but he carries with him all sorts of restricting intellectual baggage. He stereotypes the romantic, Heritage, telling him that "the place for you ... is in Russia with the Bolsheviks,"[22] and he sees his support of the pseudo-Boy Scout Die-Hards as simply social largesse. Immersion in real danger with real friends transmutes him and fixes in him a more substantial, but even wilder, romanticism, which continues in *Castle Gay* and *The House of the Four Winds*. The same sort of conversion theme lies under the plot of *Castle Gay*, where Mr. Craw, the publisher, goes through a similar conversion. Withal, Buchan purposely creates the characters in the McCunn novels on a less epic scale than those in the Hannay circle, and even the most traditionally heroic of them (Heritage in *Huntingtower*, the grown-up Jaikie, and Randal Glynde, the Secret Service man, in *The House of the Four Winds*) do not succeed through derring-do.

In the Dickson McCunn novels Buchan swung with the spirit of the twenties, the same spirit which we see replacing thriller elements in the detective novel with crackpot, whimsical characters and plots. Thus Dickson and Jaikie and Glynde came about for the same reasons that Wimsey, Poirot and Campion were created. Along the same lines, Buchan moved out of the world of dangerous fantasy found in the Hannay books to a personal fantasy world with whimsical people. In the long run, however, Buchan was too committed to what he saw as serious issues to stay for long in a world of comic romance, and so, in the twenties and thirties, he returned again and again to Hannay, Leithen, Sandy and more overly serious topics. Still, Dickson and his colleagues provided a needed relief and a measure of self-awareness for Buchan.

I have already touched on most of the other characters in Buchan's spy novels. Peter is the scout, the pal, and stands for wartime sacrifice. Archie shows his callowness and neutrality by inhabiting both the Hannay books, and *The House of the Four Winds* and *The Courts of Morning*; his only real development, his conversion, comes in *John MacNab,* which is not a spy book. Buchan's villains are pretty much of a piece, and I will say a bit about them later. One miscellaneous comment about most of Buchan's characters is that we, like the people in the books, want to call them by their first names, unlike our reponse to Smiley, Len Deighton's hero, Bond, and Colonel Granby.

There are, however, two characters who need a bit more comment. The first is John S. Blenkiron, who appears in *Greenmantle, Mr. Standfast* and *The Courts of Morning*—although he is little more than a cipher in the last book. Oddly, we don't, and Buchan's characters don't, often use his first name. Not that there is anything standoffish about him. Perhaps it is his profession and nationality: Blenkiron is Buchan's semi-comic portrait of a larger-than-life American millionaire. His humor stems from his duodenal complaint (identical with Buchan's ulcer trouble) and from his dialect, which Buchan builds out of some phonetic peculiarities ("oo" for "ew" as in "Noo York" and "noospaper") and quaint diction, like this which Hannay marks in *Greenmantle*: "I could hear him [Blenkiron] invoking some unknown deity called Holy Mike."[23] Make no mistake, though, Blenkiron is not a klutz or buffoon. He brings New World organization, bustle, and business-sense to a group of unfocused amateurs, and, by the by, is the germ of Dickson McCunn's business sense. The business side of Blenkiron can be best seen in *The Courts of Morning*, where he organizes the rebellion against Castor. In the other novels, however, it is his hearty optimism in the face of physical discomfort and perverse events which makes him stand out. It is all of this which makes Buchan position him as the motivator of Leithen's life-saving mission in his last novel, *Sick Heart River*.

In addition to Blenkiron, the other complex character in the spy novels is Sandy Arbuthnot, Lord Clanroyden. Even more than with Hannay's origins in an actual figure, Tiny Ironside, Sandy grew from one, or probably two, of Buchan's contemporaries. As Smith points out, Buchan put elements of Aubrey Herbert, the explorer, and, after 1920, added parts of T.E. Lawrence to Sandy's character. He does, in fact, change from novel to novel, growing smaller to fit Lawrence's stature for instance, but parts of his nature do remain constant. The constant part lies in the fact that Sandy is one of those Britons who feels more comfortable with, and who has more knowledge of, the exotic and occult than he does with the domestic and rational. Thus, in *Greenmantle*, he becomes the leader of the Companions of the Rosy Hours, a dervish revival in Turkey, and later assumes the prophet's mantle from the dead ayatollah. In *The Three Hostages*, he assumes the turban of Kharma, and in *The Courts of Morning*, he becomes a legendary Indian guerilla. The costumes are, however, mere props. The occult has seeped into Sandy's fiber, and even though in daytime the possession is benign, at night the mystic reality terrifes and unhinges him. Therefore, in *Greenmantle* and *The Three Hostages,* even though in the daytime Sandy fanctions in *The Courts of Morning* and *The Island of Sheep,* Sandy becomes susceptible to mystic forces of evil, to which Buchan returns constantly.

Buchan views evil as a powerful atavistic urge to return to barbarism and to destory or dominate order and civilization: this motif runs in various permutations, from *Prester John* through *The Island of Sheep*. On the simplest level, found in the early short story "The Grove of Ashtaroth" and in *Witch Wood,* this is the orgiastic urge to run around naked and give in to fear and love as superstition. Its sophisticated form manifests itself in megalomania and orchestrated chaos for profit. This we see in most of the thriller villains, from Lumley in *The Power-House* to Castor in *The Courts of Morning,* and it includes all of the villains pitted against Sandy.

Allied to this element, Buchan joins palpable personal magnetism, which makes evil prosper: thus Blackstone's grip on Hannay, Medina's mesmerism, Castor's use of drugs. With Sandy, Buchan suggests that immersion in primitive culture brings him closer to this level of experience, and, although he alone can defeat it, he faces a difficult inner struggle to do so. In *Greenmantle* only his friends' presence and encouragement, added to his duty as a British officer ("You must know, Madam, that I am a British officer."), enables him to resist Hilda von Einem. Here it does not matter a bit whether he was drawn from Herbert or Lawrence. He is there because he represents one reaction to danger and evil, significantly a reaction which differs from Hannay's. Sandy serves as a complement to Hannay so that they can illuminate each other's virtues. Thus Hannay's average, direct, domestic sphere gains from contrast with Sandy's particular genius, just as Sandy gains from contrast with Hannay. Moreover, their diverse characters contribute to the overall theme of friendship which Buchan was interested in conveying through his books.

Since Buchan's interest in espionage largely revolves around the ideas of character and friendship, he is not really interested in portraying organized espionage departments as a part of government. His heroes win the day by themselves or with the help of their friends, while organized police and armies stand by for the denouement. Lone heroes do most of the work in *Prester John, The Power-House, The Thirty Nine Steps,* and *A Prince of the Captivity.* The lone hand, a term which Bullivant applies to Scudder and which Hannay applies to himself, is important to these books, because the defeat of spies has more character building or proving importance than it has political ramifications. Novels with groups of people show the same thing, only with the theme of friendship added. Buchan accepts the principle shown in the detective books of the same period that the hero must be an amateur. With the exception of Randal Glynde and Adam Melfort, all of Buchan's people enter espionage because it is their Duty, not because it is their duty. This is not to say, however, that he has no truck whatsoever with espionage establishments; they became evident in the novels most tied to the war. Thus, in *Greenmantle,* Bullivant describes British Intelligence in the East on two occasions. First he states that

I have reports from agents everywhere—peddlars in South Russia, Afghan horse-dealers, Turcoman merchants, pilgrims on the road to Mecca, sheikhs in North Africa, sailors on the Black Sea coasters, sheep-skinned Mongols, Hindu fakirs, Greek traders in the Gulf, as well as respectable consuls who use cyphers.[24]

and later that

We have had our agents working in Persia and Mesopotamia for years—mostly young officers in the Indian Army.[25]

I suppose ingenuity could reconcile these statements and show that every other person in the East really was not a British agent, but it is not necessary. Buchan's books are unconcerned with government organizations. In Constantinople, it is Blenkiron's own ring of agents which counts in *Greenmantle,* and in *Mr. Standfast,* it is his greenbacks which buy the organization which runs Ivery to earth. Even at the beginning of *A Prince of the Captivity,* where Buchan gets as realistic about spying as he ever does, it is not a government official who recruits and controls Melfort, it is Macandrew/Meyer, the Zionist. Sure, Blenkiron alludes to the fabled expertise of British Naval Intelligence in *Greenmantle,* but it never comes into the books. Espionage in these books rests on private enterprise: private financing and personal commitment.

A large part of Buchan's success as a popular writer derives from his ability to create clear, individual characters with whom readers, especially middle class readers, can identify and who at the same time convey lucid ideals which are firmly embedded in cultural tradition. There is really nothing astonishing about his plotting. In the early novels, he pretty clearly borrows his plot ideas from Oppenheim. Thus, in *The Power-House* and *The Thirty Nine Steps,* we find the typical Oppenheim situation: the hero has some special information which he needs to deliver to obstinate, obtuse, or unreachable authority in order to foil an anarchic plot. Further, many of Buchan's novels are episodic because of his dependence on providence. Here we find providence manifests itself in Buchan's novels in two ways: either it works on the hero or it works through him. In the first instance, in books like *The Thirty Nine Steps,* providence unifies the random situations in which Hannay finds himself, and moves things toward the proper conclusion. In the second category, in books like *The Courts of Morning* and *A Prince of the Captivity,* the hero has a set purpose which unifies events and makes them less random. Largely, Buchan shows little concern for realistic motivation of events, just as he shows little concern for presenting traditional rising and falling plot construction. Most of the books have two climaxes, one which clears up plot and the second which clears up character.

A large part of Buchan's attraction for readers comes from his narrative touch, as distinct from plotting. He took the spy novel out of the overfilled and plodding world of Wallace, Oppenheim, and LeQueux and made it a spare, entertaining form. I have already suggested that part of this was due to his combining of comedy with the fictitious high matter of the spy adventure, but Buchan also knew how to orchestrate techniques of suspense. Pursuit and escape form the skeleton of almost every book, and Buchan most often works this so that the enemy pursues the hero for the first part of the novel, and then the hero pursues the villains in the last part. In his articulation of pursuit and escape he relies on the techniques of disguise and exploration of various facets of obstacles to the hero. Virtually every novel includes disguise of one sort or another, but Buchan revivifes disguise so that it is not as hackneyed or simply decorative as it is in other thriller writers. Usually in thrillers we find that it is the villains who work in disguise. This occurs in *The Thirty Nine Steps* and *Mr. Standfast,* but it is the exception, not the rule. Usually Buchan brings us the hero in disguise so as to bring him face to face with his enemies and keep readers wondering whether the villains will recognize the truth and therefore bring physical threats to bear. This may be important, but more important, since connected with character, is presenting obstacles against which the hero must struggle. For Buchan the hero must not only cope with the dangers implied by capture (and in Buchan they are largely implied and rarely employed), but he must also confront his environment and his own body. Environment coalesces with the idea of scouting, which I have already touched on. As important as environment is, though, the hero's real struggle is against the limits of his own body. Thus Hannay has bouts with malaria in both *The Thirty Nine Steps* and *Greenmantle,* he eludes German thugs with his lungs full of lentonite fumes in *The Thirty Nine Steps,* he meets the last danger in *The Three Hostages* with a wounded arm, Sandy drops from fever and exhaustion in *The Courts of Morning,* and Blenkiron faces the world with his ulcer gnawing at his entrails. Clearly Buchan's own endurance of constant pain from his own ulcer had something to do with this, but he could remove himself enough not only to use it as a character technique but a suspense technique as well. While they do fight against physical threats, Buchan's heroes have few emotional bogeys to overcome. Melfort, who puts his wife's peccadillos completely out of mind in *A Prince of the Captivity,* is representative of this. But friends do provide obstacles and dangers for the hero. Buchan complicates pursuit and escape after *The Thirty Nine Steps* by giving the heroes friends who, on the positive side, can pluck them from disaster, as Sandy does in

Constantinople, but who, on the negative side, can screw things up, as Archie does in *The Three Hostages,* or increase their exposure to evil, as Peter does in *Greenmantle.* Again, however, the suspense technique links to a character point and the novels become more than simply thrillers.

Pursuit and escape, in fact, the suspense novel itself, rests on the writer finding means of making danger seem omnipresent. The lack of this makes Oppenheim's novels so flaccid and its presence makes Buchan's novels work. Authors can make danger seem enfolding any number of ways. It can be done by creating a hero who is anxious about his body, his mind, and about the safety of his extended self—his family, friends, society, etc. That is what I treated above. Ultimately, though, it all rests on the other side, the ways in which evil makes its presence known. Buchan employs several ways of doing this. First, he uses the technique of multiple pursuit. Typically thriller heroes cannot trust anyone; they are chased by villains who have extraordinary resources and thus can turn up a squad of goons anywhere on the globe. For Buchan, though, the world is not that hostile and he wants to show the theme of friendship. As a result, the multiple pursuit in Buchan becomes more specific and therefore more credible than in the average thriller of the teens. Thus most of Buchan's heroes are hounded by more than one group: Blackstone and the police in *The Thirty Nine Steps,* Stumm, Rasta, and von Einem in *Greenmantle,* nazis and communists in *A Prince of the Captivity.* They stick to the hero's heels, but he does find rest and consolation in good people. The result of this is that we find in Buchan not only the hero caught in a hostile world, but also the presence of relief, making the tempo faster but also promising the right conclusion. To this tension and release, Buchan, in *The Thirty Nine Steps,* adds a continuing chord of danger in the form of the airplane, which is now a tiny speck and now an expanse of wing and fuselage. Living behind enemy lines provides the same sort of thing.

There are, however, other novels which grip readers harder, or tell them more of human nature, or divert them with more pure comedy or scene painting. But only Conrad does this before Buchan, and we need to wait for another generation before we find it again in Greene and Ambler. Buchan took the spy novel out of the hands of innocuous romancers like Oppenheim and gave it sinew and meaning. Regardless of chronology or irrelevant "firsts," Buchan started the modern spy novel, and in its best manifestations the spy novel returns to him. Witness this passage from LeCarre's *The*

Honourable Schoolboy:

"Mr.—?"
"Standfast," Smiley replied politely, from beneath his umbrella.

NOTES

[1]Janet Adam Smith, *John Buchan: A Biography* (Boston: Little, Brown, 1965), p. 97.

[2]Smith, pp. 177-8.

[3]Smith, p. 194.

[4]*Sir Walter Scott* (New York: Coward-McCann, 1932), p. 129.

[5]Smith, p. 144.

[6]*The Island of Sheep* (Harmondsworth: Penguin, 1956),p. 22.

[7]*The Thirty Nine Steps* (New York: The Popular Library, n.d.), p. 6.

[8]Smith, p. 284.

[9]*Sartor Resartus* (London: Dent, 1965),p. 248.

[10]*The Three Hostages* (Harmondsworth: Penguin, 1959), p. 162.

[11]*Mr. Standfast* (Harmondsworth: Penguin, 1960), p. 101.

[12]E.E. Reynolds, *Baden-Powell* (Oxford: Oxford University Press, 1943), p. 140.

[13]Robert Baden-Powell, *My Adventures as a Spy* (London: Pearson, 1915), p. 61.

[14]Baden-Powell, p. 61.

[15]Baden-Powell, p. 28.

[16]*The Thirty Nine Steps*, p. 131.

[17]Baden-Powell, p. 91.

[18]*Greenmantle* (Harmondsworth: Penguin, 1960), p. 86.

[19]*Mr. Standfast*, p. 21.

[20]Jonathan Gathorne-Hardy, *The Old School Tie* (New York: Viking, 1978); Richard Usborne, *Clubland Heroes* (London: Constable, 1953).

[21]*Huntingtower* in *Adventurers All* (Cambridge, Mass.: Houghton Mifflin, n.d.) p. 292.

[22]*Huntingtower*, p. 43.

[23]*Greenmantle*, p. 215.

[24]*Greenmantle*, p. 19.

[25]*Greenmantle*, p. 21.

Chapter 5

Sapper
(1888-1937)

Captain Hugh "Bulldog" Drummond, D.S.O., M.C., late of His Majesty's Royal Loamshires: what a man! He focuses the attributes of the popular adventure hero from the teens and he becomes the model for the adventure heroes created in the forties and fifties. Today Hugh Drummond seems outdated and he is in disfavor among literary people: critics carp about Sapper's brash and sometimes trashy writing and his neolithic social attitudes. Nevertheless, Sapper's hero provides real energy and organization to the evolution of popular fiction in Britain. From 1920 to 1937, H.C. McNeile, using the pseudonym "Sapper" (i.e., Military Engineer), wrote ten Bulldog Drummond novels: *Bull-Dog Drummond* (1920), *The Black Gang* (1922), *The Third Round* (1924), *The Final Count* (1926), *The Female of the Species* (1928), *Temple Tower* (1929), *The Return of Bulldog Drummond* (1932), *Knockout* (1933), *Bulldog Drummond at Bay* (1935), and *Challenge* (1937). During the same period he wrote several miscellaneous novels which essentially reproduce the Bulldog Drummond material in another guise: *Tiny Carteret* (1930) deals with international intrigue, and *Guardians of the Treasure* (1931) tells a treasure hunt tale featuring Jim Maitland. Sapper also developed the same things in his collections of short stories (these sometimes have a frame story to give the illusion of continuity), including *Jim Maitland* (1923), *Ronald Standish* (1933), and *Ask for Ronald Standish* (1936). Bulldog Drummond, though, contributes most to the development of the spy novel. During the course of these books Sapper's purposes and practices vary a bit, but when we reduce them to their essentials, they all boil down to the forcefulness of the hero, the evil of the villain, exciting action, some boisterously rude comedy, and some clearly articulated social attitudes.

Let's start with the hero. McNeile began writing under the pseudonym of Sapper for a specific purpose. The pseudonym sounds like those classic letters to *The Times* which individuals sign with their professions in order to indicate that they represent a class and not a single writer. The military title, Sapper, points to the military subject matter of McNeile's early fictions. Thus his first collection of short stories, *Sergeant Michael Cassidy* (1915), contains vignettes, humorous and sentimental, from the trenches. The Bulldog Drummond books, particularly the early ones, have a specific military lure. When we first meet Hugh in *Bull-Dog Drummond*, we learn that he is a demobilized soldier rusting unused in the soft arms of civilian life. Throughout this first novel the narration constantly displaces the hero's name with "the soldier." The experience and peculiar skills which Hugh gained in France go a long way toward making him efficient in the new kind of warfare which nominal peace-time presents. Sapper dwells on this. Take the following passage from *Bull-Dog Drummond:*

...Hugh had practiced in France till he could kill a man with his bare hands in a second. Olaki—a Japanese—had first taught him two or three secrets of his trade, and in the interludes of resting behind the lines he had perfected them until it was even money whether the Jap or he would win a practice bout.

And there were nights in No Man's Land when his men would hear strange sounds, and knowing that Drummond was abroad on his wanderings, would peer eagerly over the parapet into the desolate torn-up waste in front. But they never saw anything...

. . .

Perhaps a patrol coming back would report a German lying in a shell-hole, with no trace of a wound, but only a broken neck; perhaps the patrol never found anything. But whatever the report, Hugh Drummond only grinned and saw to his men's breakfasts...

. . .

The result on Drummond was not surprising: as nearly as a man may be he was without fear.[1]

Hugh Drummond is supposed to be the soldier's soldier who goes beyond the call of duty to master his craft. This is very much apparent in the early novels, but as he moved into the twenties, Sapper let it slide—in most books after *The Black Gang*, Sapper contents himself with briefly mentioning the hero's service record and lets his readers assume the details. The only really lasting result of Hugh's wartime expertise comes in his ability to move about unseen and unheard. We find little more about *ju-jitsu* after the first book and, in fact, Drummond's combats usually reduce to Hugh grabbing the villain by the throat. Sapper also substitutes Hugh's skill as a boxer, with its vague public school connection, for the hand-to-hand combat, with its military connection. This change in the specifics of fighting corresponds with a growing public distaste for wartime memories, but Sapper, as the books proceed, does not completely eliminate Hugh's war-time experience.

Few ex-soldiers really want to relive the excitement of combat since it brings with its memories of blank fear and death. Neither do they want to recall the mindless regimen or inactivity of army life. More pleasant is the memory of the camaraderie of the trenches. We see this throughout all of Sapper's books. Hugh's man, Denny, is, of course, the cliche former batman with his lasting affection for his officer. In the novels Hugh never acts alone. He is always accompanied by a group of his fellow officers: Toby Sinclair, Algy Longworth, Ted Jerningham, and Peter Darrell. When Hugh stirs up a spot of trouble in *Bull-Dog Drummond,* his thoughts turn quickly to his fellow soldiers.

Toby possessed a V.C., and a good one—for there are grades of the V.C., and those grades are appreciated to a nicety by the recipient's brother officers if not by the general public. The show would fit Toby like a glove.... Then there was Ted Jerningham, who combined the roles of an amateur actor of more than average merit with the ability to hit anything at any range with every conceivable type of firearm. And Jerry Seymour in the Flying Corps.... Not a bad thing to have a flying man—up one's sleeve.... And possibly someone versed in the ways of tanks might come in handy....[2] [Sapper's ellipses]

The soldiers' reunion sounds a bit like Hugh intends to start his own private army—which, in fact, he does—but more important from Sapper's point of view is the shared understanding and comradeship of these fellow officers. Outside the circle of soldier-friends Sapper tends to describe civilians as weak or debilitated. In the first two novels, Hugh also has at his beck loads of demobilized soldiers to provide troops in his battle against international hanky-panky. Both the enlisted men and Hugh's fellow officers, moreover, show the virtues of military discipline and of Hugh's benevolent leadership: they follow him instinctively, as opposed to the minions of the villains who do their jobs out of greed, fear, or down right insanity. Sapper returns constantly to the camaraderie of soldiers. At every break in the action they congregate not only to plan the next attack—*toujours l'audace*—but to lower a pint or two and to chafe each other with good humor.

The war not only provided Hugh with his skills and his allies, it also formed some of his attitudes toward national and international politics. No burned-out intellectual like Owen or Sassoon, Hugh Drummond learned political reality in the war. He learned that one cannot mollycoddle evil: one must face it and destroy it. Thus in *Bulldog Drummond at Bay,* Hugh reads off a namby-pamby M.P. this way:

> "You did not go through the last war as—er—as a combatant. We did, and we don't want another, any more than some of the pacifist young gentlemen to-day, who never heard a shot fired in anger. We know the horrors of it first-hand; we are all out to prevent it again if we can. But we maintain that the present policy of cutting down our fighting forces...is the most certain way of precipitating it... As you know, they intended to kill Waldron and Graham Cardwell, so that those two secrets would have been Kalinsky's sole property. Do you suppose he was going to use 'em [the military secrets] for shaving paper?"[3]

The war has given the heroes what they perceive to be certain knowledge of the ways of evil and the only method of dealing with it—exterminate the brutes.

The military background also supplies a particular role for the structured authority in Sapper's books. Society does not depute Hugh Drummond and his chums to run down the bad folks of the world; they do it on their own time, using their own financial and personal resources, and out of their own initiative. Authority, this says, well-meaning as it sometimes is, cannot handle complex situations as well as vigilantes can. This motif of effective action and human feelings being limited to small groups versus the blindness, inefficiency, and hamstrung nature of high authority is a familiar one in literature about war: the General Staff, the men with the red tabs, sit on their duffs while the company or the platoon gets things done (or fails to get things done) and feels for each of its members. In this kind of book we also find that the real soldiers inevitably feel animosity or contempt for remote, structured authority. It is notable, in this connection, that Sapper only made Hugh a Captain as opposed to Buchan's elevation of Hannay to General's rank—Buchan was an armchair soldier. Sapper's hero, as the commander of the small group, gets things done and at the same time he gives authority the raspberry. This also connects Hugh to the tradition of the thriller. Thrillers habitually found ways of keeping established law-enforcement, the police, out of the action. They did this in order to boost the role of the amateur and to show that some problems present such grave peril to society that laws must be broken to solve them. Sapper combines these two anti-authority techniques and wrangles them into his plots. Not only does Hugh constantly break the law for what he believes to be the greater good—as in *The Black Gang,* where he kidnaps Marxists, ships them to a remote island, and shows them communism in action by making them work—he also mocks authority. Thus, also in *The Black Gang,* Hugh and his pals chloroform Inspector McIver and his policemen and leave them asleep on their own doorsteps. When this sort of hi-jinks comes up before authority, however, the powers in the society indulgently allow Hugh and his chums to keep up the good work—the justification of success is success. In both *The Black Gang* and *Bulldog Drummond at Bay,* therefore, Cabinet officials laughingly approve of Drummond's unorthodox methods of handling situations. Authority at the top remains inviolate, and individual initiative is praised and rewarded while the remote institution and lower-echelon managers take it on the chin.

In addition to the soldiering background, Sapper emphasizes Bulldog Drummond's size and strength. This largely occurs after the second novel, *The Black Gang,* where the narration partly replaces the repeated invocations of "the soldier" with repeated descriptions of Hugh as "huge" or "vast." In objective terms Bulldog Drummond is not all that big: he is just under *(Bull-Dog Drummond)* or precisely *(The Final Count)* six feet tall, and he weighs fourteen stone (one hundred ninety-six pounds). Today he would be a light heavy-weight—big, but hardly vast. But this is quibbling. If Sapper wants him to be huge there must be reasons for it. One of the reasons for Hugh's bulk comes as a logical conclusion to the gothic element in the novels. The evil people in Sapper's books live amidst gothic trappings (ostensibly haunted houses, etc.) and they use these things to terrify innocents. It is simple justice, therefore, that as part of their comeuppance they receive a good hearty dose of terror in return as earnest of their total punishment. Thus Hugh's huge hands come out of nowhere and grab the crook by the throat while his fellows cower in the corner. Hugh's physical size, for another thing, exists in order to underline his prowess as an action hero. Moving quickly and stalking silently seem the attributes of a smaller, lithe individual, but Hugh's ability to do these things and be the hulk that he is make him special. In the good-evil frame of these books, Hugh's size enables Sapper to play our giant against your giant, for he often introduces a figurative or, in the case of *The Black Gang,* literal gorilla to represent the awesome strength of the bad guys against which our champion must eventually do battle. Finally, Drummond's size exists to work a whole species of comedy. Hugh's gargantuan good humor and heartiness blow away gloom and bring in celebration. He is the big man who enjoys himself, his companions, and life in general to the fullest. It takes quarts of beer to satisfy his thirst, loads of friends to fulfill his gregariousness, and tons of excitement to keep him happy. Sapper uses this and, indeed, follows the comedy of size to absurd lengths. Thus in *Bulldog Drummond Returns,* the book opens with a narrative description of a whole country house being shaken to its foundations by the snores of the slumbering giant: it is a bit difficult to become seriously involved with the danger of adventure after such hyperbole.

Instead of being a grim-visaged avenger, Hugh Drummond is a sportsman from the leisure class. This leisure class business was an afterthought, but as the novels proceed, Sapper gives his readers more background on Hugh's family (he seems to be related to a Duke by the time of *The Black Gang,* and in later books, like *Temple Tower,* he numbers noblemen among his cronies) and his independent means (shown symbolically in his move to Brook Street in the second book). Sapper makes Inspector McIver type Hugh and his pals in *The Black Gang:*

All of them built on the same pattern; all of them fashioned along the same lines. Talking a strange jargon of their own—idle, perfectly groomed, bored. As far as they were concerned, he [McIver] was non-existent save as the man who was with Drummond. He smiled a little grimly; he, who did more man's work in a week than the whole lot of them in a year. A strange caste, he reflected, as he sipped his drink; a cast which does not aim at, because it essentially is, good form; a caste which knows only one fetish—the repression of all visible emotion; a caste which incidentally pulled more than its own weight in the war.[4]

This may be a case of protesting too much, but we see Sapper's aim. These men do, though, have another fetish: sport and sportsmanship. While Sapper does not give Hugh much background as an actual sportsman, beyond telling us about his boxing and mentioning that he goes shooting, he makes up for it in the persons of Tiny Carteret, in whom Sapper essentially reproduces Hugh, and Ronald Standish. The former is an international at rugger and the latter is in constant demand for cricket elevens and golf matches. Even if Hugh does not often chase after balls of any size, he is still a sportsman. *Bull-Dog Drummond* tells us that normal varieties of sport offer no relief from boredom for Hugh. He looks for bigger game and consequently places his now-famous ad in the papers:

Demobilized officer...finding peace incredibly tedious, would welcome diversion, legitimate, if possible; but crime, if of a comparatively humorous description, no objection. Excitement essential.[5]

The same thing happens again and again in the Bulldog

Drummond books: Hugh gets bored with shooting or golf or clubbing or country housing or just plain lolling about when, presto, a spot of real excitement crops up. In terms of sport and play, both the characters and narrators of the novels insist that the action rests on these things. Look at some of the titles—*The Third Round, The Final Count, Knockout, Challenge.* Boxing is sport, isn't it? Better yet, look into any of the books and you will find Hugh describing the action as a game. When Hugh, for instance, receives the second letter from Irma Peterson, who has kidnapped his wife, in *The Female of the Species,* Dixon, the narrator, describes the hero's reaction:

> "Absurd or not absurd," said Drummond gravely, "that is exactly what the woman has done. And from what I know of her it's going to be some chase."
>
> He got up, and suddenly to my amazement, and almost ecstatic grin spread over his face.
>
> "Gosh! boys," he said," if it wasn't that it was Phyllis, what a glorious time we should have. Why did we never think of it before with Carl [the villain in the previous books]? We might have had two or three games in our spare time."[6]

The ensuing action is, in fact, built on the game of Treasure Hunt. Risking one's life, grace and friendship under pressure all provide more pleasure than games like golf which mere burghers play. In *Temple Tower* Hugh and Peter pack their wives off to France under the pretext that they are going to play golf, but this is really a cover for getting mixed up with a bunch of French jewel thieves and gangsters. All of this sport carries with it its own set of rules: the re-evaluation of fair play. The villains in all of these books play dirty; this shows particularly in their penchant for terrorizing and kidnapping helpless men and women. After raging about this lack of fair play, Drummond typically switches to their morality, usually murdering one of the villains at the close of the book—Lakington in *Bull-Dog Drummond,* Yulowski in *The Black Gang,* Peterson in *The Final Count,* LeBossu in *Temple Tower,* Demonico in *Bulldog Drummond Strikes Back.* In the later books Hugh gives the villains a fighting chance, but, as we have seen above, he and his pals know that there is only one way to deal with evil. They do not, however, let this corrupt them, and when the next adventure comes along, they are ready to play the game with or without the rules of sportsmanship.

Some writers make the point that Bulldog Drummond represents the acme, or, if you will, nadir, of the traditions of the English public school.[7] Now, seeing Sapper in the light of schoolboy fiction aids in understanding his books, but in fact Sapper makes surprisingly few explicit references to public school life in his novels. True, in *The Black Gang,* Hugh does refer to his "stinks" (Chemistry) master at school and wishes he had absorbed more of the fundamentals of science, and in the same book we learn that Hugh was Sir Brian Johnstone's fag at school. We never, however, learn the name of the school or get much more on school life than this. The most attention to schools and schoolboys enters with Joe Dixon, the narrator of *The Female of the Species,* who gets one of his old masters to help solve the riddle in one of Irma Peterson's cryptic letters. The schoolboy quality in Sapper's books depends very little upon any direct connection with school or memories of school life. Sapper, in fact, does not write for people who have memories of public school or the university, as do Buchan, Beeding, Coles, and other higher-brow writers. The schoolboy quality in his books comes rather from Sapper's use of certain well-known patterns and attitudes. First of all, through most of Sapper's books, the narrator or the villain insists on calling Drummond and his cronies young men, and the novels give us the impression that a group of good young men contends with a group of nasty old men. This is part of normal schoolboy fantasy. Second, there is the institution of fagging—the system of involuntary servitude in public schools which enslaves younger boys to older boys. As I noted above, in *The Black Gang* we learn that Hugh was Sir Brian Johnstone's fag at school. Here Sapper reverses the normal pattern and tells us that Hugh, the fag, defended and protected his studious and serious older friend from schoolboy calumny. This same pattern extends to adult life with Hugh continuing to fag for Sir Brian, now the Commissioner of Police, doing his real job for him and not seeking credit. The same relationship, only treated here in the conventional manner, exists between Hugh and his fags, Algy, Peter, Toby, Ted, etc. They drop everything and run to be of service to him and they obey his orders unquestioningly. The simple fact that Sapper inevitably uses the group of friends plus the hero, with all of its implicit and explicit lessons about cooperation and self-sacrifice, points to the schoolboy nature of these adventures. Further, through the filter of the schoolboy adventure, we get one more perspective on the nature of authority in these tales: Hugh and his chums, as the group of boys, do not go whining to the master when faced with a problem; instead they put their heads together and figure things out for themselves. Finally, some of the high jinks in the books derive from schoolboy pranks and schoolboy mentality. When Hugh first appears in *The Third Round,* he is standing by his window playing Beaver (i.e., counting the number of men with beards who pass by):

hardly an adult pastime. In *Bulldog Drummond Returns* Irma Peterson achieves part of her long-sought revenge by causing Hugh to de-bag himself: getting caught with one's trousers down may, indeed, be embarrassing, but it is a schoolboy prank and hardly an action which we expect from a crazed Master Criminal. In all, it helps to understand the purpose of these books to view them as extended schoolboy or undergraduate rags.

Just two more items from the schoolboy tradition. First, women play a miniscule role in these stories, and Sapper avoids descriptions of love or domestic scenes. In the first novel Hugh meets and marries his Phyllis, but in subsequent novels she disappears a) because, playing the typical adventure heroine, she has been kidnapped by the villains; or b) because Sapper either sends her off to France or America or fails, as in *Challenge,* to mention her at all. As in the typical schoolboy story, women in Sapper serve as means of demonstrating the hero's chivalry or, in the case of the villainess, Irma Peterson, they demonstrate the writer's fundamental fear of women. The other important element from the schoolboy tradition is the prominent vein of anti-intellectualism running through these books. In every novel Sapper points out that Hugh is no genius: he has an average mind. Thus, in *The Third Round,* the narrator says

Hugh Drummond laid no claim to being brilliant. His brain, as he frequently remarked, was of the "also-ran" variety. But he was undoubtedly the possessor of a very shrewd common sense, which generally enabled him to arrive at the same result as a far more brilliant man and, incidentally, by a much more direct route.[8]

In addition to emphasizing his militant mediocrity, which is never converted as is Tom Brown's, Sapper makes Hugh into a defiantly insular Englishman. This shows best with his skill in foreign languages. In *Bull-Dog Drummond,* Hugh and his friends follow the villain to France, where they meet a policeman who wants to inquire about their unorthodox entry (they have crash-landed in an airplane) as well as the state of their passports:

A Frenchman was advancing towards them down the stately vestibule of the Ritz waving protesting hands. He addressed himself in a voluble crescendo to Drummond, who rose and bowed deeply. His knowledge of French was microscopic, but such trifles were made to be overcome.

"Mas oui, Monsieur mon Colonel," he remarked affably when the gendarme paused for lack of breath, "vous comprenez que notre machine avait crashe dans un field des turnipes. Nous avons lost notre direction. Nous sommes hittes dans l'estomacs...comme ci, comme ca.... Vous comprenez, n'est ce-pas, mon Colonel?"[9] [Sapper's ellipses]

This from a man who supposedly spent a good deal of time in France during the Great War. Hugh does the same thing with fractured Italian in *The Black Gang*. The language business, of course, is part of the comedy upon which Sapper bases these books, but it also comes from the tradition of schoolboy ridicule of the grinds and the substantially educated. It also probably represents Sapper's reaction against the detective novel of the twenties, which was becoming increasingly complex and intellectual. In the late twenties, however, Sapper found it necessary to reverse himself on this, and he began to introduce into his novels intellectual problems (albeit sham ones) like riddles (*The Female of the Species*) and cipher *(Knockout)*. To remain consistent, though, Sapper, rather than changing Hugh's mental make-up, introduced new characters, notably Ronald Standish (who appears in *Knockout, Bulldog Drummond at Bay, Challenge,* as well as in *Tiny Carteret* and his own series of short stories), who are allegedly competent at intellectual analysis.

Looking back for a moment at Hugh's fractured French, one of the prime reasons for the popularity of the Bulldog Drummond books stems from Sapper's combination of comedy and action. His main comic technique is the creation of comic diction. At first Sapper made this comic speech the province of the hero, but in the later novels it spread to other characters, including Carl Peterson, the villain in the first four books, only to fade in the thirties when Sapper seemed to tire of it, and then to return centered around Algy Longworth in *Challenge*. The creation of comic diction was one of the staples of popular writers between the wars in both Britain and America. P.G. Wodehouse was the most active and influential practitioner but he was followed by Bentley, Sayers, Allingham, Beeding, Coles and a bunch of others. As it is practiced by most of these writers, comic diction typically combines schoolboy lingo (Hugh's reference to chemistry as "stinks" for instance), American slang and underworld argot, casual upper class speech habits (dropping g's) and slang, hunting slang (yoicks), baby talk (Drummond frequently refers to himself as "little Willie"), as well as comic displacement, the absurd series, and other standard techniques of comic rhetoric. Sapper uses most of them, with the notable exception of the comic literary allusion (the skewed, inappropriate, or unexpected quotation), which points to the nature of his audience as opposed to Wodehouse's or Beeding's. Here is a representative sample of Hugh Drummond's conversation:

"Which is where Ted comes in," said Hugh affably. "Does the Stomach-ache [Peter's airplane] hold two?" "My dear man," cried Jerningham, "I'm dining with a perfectly priceless she tonight."

"Oh, no, you're not, my lad. You're going to do some amateur acting in Paris. Disguised as a waiter, or a chambermaid, or a coffee machine or something—you will discover secrets."[10]

Much of the effect of this kind of speech is to give readers a dose of verbal comedy (which, considering its widespread nature in the twenties, readers wanted), but it also has a marked effect on character. Men who can be flippant and facetious in the face of danger or death simply ooze with nonchalance, and this, going back to McIver's description of Hugh and his chums, is one of the main elements which Sapper wanted to convey through Bulldog Drummond. It is also, incidentally, the main element which most detective and spy writers wanted to convey in their fictions in the twenties and early thirties.

Hugh Drummond, however, is not a terribly original character. We can trace much of what he does and is back to the adventures of Sherlock Holmes or Sexton Blake, or the exploits of other adventure heroes. Two of these have particular significance in respect to Sapper's place in the traditions of the spy novel. Bulldog Drummond is, first of all, Dick Hannay written down for tykes. Drummond takes over and magnifies Hannay's size and strength, he adventures with a gang of pals just as Hannay does in Buchan, and he learned his lessons in tracking people and animals from one Van Dyck who obviously comes from Peter Pienaar. In Hugh's gang Sapper only really differentiates one character, Algy Longworth. All of the others, Ted, Peter, and Toby, possess the same tongue, the same abilities, the same gung-ho spirit. Algy, though, in spite of the Wodehousean drivel added in *Challenge,* probably came from Archie Roylance in Hannay's tribe: they are both callow, girl crazy, and faintly bungling. Like Buchan, and perhaps more successfully, Sapper insists on making his sportsman hero into the Average Man.

The other important source for Bulldog Drummond can be found in the books of Baroness Orczy. Although she wrote a number of detective short stories, Orczy's fame rests on *The Scarlet Pimpernel* (1905). Sir Percy Blakeney, who masquerades as the Scarlet Pimpernel, seems a loutish bungler, sunk in the pleasures of life. In disguise, though, he zips over to France and rescues persecuted aristocrats from the guillotine. As Orczy describes him, Sir Percy is:

Tall, above the average, even for an Englishman, broad-shouldered and massively built, he would have been called unusually good-looking, but for a certain lazy expression in his deep set blue eyes, and that perpetual inane laugh which seemed to disfigure his strong, clearly-cut-mouth.[11]

Hugh Drummond may not be good-looking, but he has most of the other qualifications in the Pimpernel line. Particularly in *The Black Gang,* Hugh pretends to be a jerk in order to mask his identity as the leader of the Black Gang which, like the Pimpernel and his followers, discomfits modern revolutionaries.

So much for heroes, though. Sapper's villains deserve some attention, too. Villains in popular fiction, like everything else, follow certain observable trends. Before the First World War, British writers leaned toward using the Master Criminal who wants to turn society to his own use: thus, *The Four Just Men* (1905), *The Insidious Fu Manchu* (1913), *The Power House* (1913), and other novels fostered this sort of villain. Books predicting war, as well as those written during the war itself, combined traditional elements of villainy with the identification of the villain with perceived weakness in German mentality and politics. Therefore Williams' *Okewood of the Secret Service* (1919) ropes in bits from the story of Mata Hari to color the evil against which the hero struggles. After the Armistice there was a widespread return to the Master Criminal-gangster motif: hence, Buchan's *The Three Hostages* (1924), Beeding's *The Seven Sleepers* (1925), and *Bull-Dog Drummond.* Each of Sapper's novels, therefore, uses the Master Criminal as the antagonist. The first and most important of these is Carl Peterson, who appears in the first four Bulldog Drummond books. After Hugh calls Carl to his last reckoning in *The Final Count,* Sapper's villains go downhill: Peterson's mistress, Irma, prosecutes her revenge in *The Female of the Species,* but her villainy sadly falls off in *The Return of Bulldog Drummond.* The other villains, LeBossu, Zavier, Demonico, Kalinsky, Menalin, are all pretty much single shot, emaciated versions of Peterson. In spite of their real importance to character, plot, and theme, Sapper never hit his stride with his villains and kept on tinkering with their characters, trying to produce the desired effect. We find, for example, that in *The Third Round,* Sapper narrates in detail the villain's action while in the next book, *The Final Count,* the chief villain does not enter until the novel is nearly finished. Somehow Sapper never quite made his villains into the bogeys that he would have liked to portray.

At any rate, Sapper's villains do have a number of similarities, and they make pretty obvious character or thematic points. First, all of the villains create and use precise and carefully wrought plans and organizations. Peterson and Menalin write down every jot and tittle of their nasty plans, and all of the nefarious plots in the books turn on split-second timing. This, of course, gives easy access to their intent but, more importantly, it enhances the hero's nonchalance and quick intelligence in that he is able to thwart such finely-honed duplicity. Not only are the villains organizers, they are also part of the international capitalist conspiracy. Here Sapper taps into a theme that goes as far back as LeQueux's *The Red Room* (1911), which ascribes both international and domestic strife to the machinations of evil foreign capitalists (as opposed to good, honest, inventive British capitalists), and brings into fiction the progressive decline of British industry. Thus, in Sapper, we discover that it is not bolsheviks *qua* bolsheviks who aim to disrupt Britain in *Bull-Dog Drummond, The Black Gang,* and *Challenge,* but international capitalists who wish to stifle honest British labor and capital, or international fortune hunters like Peterson who want to cause unrest in order to line their own pockets. Likewise, in *Bulldog Drummond at Bay,* we find that nations' public policies will not bring on the next war but that the skulduggery of capitalist opportunists like Kalinsky will. The capitalist conspiracy meddles with warmongering in Sapper's early books and his late ones—those chronologically tied to the last and the next war.

In the middle books, Sapper reflects on the worsening economic climate in the world, and he posits Master Criminals who cause the disheartening fluctuations in the economy: Peterson aims to shake the international diamond market in *The Third Round,* Irma plans a stock scam in *The Return of Bulldog Drummond,* and Demonico plans to puncture confidence in sterling in *Knockout.* Capitalist greed stands behind most of the practical nastiness which the villains create in the novels (except for *Temple Tower,* which is a straight gangster plot). These monied bloodsuckers, though, never get their fingers dirty: they use loony, cunning, or misguided Marxists (see *Bull-Dog Drummond, The Black Gang* and *Challenge*), common criminals, or psychologically-warped people who engage in crime for the thrills (as with Pendelton and Corinne Moxton in *Knockout).*

The machinery of Sapper's villains pretty much resembles the standard fare of the teens and twenties. In every case, the villains have numerous toadies who are usually identified by numbers rather than names, in order to stress not only the sterility of evil but also its organization and limitless supply of labor. They do tiresome jobs and supply answers to awkward plotting problems. Since Sapper frequently deals with continuing, series villains who jump from book to book (Carl and Irma Peterson), he introduces the evil second-in-command, like Lakington in *Bull-Dog Drummond,* who takes it in the neck at the end of the action, thereby showing the conquest of evil but allowing the series villain to toddle off-stage, ready to appear in the next book. Almost all of Sapper's antagonists take top honors for disguise, as Hugh does himself. Carl, Irma, LeBossu, and Demonico all pop up as unsuspected people—as does Hugh in *Bulldog Drummond at Bay,* where he is supposedly burned to a crisp. Sapper devotes a good deal of description in *The Third Round,* in fact, to Carl Peterson's disguising skill. Further, Sapper's villains usually possess some sort of hideout which is, at the same time, the hero's goal and his greatest peril. At the hideout the hero must deal with the gang, and he must surmount various perverse mechanical dangers in the place itself: the beheading staircase in *Bull-Dog Drummond,* the electrified fence in *The Black Gang,* the reservoir of poison in *The Final Count,* etc. This impinges on the Fu Manchuish elements in Sapper's antagonists. In a number of books the villains use exotic and weird threats. Thus, in *Bull-Dog Drummond,* Carl keeps a gorilla on the grounds of his headquarters, has a cobra slithering around in the draperies at night, and hires a pigmy with a blowgun to squat on top of Hugh's wardrobe and spit poisoned darts at the hero. In *The Final Count,* Carl sends a pair of horrible spiders to Hugh and Phyllis. Could Sax Rohmer do more?

Sapper's plots run pretty much along conventional adventure fiction lines. Typically, the villain and his minions plan some sort of nefarious business which will a) threaten England's stability, and b) boost their incomes and egos. Hugh Drummond accidentally stumbles across this plot, becomes interested in it as a potential adventure, and an initial skirmish occurs. The bad people then kidnap someone (Drummond's wife, a millionaire, or an inventor). Hugh attempts to rescue this hostage, but becomes a prisoner himself. Then he escapes, usually with the aid of his friends, and shortly afterward they finish off the bad guys and thwart their scheme. This pattern admits some variation—in *Bulldog Drummond at Bay,* for instance, readers do not learn about the motivation or objective of the villains until the middle of the book—but it remains Sapper's standard formula. The main feature of this pattern is that it contains numerous chances for capture and escape and, in turn, when faced with danger, capture and escape show best Hugh's physical virtues and his happy-go-lucky nonchalance. Sapper, though, has a gift for mucking up a perfectly good adventure plot by trying to include too much. Thus, in *Bull-Dog Drummond,* he clogs up the bolshevik plot by including Lakington's theft of the Duchess' pearls, and in *The Return of Bulldog*

Drummond, perhaps the most tedious of all the books, Sapper forgets about the murder at the start of the book when he introduces Irma Peterson and her swindling scheme. He could rarely leave well enough alone.

Other than showing his readers Hugh's character, Sapper never decided what effect he wanted his novels to produce. Sure, he wanted to produce laughs with the personalities and antics of Hugh and company. He also wanted to evoke gothic thrills and suspense, as witnessed by Stockton's "had I but known" narration in *The Final Count*. But Sapper never decided about the proper mix of these things or how to convey it to his readers; consequently, we witness him constantly tinkering with technique from book to book. In some novels he centers on the actions of the villains while in others he ignores them. In some he keeps the readers in the dark about the villain's plans (as in *Bulldog Drummond at Bay*) while in others we know about them from the start. For three books *(The Final Count, The Female of the Species,* and *Temple Tower),* he uses first person narration, but he cannot decide whether the narrator should be a novice being initiated into the world of chills and thrills, or one of the principal actors in the adventure. Occasionally Sapper's technical tinkering works and sometimes it does not. The effect is not one of planned experiment, but rather of the author charging more or less blindly about trying to find the proper vehicle for his character.

Whatever their level of craftsmanship or their sensitivity to humane values, though, Sapper's books rank among that small class of fictions in which the character grows out of the writer's hands and attains a place in the public consciousness. Bulldog Drummond survived Sapper and continued to affect the tradition of the spy story, not because of the films made about him or the novels written about him, after McNeile's death, by Gerald Fairlie, but because Hugh Drummond captured for the public the blend of brutality and nonchalance which sprang up in the twenties, and which later writers would look back upon with wistfulness or disgust.

NOTES

[1]*Bull-Dog Drummond* (London: Hodder and Stoughton, n.d.), pp. 104-5.
[2]*Bull-Dog Drummond,* pp. 127-8.
[3]*Bulldog Drummond at Bay* (Garden City: Crime Club, 1935), p. 304.
[4]*The Black Gang* (London: Hodder and Stoughton, 1935), pp. 104-5.

[5] *Bull-Dog Drummond*, p. 25.

[6] *The Female of the Species* (London: Hodder and Stoughton, 1929), pp. 73-74.

[7] See Usborne's *Clubland Heroes*, for instance.

[8] *The Third Round* (London: Hodder and Stoughton, n.d.), pp. 45-6.

[9] *Bull-Dog Drummond*, p. 211.

[10] *Bull-Dog Drummond*, p. 206.

[11] E. Orczy, *The Scarlet Pimpernel* (New York: Airmont, 1963), p. 49.

Chapter 6

Francis Beeding
(1885-1949; 1898-1951)

John Leslie Palmer and Hilary Aiden St. George Saunders conspired to write thirty-one novels under the pseudonym Francis Beeding. Of these, one, *The House of Dr. Edwards* (1927), is a gothic story, and six *(Death Walks at Eastrepps,* 1931; *Murder Intended,* 1932; *The Emerald Clasp,* 1933; *The Norwich Victims,* 1935; *No Fury,* 1937; *He Could Not have Slipped,* 1939) are various genres of detective novels, and two *(The Street of the Serpents,* 1934, and *The Big Fish,* 1938) are treasure hunt books. The rest are spy novels, beginning with *The Seven Sleepers* in 1925 and ending with *There Are Thirteen* in 1946.

Beeding brings to the spy novel the typical elements of highbrow popular fiction which surfaced in Britain between the wars. He has the flippant tone, the sense of the absurd, the self-consciousness about what he does, and the impulse to quote which mark writers like Wodehouse, Allingham, Sayers or Marsh. Just look at the place of literature in Beeding. Sayers and her fellows spice their books with frequent quotations from the Bible, from Shakespeare, from Tennyson, from the whole set of standard English authors. Leafing through any Beeding book shows lots of white space caused by indented quotations. He gives us scraps of Chaucer and Keats, quotes from Dickens and Shelley, citations of Galsworthy and Hardy, and Shakespeare—he gives us Shakespeare by the cartload. A Mr. Prospero and a Senior Gonzalgo appear in *Take It Crooked* (1932) and the cipher in *The Nine Waxed Faces* (1936) uses Craig's 1912 Oxford edition of Shakespeare (even though Beeding mistakenly assumes that there is no mention of Austria in the plays). In the first chapter of *There Are Thirteen,* entitled "The Sweet Roman Hand" *(Twelfth Night),* I can quickly pick out three extended Shakespearean quotes in the first eleven pages—one from *Hamlet,* one from *Othello,* and an additional reference to *Twelfth Night.* Using quotations can, of course, serve a number of purposes in fiction. They can be used to characterize, giving particular speech or habit of mind to one character or another. They can also serve their usual rhetorical function to reinforce points of arguments. Finally, quotations do give a gloss of sophistication to elevate the tone of a novel. Beeding does, to some extent, use quotations to draw character, especially after *The Six Proud Walkers* (1928) with its introduction of Granby. But in some of the later books, like *The Secret Weapon* (1940), not only the hero but also the villain keeps returning to the words of the poets. Using quotes in the traditional way, Beeding does frequently cite literature to enhance narrative points. Thus this passage from *The Five Flamboys* (1929):

If I save the King, you will marry me. That is a bargain. But we were neither of us born to be poor. You remember Keats:

> Love in a hut, with water and a crust
> Is—Love, forgive us—cinders, ashes, dust.[1]

None of this, though, explains the frequent quotes in Beeding—or in many other writers of the twenties. Part of the explanation lies in the fact that quotations become the password to the company of cultivated people: recognizing quotations, readers admit Beeding to their confidence since he is as cultivated as they are. The quotations also provide an element of playfulness and an excuse for sinking to popular fiction. Just as Sayers, for instance, tailors Wimsey's character and diction in order to excuse using a popular form and to show readers that her real interests lie outside of this swamp, so does Beeding bombard his readers with quotations mixed with silliness of one sort or another in order to signal his readers that he is not presenting a serious view of the world in this debased form, the spy novel, but an entertainment for cultivated people. Once readers get this point, then Beeding, like Sayers, can slip a few serious points into the debased form.

If Beeding differs from other writers of the twenties in the cultural level of his books, he also differs in his doctrinal base. Although German villains spill over into the twenties, as with Val Williams' Okewood novels, most espionage writers in Britain lost some of their focus. Most spy writers in the twenties and early thirties drifted among relatively vague concepts of decency, sanity, and individuality. Buchan resuscitated the Master Crook, as did Sapper and Horler, while Oppenheim moved to the international peace-maker. The Germans, naturally, caused a rebirth of British patriotism in the mid-thirties, but in the twenties most writers used anarchic and power-crazed Master Crooks as their villains and Secret Service agents acting as policemen as their heroes. Now Beeding, too, uses Master Criminals and spy detectives, but he has a surer doctrinal base. Both Palmer and Saunders worked for the Permanent Secretariat of the League of Nations from 1920 until the Second World War. Most of their early novels have concrete connections with Geneva and the League. Beatrice in *The Seven Sleepers* works for the League, as does John Baxter, who appears in *The Five Flamboys, The Four Armourers* (1930), and *The Eight Crooked Trenches* (1936). *The Seven Sleepers, The Little White Hag* (1926), *The Five Flamboys, The Eight Crooked Trenches, The One Sane Man* (1934), and *He Could Not Have Slipped* have scenes set in Geneva, the home of the League. More important than this, the themes of most of Beeding's novels until the mid-thirties draw upon the principal objectives of the League of Nations. The League's fundamental purpose was the outlawing of war. To this end, Article Eight of the Covenant of the League of Nations states that

The members of the League agree that the manufacture by private enterprise of munitions and implements of war is open to grave objections. The Council shall advise how the evil effects attendant upon such manufacture can be prevented.... [2]

Thus the plot in *The Seven Sleepers* hinges on war profiteers secretly scheming to rearm Germany and, more to the point, *The Four Armourers* shows Hazelrig, an American munitions king who has seen the light, outbidding and out-running four munitions makers in order to purchase and present the formula for a new gas to the League so that they can destroy it. Aside from munitions Beeding deals with dangerous drugs, but on a more directed line than other writers who reacted to the dope scare in the twenties. This, too, goes back to the League of Nations whose Covenant (Article 23) stipulates that members will

...entrust the League with the general supervision over the execution of agreements with regard to the... traffic in opium and other dangerous drugs. [3]

Beeding's second novel, *The Little White Hag,* shows the debilitating effects of the international traffic in cocaine (the little white hag). The same anti-drug message is pushed in *The Six Pound Walkers* and *The Two Undertakers* (1933). Finally, Beeding uses the League's role in stabilizing international social and economic conditions in *The Six Proud Walkers, The Five Flamboys, The Three Fishers* (1931) and *The One Sane Man*. In these novels villains attempt to subvert international peace and create chaos and war in order to fatten their bankrolls or bolster their prestige. All of this usually culminates, in the early novels, in a defense of the League by one of the characters. Take this one by Bradin, the French Foreign Minister, in *The Three Fishers:*

> The League is strong. Not for nothing have the wicked nations met together for ten years and pretended to be better than they are. Some day, perhaps, we shall find that the pretence has become a reality. I am learning that lesson from my English friends. The social value to the world of organized hypocrisy is incalculable. But it is a slow process.[4]

As we move into the thirties, belief in the League peters out in Beeding's novels and we find the cynicism and bitterness of the rejected lover. In 1934 Burstead, the hero-villain of *The One Sane Man,* attempts to coerce the world to live up to the promises of the League—to vest international control of design, production and distribution in the League to enable

> ...the greatest number of persons, and ultimately every person born into the world, to make effective their demand to be supplied with the necessaries of life.[5]

This scheme, which the narrator accepts as good and necessary, comes to nought when the British representative submarines it. *The Big Fish* in 1938 presents a world in which small nations can only prosper in isolation. Finally, in 1939, *He Could Not Have Slipped* shows a League High Commissioner turning to financial jiggery pokery and crime in order to alleviate the suffering of Europe's refugees. The League is indifferent, impotent or corrupt. At its bitterest, this novel comments on League officials this way:

> Here were not men eager to help the victims of terror from Right or Left. They sat there for the most part quite unmoved; some in unhelpful pity or secret sympathy with the terrorists.[6]

Instead of pivoting his books on the League, in the late thirties he turned to actual happenings to provide the ground for his novels. Thus Beeding bases *The Eight Crooked Trenches* on the 1934 purge of Rohm and the S.A., *The Nine Waxed Faces* on the invasion of Austria, *Hell Let Loose* (1937) on the Spanish Civil War, and *The Ten Holy Terrors* (1939) on the invasion of Czechoslovakia. Beeding edged out of the fantasy world of the thirties, and, having lost faith in the League of Nations, he ends these novels with pessimism, invoking the Biblical term as he does at the close of *The Nine Waxed Faces:*

As for Wilhelm Fuchs and his brotherhood of the Edelweiss, for all I know, the nine waxed faces still move round the pleasant streets of Innsbruck or upon the wind-swept crags of the mountains about the city, helping those that fly from a tyranny still triumphant in a world heading ever faster for Armageddon.[7]

When Armageddon did come in the form of the Hitler War, Beeding, after a secret weapon book (*The Secret Weapon*), devoted his last efforts to flaying French traitors and the Vichy government in *Eleven Were Brave* (1940), *The Twelve Disguises* (1942) and *There Are Thirteen.*

If Beeding's themes adapt to the changing world, his characters, after the initial shake-down, do not change an awful lot. Every novel contains some configuration of the hero, the secret agent, the woman and the villain. Let's start with the hero. With a few exceptions (like *The Three Fishers* and *The Eight Crooked Trenches*), Beeding narrates his spy stories through the first-person voice of the hero. Now, except in the books narrated by Granby (*Take It Crooked, The One Sane Man, The Twelve Disguises*), the hero is not the main protagonist in the spy action. He is, instead, a young man either inexperienced in the toils of international intrigue or serving his novitiate in the Secret Service. He tends to fall in love somewhere along the line, there being breezy love interests in most of Beeding's novels, and he also tends to screw up or gum up the works by his naivete, ineptness or inexperience. In short, the hero inevitably falls into the hands of the villains and needs to be rescued at least once. They are, in short, the sort of people we would like to be in our pleasant fantasies. Take John Baxter, the hero of *The Five Flamboys* and *The Four Armourers*, and his character as revealed in the first novel. Baxter has firm common sense, declining to single-handedly take on a murderer because

That, I decided, was quite unnecessarily British. I did not really see why, in this case, honour required that I should take on with my bare fists a fellow who had at least a knife and very possibly an automatic as well.[8]

We can all appreciate his petty dilemmas, like whether to tip the policeman who drives him to the station and handles his bags for him. When the action starts he makes all sorts of errors: the King of Rumania gets snatched in his presence; his girl, likewise, gets bagged while he waits; and the villains literally tree him. He does, though, achieve some notable successes, delivering the plans and eluding the bad guys. Beeding portrays him (and his other heroes) as the average, cultivated, decent, compassionate man who deserves our esteem, who deserves to win, and who deserves to get the girl. In all cases this happens, but he cannot and does not win victory by himself. He needs help from a creation of wilder fantasies.

Next comes the Secret Service man who, in terms of the spy plot, acts as the protagonist, the bringer of victory, and the scourge of evil. In his first novel, *The Seven Sleepers*, and then in *The Hidden Kingdom* (1927), Beeding invented a pair of French Secret Service aces, Etienne Rehmy and Gaston de Blanchegarde, as the spy heroes. As Beeding dabbled with psychology in some of his non-spy books (see *The House of Dr. Edwards*), he split the personality of the successful agent between these two men: one is the careful planner and the other the impetuous man of action. Although Beeding continued to give both men walk-on roles in a handful of his later books—the Nazis kill Rehmy at his office in *Eleven Were Brave*—he needed a different kind of spy hero to suit the times and to suit himself. The first draft of this new hero appears in Beeding's second novel, *The Little White Hag*, with Cyrus P. Claypole. This djinn comes in an unassuming bottle: "He seemed a weak, undistinguished kind of man—the sort one would take for a clerk in a department store, except for his chin, which was firm and well-molded...."[9] This little runt, it turns out, is a resourceful and canny New York detective on the track of the dope-peddling Master Crook. For future reference, his eyes twinkle and Shakespeare rolls off his tongue, as in, "Beware of entrance to a quarrel, as Shakespeare says, but when you do jump in just to give the other fellow hell."[10] In the middle of the novel Claypole apparently commits suicide to avoid the clutches of the villains, but it is a ruse and at the end he pops up in time to save Quexter, the hero, from annihilation at the hands of the villains. He is, in fact, the preliminary study for Alistair Granby.

Colonel, eventually General, Alistair "Toby" Granby stars as the Secret Service hero in almost all of Beeding's spy novels. Without Granby Beeding's spy novels would be as drab as his detective novels. He enters Beeding's oeuvre in *The Six Proud Walkers* and comes in when needed in the subsequent novels. Several novels in the early thirties present him in slightly different roles: in *The Four Armourers* he falls for, and in *Take It Crooked* he marries, Julia Hazelrig, and in *The One Sane Man* (which mixes his narration with documents) he doubts his vocation. But largely he is the adventure hero of an active, if whimsical, fantasy. Granby, as I said above, grew from Claypole. Both men are short, both have twinkling eyes, and both have the "habit of quoting Shakespeare in, but mostly out of, season."

To this Beeding added a sense of self-conscious absurdity as well as a penchant for food and drink. His nickname, Toby, comes from Toby Jug, a vessel which he reputedly uses to imbibe famous vintages (Beeding's gastronomic interest overflows in two novels, especially, *The Street of the Serpents* and *Take it Crooked*). Granby began his career in *The Six Proud Walkers* as an extravagant character; here, Beeding created for him an excessively fruity diction compounded of literary quotations, constant repetition of the phrase "pretty sinister" (hence the title of his 1929 incarnation), and facetious use of military jargon. All of these things modulated somewhat in the later books. The military jargon, for instance, diminishes to the adjuration to "Steady the Buffs." Granby, works for, and ends up as head (P.B.3) of, the British Secret Service. Beeding tells us that this is a great octopus of an organization with a world-wide stable of agents, but we never see this; we only see the cozy headquarters flat with its single attendant and one or two agents, usually carried over from an earlier book. But Granby is still the quintessential Secret Service man. From his second appearance, in *The Five Flamboys,* he shows himself a master of disguise, the *sine qua non* of the traditional spy and an attribute which Beeding kept until the forties, as seen in *The Twelve Disguises*. Granby acts the part of the merciless taskmaster, sending agents to certain death and telling them that they are on their own. This, though, is a front. He represents the romantic impulse to self-sacrifice as in *The Two Undertakers* when he steps in the path of a bullet meant for the *Graf*. In all the books, with the exception of *The Secret Weapon,* he drags people's chestnuts out of the fire. In the typical Beeding novel we find that Granby disappears or breaks down about three-quarters of the way through the action. All seems lost, and the good folks are powerless to thwart the plans of the villains. Before the end, though, Granby either swoops down to save the day or demonstrates that what appeared to be a break-down was in fact a clever ruse. In *Eleven Were Brave* Beeding has Granby admit his own artistic function:

"You certainly have a most uncanny way of turning up quite unexpectedly," I observed.

Granby sighed.

"In the days of my youth," he said, "I made rather a point of it. They called me the Cheshire Cat because I usually turned up smiling. It's a habit I have when nervous. I was the *deus ex machina* of the Service."[12]

That, for most of Beeding's books, is the service: the slightly loony *deus ex machina* clothed as Alistair Granby.

Beeding, like most other adventure writers of the twenties,

portrayed women as fulfilling only a limited number of functions in the world of danger. They serve as incentives for the hero's exertions and rewards for his success. Nine times out of ten, in Beeding and most of his contemporaries, if there is a woman about she will sooner or later be kidnapped by the villains and need to be rescued—it was part of the formula. Perhaps the most extreme example of this in Beeding occurs in *The Hidden Kingdom*, where Kreutzemark, the current evil genius, spirits Suzanne de Polhac from Spain to Mongolia, where her lover and his friends must follow in order to save her from his wicked embrace. Yet Beeding does try to add another dimension to his female characters from the very beginning, as Preston shows in these observations:

In the first days of our acquaintance she had rather daunted me. She was so terribly adequate and assured. There was nothing about her in the least dependent or justifying the scorn of the weaker sex. I had felt the natural distrust of the gallant male for the girl who never pleads for a handicap. But I had soon found that with Beatrice there were moments that showed her unusually sensitive and intensely feminine.[13]

This may be a stammering and inadequate attempt at consciousness raising, but Beeding does try to combine the traditional adventure-novel role for women as victims and prizes with a fuller appraisal of female nature. This shows especially with Julia Granby: in *Take It Crooked* the villains kidnap her the day after her marriage and drag her off to a chateau in Southern France, but she, through her own initiative and wit, escapes while her male rescuers end up as captives themselves. This steps out of convention into Beeding's world.

The last typical character in Beeding's novels is, of course, the villain. His villains undergo the same changes that his themes do; that is, Beeding switches from the Master Criminal to the Nazi in the mid-thirties (*Eight Crooked Trenches* is the first anti-Nazi book), and then with *Eleven Were Brave* he adds the Vichy collaborator. In a sense, though, his villains remain the same from Professor Kreutzemark in *The Seven Sleepers* and *The Hidden Kingdom* through Mannteufel, the Nazi chief, in *The Secret Weapon* and *The Twelve Disguises*. But to start we need to take a look at Beeding's early villains. The early novels all deal with criminal conspiracies in which individuals plot international disorder for their own ends: these ends are clearly evil in all the books except *The One Sane Man*. Since in this sort of fiction it is neither easy nor desirable to draw individual portraits of gangs of villains—and Beeding does deal in gangs—he singles out and concentrates on one, or at most two, men,

the Master Criminals, and gives them built-up characterizations.
Thus we have Professor Kreutzemark, who plots a new European
war because German industrialists do not want to pay war
reparations in *The Seven Sleepers*, and who intends to incarnate
himself as Genghis Khan in *The Hidden Kingdom*; we also have
Caramac in *The Six Proud Walkers* and *The League of Discontent*
(1930); Ruggiero in *Take It Crooked, One Sane Man*, and *The Two
Undertakers*; and Francis Wyndham in *The Five Flamboys, The
Three Fishers* and *The Two Undertakers*. Beeding tends, especially
in the last three villains, to portray as the principal villain the
executor, the mechanic, instead of the originator of the evil, who
stays in the background. Thus in *Take It Crooked*, for example,
Granby contends with the plots of Ruggiero, but standing behind
him is the shadowly Loeval, who intends to corner the radium
market and make a killing off cancer victims—looking forward,
incidentally, to Greene's *The Third Man*. In the early thirties
Beeding wants to develop his villains as attractive personalities.
Ruggiero, the Mighty Magestro, gets the grudging respect of the
heroes for his ingenuity, his flair and his comically rendered
encyclopedic mind. Likewise Wyndham is not altogether a toad: he
is a cultivated, daring, suave, resourceful man. Wyndham would
suffer toothache rather than be impolite or awkward. Like
Ruggiero,though, he has a kink. He thinks that he is a man of the
renaissance, and he may be, but he lives in a world in which
assertive individuality and audacious individualism seem lunacy.
Beeding's villains in the early novels are attractive men, and this
culminates in Burstead in *One Sane Man*, who not only is the villain
but the hero, too. In the main, though, the flamboyant characters,
out of work in the modern world, become the agents of sleazy
capitalists and maniacal jingoists. These shadow people plot
revolutions, push dope and manipulate economies; as a sign of their
evil they stay in the dark and use the world's glorious misfits to
articulate their plans.

As men are perverted by evil, so is science. Beeding's early
villains depend a good deal upon science and the character of the
rogue scientist. The drug business works in here, what with
Caramac's plot to administer a mind-altering drug to the Italian
Prime Minister in *The Six Proud Walkers* and Du Bertrand's zombie
assassins and plan to saturate German candy and tobacco with
dope in *The Two Undertakers*. Poison gas plays a role, too, with
Kreutzemark's fumes in the first novel and the planned attack on
France in *The Eight Crooked Trenches*. Michelet's weather machine
in *The One Sane Man*, television in *Hell Let Loose* and the new

explosive in *The Secret Weapon* all lead back to the eccentric inventor out of touch with reality. Villains will have their tame scientists, but, to his credit, Beeding realized the boffo side of this in *The Five Flamboys*. Wyndham's inventor creates laughing gas and sneezing tobacco.

In Beeding we find that the devil can quote scripture. Behind the plots and under the jokes we always find the Evil One. As witnessed by *The House of Dr. Edwards*, Beeding found Satanism early in his career and he sticks to it. Villainy and Satan are one. Witness the following passage from Preston in *The Seven Sleepers*, as he helplessly watches Kreutzemark hypnotize his beloved:

But I would ask any who may read these lines to realize that I loved Beatrice, and to imagine what it was for me to see her subdued to the purposes of a man who carried with him so positive and penetrating a suggestion of evil that since meeting him I have ceased to believe that wickedness is not merely the absence of good, as the modern sentimentalists have persuaded themselves, but a firm reality as objective, concrete and tangible as the devil who gnaws his bone upon the eaves of Notre Dame.[14]

Although this theme moves into the background with the "genial villain" books, it reappears and is justified in the books about the Hitler War. In the late books, not only is one of the main villains named Mannteufel (probably "the devil's retainer"), but in *The Secret Weapon* we get this passage on the guards at Buchenwald:

I felt—and it was an impression which will abide with me to the grave—that these men in their brown uniforms, with the breeches and shiny leggings, their heads wreathed in the blue smoke of their cheap cigars, were degraded embodiments of that spirit which Michael himself had aforetime driven from the battlements of heaven. In that place good and evil could be apprehended as no mere products of human error or expediency, but as fundamental realities, each in their kind positive and absolute.[15]

This is pretty strong stuff for popular fiction, warping us over to the shoals of theology, but Beeding never goes that far even in the war-time novels. For, as I said, the devil can quote. Beeding's irrepressible desire to buffet his readers with allusions causes him to make his villains spout esoteric facts and classic poetry. Ruggiero and Wyndham quote frequently, but so does Mannteufel, the Falstaffian Nazi in the war-time books. This is so because the true evil ones, with a few exceptions, stay in the background, but is also the case because, true to his beginnings in the twenties, Beeding sees spy stuff as giving the writer the chance to describe a genial game.

Beeding's later villains are, nevertheless, different. We can almost graph this in the gradual debasement of Krause, the Nazi agent, who appears in *The Eight Crooked Trenches, The Nine Waxed Faces* and *Hell Let Loose.* But even Krause retains some of the typical trappings of Beeding's fictional villains. The later books suggest that if we want true wickedness we have to turn to real people. Thus the war-time novels bring us actual people. Before the war there was a widespread reluctance to use actual names in British spy novels. Household does not name Hitler even if he appears in *Rogue Male* (1939), and Oppenheim limits himself to initials in *The Spymaster* (1938) when referring to "two European dictators." Beeding started to introduce real people as early as *The Nine Waxed Faces,* where Hagen (Hitler) and Caferelli (Mussolini) meet to decide Austria's future, but he does cover them with pseudonyms. He uses Hagen for Hitler again in *The Ten Holy Horrors* (1939), and Caferelli for Mussolini in *The Black Arrows* (1938) but thereafter the gloves, and presumably the publishers' restrictions, came off. It is Hitler, forget the Hagen, in *The Secret Weapon,* Goebbels in *The Twelve Disguises,* Himmler in *There Are Thirteen.* The same process works with the Vichy collaborators. *Eleven Were Brave* shows Privet duping Marshall Villebous at the fall of France, certainly referring to Pierre Laval, the Vichy Vice-Premier, and Marshal Petain; in *There Are Thirteen* the pseudonym goes out and he calls the villain Laval. He does, however, continue to keep the pseudonym Algernon Woodstock for Churchill in *Eleven Were Brave* and *The Twelve Disguises.* All this, obviously, is a practice in propaganda and it does show Beeding turning to the source of evil rather than the creator of fancy effects in the plot, but it does a bit more. Beeding knew that his readers would not accept villains who were slavering monsters—even if such men exist—since that was not in the province of the spy novel, their spy novel. So he presents Hitler, at least, as a dialogue figure, and shows him not only drooling over death and destruction in Poland but also debating fascism versus humanism with Hammerstein in *The Secret Weapon.* Ultimately, though, Beeding's war-time books flop because they have lost their world in which zest and exuberance could play. They may be franker about technique (Granby admits to being a *deus ex machina* in *Eleven Were Brave*), but they lack the very technique which they outline.

Beeding introduces very little which is particularly novel in the way of plotting adventure tales. He works more on details than on invention. Like most of his contemporaries' books, Beeding's books move from capture to escape to capture to escape. Typically the hero naively stumbles into the first capture, but later in the book knowingly puts himself into the enemy's hands in order to save the inevitable kidnap victim, the girl. Occasionally, though, we get comic details like Granby being bombed with a soup tureen in *Take It Crooked*. Siding with the more intellectual school of detective-spy writers, Beeding usually introduces the a) acquisition, and b) deciphering of a code document as one of the bases for the plot. This is another way of shoehorning in educated or cultivated material: thus *The Hidden Kingdom* depends on finding and interpreting a Latin text, *The Two Undertakers* has a code based on music, and *The Nine Waxed Faces* uses Shakespeare. If it is not a code at stake, then the novel revolves on the possession of some sort of secret document—from the German industrialists' signed agreement in *The Seven Sleepers* through the thirteen record discs exposing Laval's rottenness in *There Are Thirteen*—for both sides to lose and find. As Ogilvie says in *The Ten Holy Horrors,* " 'There is always a paper in your possession,' I said, 'and it usually gets lost. You spend your life in a paper-chase and expect your friends to join the hounds.' "[16] Granby replies to this that papers contain men's thoughts, but this is so much bilge. The paper chase is a game (like hare and hounds, says the O.E.D.) and Beeding predicates most of his books on games. Leaving, for a second, the paper chase, we can find characters playing a combination of the murder game and treasure hunt at the opening of *The Eight Crooked Trenches,* and Beeding includes unalloyed treasure hunts in *The Street of the Serpents* and *The Big Fish*. Sure, Beeding introduces games because they provide a tame and controlled form of mental exercise (which he does not permit the readers to experience), but more importantly he brings games in because he loves chases. Beeding, in the early novels at least, wants to create a chase to rival "Harold Lloyd and masters in that kind,"[17] as he says in *The Five Flamboys,* and, indeed, he does pretty well in the comic-suspense chase in that novel. In it Baxter escapes from Wyndham and assorted goons after Granby creates a diversion by stuffing chewing gum into a siphon, causing it to explode. He first steals a delivery man's bicycle, which he crashes into a tavern. After winging a bowling ball at the pursuers, he takes off through a vineyard, drops off an embankment and hops a maintenance tram headed for Geneva. Though winded, his enemies keep on the trail until Baxter bribes one of the men hired to walk around in an eight-foot-tall cardboard bottle, advertizing "DR. PERROT'S QUINQUINA. A DIGESTIVE TONIC," and toddles along to the safety of the Secretariat of the League of Nations inside said bottle. This chase illustrates best what Beeding wanted to do in his spy novels—create extravagant comedy.

The pre-war novels go to some length to entertain, not only with comedy but also with adventure and local color. Other than the kidnapping and the chase, Beeding often in the early books uses the technique of the double (in *The Seven Sleepers*, for example, the German plotters mistake Preston for one of their own ace agents), and he also manipulates clues. Unlike the detective novelist, the suspense novelist fully expects readers to put the clues together before the hero so that the gap in knowledge will stimulate excitement. This Beeding does in *The Three Fishers*, where we know all about the fake Foreign Minister long before Briarcliffe and Rehmy do. In addition to the suspense techniques, Beeding, again in the early books, sought to convey a sense of scene, almost in the travelog sense, to his readers. Only a few of the novels have scenes in Britain, and even those soon embark us for foreign shores. We wind up, because of the League, most often in Geneva, but the settings range over Europe (France, Germany, Spain, Switzerland, Austria, Italy) and, in the case of *The Hidden Kingdom*, as far away as Mongolia. Beeding gives more than naked road signs: he describes architecture and customs in detail, from the ritual of the bullfight (*The Hidden Kingdom*) to the passageways and chapels of the Escorial (*The Four Armourers* and *The Street of the Serpents*). He narrates the sights, moreover, without condescension and with the verve of someone enthusiastically interested.

In all, Beeding represents the best of conventional spy writing between the wars. Except for a mundane blush on Davis (especially in *The Three Fishers*), he shows espionage as the Victorian testing ground of character which, because this sort of thing does not prove real character, turns into a playground. If his books do not pierce into the spy's life as Greene's or Ambler's do, they provide entertainment for cultivated people for whom the fatuous products of Sapper and Horler hold little interest. The books hold up witty, charming, yet common individuals who show grace under pressure. It was the fault or the virtue of the times, though, that the pressure was not real and that, therefore, the grace was an arcadian fiction.

NOTES

[1] *The Five Flamboys* (Boston: Little, Brown, 1929), p. 257.

[2] Raymond P. Stearns, ed., *The Pageant of Europe* (New York: Harcourt Brace, 1947), p. 745.

[3] Stearns, p. 749.

[4] *The Three Fishers* (Boston: Little, Brown, 1931), p. 241.

[5] *The One Sane Man* (Boston: Little, Brown, 1934), p. 200.

6*He Could Not Have Slipped* (New York: Harper, 1939), p. 13.

7*The Nine Waxed Faces* (New York: Books, Inc., 1944), p. 291.

8*The Five Flamboys,* p. 17.

9*The Little White Hag* (Boston: Little, Brown, 1926), p. 4.

10*The Little White Hag,* p. 70.

11*There Are Thirteen* (New York: Harper, 1946), p. 2.

12*Eleven Were Brave* (London: Hodder and Stoughton, 1940), p. 74.

13*The Seven Sleepers* (Boston: Little, Brown, 1925), p. 31.

14*The Seven Sleepers,* p. 167.

15*The Secret Weapon* (New York: Harper, 1940), pp. 139-40.

16*The Ten Holy Horrors* (London: Hodder and Stoughton, 1939), p. 42.

17*The Five Flamboys,* p. 210.

Chapter 7
Sidney Horler
(1888-1954)

PROLIFIC WRITERS ARE nothing new; in the nineteenth century writers like Mrs. Trollope or F. Marion Crawford wrote shelves full of books. Neither is it new that the literate public quickly forgets most prolific writers. We have to look them up in handbooks, and they survive mostly in footnotes, paragraphs and doctoral dissertations which claim to rediscover the merits of forgotten writers. Sidney Horler was a prolific writer. From 1920 to 1954 he wrote one hundred and seventeen mystery and espionage novels, as well as a number of short story collections. He was, in his own day, enthusiastically reviewed, especially in the provincial press, as three excerpts from reviews of his novels in the 1920s illustrate:

Here is a novel brim-full of excitement; a story to suit all who love to read of an adventure. The characters are very well drawn....

Hull Daily Mail

Sidney Horler utilises his rare capacity for descriptive writing to such purpose that the secret service mystery grips from the beginning to the end.

The Northern Echo

From start to finish Mr.Horler's story rushes along at breakneck speed, and the author has such a grip on his characters that each happening appears inevitable.

Bookman[1]

These reviews are unadulterated drivel and Horler is an egregiously bad writer even by the less than exacting standards of the popular novel. His style bores even if readers skip the paragraphs after the topic sentences; his characters exist only as tissue, not even cardboard, and their motives are either blatantly conventional or absurd; and his capture and escape plots drag with leaden predictability through incident after incident. Bad writing, from the historical perspective, can be saved by innovation, as it is with LeQueux. Horler, however, invents nothing, but merely repeats formulae from Buchan or Wallace or Sapper: in some cases he resorts to out-and-out plagiarism, as with the effeminate Nazi general in *The Ace* (1941) who comes directly from Buchan's *Greenmantle*. I include a discussion of his espionage novels here to fulfill the function of criticism which tells readers what to avoid.

In order to give readers an idea of the way that Horler's novels run, I will summarize the plot of *The Curse of Doone* (1930) which is perhaps a bit superior to Horler's other books. At the start, the hero, Ian Heath, returns from the Continent exhausted by the strenuous life of the Secret Service man:

> That affair in Venice from which he had so narrowly escaped with his life, and something more valuable—his reason—had been damnably nerve-racking: his series of adventures as a member of the British Secret Service, originating in an obscure dance hall in the underworld of Budapest and culminating in a duel with rapiers— looking back, how monstrous and yet how real that bizarre affair had appeared—in the palace of the Prince of Vantori hidden away so discreetly in the shadows of the secret waterways of old Venice, had left him spent and weary.[2]

As Heath steps off the train, this "unorthodox, if brilliant Rugby three-quarter" lands on the foot of a beautiful woman who has the "pluck" not to faint from the experience. Before he has a chance to make a bit of time with her she vanishes. That evening, still with the woman on his mind, Heath attends a performance of the play *Mischief* where he saves the same woman, Cicely Garrett, from being abducted by a particularly loathsome-looking customer. Cicely, unaccountably, declines Heath's offer of protection and disappears into her hotel. She is, we learn, an orphan who has left America in order to run her uncle's household. Her uncle, Warren Murdoch, lives in a spooky old castle on the edge of Dartmoor where he pursues his occupation as an inventor. At present he is working on a device to immobilize engines, particularly aircraft engines, and, thus, is apt to get testy when he is disturbed. Doone Castle, coincidentally like Doyle's Baskerville Hall, comes complete with a set of mysterious servants, who are harboring a relative who has escaped from prison, a vampire legend, and a suspicious neighbor who oozes around the place ingratiating himself with Murdoch. Meanwhile, back in London, someone tries to murder Heath by fogging poison gas into his rooms, and Heath and his friend, Jerry Hartsgill (who also appears in *False Face*, 1926), stage a mock funeral for Heath and decamp for Jerry's chicken farm on, of all places, Dartmoor, in order to throw the enemy off the track. Quickly Horler brings boy and girl together, and things really begin to fly. The vampire (it seems) rips up a visiting professor as well as one Moses Grinstead. Philip Voyce, the unctuous neighbor, menaces Ian and Jerry and they menace him back. A couple of notable German spies turn up, Murdoch dies from a stroke, Jerry and Cicely are kidnapped, and Heath is injured in a car crash. Things look grim, but Heath leaps out of his hospital bed and tracks down Voyce, who is really another German spy, and the Secret Service chief, Harker Bellamy (who also appears in *The Spy*, 1931; *My Lady Dangerous*, 1930; *The House in Greek Street*, 1935; and *The Destroyer and the Red Hair Death*, 1938), saves Cicely from the German spies, Gusta Staube and Victor von Kroom. They save Murdoch's plans for England and, as a bonus, discover hidden treasure which will serve as Cicely's dowry when the inevitable occurs.

Now,given the coincidences and the use of stock characters and situations, this could have been a mildly entertaining adventure romp in the Sapper manner. It has all the ingredients of the popular spy novel of the thirties from the secret weapon, to the virginal heroine, to the manly Secret Service ace, to the gruff chief, to the *deus ex machina*, and so on. Under Horler's hand, however, all the flaws of the form grow until they approach the further limits of the term ridiculous. Perhaps extremely credulous readers can accept the fact that people mistake Voyce zooming around in a tiny airplane for a vampire. Perhaps the technically-minded will approve of Horler's doubts about the possibilities of stopping engines, expressed at the end of the novel, and not question the wisdom of Horler's creating the notion of this secret weapon in the first place. Yet even the most open-minded reader has to balk at the revelation of Voyce's real identity and motive:

"The man himself was a mouthful, as we know. Von Salkenheim [i.e. Voyce] was born in the shadow of the Prussian Court, and was destined for the life of that amazing creature, the Prussian nobleman. He was to have been a big-wig in the Prussian Guards, a courtier, a swaggerer of the old type.

"But Fate intervened. When he was twenty years of age . . . he had a severe attack of fever. As a consequence of his illness, Count Erich von Salkenheim became completely bald....

"The Prussian idea of wit is heavy-footed and cruelly coarse. Van Salkenheim . . . was unmercifully chaffed about his baldness. Provoked beyond all sense of control one night at mess, he flung himself upon a senior officer and stabbed him in the heart."[3]

This leads him to be drummed out of the regiment and offered a job as a spy as his only path to redemption. Horler does not run to irony in his humor but sticks to the jokes of the hearty sportsman. He means us to take this seriously, and, therefore, takes away the option of seeing *The Curse of Doone* as a slapstick, parody spy novel. We are stuck with viewing it as a badly written, trite, silly, improbable book, whatever the reviewer in *The Bookman* says.

Horler builds his novels on seven recognizable and hackneyed character types: hero number one, hero number two, the girl with the secret, the Master Criminal, the assistant Master Criminal, the rogue scientist, and the moll. Sometimes one or two of them do not appear in particular novels, but they are, by and large, Horler's stable. Given the mass of novels which he produced, he had to work from patterns like these.

Horler's heroes usually come in pairs. This, of course, conveys the impression of healthy friendship and has lots of advantages in plotting adventures. Both men act, and, after their own fashion, think, but one of them inevitably winds up in trouble—usually because of the girl—and the other one drops out of the heavens at the end and saves everyone from perdition and fates worse than death. Take the example of *Vivanti* (1927). Dick Quinn falls for Sonia Hennessy and tries to straighten out her life, only he falls into the coils of the villain. Vivanti is about to practice nasty medical experiments on them when Peter Foyle swoops down and shoots the villain. Simply change the names and you have Horler's hero pattern from the twenties to the fifties. Sometimes we get a variation where the romantic lead saves the friend or, in the case of *The Curse of Doone* and *Tiger Standish* (1932), the Secret Service chief saves the day, but the pattern stays the same. Since Horler's journalistic experience included writing about sports (his first novel was entitled *Goal*, 1920), his heroes frequently have backgrounds as athletes— amateur athletes, to be sure. Gerald Holiday, in *The Lady of the Night* (1929), plays polo, Ian Heath, as already noted, plays rugger, and Tiger Standish plays, without fee, professional soccer. *Tiger Standish*, in fact, includes two football matches, and the villains snatch the hero after bribing one of the professional players to injure him with dirty play. Horler, then, uses sports as an emblem of his heroes' physical and moral strength, and he expects that merely mentioning it in passing will serve as a code word to his audience and, therefore, relieve him of detailed characterization. He uses the Secret Service in the same way, never detailing the organization but employing the aura of the term to clothe his heroes. Nicknames fall into the same category: he calls Justin Marsh, for instance, The Ace, because of the associations of the term rather than its connection with the character. In his own feeble way Horler tries to attach some traditional archetypes to his heroes. Thus, he repeatedly ties Bunny Chipstead to Dumas' D'Artagnan. His big myth, however, is the knight, damsel in distress, dragon gambit. Horler's world is strewn with helpless virgins in distress who are made-to-order for his clean-living, determined, sportsmen heroes.

Horler's series heroes are, in chronological order, Bunny Chipstead, Tiger Standish, the Nighthawk, the Ace, and H. Emp. It made commercial sense for Horler to create series heroes in most of his novels for they ran first as newspaper serials, and he and newspaper editors realized the virtues of name recognition to boost circulation. Not that Horler's heroes differ from one another in anything but their nicknames; they are simply the same product with a different label.But the series hero made commercial sense.

Horler did not, however, begin with the series hero. His first three thrillers—*The Mystery of Number One* (1923),*The House of Secrets* (1926) and *False Face* (1926)—have heroes who are not repeated. His first series hero was Bunny Chipstead, whom Horler concocted as half of the hero team in *In the Dark* (1927), and then continued in *Chipstead of the Lone Hand* (1928), *The Secret Agent* (1934), and *The Enemy Within the Gates* (1940). Here is Horler's first description of Chipstead:

> Bunny Chipstead was a slight, wiry, immaculately dressed man of forty-four. At first glance he might have been taken for a soldier of fortune come into a rich inheritance, or a big-game hunter on holiday after completing a hazardous trip. As a matter of fact Chipstead was a little of both. He had soldiered in many countries, whilst the big game he had hunted included many men who were more desperate than wild beasts. His lean face, that had a wind-swept, bleak expression, was redeemed from utter grimness by humourous grey eyes. He was tanned almost to a leather hue; he weighed exactly one hundred and thirty five pounds, could use his fists or a revolver with equal facility, had once half-killed an Apache in a back-alley of Paris by a simple ju-jitsu trick.[4]

Chipstead's nickname (this is Horler's idea of humor) is a shortened form of Buncombe which his schoolmates shorted to "bunkum" until he knocked some respect into them. Like Oppenheim, Horler recognized the commercial benefits of American connections, so he gives Bunny a father who is a wealthy American automobile manufacturer, and gives him an American *alma mater*, Cornell University. During the Great War Chipstead was in the Intelligence Corps:

> It was a hazardous game, and Bunny responded to the thrill of it. When the whole business was over, he had adopted the suggestion made to him that he should become a free-lance of the American Secret Service.

. . .

> Bunny travelled extensively, executing delicate commissions, not only for the American, but also for the British Government, working for the love of the job

alone.... The thought of any payment was out of the question, but Bunny always made one stipulation: he had to work entirely on his own, and refused to be fettered by any official rules.[5]

Any number of suggestive things crop up here. First, Chipstead seems to owe more to Rider Haggard's Alan Quatermain in his size and his big-game background than he does to the heftier Bulldog Drummond (the Ace also falls into this category as well). All sorts of stereotypes, the underdog, the giant killer, etc., accrue to this physical type. Chipstead's suave enthusiasm for danger is something common to all of Horler's heroes, who prefer anything to a quiet rusticating life: no danger is too great for them. The unpaid, free-lance business ties Horler to the attitudes of LeQueux and Oppenheim, who viewed spying as dirty business, but one which became admirable, as in Le Queux's *Hidden Hands* (1925), if the agent worked for nothing.

There are also the elements of world travel and Bunny's advancing years. These two items place him in the traditions of the love romance, which uses the middle-aged hero with a dangerous, exotic past as stock in trade. Finally, Horler gives us all the business about the hero working alone, and acting unfettered by official rules. This we can trace in the private detective tradition as far back as Poe, but we need not since in Horler it is largely bunkum. In spite of the stress of the title of Chipstead's second adventure, *Chipstead of the Lone Hand,* Horler constantly uses subsidiary characters or secondary heroes to help Chipstead, or to save his bacon.

Much of this also applies to Horler's other heroes. The second series hero, Tiger Standish, appeared in nine novels: *Tiger Standish* (1932), *Tiger Standish Comes Back* (1934), *The Mystery of the Seven Cafes* (1935), *The Grim Game* (1936), *Tiger Standish Takes the Field* (1940), *The Lady with the Limp* (1944), *Exit the Disguiser* (1948), *They Thought He Was Dead* (1949) and *The House of Jackals* (1951). This second continuing hero of Horler's menagerie plays football, as I noted before, but hardly as a professional. By playing soccer and by being a "free lance" Secret Service agent, he fulfills, vicariously, his crippled father's love of sport. Horler, here, probably borrowed the use of the sport contest in *Tiger Standish* from *Castle Gay*. He makes Tiger a bit beefier than Chipstead, and gives him a bit of pseudo-zingy diction which leads Colin Watson to trace him to Bulldog Drummond.[6] If Watson is right, we witness a sad decline from the thundering, if vulgar, text to the snivelling commentary. Next, we have the Nighthawk, Horler apparently deciding that predators give better associations than rabbits in the nickname department. The Nighthawk books are *They Call Him Nighthawk* (1937), *The Return of Nighthawk* (1940), *The Nighthawk Strikes to Kill (1941) Nighthawk Mops Up* (1944), *Ring Up Nighthawk* (1947), *Nap on Nighthawk* (1950) and *Nighthawk Swears Vengeance* (1954). In these books Horler uses his favorite motif, the Jekyll-Hyde motif, by picturing Gerald Frost as a mild-mannered newspaper reporter who avenges crime and treason in the person of the Nighthawk. Frost definitely does not play a lone hand, for he uses his chums to help him fight (mostly) Nazis. His use of a drawing of a night hawk as a calling card comes pretty directly from Simon Templar's stick figure. Justin Marsh, the Ace, is mainly a continuation, under a new name, of Bunny Chipstead. Horler invented him during the war to have a stable of heroes to unloose on the Nazis. The Ace, however, appears in only one war-time book, *Enter the Ace* (1941), and two subsequent ones, *Hell's Brow* (1952) and *The Dark Night* (1953). At the very end of his career, Horler tried out yet one more series: H. Emp. He was to tell his readers about the joke by nicknaming him "rope." Emp appears in only two novels: *The Master of Venom* (1949) and *Murder at Large* (1952). The writer tried out a new model here, as Emp is huge (six feet six, and weighs in at two hundred and fifty-two pounds), and, even after going to a good school, he has suffered reverses and turns to private investigating to support himself. In the end, though, all of Horler's heroes are the same. They contain a mixture of LeQueux, Sapper and any other writer whose ideas seem safe and saleable to Horler. They are long on determination and sex appeal, but short on intelligence, wit or even loud vulgarity. They, indeed, lack every element which could be called unique, vivid or interesting.

As sure as all of Horler's novels contain virile, "exciting" heroes, they also introduce the Girl with a Secret. Horler has pretty definite ideas about women. Peruse this description from *Chipstead of the Lone Hand*:

This girl was totally unlike any other woman he had ever met. She combined the frank, clear eyed sportsmanlike qualities of the modern day with all the fragrant femininity for which the man of his type craved. It was the total lack of this essential quality which rendered her prototypes, in his eyes, so sickeningly unsexed. Chipstead had a horror of the flat-chested, unhipped, raucous-voiced, cocktail-crazed creature that nowadays went by the name of girl.... Young women were trying to make the best of two worlds and failing horribly in the consequence. There was far too much of this aping men—in pursuits, mannerisms, even clothes.[6]

If Horler had had his way, the whale would now be extinct and Peter Cheyney's mother would have remained in the corset business much longer. Natural beauty, as opposed to what Horler calls "cosmetic miracles," pluck, naivete, isolation, and the Secret form the character of Horler's heroines. To establish natural beauty he contrasts the heroine with the vamp in the story, who is an overly made-up woman allied with evil motives and evil people. Take Mrs. Rosalie Shan from *Heart Cut Diamond* (1929):

There are women who might be summarized under the heading of "lovely ladies"— although they may not be lovely in themselves, they are lovely to look upon. Endowed by nature with lovely bodies, they make loveliness a cult. They exploit this ruthlessly and systematically. It is a business with them—and a hard, merciless business at that; knowing that the world worships Beauty, they extract the last coin from the pockets of its devotees before flinging them aside.[7]

A nice girl does not think of herself as beautiful, and even if she did, she would never dream of exploiting her beauty. If they are not entrepreneurs, Horler's heroines are certainly plucky. They do not scream when someone steps on their feet, and when threatened they try, albeit ineffectually, to do something about it. And, of course, they are always threatened with death or bondage or fates worse than death. This threat usually arises from their isolation. Respectable girls have fathers and brothers to defend them and mothers to counsel them. Mothers in Horler, however, have a high rate of mortality, so there goes one prop to a girl's life. Fathers and brothers, moreover, have flaws and peccadillos which incapacitate them from playing active roles. Either this, or Horler eliminates them altogether and gives us the ideal heroine of the love romance, the orphan. Even if they are dead, however, the heroine's family gives her the most important part of her romantic character, the Secret—the girl, being blameless, cannot have done anything to have acquired this priceless dowry for herself. We get the following orientation on the Secret in *The House of Secrets* (1926) when the hero meets the heroine:

A man whose experience had made him an accurate observer, Wilding came to the conclusion as he lit a cigarette that if it had not been for a Something undisclosed the girl would conceivably have accepted the friendship which he felt compelled to offer her. What was that mysterious Something?[8]

This secret and others like it lever Horler's heroes into the pell mell action of the plot. They have to solve them in order to a) help the woman and b)facilitate their courtship. The solution usually hinges on something which her male relatives have done: it is her father who causes Phyllis' peculiar behavior in *The House of Secrets* in *In the Dark* (1927) it is dad again, and in *The Lady of the Night* (1929) it is the heroine's brother who causes the creepy behavior of the heroine. Practically these women seem to be thoroughly imbecilic for not actively seeking working solutions to their problems. From Horler's point of view, they dummy up out of laudable loyalty to their male relatives. From a historical point of view, though, they possess secrets because Horler takes their characters over from LeQueux, Oppenheim and the love romance. He, like these writers, wants to present women with excitement in their lives to female readers who had only the endless prospect of typing or nursing or mothering.

Horler's villains are a bit more up to date than his heroines. In *Tiger Standish* he connects the villains to Al Capone and the reign of gangsters in America, and he does work up the character of the rogue scientist in order to be up to date. But, going back a minute, just as Horler's books contain more than one hero, they also contain multiple villains. These are the boss, the rogue scientist and the moll. Sometimes these roles coalesce in one person, but often they abide in individual villains. The villains almost always have some sort of colorful and baleful moniker: Juhl in *In the Dark* is "The Colossus" but he also calls himself "The Seeker of Secrets"; there is "The Disguiser" who skulks through the Chipstead books from *Chipstead of the Lone Hand* and exits in the Standish novel *Exit the Disguiser*; as late as 1949 we have "The Master of Venom" and, in the same book, "The Voice of Ice." Frequently Horler makes his villains physically disfigured. Chadderly in *Vivanti*, is disgustingly fat, Professor in *In the Dark*, is a dwarf, Philip Voyce is, as already mentioned, bald. Frequently, too, the Master Criminal is either himself a scientist, as is Dr. Paul Vivanti (in *The Mystery of Number One, Vivanti* and *Vivanti Returns*, 1931) or he has a rogue scientist in tow, like The Master of Venom, to do his bidding. Horler's predilection for scientists, mostly physicians gone wrong, probably stems from his fascination with the Jekyll-Hyde motif. This works its way into the early books in that in *Vivanti*, he shows us a nerve specialist out to wreck society, while in *The House of Secrets* another psychiatrist works for the weal of society.

We need worry little about the motives of Horler's Master Criminals—he certainly does not. He takes us back to the days even before Lambroso. Witness Wendover's first view of the chief villains in *The False Purple* (1932):

"Yes, the most interesting bit is coming now. I don't pose to be such a physiognomist as your illustrious self, but I placed this man and woman from the start as wrong 'uns.

High-class wrong 'uns, no doubt—but still wrong 'uns."[9]

Simply put, to healthy perceptions, good folks look good and bad folks look bad. Whether evil comes from unpleasant appearance—as with Greene's Raven—or, more likely, being ugly comes from being evil, Horler never tells us. But in the end it makes little difference: people act as villains because the plots need villains. The only other common background, besides their ill-looks, that Horler supplies to his crooks is that of their education. His heroes are superior products of British (or American) education, while the villains are not. Horler makes this point pretty clearly with Newton-Smith in *Nighthawk Strikes to Kill*:

There are degrees of evil-doers. There is, for instance, the man who is born wicked, as distinct from the man who has wickedness thrust upon him. The latter, in turn, is distinct from the man who takes to crime through the sheer necessity of being forced to live.

Wilfrid Newton-Smith belonged to the first class. The son of a scoundrel, he had gloried in wickedness from an early age. Even at prep. school he had been marked out for a criminal career, for he had been expelled for systematic thieving. This episode hushed up, he had climbed to much better heights at Winnington, that public school of the Second Class. Here he had organized and led a small gang of youthful hooligans who had made life an unmerry hell for all who came in for their attention. Expulsion again sent Wilfred Newton-Smith into the cold, critical, hostile world.[10]

It is not, moreover, only Second Class public schools which harbor these Master Crooks of tomorrow. In *Tiger Standish* the villain, Aubrey Hamme, is an old boy from Eton: Eton, however, has had the superior values to raze Hamme's name from the honored list of its graduates.

Horler, as I have said, cares little about the causes of evil beyond throwing us the snippet from *Twelfth Night* in the passage above. He does, however, explore one facet of the villain's motivation: his reaction to the boredom of life. Thus the series villain, the Disguiser, compares himself to Sherlock Holmes in *The Secret Agent*:

"That self-complacent ass whose creator called him a detective—I refer, of course, to the illustrious Sherlock Holmes—once replied, when asked by the egregious Watson (surely the stupidest nit wit that ever appeared in ficton) why he dosed himself with cocaine three times a day: 'My mind rebels at stagnation. Give me problems, give me work.... I am in my own proper atmosphere.... I abhor the dull routine of existence. I crave for mental exaltation.' Holmes claimed to be a detective; I'm a crook, but the same thing applies.

"You mean you can't live without excitement?"

"Crudely put, but yes...."[22]

Even Horler realized that he was in trouble here. Now, this element of the jaded sophisticate going into villainy because it provides thrills to pique him, is common in the Master Crooks of the writers of the first third of the century. Just as common, though, is the hero who engages in the hurly-burly of adventure because he is bored: Buchan's heroes are bored just as Sapper's are. So are Horler's; they love excitement and abhor inaction. With Chipstead "it was a hazardous game, and Bunny responded to the thrill of it." Thriller writers sensed that their readers read in order to relieve boredom at home and to travel out of the routine of their daily lives. But when both hero and villain operate out of the same motive, what distinguishes them? Buchan goes to Carlyle to explain this, and he and other writers tie the hero to the knightly quest in defense of innocence. As I have said, Horler's heroes do act, unlike the villains, out of chivalric motives, but Horler adds another level to delineate the difference between hero-excitement and villain-excitement. He summons up the Jekyll-Hyde motif and attaches it to his villains: they are, at once, respectable, successful men and nasty villains. They could have been pillars of the community, but turn to destroying it. In the ultimate sense, this does little to explain the causes of evil, as Horler does not go into the whys, but he uses it as camouflage or as a circular definition which seems to explain things but does not.

Tied up with Horler's Master Criminal we usually find a female villain who has forsaken decent, clean, domestic society for a life of crime. None of these women, from Xavia Sergioff in *In the Dark* onward, plays the role of the major antagonist. I have mentioned this type in connection with the heroine and there is not much more to say, since Horler's molls chiefly function to define the virginal heroines. Like the sleazy Diana Norquay in *Tiger Standish*, these women reject the respectable world of family and seemly courtship for an environment saturated with booze and dope. They become tools of the Master Crook and, partly out of fear and partly out of jealousy of the heroine's freshness, they aid in the plans to destroy the good. Also Horler uses women sub-villains because his books deal with "High Society" people, and often turn on the high society crime of blackmail. Women work in here because of the susceptibility they have to blackmail and because they are the ideal agents for collecting dirt on and from normally respectable men.

Just as Doyle uses the significance of Sherlock Holmes' cozy flat and the gas-lit streets to add relevance and meaning, so Horler uses locales dripping with association. First he uses the haunts of the rich, usually Paris or Monte, to lend upper class ambience to his characters. Like Edgar Wallace, Horler loves dungeons because of their obvious gothic associations, and since most of his novels turn on kidnapping, what could be more appropriate? Horler, somehow or other, shoehorns castles into books just so there can be a dungeon handy. Nightclubs also loom large in his novels. They are there because they are not boring; they are dangerous and exciting. Here is the "Gilded Lily" club from *Nighthawk Strikes to Kill*:

Professional perverts of both sexes met their Society clients in these stifling overcrowded rooms; what gigolos had not gone to Torquay, or to the bars of Lisbon, were present with their old woman consorts; scattered here and there were small groups of officers looking on the unsavoury scene, some with amused, some with contemptuous eyes.[12]

In spite of or because of these denizens, Horler commonly pivots his plots at a nightclub: someone is seen or something is overheard which starts things off.

Starts things off: this is how Horler's plots work. Contemporary reviewers always stressed, and praised, the speed and number of incidents in Horler's books. These incidents usually have little or no integration. In *Enter the Ace*, for instance, the action in the first half of the novel has virtually no relationship to the action in the second half. But this never troubled Horler. His typical plot proceeds something like this. The Head of the Secret Service calls the hero in and tells him to solve an impossible problem. The agent then beetles out and without any sort of plan comes into contact with a) the helpless and threatened Girl with a Secret, and b) the Master Criminal and his helots. After this the plot settles down to a series of chases, kidnappings and escapes. On the level of plotting, Horler is occasionally cynically frank. In the Anastasia-based book, *The False Purple*, he talks to his readers about the use of coincidence:

"Ladies and Gentlemen," said Beryl gravely, "I will now introduce to you that character beloved of novelists, not to mention book reviewers, who is known to us as The Long Arm of Coincidence. I am going to pull him almost out of his socket—but as this happens to be the truth and not fiction, you must all believe me. Promise?"[13]

In *The Secret Agent* Horler introduces himself to his readers in the guise of J.R. Blandish, a popular writer. Through Blandish he again makes pretty clear the intention of his plots and characters. Blandish says that he is "very glad to know that his 'fairy tales for tired businessmen,' as he called them, were read by the owner of an intelligent face as mine, and he promptly invited me to have a drink."[14] The narrator also adds that "It's silly of me, no doubt, but whenever I read a Blandish yarn I always want to sleep with the heroine!"[15] Much could be made of this last remark (prurient interest, the neglect or the direction of the adventure plot toward the love romance, the level of frankness for 1934), but perhaps the most effective criticism is that one would need to be pretty demented to want to sleep with any of Horler's neurotic, confectionary heroines.

Horler's characters may be crudely drawn and his plots painfully slap-dash, but his books do not represent the absolute nadir of popular spy fiction. One does come away from his books with a fragment of a piece of an idea, which is more than one can say about writers like Edgar Wallace. Horler is a Darwinian of sorts—the Tennysonian "nature red in tooth and claw" variety. Consistently in his books he brings his heroes to a point where they emotionally strip down to the primitive and out-animal the villains. This, coincidentally, brings us back to *The Curse of Doone* where Warren Murdoch gives us what may as well be Horler's credo:

"What causes war....Many things...—but principally human nature. So long as there are human beings inhabiting the earth, so long will there be wars—nothing can prevent them. Elaborate international tribunals may be set up, conferences held—pshaw! So much eye wash; for all of our civilisation humanity remains primitive beneath the surface, and the instinct of the primitive creature is to fight for what it desires.[16]

Why, though? Is there no God? Do we live in a Fallen World? Are the powers of the universe malign? Horler does not want these questions to be asked. Instead, the above passage is like a discussion in a pub on the topic of the League of Nations. And his plotting is much like a yarn told in a pub: it will pass as entertainment, but only if nothing else is available.

NOTES

[1] *The Heart Cut Diamond* (London: Hodder and Stoughton, n.d.), endpapers.
[2] *The Curse of Doone* (New York: The Mystery League, 1930), p. 10.
[3] *The Curse of Doone*, p. 303.
[4] *In the Dark* (London: Hodder and Stoughton, n.d.), pp. 64-5.
[5] *In the Dark*, pp. 66-7.
[6] *Chipstead of the Lone Hand* (London: Nelson, n.d.), pp. 127-8.
[7] *The Heart Cut Diamond*, p. 62.
[8] *The House of Secrets* (New York: Grosset & Dunlap, 1927), p. 16.
[9] *The False Purple* (New York: The Mystery League, 1932), p. 58.
[10] *Nighthawk Strikes to Kill* (London: Hodder and Stoughton, 1941), p. 21.
[11] *The Secret Agent* (London: Collins, 1936), p. 220.

[12]*Nighthawk Strikes to Kill*, p. 27.
[13]*The False Purple*, p. 281.
[14]*The Secret Agent*, p. 82.
[15]*The Secret Agent*, p. 82.
[16]*The Curse of Doone*, pp. 138-9.

Chapter 8

Graham Greene
(1904—)

GRAHAM GREENE HAS WRITTEN eight novels which deal with espionage: *The Stamboul Train* (1932), *A Gun for Sale* (1936), *The Confidential Agent* (1939), *The Ministry of Fear* (1943), *The Quiet American* (1955), *Our Man in Havana* (1958), *The Honorary Counsel* (1973) and *The Human Factor* (1978). Though all these novels touch upon espionage to some degree, spying *qua* spying always takes a back seat. The mechanical techniques and practical consequences of spying do not interest Greene, and he usually minimizes them, ridicules them or moves them into the background. Even in *The Ministry of Fear*, written during the Hitler War, Greene does not propagandize or concentrate on the traditional matters of the spy novel. In spite of its secondary function, however, espionage fascinates Greene because of its potential to open up for examination certain human issues: commitment, conscience, individual will, betrayal and alienation. All these issues, of course, impinge upon Greene's examination of his own faith and his church. They exist because of Greene's Catholicism and consequently tie his spy novels to his overtly religious fictions. Through half his writing career, Greene separated his spy books off into a category labeled "entertainments." Espionage and other traditions of popular fiction, however, provided Greene with so much form and direction for all his writing that he eventually dropped the sardonic "entertainment" tag from his spy books and admitted that they were an organic part of his artistic production.

The Stamboul Train

1932: Sapper, Beeding, Christie, Sayers. Popular fiction was pretty and peppy, full of clubmen, wise cracks, smart diction, artificial puzzles and other kinds of entertainments for people who were not yet on the bread line. The most unreal form of the detective story, the puzzle piece, was on the wane, and some detective writers were turning toward the psychological puzzle in which readers, instead of musing on material clues, looked for psychological clues

112

in order to pin the tail on the murderer. Just look at those six people isolated on a yacht or at a weekend bridge shindig at a big house in the country; look into the pre-arranged psyches and figure out who murdered nasty, rich old Clive. This kind of fiction, using A.B. Cox's term, is a "closed" detective story: limited suspects, clear issues, definite ending. It is a tame, wholesome, superficially intellectual, reassuring entertainment.

Enter the young Graham Greene. Greene called *The Stamboul Train* an "entertainment" and in constructing the novel he used some of the standard devices of detective fiction. He takes seven very diverse people (Dr. Czinner, Coral Musker, Quinn Savory, Joseph Grunlich, Janet Pardoe, Mabel Warren and Mr. Myatt) and reveals their characters as they are thrown together on their journey on the Orient Express. The basic situation sounds a bit like Agatha Christie's *Murder on the Orient Express* (1934). Well, *The Stamboul Train* is not like Christie's book—not one bit. First of all, it is not a murder mystery, for we know who the killers are. It is not a detective story, for the murderers live on in a world of reasonable comfort: no detective hauls, or can haul, them to the dock. The world of the novel continues on after the main action, soaked in hypocrisy and corruption, defeating the romantic possibilities of the opening of the book. Greene surely was joking when he called the book an entertainment, but then again readers of detective stories do divert themselves with death and stylized guilt.

Greene emphatically does not want to divert us through laughter or abstract intellectual involvement—unless we are entertained by disinterments and autopsies. I do not mean to disparage *The Stamboul Train*, which is remarkable in many ways as a novel as well as a realistic spy story. It is just not entertainment and, in spite of the label, Greene knows it and makes it clear. First, Greene continually makes mention of Dunn's Babies, a leggy musical review troup which Coral intends to join in Istambul. At the end of the novel he even gives us a snippet out of one of their performances:

> Waiting at the station
> For a near relation,
> Puff, puff, puff, puff—

Along with these lines Greene introduces us to Quinn Savory, the author of the best-selling novel entitled *The Great Gay Whirl*. He lets Savory pronounce on art in passages like this:

I take my stand with sanity as opposed to the morbid introspection of such writers as Lawrence and Joyce. Life is a fine thing for the adventurous with a healthy mind in a healthy body.[2]

We can see why Greene calls him savory, using the sense of appetizing. Also we can see through the novelist's name how Greene himself intends to entertain us here: Savory, in British usage, is the piquant dessert course which is served so as to contrast with the sweet. That is how Greene's entertainments are supposed to work—they are the sour contrast.

The Stamboul Train plunges us right into introspection and gloom. It penetrates the personalities of mean, untidy, self-centered, grubby people. Myatt, the raisin entrepreneur, interrupts his immersion in currant affairs for a brief romantic fling. Miss Warren, who probably causes Czinner's death, pursues her lesbian fantasies while grinding out yellow journalism. Grunlich revels in his hoodlum reputation for never having been in jail and fondles the memory of his quick draw. Janet Pardoe peddles sex appeal up and down the train. Savory dispenses his bromides to tired listeners. Even the minor characters, as usual in Greene, ooze corruption and absurdity, from Mr. Opie and his cricket, to the tourists in Coral's compartment, to Major Petkovitch, to Stein, to all of them.

Only Coral Musker and Dr. Czinner come close to being admirable people, but Greene denies even this to his readers. He introduces Coral as a potentially sympathetic character by making her a well-intentioned but lost innocent and by surrounding her with people who are palpably corrupt. By the end of the novel, though, Greene demeans her by spotlighting the shallowness of her romantic fantasies and by showing her alienation from Czinner—a motif more graphically repeated in Anne's repugnance to Raven in A Gun for Sale. Greene treats Dr. Czinner slightly differently. He allows Czinner to examine his conscience—hence the obvious link with "sinner"—and follows this with an impulse toward confession. This part of Czinner we need to see in the light of Greene's treatment of Roman Catholic themes in all his books. More important here, however, is the fact that Greene portrays Czinner as the failed revolutionary, and he is the first character of this type which will continue through The Honourary Counsel. In line with the intellectual fashion in Britain in the thirties, Greene makes Czinner an international socialist:

Sad and beautiful faces, thin from bad food, old before their time, resigned to despair, had passed through his mind; they were people he had known, whom he had attended.... The world was in chaos to leave so much nobility unusued, while the great financiers and soldiers prospered.³

But socialism will not work or it will not be given a chance to work. Czinner's return to his homeland to help the cause is quixotic in the face of the entrenched power of financiers and soldiers. The animus of Mabel Warren and the ironies of circumstance stifle Czinner's chances of pulling off even a propaganda coup at his seemingly inevitable trial. His consciousness of his own past failures nullifies his ability to act, and the raw material of the hypothetical revolution, the peasants, show no hope for change: "The peasants gave way and moved on to the line, but presently they swarmed back, obstinate, stupid, and hopeless."⁴ There can be no revolution, now or ever. The raw material, Greene shows us constantly, simply is not there.

Czinner, the old man, dies a messy, ignominious death. The others go on with their doggy lives, with their doggy illusions. Myatt, the raisin king, drifts back to memories of his childhood—as do most of Greene's characters. He remembers, significantly, that, "When he was younger he used to read stories of King's Messengers seduced by beautiful countesses travelling alone and wonder whether such good fortune would ever happen to him."⁵ His head is stuffed, obviously, with LeQueux and Oppenheim. He misses out on the countesses, but gets a few hours of passion in a cramped bunk on a jostling train. The King's Messenger is a broken old man whose message is too late, and useless anyway, and who is pulled off the train and murdered. It is that kind of spy story.

A Gun For Sale

Even more than in *The Stamboul Train*, Greene collected most of the materials for *A Gun for Sale* from a number of identifiable traditions of the detective novel and the thriller. In any number of senses the novel was born of the popular fiction of the twenties and thirties, but under Greene's hand it grows into something more complex than its parents.

On one level *A Gun for Sale* resembles the novels of any number of Golden Age detective writers. Initially, Greene introduces a number of characters into the novel who resemble conventional character types from the regular detective novel. The policeman in *A Gun for Sale*, Mather, is as solid, energetic and dutiful as any detective in the mystery fiction of the period. Greene makes Mather come to the wrong conclusions about the essentials of the case, but this, too, comes from the traditions of the detective novel—Bentley and Cox both make the erring detective a convention of the form. If Mather is conventional, so is his assistant, Saunders. Saunders trots dutifully at Mather's heels and worships his superior every bit as much as Fox worships Alleyn in Marsh's detective novels: he too comes right out of detective literature. Greene, like so many detective writers, pulls many of the minor characters of *A Gun for Sale* from comic molds. Major Calkin, the Chief Constable, the Mayoress, Ruby the chorus girl, the vicar, all come from comic types common to the detective novel. Indeed, the alternation of comic scenes with scenes of tension and high seriousness which Greene begins to use in this novel is typical of the Golden Age detective novel at its best. Here Greene moves readers through the comedy of the church jumble sale, dinner at Major Calkin's house, and a medical students' rag, while Raven prowls the dark streets of Nottwich. This is akin to Poirot and Hastings fooling around while the murderer runs up his tally in Christie's *A.B.C. Murders* (1935). Like Sayers and Allingham, Greene in *A Gun for Sale* extends comedy from character to situation to dialogue. Take Calkin's remark about,

> Somewhere there's a foreign field
> that is forever .... Shakespeare
> knew. Old time-honoured Gaunt
> when he said that—[6]

This is the sort of sneering literary jibe which we find in most detective novels aimed at upper middle class readers. Greene also has a go at giving his characters peppy, nonchalant dialogue when they are under stress:

You're the third person who's tried to kill me.... Come to sunny Nottwich. Well, I've six lives left.

***

This is where you hit... if that's what you want to know.... It was only an outer. You don't even get a box of chocolates.[7]

Examined selectively, *A Gun for Sale* possesses many of the elements characteristic of the British detective novel between the wars. In plot it bears some similarity to "howcatchem" novels like Philip MacDonald's *Murder Gone Mad* (1931) or Allingham's later novel *Tiger in the Smoke* (1951), which may have been influenced by *A Gun for Sale*.

Added to these similarities to the Golden Age detective novel, *A Gun for Sale* connects in many ways with the spy thrillers of the teens and twenties. This shows through largely in the externals of the villains in Greene's book. Sir Marcus and the international group of capitalists who meet to plot a new European war in order to line their own pockets repeat the same gang which we find in so many thrillers such as Sapper's *Bull-Dog Drummond at Bay* (1935). Sir Marcus seems in many ways like the stereotypical Master Crook, with his power, his deformity, his toadies and his hide-out. *A Gun for Sale* seems to depend on the same simplistic, anti-semitic, anti-capitalist, anti-international leaven of so many other earlier thrillers. Further, if *The Stamboul Train* acts as the antidote to the notion of the romantic story running on coincidences, *A Gun for Sale* is the poison which the earlier book sought to counteract. The plot turns on improbable coincidence, like Raven spotting Anne's purse at the church, or Raven's good fortune in being in the middle of the practice gas attack: this is plotting similar to that in *The Thirty Nine Steps*.

Finally, in terms of conventions, Greene, in *A Gun for Sale*, brings in several motifs from the American hard-boiled detective novel or film. Raven is much like the punk gun man, Wilmer, in Hammett's *The Maltese Falcon* (1929) in his insignificance compensated for by the possession of a pistol. He, in fact, speaks like the plug-uglies in Hammett, Whitfield, or Chandler: he insists on grating on Cholmondeley's nerves by constantly calling him "Cholmon-deley" instead of "Chumley." Raven speaks gangster patois, calling women "skirts" and talking about "plugging" people. Also, either from the hard-boiled story or from the native tradition of the thriller (it makes little difference as the two forms mutually influence each other), Greene adopted a casual attitude toward the resilience of the human fabric. Thus, Anne feels pretty chipper when Raven rescues her from her captors at Khyber Avenue, in spite of the fact that she has spent a considerable time bound and stuffed up a chimney. Hard-boiled heroines are made of strong stuff.

With Greene, however, popular material does not function solely in order to satisfy the demands of the audience. He, I suppose, would not dissuade a detective story addict from buying *A Gun for Sale*, but he did not write the novel with detective story addicts in mind. Certainly he got a boost out of making up the jokes and writing the comic sequences for this book, just as detective writers do. At the center of Greene's use of conventional elements, however, lurks the luddite: he wants to smash the accepted notions of the detective story. We can see this in the final chapters of *A Gun for Sale*. The typical thriller ends with the triumph of law over evil. The detective story ends with the recapitulation of the major problems of the plot and thereby solves them. That is all; conventional novels end here. They exist to show the vicarious defeat of evil or solution to fake problems, and when these things happen the books have no reason to continue. But *A Gun for Sale* does neither of these things. If this were a detective story or thriller, the necessary happy ending with Mather and Anne and their special license would follow hard upon Raven's death and the exposure of the perfidy of Midland Steel. *A Gun for Sale* does not do the expected. Instead, Greene traces the continuing lives of Calkin, Saunders, Ruby and Acky, showing them continuing, unchanged, their insignificant, dreary lives. Greene dissipates Raven's blaze of glory by sinking us back into the slough of routine existence. The way in which he manipulates the ending helps to defeat the conventional expectations of the form. More important, though, Greene mines the novel with any number of serious ambiguities which explode the expectations of the average detective or spy reader. These run from the pointed ambiguity in motivation to the serious ambiguity in characterization. Greene, thus, gathers ambiguity around the character of Sir Marcus, the ostensible villain of *A Gun for Sale*. On one hand, he is a nasty, wizened Jewish capitalist who orders the murder of his childhood friend to precipitate a war. This is the stuff of cliche. But Greene raises doubt about his Jewishness, and, more importantly, shows him to be a pitiable tissue of mortality waiting for death. His villainy and his character do not condense down to the simple formula which we find in, say, Sapper's villains. This same sort of ambiguity comes in when Calkin refuses to issue a shoot-on-sight order about Raven. Does he refuse Sir Marcus' request as a single act of rebellion, or out of pusillanimity? Look at the text:

He went into his study and sat by the telephone. In five minutes Sir Marcus would be at home. So much stolen from him already, surely there was little more he could lose by acquiescence. But he sat there doing nothing, a small plump bullying hen-pecked profiteer.[8]

Which is it, strength or weakness? The narration inclines us to the latter, but there is no way to be sure. Greene will not be pinned down. These ambiguities, moreover, condition us for the central ambiguity of the novel: is Raven the anti-Christ, or is he the abused Savior? Greene makes the question, at least, pretty clear by setting the novel during the Christmas season, with trees, creches, and the talk of

Christ's birth. Raven, obviously, finds no room at the inn, and Anne, who reluctantly gives life to Raven, and Mather act out the roles of Mary and a grudging and dubious Joseph. Raven, like Christ, dies to give his society one more chance. But, on the other hand, Raven is the grotesque, hare-lipped killer who gains manhood only from his possession of a pistol, and who has a moral sense governed only by a rudimentary sense of pleasure and pain.

If he refuses complete answers to these points, Greene does give some pointers to the answers. Chief here is the fact that Raven is about as much Christ as a fallen world deserves. Basic to this novel, indeed basic to all of Greene, is the squalidness of the human condition—not part of it, like the awful background about Raven's parents, but all of it. Although the book does make a few socialistic points—that society created Raven, that international capitalism destroys little people, that the murdered Czech Minister really did try to help the working poor—their significance dwindles when we add the perspective of the action, and the folly and viciousness which it uncovers. As in *The Stamboul Train*, corruption trickles out of not only the major characters but also out of the minor ones. Just consider Alice, Raven's putative girlfriend, at the beginning of the novel, or Sir Marcus' valet at the end. All are weak, cruel, ugly, snivelling, loveless and self-absorbed. Even the nominally decent characters, Mather and Anne, have diseased abscesses: Mather huddling in the false security of discipline, and Anne's about-face when she actually perceives Raven's grotesqueness.

In *A Gun for Sale*, then, Greene takes the detective story, the thriller, and the spy story, their tone and diction, their organization and plot, and shows a new world. Here Buchan's values do not hold, or even exist; we enter the spiritual wasteland drawn by Eliot and Auden, where even an individual shot through with venom is more admirable than people drowning in casual corruption.

The Confidential Agent

The Confidential Agent lacks punch. Greene wrote it, he tells us, under difficult conditions: he was about to enter the army, was trying to finish *The Power and the Glory*, and was souping himself up with benzedrine. From the perspective of 1971, Greene said that *"The Confidential Agent* is one of the few books of mine which I have cared to reread."[9] He no doubt had good reasons for saying this, but it certainly does not hold true when considering *The Confidential Agent* against his other "entertainments."

This does smack of effrontery, but it can be substantiated. To start with, Greene's spy books work best when they merge with the concerns which occupy him in his other fiction. *A Gun for Sale*, for instance, is in many ways the raw material for *Brighton Rock*. Raven and Pinkie come from the same model and, in fact, Greene ties the two novels together by making Raven's first victim, Mr. Kite, Pinkie's mentor, and having the occasion of his death be the reason for Pinkie's assumption of power in the gang. Further, the issues of depravity and salvation connect the two novels. Greene fortifies most of his spy plots by combining action with serious issues. But not *The Confidential Agent*. This novel walks a middle ground between action and issues and, consequently, never involves us in pure action, as in the closing scenes of *A Gun for Sale* or *The Ministry of Fear,* or engages readers with the issues or personalities in the book. This may have been Greene's aim, but this can hardly be ballyhooed in a study of the spy novel.

Like Orwell's *Homage to Catalonia*, Koestler's *Dialogue with Death* or, on a more mundane level, Beeding's *Hell Let Loose*, Greene centers *The Confidential Agent* on the Spanish Civil War. More specifically, he deals with rumors of war as the novel takes place exclusively in Britain. Abstracted from the novel, Greene's attitudes toward the war are much the same as other writers' views: the rebels are cruel and inhuman, but the loyalists do a pretty good job of these things too. Greene, though, shunts these political issues into the background and devotes his attention to people. He fills the novel with passionless people and makes their emptiness the subject rather than focusing on the unfolding of any sort of political plot.

In *The Confidential Agent,* the anonymous D. and Rose Cullen occupy most of the readers' attention. Rose is a frigid, closed-mouthed woman who merely drifts through life. Even her rebellion against her daddy's ill-gotten millions (a rebellion which D. sees as akin to his own personal and political rebellion) seems low-keyed, passive and ineffectual. At the end of the novel she merely shrugs off Forbes, her intended, and sails off to Spain with D., with whom she has had about three hours, total, perfunctory conversation. When she does show a bit of human zing in her personality, in her jealousy of Else, it seems arbitrary and out of place. Likewise, D., the title character, is a pretty emasculated individual. Greene tried to construct him out of a tag from *Doctor Faustus*, "Why this is hell, nor am I out of it," from a contrast between modern life and Roland's heroism in *The Song of Roland*, and from the persistence of memories budding into the present's acts and thoughts. D. brings to England with him the Spanish Civil War: the inner chaos and duplicity of the loyalists, the bonhomous inhumanity of Franco's aristocratic agent, L., as well as the remembered horrors of the war itself. But these things dissolve for D. when he actually sees the squalor and misery of Benditch, the English coal mining town where work or strike will affect events in Spain: he realizes that the condition of the town "was like war, but without the spirit of defiance which war usually raised."[10] On the level of plot and that of theme, D. does nothing. Early in the novel he passively takes a thrashing on the London Road, later he rages, threatening conventional adventure story vengeance on Else's murderers and other assorted malefactors, but at the end he subsides back into passivity. This development probably fits into an obvious theological framework in the novel, which we can see in D.'s thoughts over Else's corpse:

If you believed in God, you could believe that it [the corpse] had been saved from much misery and had a finer future. You could leave punishment, then, to God... just because there was no need for punishments when all a murderer did was to deliver....[11]

Immediately it occurs to D. that in this framework of belief, God punishes evil doers. In *The Confidential Agent* this proof of Providential justice does appear: Else's killers are punished (K. dies spontaneously, and the manageress of the hotel goes insane). The hero, consequently, becomes someone who waits. Thus Greene gives us an ironic inversion of the usual thrust of the adventure action plot. His labeling of the first two sections of the novel as "The Hunted" and "The Hunter," moreover, ceases to be false packaging and falls into the same category as calling the spy novels "entertainments."

Part of the import of action in this novel points to the significance of wise, if accidental, passiveness. D. does not get the coal contract which he is sent for, he does not shoot K., and his grotty bunch of Gorbals Die-Hards do not blow up the Benditch coal mine. In spite of these negatives, however, Franco's side does not get the coal, and the murderers get their due. Failure means success in terms of the personal and political goals of the novel, but unfortunately, this adds little to the pace of the action or, more importantly, to the dynamic presence of the characters. Fate, after all, does not keep Hamlet wisely passive throughout the play.

Like *A Gun for Sale*, *The Confidential Agent* mixes serious action with comedy. The doses of the new international language, Entrenationo, and its zealots, as well as the brief scene with Hogpit and the policemen contain some funny material layered between suspense and danger. There is, however, less humor here than in *A Gun for Sale*. The scenes at the holiday camp at the end of the novel have comic potential, but Greene prefers to use satiric contempt here. Likewise, Captain Currie, the recurring bad penny, might be funny if readers knew why he keeps popping up so often.

Like the business with Captain Currie, *The Confidential Agent* records failed opportunities and, in general, conveys a sense of listlessness rather than suspense or terror. The villains, except for perhaps the manageress, have none of the vivid grotesqueness of Sir Marcus, and even the principal character point, D.'s indecision and humanity, never comes across well. The failure of purpose in this novel shows through the best in Greene's fulminations about the fallen nature of the world. When D. arrives in England at the beginning of the novel, Greene gives us this passage:

> He had imagined that the suspicion which was the atmosphere of his own life was due to civil war, but he began to believe that it existed everywhere: it was part of human life. People were united only in their vices.... It was as if the whole world lay in the shadow of abandonment. Perhaps it was still propped up by ten just men—that was a pity. Better scrap it and begin again with the newts.[12]

The reference to the ten just men comes from the Cities of the Plain (Genesis 18), and the newts from Capek's *The War with the Newts* (1936). They both reinforce the idea of destroying mankind for its sin and folly. This message is a pretty consistent one in Greene. It does not jibe with much in *The Confidential Agent*, though. The end of the novel mixes romantic optimism with hedonism. When he is definitely up the creek, bogus coppers rescue D. from imprisonment and Rose promises him love here and now even if the future holds death. They then sail off into the future together. Even a pagan Roman could approve of this. We forget about the pillar of fire, and about newts flooding China to make new breeding grounds. We could take refuge in the idea of ambiguity here, but this would muddle the real importance of ambiguity in Greene's other novels. It is probably best to admit that he was off his mark in *The Confidential Agent*.

The Ministry of Fear

In the last years of the thirties, many detective story writers who had frisked and gambolled with safe, imaginary crimes, like Sayers, quit writing detective stories or they turned to the spy thriller as a means of expressing and controlling the new, troubling world full of tension and fear. Nicholas Blake (C. Day Lewis), for instance, turns to the spy thriller with *Smiler with a Knife* (1939). Greene as a user of popular forms did not need to quit or to switch forms; he had always insisted that tension and fear lay at the core of human existence, but that it was beyond the help of any human exorcism. Nonetheless, in *The Ministry of Fear* Greene takes readers through the process of rejecting the detective story and then through the process of rejecting the thriller one more time in order to make them face the world with only pity and terror.

The Ministry of Fear begins as a detective novel and Greene uses and draws attention to various detective story conventions. Unlike the other novels which contain detective motifs, Greene here concentrates the plot on several mysteries which Rowe, the hero, stumbles into. He introduces chains of evidence and pertinent questions upon which the plot rests: why does Poole crumble his cake? what is in the cake? who killed Cost? As significant as the questions and evidence is the way in which Greene handles them: he handles them as a detective writer would, planting clues in the narrative which the reader can only understand in retrospect. Thus, when Hilfe and Cost go off together at Mrs. Bellaire's seance, they plot the bogus murder, but readers can only realize this by exact attention to all the details of the novel coupled with constant evaluation—which is unlikely—or later by reviewing events after they know what happens in the entire plot. This is fundamental detective story technique. In the same vein, Rowe, late in the novel, uses the term "jigsaw puzzle" to explain his experiences, and this brings in the whole load of pseudo-intellectual posing which detective writers and readers in the twenties and thirties developed to explain and justify the detective story. Another uniquely detective novel element which Greene uses in *The Ministry of Fear* is the peculiar event involving a peculiar set of odd-ball characters. In Greene's earlier spy novels, granted, he does give us some peculiar characters, and he also uses detective-thriller locales—fog, for instance, plays a major role in *A Gun for Sale* and *The Confidential Agent*. In *The Ministry of Fear*, however, Greene uses the same kind of zany situations which we find in detective novels of the twenties and thirties, like Sayers' *Whose Body?* which starts with the discovery of a strange corpse in a bathtub. *The Ministry of Fear* begins at a fete held by the Mothers of Free Nations where Rowe wins a cake, and this begins the whole business of the villains chasing him for the cake, which has secret information baked inside. It does sound a bit wacko. One cannot see this happening in Greene's earlier novels which he wraps up in mist and fog. Also Greene presents us with a bunch of balmy minor characters from the woman at the fete who confuses "free mothers" with "Mothers of Free Nations" to Rowe's sweet-toothed landlady, to Rennit, the head of Orthotex, to the book seller who specializes in garden literature. These people come from the comic detective tradition and many lack the malign aspects of the minor characters in Greene's other books. Finally, although he did not write any extended comic scenes in *The Ministry of Fear* as he did in *A Gun for Sale*, he does use the same sort of inside literary jokes which turn up in the detective novels of Nicholas Blake or Michael Innes. When Rowe, for example, speaks to the bookseller about the place of the tomb in garden architecture, we get, imbedded in the conversation, " 'Black thoughts,' said Rowe, 'in a black shade?' "[13] Greene, naturally, has reason to remember "Green thoughts in a green shade" from Marvell's poem "The Garden," and he puts it into this novel as a witty literary reference much in the manner of the witty, literary detective novelist. The quote from "The Garden," furthermore, operates in the same way that Blake's allusion to Tourneur's *The Revenger's Tragedy* works in *Thou Shell of Death*. Understand the quote and you understand the structure of the novel. In *The Ministry of Fear* Greene's hero begins the novel wrapped in contemplation, he suffers a benign fall into adolescence, and then suffers the real fall into experience; "The Garden" rests on the idea of contemplation, and moves men through several falls, the last of which is the fall into real life. Taking this with the other detective implements, Greene does them all very neatly; he has mastered the detective writer's craft. *The Ministry of Fear*, however, also demonstrates that detective novels are impossible.

After the war, Michael Innes in *The Case of the Journeying Boy* (1949) demonstrates how much more closely thrillers approximate modern reality than do detective stories. Between the wars, detective critics pooh-poohed the thriller as being improbable and as the product of unhealthy or low class minds. Events after 1939 proved these people to be wrong: the world very definitely is like the thriller. This is the next moment in *The Ministry of Fear*. The book plunges the reader into the world of capture and escape, omnipresent danger and Master Villains. Rowe, in his dream in the bomb shelter, tries to explain this to his mother:

It sounds like a thriller, doesn't it?—but the thrillers are like life—more than you are, this lawn, your sandwiches, that pine. You used to laugh at the books Miss Savage read—about spies, and murders, and violence, and wild motor-car chases, but, dear, that's real life: it's what we've all made of the world since you died. I'm your little Arthur who wouldn't hurt a beetle and I'm a murderer too. The world has been remade by William LeQueux.[14]

Greene plunges his hero into the world of the thriller. Rowe, for the most part of the book, acts the part of his adventure hero. In the action sections he does not hesitate or intellectualize: he rushes out to chase spies or to rescue innocent people, like the Major, from the clutches of the villains. As in the detective parts of *The Ministry of Fear*, Greene devotes considerable attention to making the novel work as a thriller. As with Raven, Greene makes one of the villains, Poole, a strikingly grotesque figure with simian grooming habits. He strips Rowe of reliable friends at the start of the novel, and makes him rely on the aid of Hilfe, who turns out to be an enemy agent. The eeriness of the trap at the hotel, and the threat of incarceration at the "sick-bay" provide suitable and effective tension. Here, as in the early books, Green pivots the action from chase to hunt but does it with more facility than in *The Confidential Agent.*. Also he moves the plot through jolts in the action: the cake, the bomb blast, Cost's murder, the hotel, the sanitorium, Scotland Yard, etc. The added menace of flights of Nazi bombers calling "where are you?" and the nightmare presence of Poole in Rowe's rooms are well up to if not above standard. Yet *The Ministry of Fear* rejects the basic morality of the thriller.

In this novel Greene uses two different kinds of popular literature, partly to develop the plot, but also to destroy these same elements. First he rejects the detective story. He does this initially by bringing it up against the action-oriented thriller, and then by opposing it to reality. We can see the later motive in Greene's portrait of the private detective, Rennit, and his chief and only agent, Jones, Agent A2. Rennit's detective agency, Orthotex, is a far cry from the headquarters of the storied private detective of independent means and high-class taste; it sounds like the name of a mouthwash or denture manufacturer. Orthotex's business relies on the divorce trade—not recovering duchesses' pearls—for Greene wants it to be seedily realistic. We have not only this sobering element to degrade the idea of the conventional detective story, but Greene turns *The Ministry of Fear* toward the negative tradition of the British detective story. From *Brighton Rock* (1938) Greene allied himself with detective writers like Anthony Berkeley Cox and the American James M. Cain who attempt to examine real crime and real criminal psychology. This occurs also in *The Ministry of Fear*. Rowe's situation in this novel presents us with a plot very like Cox's *Before the Fact* (1932) with a murderer committing euthanasia. Greene, moreover, goes further than Cox in that he focuses on the murderer having to continue to live battered by his own conscience.

The focus on Rowe's semi-rational struggles and corrosive

conscience put the lid on the mannered, superficial detective story which is far too fastidious to handle anything as messy as a human psyche. After Greene puts the quietus on the old-fashioned detective story, he takes on the spy thriller. In the middle of *The Ministry of Fear* the hero loses all consciousness of his previous adult existence, and approaches life as an adolescent, relishing action and simplistically judging good and evil. At the end of the book, he grows up for a second time, reacquiring pity and learning how to bear its burden. By showing this, Greene looks at and then leaves the action-fixated conventions of the spy book for the more complex, unanswerable series of ambiguities which he sees as the human condition. The same thing holds true for the Nazi spies as well as the hero. Like Conrad's secret agent, or the spy in Ambler's *Epitaph for a Spy*, the Nazi agents in *The Ministry of Fear* are inept, pathetic, little people. They intrude into Rowe's life and play various games with him when, to achieve their goals, they should have left him alone. Hilfe, thus, urges Rowe to continue his investigations just as he is about to drop them, and the bookseller intervenes just as Rowe is about to commit suicide. As in *The Confidential Agent*, Providence works against evil: the devil is an ass. But Greene does not present the German agents as demons. Hilfe and his people are pitiable and human. This is what he looks at rather than at thriller bogies or Britain's real military position in the war. In fact, Greene turns the real situation of the actual war toward his theme of the sordidness of the human estate when he praises Churchill for telling his nation unpleasant truths about itself and its future ordeal.

The Quiet American

By the time of this novel, 1955, Greene had totally absorbed the essence of the detective novel and instead of standing as an ironic contrast to the real world which needs to be rejected, the detective novel makes *The Quiet American* work. The novel has several direct allusions to detective heroes and their creators: Greene mentions Lecoq and Gaboriau as well as Maigret and Simenon. On the simplest level, the book tells the story of a sympathetic policeman, much like Calloway in *The Third Man*, as one of its plots. The policeman works in a world where legal distinctions pale before unsolvable moral dilemmas, and he does not actually solve the crime which is at the center of the narrative. This pattern and character Greene would repeat in *Our Man in Havana, The Honorary Counsul* and *The Human Factor*.

More importantly, the detective novel, for the first time,

contributes to Greene's narrative structure. *The Stamboul Train, A Gun for Sale, The Confidential Agent* and *The Ministry of Fear* all use third person narration and, although Greene does use flashbacks in order to render his main characters' personalities, these books proceed through time in the normal fashion: beginning, middle and end. *The Third Man* breaks this pattern by employing the first person voice of Calloway, the observer, and by telling the story in retrospect, in the past tense. For *The Quiet American* Greene moved to first person narration by Fowler, the main character, and he fragmented time in the novel so that the narrative moves from the present, through scenes which sift through various levels of the past, to the present with Fowler's interview with Vigot, the policeman, to the immediate past which actuated all the present circumstances in the book, and finally back to the present which opens onto an undisclosed but anxiety-ridden future. This somewhat incomprehensible account of Greene's time shifts in *The Quiet American* seems to have little to do with the detective novel, but it does. If the traditional detective story is proficient at nothing else, it is technically proficient, even sophisticated, in its use of point of view. Now, the majority of detective stories fool readers by using the nooks and crannies of third person narration. There are, however, famous exceptions. Christie, in a couple of instances, used first person narration by the murderer—initially in *The Man in the Brown Suit* (1924) and then in the widely-known *Murder of Roger Ackroyd* (1926)—in order to misdirect her readers. The misdirection comes in the fact that readers trust the narrator until the last chapter when he reveals that he is the killer. Anthony Berkeley Cox used similar first person narration in *The Second Shot* (1931), but not merely as a device to deceive readers. Cox wanted to surprise his readers, but he also wished to use the first person narrative in order to examine, albeit superficially, the psychology of the murderer. Greene wants to do this too. Fowler's admission at the end of the novel that he had contrived Pyles' execution comes right out of the detective tradition. It is more than playing games or dabbling in criminal psychology, though. As in *The Ministry of Fears* Greene probes deeply into the psychic abscesses of the criminal's soul. The structure for doing this draws heavily on detective fiction, but Greene only takes the parts which serve his purposes. Detective stories pose the legal question of who committed the crime, and the pursuit of this question washes out readers' concentration on anything but the surface of personality. The who did it question in *The Quiet American* quickly disappears as Greene makes readers watch the emergence and development of character. On the level of the detective story, therefore, *The Quiet American* is the novel which some critics of the thirties predicted: the detective novel as regular literature.

Although *The Quiet American* uses some espionage embellishment to the plot—the United States' effort to start a Third Force to oppose both the French and the communists in Vietnam is the literal motive for much of the action—Greene overlooks the mechanical details of international politics and intrigue and singles out the act of conversion. The novel rests on Greene's juxtaposition of the characters of Fowler, the burned-out British reporter, and Pyles, the quiet American zealot: he contrasts them and compares them. In Pyles Greene draws the school-boy type—the same adolescent stage which plays a part in Rowe's development in *The Ministry of Fear*. Pyles embodies the traditions of honor, conventional politeness and selfless heroism. Saving Fowler from the wrecked watch tower, Pyles plays a part from romantic fiction, the same form evoked by the film of *Scaramouche* which Fowler sees the night of Pyles' death (the whole of Fowler's relationship with Pyles, in fact, plays upon the relationship between Andre-Louis and his father in Sabatini's novel). Further, Pyles is the literal school boy in his unexamined devotion to his teacher's doctrines: in this case, the doctrines are York Harding's half-baked views on Southeast Asia. His yearning for action and his anxiety to put his faith to work warp Pyles from the truth, even the truth of his victims' blood on his shoes. On the other hand, Fowler, the adult, embittered by failed love, uncritically anti-American, possessive of the feather-brained Phuong, refuses to commit himself to anything beyond hedonism. After seeing the carnage of war, however, Fowler commits himself to humanity. This means precipitating Pyles' murder, but it also means suffering and identifying with the dead boy.

Fowler's engagement with life after a stretch of withdrawal, like Rowe's, carries a new burden (indeed, both men perform acts which they see as euthanasia), but Fowler bears the weight more easily than Rowe does because he develops a political ideology, or rather a non-political foundation for existing in a political world:

Isms and ocraies. Give me facts. A rubber planter beats his labourer—all right, I'm against him. He hasn't been instructed to do it by the Minister of the Colonies. In France I expect he'd beat his wife. I've seen a priest so poor he hasn't a change of trousers, working fifteen hours a day from hut to hut in a cholera epidemic, eating nothing but rice and salt fish, saying Mass with an old cup—a wooden platter. I don't believe in God and yet I'm for that priest.[15]

This is similar to the position of Household in novels like *Red Anger* and *Hostage London*. It is also akin to Camus' move toward humanism in *The Plague* (1947). In *The Quiet American* Greene moves slightly away from despair toward optimism, human values and empiricism. We do, however, need to be careful about fastening too hard to these, for they are isms as well.

Our Man in Havana

Our Man in Havana gets less funny with each reading. Its comedy does not derive from drawing room farce as do the comic scenes in *A Gun for Sale* or *The Confidential Agent,* we can abstract no characters and no set scenes from the novel which entertain the way that the scene at the Chief Constable's house does in the earlier novel. Further, *Our Man in Havana* is not, technically, satire either; satire measures the distance between what ought to exist and what does exist, and Greene does not for a moment believe that beings or organizations can be anything but putrescent in the long run. The book mostly attacks. In the context of the spy novel, however, *Our Man in Havana* opens up the genre of the wholesale attacks on the form by the next generation of spy writers, and therefore contributes to the major shift in the direction of the spy novel which we see in the sixties and seventies. On the level of character, *Our Man in Havana* simply carries through a motif which Greene began in *The Ministry of Fear*. In that book Rowe acts out the fantasies of adolescent literature by playing the detective and then playing the spy. Before Rowe's final fall into real human experience, *The Ministry of Fear* is a "get out into the fresh air and make something of it yourself" story. To even a greater extent, Greene uses the framework of the schoolboy adventure character to form the character of Wormold in *Our Man in Havana*. For one thing Wormold frequently thinks about what he is doing (conning the big-shots in London) as a school rag, comparable to his daughter, Milly, setting fire to Thomas Earl Parkman at school. Equally significant, Greene brings in references to *Boy's Own Paper,* the Victorian well-head of the schoolboy story, in the conversations between Wormold and Beatrice. And to reduce the cultural level of the adventure hero even farther, before Wormold leaves to face the danger of being poisoned by enemy agents, Greene shows him reading the cartoon adventures of Little Dwarf Doodoo on the back of a cereal box. These references, of course, connect Greene's hero with the traditions of the juvenile adventure story where even the puniest of boys, if his heart is pure, can strike a blow and help win the day for the Empire. This, on one level, happens to

Wormold. He unselfishly risks himself in order to save his daughter from financial worry, he avenges the murder of his friend, Hasselbacher, showing guts and fair play, and he bests the intelligent but sadistic police officer, Segura, in a battle of wits and sobriety. Add to this that part of his invigoration which comes from his developing love for a woman named, significantly, Beatrice, and we have most of the ingredients of the adult schoolboy spy story.

But something goes wrong: something always goes wrong in Greene's world. Wormold starts off his course of deceiving Her Majesty's Government in order to insure that Milly will have a sufficient dowry when the time comes, but is she worth the trouble? Greene repeatedly shows Milly as a frivolous, cunning, stereotyped girl involved in a world centered around promiscuous coyness and trite materialism. If Wormold had only provided Milly with a dowry, things might not have been so bad. His con game, however, causes his friend, Dr. Hasselbacher, to be persecuted, forced into spying, and finally murdered. The stone which Wormold starts rolling even squashes people outside his immediate sphere, like Raul, the drunken pilot. At first, Wormold, through artistic egotism, believes that his fictions have sprung to life and careened out of his controlling grasp; only later does he realize that he has sold the copyright to his adolescent imaginings, and that the buyer is adapting them to another, sinister reality. To go back to *The Ministry of Fears* "the world has been remade by William LeQueux." Finally, something goes wrong with Wormold's heroism. At the end of the novel he really wants to do a useful bit of espionage, to accomplish the great coup, which will be partial atonement for bamboozling London, but he fails in this. His prized micro-dot reveals only a blur, reveals only Wormold's failure as a real spy.

In Havana Greene insists on parading past his readers the pimps and prostitutes who hawk pornographic pictures and acrobatic sex shows to the tourists. The parallel is pretty clear: Wormold, too, sells pornography. He peddles his fantasies and illustrations which, of course, reflect as little of real life as the mechanical act reflects of love—Greene draws the same spying/pornography metaphor in *The Quiet American* and *The Human Factor*. But, by and large, Wormold's occupation is innocuous, recreational, and carefree. The perverted sybarites who buy Wormold's pornography are really the nasty ones. In Cuba it is all out in the street, while in London men huddle in underground rooms to leer at pictures and text. The Chief's black monocle covering an artificial eye bludgeons us not only with his inability to see and his stereotypical Englishness, but it also suggests impotent voyeurism. As in LeCarré's *The Looking Glass War*, the intelligence people in London build an international incident out of their feeble desires to grasp power and prestige. These people abet Wormold's plans for himself and Milly, when he, realistically, believes that he is going to get it in the neck, because they fear appearing to be fools more than they value the truth.

Although in the long run Greene does not believe in its message, *Our Man in Havana* does carry a political theme. Perhaps because of his experience in Vietnam and the filtering of this in *The Quiet American*, Greene now shows values worth fighting for—as opposed to the horizons of agony glimpsed in the early books. Here Beatrice leads the way with her speech to the trial board:

"There's something greater than one's country, isn't there? You taught us that with your League of Nations and your Atlantic Pact, NATO and UNO and SEATO. But they don't mean any more to most of us than all of the other letters, U.S.A. and U.S.S.R. And we don't believe you any more when you say you want peace and justice and freedom. What kind of freedom?... I said I sympathised with the French officers in 1940 who looked after their families; they didn't anyway put their careers first. A country is more a family than a Parliamentary system."

***

"Not all of it. They haven't left us much to believe, have they?—even disbelief. I can't believe in anything bigger than a home, or anything vaguer than a human being."[16]

On one hand, the absence of homes and human beings brought Raven and Pinkie to grief, and, on the other hand, the peasant endures in spite of who sends out orders from the capital. But we ought not to set too much store by this statement. Greene did, after all, label this book as an "entertainment" and even if he plays fast and loose with this term, *Our Man in Havana* contains more romantic concessions than any of Greene's other "entertainments." Further, we ought to notice that Beatrice defines her ideals not in positive language, but in negative terms.

The Honorary Consul

The Honorary Consul makes a lot of comments about the detective novel. Father Rivas, who as a boy hoarded Perry Mason books, reads an English detective novel while the paratroopers surround his hide-out in the *barrio,* and Dr. Plarr asks him,

"A good one?"
"I am no judge of that. The translation [into Spanish] is not very good, and with this

sort of book I can always guess the end."

"Then where is the interest?"

"Oh, there is a sort of comfort in reading a story where one knows what the end will be. The story of a dream world where justice is always done. There were not detective stories in the age of faith—an interesting point when you think of it. God used to be the only detective when people believed in him. He was Law. He was order. Like your Sherlock Holmes. It was He who pursued the wicked man for punishment and discovered all. But now people like the General make law and order. Electric shocks on the genitals. Aquino's fingers. Keep the poor ill-fed, and they do not have the energy to revolt. I prefer the detective. I prefer God.[17]

This sounds a bit like Dorothy Sayers' comments on the detective story which she put into *The Omnibus of Crime* (1929) and which she made in the essays which she wrote after she resigned from being a detective writer. But there are other comments relevant to the detective story in *The Honorary Consul*. Dr. Saaveda, the novelist of *machismo*, tells Humphries that

I trust I shall never write a detective story, Doctor Humphries, if by a detective story you mean one of those absurd puzzles, which are the literary equivalent of a jigsaw. In my new book I am concerned with the psychology of violence.[18]

In these passages, Greene shows that he has mellowed a good deal on the subject of the detective story. He puts the retributive justice which we see in *The Confidential Agent* into its perspective, and he also puts into perspective *A Gun for Sale* and *The Quiet American*.

For *The Honorary Consul* Greene chose familiar materials. Saaveda, the writer, owes something to Hasselbacher in *Our Man in Havana*. The most important characters, though, look back to *The Quiet American*. Dr. Plarr, the hero, repeats Fowler in his cynicism and his disengagement from causes—even those which affect him intimately. Father Rivas, the priest turned revolutionary, presents us with a more intense study of idealism, but he comes from Pyles in the earlier novel. Clara Rivas has some ties to Phuong, but it is hard to say this with certainty since, across the board, Greene's female characters are underdeveloped and shallow. In spite of character similarities, this novel ends a bit differently from *The Quiet American*. *The Honorary Consul*, like all of Greene's novels which touch on international intrigue, shows the plotters to be hopelessly inept: they intend to kidnap the American ambassador, but mistakenly snatch good old Charley Fortnum, the pie-eyed British Honorary Consul. The revolutionaries are a bunch of bungling amateurs who are directed by a firebrand called *El Tigre*, but his name does not come from his ferocity or cunning but from his penchant for striped shirts. The revolutionaries convince Dr. Plarr to travel along by convincing him that they will free his father from imprisonment in Paraguay, but this is a conscious lie. Everything falls about their ears: no one will put pressure on Paraguay's dictator, the U.S. opts out, the British do not care about the fate of one broken-down, alcoholic honorary consul, and the police hunt the revolutionaries down without meeting any popular opposition in the slums. Even with all this, or because of it, both Plarr and Rivas assert their humanities. Plarr demonstrates love for the first time in his antiseptic life and Rivas upholds both his sacred and secular missions before the paratroopers put the final bullets in their heads. Now, all this is pretty much within the scope of *The Quiet American* with the extension of both Fowler's and Pyles' characters. But Charley Fortnum is a new element. Charley survives. The cuckold, the drunk, the incompetent, romantic Charles survives and grows to be more than a poor sap. The average man, Charley learns what only Greene's earlier heroes (who, in one way or another, are exceptional men) know; he learns how to live with grief and love. He learns to forgive the good their trespasses and tries to expose the evil—which, given Greene's world, he will never do. He is the real *machismo* in the novel, which Saaveda tries in vain to capture in his own works.

Greene seems a bit looser in this novel than in *The Quiet American*. This probably comes from the reinstitution of humor in *Our Man in Havana*. Comic scenes punctuate *The Honorary Consul*—the ones which come to mind are Plarr blackmailing Humphries at the *Nacional,* and the British Ambassador's *bonhomie* when faced with fried eggs. This being Greene, though, comedy cohabits with misery; the mood of *The Honorary Consul* approximates that of *A Gun for Sale* more than it does that of *The Quiet American.* Also, it is noteworthy that with *The Honorary Consul* Greene stopped classifying his books into the classes of novels and entertaiments as he had done through *Our Man in Havana.* Here Greene realized that the amorphous form of the spy novel could convey most of his serious themes—as, in fact, it always had. The inclusion of the explicit Roman Catholic material in *The Honorary Consul* points to this. After *The Stamboul Train,* Greene largely excluded extended discussions of religious concerns from his "entertainments"—they may be there, but not explicitly. His earlier heroes, whatever their actual spiritual state or position, are avowed athiests or agnostics. Here it is different. Much of the novel involves the Church's role in promoting social justice, the priest's function, and Rivas' views of God perfecting Himself and His creation. The novel, in effect, says that detective stories show us nice, clean, just worlds which we can wish were ours; they, however, are not our world and since they are not, we had best look at the real, violent, inefficient world of politics and social struggle, and try to understand not only the mechanisms of violence but also the psychology of salvation.

The Human Factor

In 1968 Greene wrote:

I and another old friend of Kim were together in Crowborough and we thought to look him up. There was no sign of any tending in the overgrown garden and no answer to the bell when we rang. We looked through the windows of the ugly, sprawling Edwardian house, on the borders of Ashdown forest in this poor man's Surrey. The post hadn't been collected for a long time—the floor under the door was littered with advertising brochures. In the kitchen there were some empty milk bottles, and a single dirty cup and saucer in the sink. It was more like an abandoned gypsy encampment than the dwelling of a man with wife and children. We did not know it, but he had already left for Beirut—the last stage of his journey to Moscow.[19]

Kim Philby's empty house, Philby's craftmanship, Philby's faith and Philby's defection greatly impressed Greene, and they lie at the foundation of *The Human Factor*. Perhaps because of his closeness to the subject, it took Greene much longer to use the subject matter of the English defectors fictionally. Before Greene most spy writers had taken a crack at the Burgess, Maclean, Philby defections. Fleming alludes to them in *From Russia, with Love* (1957), as does Haggard in *Slow Burner* (1958) and Deighton and LeCarré base *The Ipcress File* (1962) and *Tinker, Tailor, Soldier, Spy* (1974) on the defections. Hall, in *The Warsaw Document* (1971), in fact, brings the defected Philby into the plot. In spite of Greene's identification with Philby as a man, though, *The Human Factor* could have been written if Philby had never become a Marxist, for, in a number of ways it is a realistic remake of *Our Man in Havana*. Lots of things link the two novels. *The Human Factor* uses the same fictional intelligence service as the earlier book, telling us that its present head, Sir John Hargreaves, has recently replaced the Cyclopean C. who bought Wormold's vacuum cleaner designs. Both chiefs linger in memories of older, dead worlds—one colonial and one Edwardian. Hargreaves, granted, has the perverted genius of Dr. Percival to guide him, but this is due to the fact that *The Human Factor* looks at the inner workings of the intelligence agency, while *Our Man in Havana* concentrates on Wormold's extramural fooling around. Greene, further, ties C., Hargreaves and Percival together with their dilletantish epicureanism. Pornography, likewise, appears in both books with the postcard sellers in Havana and the shops of Mr. Halliday's son in Soho and Newington Butts—granted, though, Greene makes the pornography-espionage business more complex in *The Human Factor*. In both books we find organizational commitment to covering up human error, in one case simply folly, but in the other a murder. Finally, both novels find resolution to human perversity, organizational and societal, in commitment to small, achievable values. As Sarah puts it in *The Human Factor*, "We have our own country. You and I and Sam. You've never betrayed that country Maurice."[2] This is not far from Beatrice's statement of values at the end of *Our Man in Havana*.

The *Human Factor*, though, is the realistic version and not the comic reduction. Greene points this out by referring to Ian Fleming in *The Human Factor*. In the first half of the novel, Greene alludes often to Bond, pointing out his remoteness from espionage and life as well as his fundamental romanticism. Most pointedly, Greene gives us this passage:

"We met," Buffy explained, "at Hargreaves's place. The Colonel is one of the hush-hush boys. James Bond and all that."
One of the two said, "I could never read those books by Ian."
"Too sexy for me," the other said. "Exaggerated. I like a good screw as much as the next man, but it's not all that important, is it?"[21]

Opposed to Fleming's fantasy espionage and sexual fantasies, Greene shows his spies, Davis and Castle, at work at the Africa desk, doing routine jobs which are boring and largely useless. Insofar as *The Human Factor* deals with the nuts and bolts of espionage—and it does so more than any of Greene's other novels— it partakes of the spirit of the sixties and seventies, and indicts organizations. As in Deighton's early novels, the British intelligence establishment in *The Human Factor* comes across as being founded on public school class prejudice and as prostituting the nation's values to U.S. power and South African genocide. Thus, Percival murders Davis and not Castle because of the old boy syndrome, and the intelligence system cozies up to South Africa and its plan to use tactical nuclear weapons against Black invaders. Greene does not show us much detail about the Soviet side of spying, but he does show enough to taint them with the same blight that affects Western intelligence. Just as Percival talks about olympian gamesmanship in espionage, the Soviets use Castle not to further racial justice in Africa but as a blind in some sort of unspecified strategic game of misinformation which they are playing on the

West. Boris, Castle's control, may display a human face to the reader as well as to Castle, but then so does Daintry, the British security man. The pathos is that there is no choice.

Everything in *The Human Factor* boils down to the hero, Castle. In spite of his controlled narrative coolness, Greene allows more of spy psychology to govern Castle than any of his other heroes. His isolation, his love, his fear, his rage and his compassion all have something to do with his role as a spy. As could be expected in Greene, Castle's idealism gets him nowhere but into barren exile in the Soviet Union. Castle wins victory for no one but himself, and that is short-lived. He commits himself to the cause of Black Africa, but fails because none of the Powers cares. He becomes a double agent out of admirable motives, out of friendship for Carson, and out of love for Sarah and Sam. Yet he does not save them: Carson dies in a police cell, and Sarah and Sam wilt in polite captivity. Like Greene's other heroes Castle survives by welding success and failure together, the optimistic tone and the aching heart.

Growing up is as important in *The Human Factor* as it is for Greene's other novels. Here the intelligence chiefs live in a world of eternal childhood with their school nicknames and selfish gratifications. They remain obsessed with playing games. As Percival tells Daintry: "We are playing games, Daintry, games, all of us. It's important not to take a game too seriously or we may lose it."[22] This is a tenable approach to life if a) we ignore professional sports, b) we live in a world where style means more than substance, c) we live in a world without ultimate values of love, God, etc., and d) we live in a world in which everyone agrees to accept this as the only approach to life. The entrenched upper class of the intelligence community can do these things: they can remain old boys. Castle and Daintry, however, have lost their childhoods and with them the security, and confidence, of the schoolboy. Greene's inversion shows these two men as bewildered adults in a world run by confident, sadistic children, or else he gives us a true schoolboy story of the suave, wealthy bullies persecuting the poor, clumsy, introspective and intelligent boys. The suffering and the slow climb to values and courage in Castle and Daintry, isolated and rare as they are, are the real human factors.

Since the 1930s Greene has lingered beside the waters of the spy novel, now putting a toe in, now a whole leg, and now reviling the whole form as polluted. He has, though, gotten used to it, and accepted it as a vehicle as capable as any other literary form for carrying his particular vision of men and the world. He has accepted the fact that they are novels and not entertainments. In spite of his misgivings, Greene has contributed mightily to the evolution of the form. First, in the thirties, he insisted on the anti-heroic side of political intrigue. In the fifties he showed how the detective story could be adapted to the spy novel, and he redirected the spy novel toward satire and the criticism of organizations. Through all this he has shown, in various degrees, competence in handling the techniques of suspense, action and horror. It is just as well, though, that Greene did not devote himself exclusively to the spy novel. We then would have lost Greene's periodic rejections of the spy motif, and these have done the form a world of good.

NOTES

[1] *Stamboul Train* (London: Heinemann, 1932), p. 264.

[2] *Stamboul Train*, p. 111.

[3] *Stamboul Train*, pp. 199-200.

[4] *Stamboul Train*, p. 181.

[5] *Stamboul Train*, p. 142.

[6] *A Gun for Sale* (London: Heinemann, 1961), p. 143.

[7] *A Gun for Sale*, p. 175.

[8] *A Gun for Sale*, p. 147.

[9] *The Confidential Agent* (London: Heinemann, 1971), viii.

[10] *The Confidential Agent*, p. 193.

[11] *The Confidential Agent*, p. 138.

[12] *The Confidential Agent*, p. 72.

[13] *The Ministry of Fear* (New York: Bantam, 1963), p. 86.

[14] *The Ministry of Fear*, p. 57.

[15] *The Quiet American* (London: Heinemann, 1956), pp. 120-21.

[16] *Our Man in Havana* (New York: Viking, 1958), pp. 239-40.

[17] *The Honorary Consul* (New York: Simon and Schuster, 1973), p. 247.

[18] *The Honorary Consul*, p. 184.

[19] *The Collected Essays* (New York: Viking, 1969), p. 419.

[20] *The Human Factor* (New York: Simon and Schuster, 1978), p. 171.

[21] *The Human Factor*, p. 148.

[22] *The Human Factor*, p. 26.

IN THE MID-1950s Eric Ambler and Graham Greene remade the spy novel. This seems strange, given the political state of Europe and the logical development of popular fiction. Fascists, Nazis, the economic situation: all these made simple reactions easy, almost inevitable. The closer Europe came to war, the more appealing became the satisfactions of the thriller which had foundered around a bit when there were no obvious villains in the world—Buchan, for instance, never satisfactorily replaced the German villains of his early novels. As the war approached, the English detective novel lost some of its intellectual playfulness and turned toward the thriller for inspiration. The detective hero became the spy hero. But Ambler and Greene stand outside all this. Instead of joining the pack yelping for Nazi blood and extolling traditional English virtues, these writers turned inward to look at the spy as he really is, and at the political, economic and spiritual parents who procreate spies.

Ambler's seventeen novels fall into two broad categories which are not only chronologically separate but also thematically distinct. These categories are, simply, those novels which Ambler wrote before the war and those he wrote after it. Each group has a number of similarities and directions of development which, when examined, tell us a good deal about what Ambler tried to do with the spy novel. Ambler's six pre-war books include *The Dark Frontier* (1936), *Background to Danger* (1937), *Epitaph for a Spy* (1938), *Cause for Alarm* (1938), *A Coffin for Dimitrios* (1939) and *Journey into Fear* (1940). The novels written after the war, excluding Ambler's collaborations with Charles Rodda, are *Judgment on Deltchev* (1951), *The Schirmer Inheritance* (1953), *State of Siege* (1956), *Passage of Arms* (1959), *Light of Day* (1962), *A Kind of Anger* (1964), *Dirty Story* (1967), *The Intercom Conspiracy* (1969), *The Levanter* (1972) *Doctor Frigo* (1974) and *The Siege of the Villa Lipp* (1977). Looking through these books we can see Ambler developing new slants on the spy story and we ought to also notice his ability to make new plots. Both are real accomplishments in a genre not then noted for its development or originality.

Ambler's particular brand of trapped men in the middle, for which he is well known, did not spring into his fiction fully formed. They developed: they grew out of the traditional romantic conventions of the spy novel going back to LeQueux, but under Ambler's hand they slowly emerge as something other than conventional even if they partake of a new sort of romanticism. As a popular writer, Ambler put in his time on the shop floor before he moved up to have an office of his own. His early novels, in fact, have much in common with the restrained, half-refined writers of the previous generation, exemplified best in the novels of Francis Beeding. Ambler uses most of the stock spy characters from the thriller tradition in his early books. Colonel Robinson, in *Background to Danger*, and General Vargas, in *Cause for Alarm*, are very much in the mold of the gentleman super villain beloved of the thriller writers of the twenties. They combine suavity with grotesqueness and have access to power, just as innumerable other villains do. Likewise, the Zaleschoffs, brother and sister, seem very much the stereotypical secret agent heroes of the popular tradition (they appear in both *Background to Danger* and *Cause for Alarm*).

Tamara Zaleschoff is the beautiful, mysterious, perky yet feminine agent. Both she and her brother, Andreas, use the same sort of witty dialogue and engage in the same sort of swashbuckling adventure as the traditional secret service hero. This being the 1930s, Ambler gives them some organizational trappings—they have sets of files, access to helpers, safe-houses, etc.—but this does not diminish their conventional characters and actions. They exist to please the readers, not to worry them or inform them or to lever them into another area of thought. Another cliche character in *Background to Danger* and *Cause for Alarm* is the civilian hero who becomes mixed up in spy business and who voluntarily, indeed eagerly, participates in some or all the dangerous adventure action. We need to recognize this character type, who bumptiously chooses to participate, and to see him as a conventional character in order to understand Ambler's later heroes who will be trapped in the middle of the action. The man trapped in the middle was to be important in his later novels, but he does not come into the pre-war books. Instead of being trapped, truly trapped, Ambler's early heroes choose. Kenton, in *Background to Danger*, could have (and in Zaleschoff's opinion should have) stayed out of the action and left the whole thing to the professionals, but the lure of adventure and action gets too strong for him. Likewise, Marlow, in *Cause for Alarm*, throws in with the Zaleschoffs and their plan to put a kink in the Rome-Berlin Axis after he is worked over by a fascist goon squad when he could have thrown over the whole thing and returned to England. Further, even in Yugoslavia, where he is safe, Marlow continues to act the spy. These people have a romantic attraction to danger, and Ambler shows them being initiated and vindicated by the events in the plots. Marlow is the romantic Spartacus (the name of his employer) who defeats the opposition instead of the historical slave-rebel put to the sword by the armies of Rome. Both Kenton and Marlow (what English names they have) come from the background of Buchan's Hannay, reluctant to become involved, but then committed with a vengeance to the side of the right.

The Dark Frontier, Background to Danger and Cause for Alarm all use the traditional material of the spy-adventure novel and to some degree accept its conventions of character and plot. So, too, do Epitaph for a Spy, A Coffin for Dimitrios and Journey into Fear, but in these novels Ambler uses the conventions in a more limited manner—there is, for instance, an episode of danger at the end of each book to slam the door of the plot—or he purposely overturns the conventions. But more on this later. All the pre-war novels end with or consist entirely of hunt-chase action which culminates in a shoot-out of some sort, in which the villains are either discomfited or killed. Further, in these early books Ambler inserts into the dialogue ideological speeches outlining the hero's motives, thereby bringing them into line with the conventional spy book which, like the American hard-boiled story, is given to providing readers with rhetorical capsules.

Yet, for all this, Ambler is not a typical spy writer, even at the beginning. His first novel, The Dark Frontier, tries, but fails, to burlesque the artificiality of the usual spy book. In it the hero, Professor Barstow, a mild-mannered physicist, gets clonked on the head in a car crash and takes on the larger than life personality of the hero of the thriller which he has been leafing through—Conway Carruthers, Dept. Y. The character of Carruthers summarizes the hero of the popular spy novel:

Nothing was beyond the powers of this remarkable man. His age, judging by his relations with other characters in the book, might have been in the neighbourhood of forty. Against this estimate, however, must be set the evidence of his physical prowess which would have done credit to an Olympian athlete of twenty-five. On the other hand, he had somehow found time during his adult lifetime to save the lives of, or otherwise befriend, natives of a remarkable number of countries. The gratitude of these fortunates contributed largely to his success. Certain death might stare him in the face and he would extricate himself from his predicament by means of a trick learnt from a Patagonian Indian or a Bessarabian moujik.[1]

This is Harriet Vane's Robert Templeton moved from Sayers to the spy novel. In the course of *The Dark Frontier*, Barstow-Carruthers thinks and fights his way through various thrilling problems and pit-falls, ending up a national hero, a savior of civilization, etc. Of course, much of this is burlesque of the popular spy hero, but in the course of the novel it becomes difficult to determine just how much of the readers' minds should be conscious of the burlesque and how much wrapped up in the exciting action. In spite of its early, but laughable, introduction of atomic weapons, *The Dark Frontier* stands as a failed attempt to do something new and simply becomes another one of the half-serious, half-spoof adventure-espionage books turned out in the twenties by writers like Beeding.

Nevertheless, *The Dark Frontier* does show Ambler's interest in psychology, even if here it is flippant. In other pre-war novels, Ambler took several, more serious runs at deepening the psychology of the spy story. Most often he does this by closely examining the hero's psychology at that point in the novel where the hero makes a mental commitment to the dangerous course of action. Typical of these sections is Kenton's reaction in *Background to Danger* when, under pressure of physical coercion, he decides to oppose the bad guys and throw in with the good guys: "In those five seconds the entire structure of resentment, anger and defiance that reason had so completely demolished was reerected."[2] Almost always Ambler shows that the hero becomes the hero because anger overcomes reason which counsels safety; rage drives the adventures in *The Dark Frontier, Cause for Alarm,* and *Journey into Fear.* Using Greene's terminology, Ambler's heroes are not of the torturable class. None of this, though, shows much beyond the most superficial attempt to give heroes reasonable motives for their acts, beyond the unreasoned behavior of the thriller hero. In *Journey into Fear,* however, Ambler deepens his psychological attention and follows the fluctuations of tension and release on the character of the hero when he confronts real or imagined dangers. Ultimately even this does little to lift Ambler above the crowd of semi-conscious thriller writers. Later, when he would connect adventure with adolescent psychology, Ambler made a contribution to the psychology of the spy book, but in his most important pre-war novels, *Epitaph for a Spy* and *A Coffin for Dimitrios,* Ambler left simplistic psychology and emotional temperature-taking to others.

Ambler's political slant also lifts him out of the realm of the usual spy novel of the thirties. Most early spy writers came from the poltical right: Buchan, for instance, was a Tory, and Oppenheim was a raging Tory. Ambler, and Greene too, for that matter, start their political thinking from socialist assumptions. Tamara and Andreas Zaleschoff, as spunky and typical as they are as secret agents, are explicitly identified as Soviet agents in *Background to Danger*—although Ambler does back off a bit in *Cause for Alarm* when he strongly implies but never says outright that they are Soviet spies. Spies, though, without ideology, do not make a political stance. Ambler provides the requisite ideology, too. Big business in Ambler's novels serves the same role that the traditional spy thriller reserved for perverse individuals and belligerent states. From the first book, Ambler creates and attacks the giant armaments cartel of Cator and Bliss—the name Cator may have come from either Cato the Elder, an untiring advocate of war with Carthage, or from Cato the Younger, who fought against Spartacus. In *The Dark Frontier*, Barstow/Carruthers fights not only to keep the secret of atomic weapons from Balkan loonies, but also from the sinister director of Cator and Bliss who would make money out of misery and death. Graham voices the same concern in *Journey into Fear* when he, a ballistics expert and employee of the same Cator and Bliss, begins to examine not only the international capitalist conspiracy, but also his own part in it. Ambler treats the same theme, but with an ironic twist, in *Cause for Alarm,* when Marlow deserts Spartacus Machine Tool, which is run by likeable zanies and uses the name Spartacus, so popular in socialist iconography, for the employ of Cator and Bliss. In addition to the armaments manufacturer, Ambler introduces and blackens other capitalist institutions. Pan-Eurasian Petroleum motivates all the trouble in *Background to Danger*, by conniving to obtain an oil concession in Rumania, and the shadowy, Monaco-based Eurasian Credit Trust (which Ambler was to revive after the war in *The Schirmer Inheritance*) stands behind much of the human misery described in *A Coffin for Dimitrios*. Ambler evokes the perfidy of capitalist oppression by showing the roles of nasty multi-national corporations and characters' responses toward them, and he also drives his points home in rhetorical capsules imbedded in the early novels. For example:

"Banking!" Mathis was saying. "What is it but usury? Bankers are money lenders, usurers. But because they lend other people's money or money that does not exist, they have a pretty name. They are still usurers. Once, usury was a mortal sin and an abomination, and the usurer was to be a criminal for whom there was a prison cell. Today the usurers are the gods of the earth and the only mortal sin is to be poor.

***

"Ha! That is what the banker likes. Banking is a mystery! It is too difficult for ordinary men to understand.... If you make two and two equal five you *must* have a lot of mystery....The international bankers are the real war criminals. Others do the killing but they sit, calm and collected, in their offices and make money."[3]

It is this voiced political attitude which makes Ambler unconventional as a spy novelist, but hardly different. The two books which really make him different and which point to a new line of development which he followed after the war are *Epitaph for a Spy* and *A Coffin for Dimitrios*.

Instead of being action-fixated, *Epitaph for a Spy* goes back to the tradition of Conrad's *The Secret Agent* (1907), which emphasizes the mundane, seedy, sordid and pathetically inconclusive nature of espionage. Ambler, in terms of the spy novel, takes Conrad's premise to its furthest extent. Josef Vadassy is the hero of *Epitaph for a Spy*. He teaches languages, like the narrator of *Under Western Eyes* (1911), and is a stateless individual—not because of anything that he has done, but because of his father's politics and the arbitrary shifting of boundaries of states in central Europe. Although a meek and innocuous individual, the French authorities arrest Vadassy because his name has become linked to some blurred photographs of the port defenses at Toulon.

In spite of the fact that Beghin, the Naval Intelligence officer, knows full well that Vadassy did not take the photos, he forces him to return to the Hotel Reserve in order to smoke out the real spy, thereby allowing the authorities to roll up the whole espionage network. Nothing works out at the hotel. Vadassy bumbles around, making everyone suspicious, until, finally, the intelligence people make a show of arresting him, whereupon the real spy takes flight and is cornered and killed in a roof-top gun battle. The spy, whose efforts in photography are at best third class and of minimal danger to French security, is a ratty down-and-outer, whose epitaph is "He needed the money." Ironically connected to this, the sub-plot shows how Vadassy's trampling around helps Nazi agents track down an anti-Nazi agent and blackmail him into returning to Germany and his execution.

This novel is not only vital for Ambler's later development, but also for the development of the spy novel as a whole. It contains Ambler's first genuinely unwilling spy who does not choose to participate in the action but whom malign authority forces to do distasteful and dangerous things. He is the man in the middle who is battered by both sides. The only other pre-war character who approaches this is Graham in *Journey into Fear*, but his case does not have the force of Vadassy's, since Graham acts for an armaments manufacturer on the eve of war. Vadassy, in a sense, extends the situation of Conrad's secret agent, Verloc, who is also trapped by irrational demands. Ambler's character, however, deserves sympathy as Verloc does not. Another important ingredient in *Epitaph for a Spy* is the character of the agent who photographed Toulon harbor. No longer does Ambler show the villain as a dashing, bizarre character like Colonel Robinson or General Vargas. Neither do the results of his spying shake the foundations of Europe. He is merely a disagreeable, shoddy human being who works in the hope of the big pay-off, or of any pay-off. Finally, *Epitaph for a Spy* shows a different slant in its fictional organization. Ambler gives up oratorical ideology and only indirectly attacks the capitalist system through Duclos, a sanitary engineer who, in his skewed sense of reality, believes himself to be a paternalistic industrial mogul. More important than this, Ambler gives up the hunt-chase organization of his early books and centers most of *Epitaph for a Spy* around a series of interviews at the hotel, drawing technique from the detective novel. Also, in the detective novel tradition, the realistic detective novel versus the romantic one, the amateur detective is absolutely wrong about most of his observations. In his footnote to the 1951 edition of *Epitaph for a Spy*, Ambler calls the book "a mild attempt at realism." "Mild," of course, depends on what it is compared to. Compared to Horler's spy books, *Epitaph for a Spy* is *Nana, MacTeague* and *Sister Carrie* rolled into one, but compared to *A Gun for Sale* it is rosy hued. Still, *Epitaph for a Spy* marks an important change for Ambler and it later provided him with much to build upon.

Most of Ambler's building on ideas which he explored in *Epitaph for a Spy* occurred after the war, with the significant exception of *A Coffin for Dimitrios*. Like *Epitaph for a Spy*, *A Coffin for Dimitrios* does not contain any rhetorical capsules, and the only character who has a political background, Marukakis the Greek newspaper man, does not orate. Ambler also organized *Dimitrios* as a detective novel, for it relies on the detective story pattern of the hero hunting dispersed bits of information as opposed to the detective pattern in *Epitaph for a Spy* which relies on interviews. Further, *Dimitrios* is not overtly a spy novel: the only spy connection resides in the fact that Dimitrios once did some dirty work for the Master Spy, Grodek, and then double-crossed him. Instead, Ambler here examines the sewage purification system which takes a raw, brutal killer and refines him to the extent that he becomes an accepted and protected member of the highest level of legitimate society. This process, as is typical in pre-war Ambler, is aided by our old friend, the Eurasian Credit Trust, which at first uses Dimitrios' violent talents and ends up in making him a corporate executive. As important for the novel as Dimitrios is the searcher, Charles Latimer. Latimer is a jerk. He enters the novel as an academic turned detective story writer who has published four novels—*I, Said the Fly; Murderer's Arms; A Bloody Shovel;* and *No Doornail This.* Latimer comes from the tendency in the detective novel of the twenties and thirties to parody itself (see Sayers' Harriet Vane, Carr's Henry Morgan, Christie's Ariadne Oliver, etc.). In the novel Ambler shows Latimer playing a game of trying to track down a real criminal now that he has mastered tracking down fictional ones. He paddles around in the drains of criminal society in Turkey, the Balkans and France on the trail of one Dimitrios. Along the way he meets the totally corrupt Mr. Peters, a sort of neo Caspar Gutman, who has smuggled dope and prostitutes for Dimitrios. Latimer, however, learns nothing from his dip into society's cesspoll or even from his encounter with death. At the close of the book we see him sitting on a train trying to compose another clever and antiseptic detective novel. Later Ambler would bring home Charles Latimer's essential foolishness during the course of *The Intercom Conspiracy.* In this book we find out how dumb Latimer really is, for there his ignorance of people, his rampaging ego and his obsessive desire to see human activity as play get him only a cement overcoat.

After *A Coffin for Dimitrios* Ambler stopped writing novels until the early 1950s. In 1951 he began writing again, first with Charles Rodda under the joint pseudonym of Eliot Reed (Ambler collaborated in four Reed novels: *Skytrip*, 1951; *Tender to Danger*, 1953; *The Maras Affair*, 1953; and *Charter to Danger*, 1954), and then under his own name again. The first post-war book was *Judgment on Deltchev* in 1951. In 1951 Ambler also wrote a historical footnote for the new edition of *Epitaph for a Spy* in which he shows a heightened consciousness of the literary form of the spy novel by presenting a thumb-nail sketch of the history of the genre. Ambler as a writer changed considerably after the war. For one thing, he stopped being a book a year fiction machine and began publishing novels every two or three years. Partly this was due to his commitments to motion pictures and television, but it was probably also due to Ambler's own consciousness that he was one of the leading writers in a historically important form of fiction. Ambler, never a weak technician, became even more careful and thoughtful in his writing, trying out not only new character patterns, but also new ways of telling stories. Of course, being ten years older and having witnessed a devastating war had its effects, too.

Ambler, after the war, is as different from other spy writers as he was before the war. While conventional writers like Cheyney and

Fleming exploited the hard-boiled hero, violence and political cliches, Ambler followed different paths. Nowhere does this show more clearly than in the international situations which Ambler drew in his post-war books. Before the war he set most of his action in Europe and in the center of political hot spots. After the war he pays almost no attention to the so-called "Great Powers"—the Soviet Union, the United States and, as we move into the seventies, China. Most other writers use them, drawing British agents into their orbits, but not Ambler. The physical and ideological presence of the Great Powers, as well as the role played by the British in keeping the barbarians from the gates, may obsess others, but Ambler has other areas of interest. He even ignores the British security scene when others in the sixties wrote veiled Burgess and Maclean books. Instead he presents local or regional situations which, by design, are separate from Great Power influence. The settings of his post-war books at first seem to be an appeal to the exotic: the Balkans in *Judgment on Deltchev* and *The Schirmer Inheritance*, the Far East in *State of Siege* and *Passage of Arms*, the Middle East in *The Light of Day* and *The Levanter*, Africa in *Dirty Story*, and Central America in *Doctor Frigo*. Ambler, though, uses these settings not for local color or as battlegrounds for proxy wars between the Great Powers. He chooses them because they are outside Great Power influence—or at least they are within the confines of the novels. The influence of the politics and the ideologies of the United States and the Soviet Union is only lightly present in the majority of Ambler's books. The only novel which makes major use of the international influence of the Great Powers is *The Intercom Conspiracy* where Jost and Brand describe the international situation this way:

They could accept the necessity for the alliance to which their countries were committed. They could accept with resignation that their countries meant no more to NATO than Romania or Bulgaria meant to the Warsaw Pact and that they were pygmies in a struggle between giants. What they could not do was change their ways of thinking about giants.

***

The appraisals they made were not flattering. What impressed them most about these giants, they ultimately decided, was not their strength, still less the loud and threatening noises they made, but their inherent clumsiness.[1]

Nevertheless, *The Intercom Conspiracy* hardly takes international politics as its main concern. Just as before the war, Ambler also refrained from using Britain as a principal setting, just as he avoided America and Russia. The problem for Ambler is not so much states as states of mind.

If one excepts the nasty KGB agents who briefly enter *The Intercom Conspiracy*, there are no Soviets in the post-war books. Likewise, if one excepts the CIA Agents Goodman and Rich and overlooks their names, Ambler introduces no American agents. Average American citizens (that is, including Theodore Carter of *The Intercom Conspiracy*, who is a Canadian) enter more frequently. Ambler, however, rarely uses them as ideological vehicles. Sure, Georghi Pashik, in *Judgment on Deltchev*, with his pathetic fantasies of the consumer society founded on ball-point pens and dreams of Passaic, New Jersey, is a criticism of America, but the other Americans in the books like George Carey in *The Schirmer Inheritance* and the Nilsens in *Passage of Arms* contrast refreshing innocence to Old World corruption. Mrs. Nilsen, for instance, joins the action of the plot because of her disgust at a British officer's racial prejudice, and in *Passage of Arms* Ambler also satirizes Fowler's anti-Americanism in Greene's *The Quiet American*. But in the main, Great Power conflicts and personalities have little to do with the essentials of Ambler's novels.

Ambler uses political situations in his novels that are local, empty and futile. Typically, one group of governors replaces another without any promise of better government or more prosperity for the people. Thus, in *Judgment on Deltchev, State of Siege, Dirty Story* and *Doctor Frigo*, governments or leaders rise and fall but virtually everyone knows that nothing will change. This is true because of the international conspiracy of capital, as shown in *Dirty Story*, where the mining cartels SMMAC and UMAD instigate a brief war over the deposit of rare earths only to join forces after men have been killed in their little war. The same thing, though, also happens in novels concerning Marxist governments, like *Judgment on Deltchev*. Because of what Ambler perceives the international and national realities to be, he uses political situations only as backdrops against which individuals must act or react, as large, irrational but unchanging forces, regardless of their names or political coloring, lumber along crushing the vitality and hope out of people caught in their paths. This represents a slightly new track for Ambler. In the post-war books he leaves his anti-capitalist rhetoric behind, or rather he sets it in a world where ideology makes little difference in the face of power.

Particular brands of action, however, do make a difference in this new world. Before the war, with a few exceptions, Ambler, like other spy writers, depended a good deal upon action and its efficacy for both plot situations and characters' recognition of their real selves. After the war he dropped a good bit of the cliche action found in his pre-war books. There are, for instance, few hunt-chase scenes at the end of the post-war books. He also gives the meaning of action new scrutiny. Going as far back as Buchan, or even farther back to Stevenson and Rider Haggard for that matter, action has not only been one of the bases of the adventure-spy story, but it has also been one of its cardinal moral points. Since spy novels go back to Victorian schoolboy stories, and many really remain schoolboy stories, they preach that man's physical and mental worth are best shown in action and that action and social responsibilities, like duty, inextricably intertwine. Spy stories like this are like Carlyle for the unsophisticated. Although the twentieth century likes to pretend to have rejected Victorianism, these same schoolboy standards apply to writers like Hemingway, who operate under the loose label of existentialism. In the twentieth century, however, action may lose its association with duty, but it becomes associated with another shibboleth, knowing one's self. Just as Ambler had used this motif of the proving virtues of action before the war, he uses it after the war with a bit more examination. Thus, Colonel Jost reminds Carter in *The Intercom Conspiracy* that all the danger which he has faced and to which he has been forced to react has had a therapeutic and liberating effect:

> You are a different man from the one I met a year ago. Then you were tired and contemptuous of the work you did. You disliked yourself. Now I detect a new confidence in you. Think. You are engaged in completing a new book for the late, respected and much lamented Mr. Latimer. Would his publishers have employed the man you were a year ago? I doubt it. You have come to terms with yourself.[5]

Along these same lines, Piet Maas in *A Kind of Anger* gets off pills and loses his sense of failure after dueling with death. Seeing life and yourself has a joyously liberating effect. After meeting danger, characters can joke. Carter's last sentence in *The Intercom Conspiracy* is "Once past the gateway to Latimer's villa I enjoyed the walk back to the inn," and George, at the close of *The Schirmer Inheritance*, laughs as he walks back to Greece. Ambler does not have the inclination to microscopically examine the psychological changes which action makes in his characters, but in the tradition of the action spy novel he notes that they do happen.

This, however, is not Ambler's only slant on the human effects of action. Like Greene, Ambler does take a critical look at the place of action in the spy-adventure book. Any rational adult who has experienced real uncertainty and danger, say, in combat, will acknowledge that it does not have a great deal to recommend it. Adults recognize the manifest potentials for pain and death in dangerous adventures, and need to be very powerfully motivated before they will willingly seek them. Adults are tender with their lives, having recognized their mortality, and having been grafted to social responsibilities in the form of professions and families. The fanatic, the imbecile or the adolescent usually becomes the street fighter or the rebel. Ambler knew all about this, and he added it to his descriptions of people involved in dangerous action. George Carey, for instance, in *The Schirmer Inheritance,* finds himself caught in situations which are not only illegal but also dangerous. He, however, dives right into them in spite of his mature instincts; he does this

Because he loved his fellow men and was curious about them? Rubbish. More likely that the elaborate defenses of his youth, the pompous fantasies of big office chairs and panelled boardrooms, of hidden wealth and power behind the scenes, were beginning to crumble, and that the pimply adolescent was belatedly emerging into the light.[6]

Quite the same thing happens to Greg Nilsen in *Passage of Arms:*

He regarded himself, not without reason, as a mature and level-headed man. If anyone had suggested that somewhere in the back streets of his mind another Greg Nilsen—a roistering, romantic, ten-year-old swashbucker—had escaped from custody and was out enjoying a game of cops and robbers he would have been angrily incredulous.[7]

To drive the point home in this novel, Ambler makes Greg's wife, Dorothy, a kindergarten teacher, and he makes Nilsen get into trouble behind her back and partly to spite her.

In all this, Ambler goes back and re-presents the double selves of Barstow/Carruthers from *The Dark Frontier*: there is a responsible, adult self which shrinks from action and an adolescent self which seeks and revels in it. By tying the action-seeking motive to adolescence rather than Providence or character molding, Ambler denigrates the value of adventure for its own sake, and the construction of his novels shows that normal people do not engage in risks unless they are trapped into it—and well and truly trapped at that.

This brings us to Ambler's man in the middle. First of all, we need to recognize that this character type has several manifestations in Ambler's post-war books. We can see Ambler's simplest use of this character in the men in the middle in *Judgment on Deltchev, The Schirmer Inheritance, State of Siege, Passage of Arms, The Intercom Conspiracy, The Levanter* and *Doctor Frigo.* These books turn on men (women in Ambler, when they are important to the plots, play subsidiary roles like Dorothy Nilsen in *Passage of Arms* or Lucia Bernardi in *A Kind of Anger*) coerced by forces which they definitely cannot control. Typically, intransigent and unforgiving forces, like the Palestine Action Force and the Syrian government in *The Levanter,* collide, but they also catch the heroes at the exact spot at which they collide. Thus Ambler's heroes get caught in the middle of the opposing forces because of perverse circumstances—they are in the wrong place at the wrong time—or because biases of their personalities work with circumstance to entrap them. Michael Howell, in *The Levanter* happens to be engaged in trying to maintain his investments in Syria when the government goes on a nationalizing binge, and he happens to own a factory suitable for the clandestine production of arms. Further, he is a dogged and compulsive entrepreneur and engineer who believes that he can fix things with his own talents and skills. People like Howell may face dangers, but they do not make any appreciable impact on the forces which manipulate them. They become, in many cases, not so much minor participants as observers of political perversities. It is not surprising to find that in two of his post-war man in the middle novels, Ambler uses journalists (*Judgment on Deltchev* and *The Intercom Conspiracy*), in three (*State of Siege, Passage of Arms* and *The Levanter*) he uses engineers, and that in *The Schirmer Inheritance* and *Doctor Frigo* he uses a lawyer and a physician, respectively. All these professions for his heroes carry with them objectivity and technical know-how. Ambler's heroes, like Fraser in *State of Siege,* watch armies slug it out, and they are forced to watch from a dangerous vantage point. From watching the collisions, Ambler's simplest heroes learn something about themselves and about love—it being impossible, from Ambler's view to learn anything but despair from politics. A few of them, though, get caught in the grinder and destroyed, as in *Judgment on Deltchev.* In spite of this pathetic outcome, and in spite of the fact that many of Ambler's simple heroes in the middle do not chose to be where they are or to act as they act under pressure, this sort of hero works out to be reasonably romantic, and can be seen as a logical extension of spy novel conventions since LeQueux.

Ambler, however, was not content with this, and wished to make the man in the middle into a new character. He did this first with the character of Arthur Abdel Simpson. Arthur appears in *The*

Light of Day (which is not a spy novel) and *Dirty Story*. He is the
only distinctive voice in all of Ambler, and in many ways he is the
culmination of much of what Ambler had done both before and after
the war. Unlike the romantic men in the middle who engage the
reader's identification and sympathy, Arthur gains no personal
knowledge or stature from the events into which he is hurled. He
ends as he begins, as a crud. He does, though, learn something about
living in a world of bullies by the end of the second novel, and from
Arthur's discovery Ambler then built a whole other class of
characters in his most recent novels.

To begin with, Arthur is a new model of Josef Vadassy from
Epitaph for a Spy. From Vadassy, Ambler took the idea of a man
whose defenselessness originates in his statelessness, his lack of
citizenship, but he gave it more punch by showing that Arthur has
forfeited his citizenship (his British passport) by conniving,
corruption and meanness. Like Vadassy, Arthur falls into traps set
by the powerful, but with the new character Ambler makes this more
credible: the French trap Vadassy because of the very long
coincidence of turning in and getting some else's photos developed,
while Arthur gets into trouble because he is a pimp and a sneak
thief. To the Vadassy ingredients, Ambler added Mr. Peters'
background from *A Coffin for Dimitrios*, thereby linking him to the
sleaziest sorts of crime. From *The Schirmer Inheritance* he got the
name Arthur, and the background of the non-com soldier from
Sergeant Schirmer's cockney second-in-command. The anti-
authoritatian and self-protective realism of the soldier are apt
defenses in the sort of world which Ambler protrays, and although
he does not even have the stature to have been a soldier, Arthur
constantly alludes to and tries to live by the maxims of his soldier
father, maxims like

Bullshit baffles brains
Never volunteer for anything.
If you can't keep your nose clean, don't let them see you picking it.

Most officers are pricks until you get to know them better. Then you find out that some
are bigger pricks than others.[8]

This fatalistic, anti-authority stance accounts for much of Arthur:
he is an old soldier, a type as old as Falstaff, who tries to make the
army, or in this case society, line his pockets and give him an easy
life. Arthur Simpson, however, is the opportunist who never gets

opportunities. Instead, individual, corporate, or governmental power defeats him every time. In *The Light of Day,* not only international jewel thieves but also Turkish Intelligence officers bully him, and in *Dirty Story* a producer of pornographic films and two international mining cartels use him. The difference is that, even if Arthur has to take all of this, he complains about the injustices, real or imagined, done to him. *Dirty Story,* therefore, begins with

Write it on the Walls. H. Carter Garvin, Her Britannic Majesty's vice consul in Athens, is a shit.[9]

This is a pungent departure from the normal narrative voice in Ambler. He had used first person narration before *The Light of Day (Dark Frontier, Epitaph for a Spy, Cause for Alarm, Judgment on Deltchev,* and *State of Siege*) but all of these novels have the same narrative tone of the reasonable, average man—the staple of the spy writer. Arthur is not reasonable, just as the situations in which he finds himself are not reasonable. His narration brings in tirades as well as lies and self-deceptions, and these, too, open new narrative angles for Ambler.

At the end of *Dirty Story* Arthur conceives a fantastic plan to place himself on a par with all the people, institutions, and states which have been doing him the dirty. Of course Arthur is a *picaro* (and Ambler does much better at this character type than do his contemporaries, Coles and Household, who also used the *picaro* in the spy novel), but in him Ambler placed certain serious alternatives for those trapped by the powerful of the world. In him he developed a new sort of man in the middle. Now, Ambler's original victim characters may learn something from their brushes with authority and danger, but they do not substantially master them. Beginning with *The Schirmer Inheritance,* it occured to Ambler that, although political and social entities often shift or collide so as to discomfit or crush individuals caught in the way, there exist gaps and vacuums between them which can be exploited. In *A Coffin for Dimitrios,* he demonstrated the ways in which criminals use these gaps and blind spots, and after the war he added to this the idea of the guerrilla. Both *The Schirmer Inheritance* and *The Intercom Conspiracy* use characters who have backgrounds as guerrillas. I do not want to say that Ambler advocates actual guerrilla warfare with established institutions, or considers that this sort of action might have an effect; he does not. He does, however, use it as a metaphor for the way in which his new sort of hero may prosper in a hostile world.

Historically, the first of these new men in the middle is Sergeant Franz Schirmer, in *The Schirmer Inheritance*, who imitates his nineteenth century ancestor, opts out of the *Wehrmacht* which is indifferent to honor or competence, opts out of the army of the Greek communists which blackmails him, and sets up as Robin Hood along the Greek-Yugoslavian border. From his hide-out in no man's land, Schirmer can plunder institutions, like the Eurasian Credit Trust, avoid both Greek and Yugoslavian laws, and make a world for himself and his woman. Like Schirmer, Girija Krishnan in *Passage of Arms* manages to skirt legality, get the best of Mr. Tan, the Chinese capitalist, and fulfill his boyhood dream of setting up a bus company with genuine British busses. Lucia Bernardi and Piet Maas sell secret papers, not only to the Iraqi government, but also to an Italian oil company in *A Kind of Anger*. Arthur Simpson, though, does what all of these characters really want to do when at the close of *Dirty Story* he decides to set himself up as a passport-issuing country.

Before Arthur, Ambler shows these people who make and sell juice from the squeeze between powers to the likeable folks whom we should admire for their pluck and ingenuity. After Arthur, however, the position of this character becomes less simple. Arthur, *picaro* that he is, is still a pimp, a pornographer, and thief who, in spite of his whining protests of innocence, deserves all that he gets. Although they seem cleaner, the same is true of Colonels Jost and Brand in *The Intercom Conspiracy,* and Paul Firman and Mat Williamson in *The Siege of the Villa Lipp.* All these men win against the system, and have nice clothes and better accents than Arthur. But they cause far more in the way of misery and death in their milking of the system than Arthur does—misery and death, moreover, which they never see, operating as they do through cut-outs, covers, and mail services, or which they stubbornly refuse to acknowledge. They come to act as states and institutions do, and they go from men in the middle to men who put others in the middle.

Just as this shift shows a more complex moral world, so do Ambler's methods of presentation become more complex in the most recent novels. Beginning with *The Intercom Conspiracy* and including *The Levanter,* and *The Siege of the Villa Lipp,* Ambler has moved from the single narrative voice to presentation of collections of views which cast doubt on the truth of the main narrator. *The Siege of the Villa Lipp,* for instance, gives Firman's story as told to a writer whom he has hired, but it also contains an Afterword by Professor Krom, and this sheds new light on the whole narration: in the body of the novel, Firman shows Krom to be incompetent and weak, but the Afterword shows him to be rational, perceptive, and human. Which one do we accept? This same technique blurs the characters' moral positions and the issues of *The Intercom Conspiracy* and *The Levanter,* and becomes for Ambler another way to undercut the cliches of the spy novel.

In the thirties Ambler began writing spy novels which entertained people, but he also endeavored to make them think: think about capitalism, think about real spies, think about detectives. With sure craftsmanship Ambler changed the traditional novel of espionage. He brought to it a realistic sense of what people really are, and a new point of view toward political and economic reality. He did away with the Secret Service hero and ignored the cliches of the thirties, like secret papers. The air of distanced analysis which increasingly affects his novels may not bring him into the pale of enduring literature, but it certainly makes Ambler the superior spy writer of his generation.

NOTES

[1] *The Dark Frontier* (London: Hodder and Stoughton, 1936), pp. 41-2.
[2] *Background to Danger* (New York: Dell, 1965), p. 76.
[3] *Journey into Fear* (New York: Ballantine, 1977), pp. 150-51.
[4] *The Intercom Conspiracy* (New York: Bantam, 1970), p. 23.
[5] *The Intercom Conspiracy*, pp. 207-8.
[6] *The Intercom Conspiracy*, p. 209.
[7] *The Schirmer Inheritance* (New York: Knopf, 1953), pp. 138-9.
[8] *Passage of Arms* (New York: Bantam, 1965), p. 64.
[9] *The Light of Day* (New York: Knopf, 1962), pp. 10, 11, 155; *Dirty Story* (New York: Atheneum, 1967), pp. 25, 156.
[10] *Dirty Story*, p. 3.

Chapter 10
Geoffrey Household
(1900—)

BETWEEN 1955 and 1960 Geoffrey Household's view of his writing changed. On the end papers of *Fellow Passenger* (1955) he divided his books into four categories: novels, romances, short story collections, and books for children. With *Watcher in the Shadows* (1960) the categories changed; Household dropped the old-fashioned and consciously anti-artistic label of romance and listed his books simply as novels, short stories, and books for children. Here Household may have been following Graham Greene's lead in dropping a label which connects the spy novel only with unadulterated popular entertainment, or he may have realized while writing his autobiography *(Against the Wind,* 1958) that there are numerous similarities between making regular novels and making spy stories. Ultimately, however, Household discovered that he could treat his serious themes in spy fiction as well as in what he considered regular novels—indeed that he could convey these themes more successfully in the spy plot than in his lugubrious attempts at regular fiction. Call them what you will, though, as of 1980 Household has nineteen pieces of long fiction, four collections of short stories, and four books for children. Of the nineteen novels, seven have little or no spy business in them: one, *The Third Hour* (1938), is a philosophic-character book; one, *Arabesque* (1948), is a love-character book; two are political character books, *Thing to Love* (1963) and *The Three Sentinels* (1971); one, *The Sending* (1980), is an occult-adventure novel; and two, *The Courtesy of Death* (1967) and *The Dance of the Dwarfs* (1968), are miscellaneous adventure tales. This leaves twelve novels which center on the issues of international intrigue and espionage: *Rogue Male* (1939), *The High Place* (1950), *A Rough Shoot* (1951), *A Time to Kill* (1951)[1], *Fellow Passenger* (1955), *Watcher in the Shadows* (1960), *Olura* (1965), *Doom's Caravan* (1971), *The Lives and Times of Bernardo Brown* (1973), *Red Anger* (1975), *Hostage London* (1977), and *The Last Two Weeks of Georges Rivac* (1978).

Household's life gave him a good bit of raw material for adventure fiction. Before the war he was a banker in the Balkans and a commercial traveller throughout Europe and South America. He sold bananas in Spain and wrote articles for a children's encyclopedia in New York. During the war he was a military attache in Rumania where he was to assist in blowing up the Rumanian oil fields if threatened by Hitler. After the Rumanians and the Nazis frustrated this, Household served as a Field Security officer in the Middle East. Most of this comes up sooner or later in his fiction. *The Third Hour* follows Household's peripatetic youth and then argues for the need to create a new class of aristocrats (the Order of the Third Hour) to quietly preserve real values and to wean the world away from commercial values. Several novels touch upon Household's experiences with Field Security *(Arabesque, A High Place,* and *Doom's Caravan),* but in these books he is too close to his material and the background and scenery are insufficient to redeem the low-keyed action and the narrow spectrum of characterization. When Household has digested his material and subordinates it to adventure/action plotting he does much better. Thus, in the early seventies Household consciously dipped into his past and adapted it to external fictions—the demolition of an oil field forms only part of the plot of *The Three Sentinels,* just as the people and the countryside of Rumania form only part of *The Lives and Times of Bernardo Brown.*

Even though Household stopped distinguishing between his books as novels and romances, they do fall into reasonably definite groups. As he uses it, "novel" structure builds slowly to one culminating event which illuminates fully the characters which the early parts introduce and develop. Among these books are *The Third Hour, The High Place, Arabesque, Thing to Love, Doom's Caravan* and *The Three Sentinels.* All these show Household's chief thematic concerns and mark the progress of his political thinking, but they are logy and lifeless in spite of the author's efforts. On the other hand, Household's "romances" build on episodes of threat or danger which he binds together with thematic concern, and, more importantly, character. This structure is the main vehicle for his spy books from *Rogue Male* to *The Last Two Weeks of Georges Rivac;* it is the sort of thing which he does best, and it is where Household participates in the main line of the spy novel's technical development.

At the core of the adventure spy novel we always find the plot motifs of the hunter and the hunted. The Hannay books may as well be the memoirs of a fox hunted man. Greene labels parts of *The Confidential Agent* with the terms "Hunted" and "Hunter." I could multiply examples almost indefinitely. Household, more perhaps than any other spy writer, made actual the potential of hunting in the adventure plot, and he exploited it more fully in his plots than anyone else does in his. Now, to sedentary and vaguely anti-vivisectionist people like myself, hunting seems to be the vicious pastime of cretins and sadists. Even without recourse to anthropological and psychological arguments, this is an indefensible position. Hunting, for one thing, when reduced to its abstract structure, can be an immensely complicated intellectual construct. This is occasionally true for the actual hunter in the fields with a gun, but it is absolutely accurate for the writer, like Household, who uses the hunt as one of the ingredients of his fiction. Let us, for a start, approach hunting as if it were an abstract game to see the nature of its complexities:

Participants

A. number

    1. hunting in its simplest form needs only one hunter and one quarry.

    2. hunter and quarry, however, can exist in groups

B. attitude

    1. awareness by the prey or the hunter of the other's presence and purpose complicates matters. Again, one or both parties or groups can be aware of the other.

    2. willingness (or unwillingness) to continue with the hunt or the escape on the part of the participants adds possibilities.

Setting

A. either or both parties can remain stationary in a blind or under cover.

B. either or both parties can move

    1. from one place to another

    2. to use motion for its own sake

C. space for both parties is next to infinite.

D. time affects space with the variable influences of weather and light.

So far we have a pretty large number of variables which can apply to the simplest sort of hunt: animal versus man. When we factor in large animals with the strength to kill their hunters and also human beings who have the intelligence to create offensive and defensive weapons, and who can alter their appearance through disguise, the construct becomes incredibly more complex. Hunting shifts from a simple game with only a few possible endings (death or escape of the quarry; success or resignation of the hunter) to a fluid series of reversing games. Thus the hunter becomes the hunted, the quarry becomes the aggressor, and *vice versa*. Add to this man's capacity for self-examination, his sometimes errant ability to draw conclusions from observations of the past, an individual's complicated emotions, memories and conscience, and we have a series of possibilities in the hunt which can approach the actual meaning of infinite.

In his early books Household moved toward the complete realization of hunting for the adventure/spy novel. For one thing, he identifies a couple of his heroes with small animals, the traditional victim of the hunt. The hero of *Rogue Male* makes his stand in a burrow much like a rabbit or badger, and Dennim in *Watcher in the Shadows* is a naturalist immersed in the life and habits of the squirrel. On the level of plot, *Rogue Male* traces the hero from being hunted by Nazis to escaping across Germany to stalking an assassin in the Underground to being trapped in his burrow to dodging behind chimney pots waiting for Hitler to cross his sights. All the action is hunt. Roger Taine in *A Rough Shoot* and *A Time to Kill* does very much the same thing: the first book focuses on a long chase with Taine and Sandorski as the quarry and ends in a brief but violent hunt across the roof tops of London, while the second book shows Taine and Pink in their patient but anxious stalk of the Russian agent who has kidnapped Taine's sons. With *Watcher in the Shadows* Household wrote his most articulated hunting story. Here Charles Dennim and St. Sabas repeatedly exchange roles of hunter and hunted until the final, prolonged contest in the darkened English countryside. In the book Household builds up the complexities of the hunt, using the metaphor of chess, until we get this passage during the final struggle:

Both of us were now on foot and under the beeches. The windbreak was a rough oval with a diameter of a hundred and fifty yards one way and about a hundred on the other. That sounds a small area for terror and uncertainty, but visibility was down to twenty feet if the enemy moved and nothing at all if he didn't. Wherever a man lay down he automatically created an ambush. So, on the face of it, the odds were heavily against the attacker. But it was not much use to crouch and wait and switch a tail unless the prey could be attracted out of a thousand possible squares of darkness into the right one.[2]

With *Watcher in the Shadows* Household perfected the hunting-based plot and although he used hunting and its allied techniques (use of cover, use of disguise, use of bluff, etc.) in his books after 1960, he depended a bit more heavily on his other techniques for organizing the episodic adventure plot.

The title of Household's first spy/adventure novel, *Rogue Male,* had an impact upon the writer beyond its implications for the isolation of the hero of that novel. Rogues, the epigraph of *Rogue Male* tells us, act as "...individual[s], separat[ed] from its fellows appearing to increase both cunning and ferocity." This usage, however, is a comparatively recent one, appearing first in the nineteenth century. The older meaning of the term pictures the rogue as the homeless vagabond or the mischief-making rascal. This, of course, connects us to the *picaro,* automatically brings the picaresque novel to mind. The picaresque novel unites a series of variegated episodes with the roguish character of the itinerant hero: *Gil Blas, Tom Jones, Huck Finn.* Now, partly because of his own adventurous youth, and partly as a reaction against the kind of adventure plots which he used before 1955 (I will have more to say about this later), Household consciously switched to picaresque character and organization in *Fellow Passenger*[3]and he also used it in *Olura, The Lives and Times of Bernardo Brown, Red Anger,* and *The Last Two Weeks of Georges Rivac.* Indeed, at the end of *Bernardo Brown,* Alfonso, King of Spain, tells Brown: "Rogue! *Picaro!* You belong to us."[4] The picaresque has two noticeable effects on Household's fiction. First, it changes his hero. *Rogue Male, The High Place, A Rough Shoot* and *A Time to Kill* all employ traditional heroes of English adventure fiction: the cold aristocrat who realizes his duty to his heart, or the resourceful country squire. One thing which we can notice about Household's picaresque books is that the heroes augment good old British stock with foreign backgrounds: Howard Wolferstan *(Fellow Passenger)* is half English and half Ecuadorean, Olura is half Greek, Bernardo Brown is half Spanish, Adrian Gurney *(Red Anger)* is half Rumanian, and Georges Rivac is three quarters French. Aside from connecting with Household's pan-European sentiments (see *The Third Hour* and *Against the Wind*) he feels that these polyglot heroes possess a kind of looseness and elan which totally British characters lack. The cultural contrast particularly shows in *Red Anger,* where Household joins the picaresque Gurney with the single-minded and fully English Alwyn Rory.

Although, with the possible exceptions of *Rogue Male* and *Hostage London,* all of Household's heroes are innocents snarled in the brambles of events, this is even more the case with those in the picaresque books. These people mind their own business when, bang, they land in the middle of international intrigue which sets them off on their journeys and this, in turn, brings their roguish imaginations and reflexes to bear. Household's picaresque books also move through a wider variety of incident than do the hunt-chase novels. In *Fellow Traveller* Howard-Wolferstan burgles an atom think-tank, plays cricket with a country eleven, poses as an itinerant painter, tends elephants in a circus and strolls the Cotswolds as a folksinger. Bernardo Brown goes through incarnations as an engineer, a pimp, a concierge, a stage manager and a fugitive, playing different roles and seeing more of the world with every move. This is not merely variety for the sake of variety. The picaresque enables Household to expand on the minor thread of comedy which he began with General Sandorski in *A Rough Shoot*, but which the form of the hunt-chase story crowds to the sidelines. It also lets him show a larger slice of humanity with two results: first, he can show the competence and nobility of a broader range of society, and secondly, he can more easily portray women and love in the picaresque story than in the hunt-chase book. Finally, on the level of adventure plotting, it allows Household to deal not only with hiding and seeking, but it gives him a larger scope to use disguise. Thus in the picaresque novels, the heroes run through any number of disguises, while in, say, *Watcher in the Shadows*, disguise hardly figures in the plot. Ultimately, though, Household never feels at home with the picaresque as does, for instance, Manning Coles. His interests in character and in political-moral issues do not blend well with the character of the rogue or with the succession of absurd incidents. Therefore, even if he does include picaresque features in a number of books, the only novels which are thoroughly picaresque are *The Lives and Times of Bernardo Brown* and *Fellow Passenger*. In the rest Household uses picaresque motifs to accomplish other ends.

In choosing the picaresque Household, as I said above, reacted against his pre-1955 fiction. He directed this reaction against John Buchan. In the early spy novels, through *A Time to Kill*, Household more or less followed precedents set in the Hannay saga. Thus, in *Against the Wind* he tries to sort out the genesis of *Rogue Male* and says:

To what incidents these pages were to lead I did not know, but the whole of the story was inherent in them, and *Rogue Male* began, week after week, to live. I observed, faintly protesting, that whereas I had intended a picaresque story in which Fear would supply the suspense, what I was really writing had some affinity to Buchan without his coincidences and with the cry of human suffering unsuppressed.[5]

A bit later in the autobiography Household notes that *Fellow*

Passenger was a concerted attempt to move to the picaresque and away from Buchan. In many ways, though, Household never broke Buchan's grip on his fiction. We can see this influence in prose style in that both men write their best material when describing action: they deal in unadulterated, active prose.

The influence also shows through in the use of landscape. Hannay would be nothing if he did not have a specific countryside to act in and the same is true of Household's heroes—even if Household imputes more to nature than the calvinist Buchan ever could. It also appears in definite plot parallels. Billy Bones storms into the Admiral Benbow Inn, gets himself killed and leaves a piece of paper which ignites the adventure in *Treasure Island*. From this Buchan drew Scudder who invades Hannay's rooms and with his piece of paper sets off the incidents in *The Thirty Nine Steps*. The same thing happens in Household. Look at *The Courtesy of Death* (written long after Household ostensibly rejected Buchan for the picaresque). Household's hero, Yarrow, an ex-mining engineer (so is Hannay) sits quietly in his rooms when Fosworthy bursts in. Yarrow, in spite of believing his guest to be half balmy, helps him and as a consequence becomes caught up in a plot replete with threat and danger. Quite the same thing happens in *The Last Two Weeks of Georges Rivac* when Kren bursts into Rivac's office and gives him a pamphlet to deliver to London. In fact, in *The Last Two Weeks* Household does precisely what he described in *Against the Wind*: he gives us Buchan without the abnormal number of coincidences. Thus Rivac, like Hannay, has significant information to deliver to the people in charge of security in London. He, however, does not and cannot dope out the code in Kren's pamphlet, and when he arrives in London he has a devil of a time trying to find someone who will, first, believe him and, second, direct him to the proper office in the rabbit warren of the intelligence bureaucracies. Officials lie to him, others threaten, and before the right people get the message, KGB thugs chase Rivac and Zia halfway across England. It is, however, not only in these incidents that we see Buchan in Household's books. Roger Taine in *Rough Shoot* and *A Time to Kill* is clearly very much Buchan's Hannay. The setting of *The Three Sentinels* suggests Buchan's *The Courts of Morning* (as well as Haggard's *The Telemann Touch*, 1958). Like Buchan, moreover, Household uses his fiction to delineate certain ethical and moral perspectives; Household, indeed, goes several steps further than Buchan in that he makes his moral and ethical points explicitly instead of implicitly, and he shows his characters having more complete human consciousnesses as opposed to the relatively limited inner lives of Hannay and Dickson McCunn.

When Household considers the actors in his plots, one of his first concerns is to give them the perpective of class. We can see this from the very beginning in *The Third Hour* which largely revolves on the definition of class, and Household very definitely carries this topic over into his spy books. Thus, in *Rogue Male* he makes the narrator bring up the question of class rather early in the text; in fact, here Household distills off much of the tedious material about class which he put into *The Third Hour* with the following result:

I say Class X because there is no definition of it. To talk of an upper or a ruling class is nonsense. The upper class, if the term has any meaning at all, means landed gentry who probably do belong to Class X but form only a small proportion of it. The ruling class are, I presume, politicians and servants of the state—terms which are self-contradictory.

I wish there were some explanation of Class X. We are politically a democracy— or should I say that we are an oligarchy with its ranks open to talent?—and the least class-conscious of nations in the Marxian sense. The only class-conscious people are those who would like to belong to Class X and don't: the suburban old-school-tie brigade and their wives, especially their wives. Yet we have a profound division of classes which defies analysis since it is in a continual state of flux.

Who belongs to Class X? I don't know 'till I talk to him and then I know at once. It is not, I think, a question of accent, but rather of the gentle voice. It is certainly not a question of clothes. It may be a question of bearing. . . .

I should like some socialist pundit to explain to me why it is that in England a man can be a member of the proletariat by every definition of the proletariat (that is by the nature of his employment and his poverty) and yet obviously belong to Class X, and why another can be a bulging capitalist or cabinet minister or both and never get nearer to Class X than being directed to the saloon bar if he enters the public.[6]

This definition which Household worked on for two novels is not, after all, very precise; a cynic could reduce it to the formula: everyone I like is Class X and those I do not like are not in Class X. As Class X works out in the novels, particularly *Hostage London*, we find that politicians, in and out of government, are not in Class X, while people who work and think are in Class X. But this does not get us too far. To really understand Class X we need to recognize Household's concepts of aristocracy and commitment.

Trying to explain the legitimacy of anarchy in *The High Place,* Amberson calls it ". . . the only political label which, in the modern world, could be applied to the once respectable opinions of an Eighteenth Century Whig."[7] The mention of political commitment in the context of the old, landed aristocracy has reasonably broad implications for Household. There are several aristocrats who play significant roles in Household's books. There is the narrator of *Rogue Male*, Count Kalmody and Sigismund Pozharski in *The Lives and Times of Bernardo Brown,* and Charles [von] Dennim in *Watcher in the Shadows.* These men, first of all, have the confidence, grace and charm to get along with anybody. They can enjoy and participate in life fully—even if Pozharski is a bit too randy, and the others show mainly the potential for enjoyment. Most importantly, they do not depend on or tolerate niggling officialdom. Kalmody and Pozharski are the *deus ex machina* in *The Lives and Times,* who pluck victory from the toothless maws of laws and red tape. Von Dennim presents a slightly different side of the aristocrat: he shows the side of honor, particularly military honor. Thus he refuses the succor of an anemic government and determines to fight his own battle rather than a) subjecting innocents to danger or b) waiting while an incompetent establishment allows an assassin to murder him. The confrontation at the close of *Watcher in the Shadows* becomes in every sense a chivalric duel with the two combatants sharing love and respect in the same way that Hal and Hotspur do after the climax at Shrewsbury. Indeed, in order to understand *Rogue Male,* we need to read the concept of the aristocrat into it. Thus in the larger context of Household's books, the hero of *Rogue's Male* is an aristocrat debauched and dehydrated by the twentieth century's consumer society (one main complaint enunciated in *The Third Hour*) who dawdles around the world shooting big game and casually enjoying his wealth. At the crisis of the novel he recognizes the kernel of his aristocratic identity as a soldier and he then thinks clearly and effectively, and acts decisively.

The label of aristocrat with its military-chivalric association, however, is only part of Household's complete formula for Class X. The hero in Household—or any viable individual in the books— must recognize and align himself with certain psychic realities. In terms of psychology, Household emphasizes several distinct levels of awareness. He shows in the early novels the hero's affinity with animals as well as his intellectual movement away from purely instinctive being. This begins with *Rogue Male* where the hero undergoes an accelerated course of human evolution. The novel opens with the hero crawling painfully out of the primordial ooze: "I had supposed that this bog was me; it tasted of blood. Then it occurred to me that this soft extension of my body might really be bog."[8] He emerges from the swamp as a reptile: "I travelled on my belly, using my elbows for legs and leaving a track behind me like that of a wounded crocodile."[9] Then he takes to the trees like a monkey. Later in the book he, to his peril but ultimately for his benefit (in that it forces him to achieve his complete humanness), accepts the complete wisdom of instinct:

> I had begun to think as an animal. Instinct, saving instinct, had preserved me time and again. I accepted its power complacently, never warning myself that instinct might be deadly wrong. If it were not, the hunted could always escape the hunter, and the carnivores would be as extinct as the great saurians.[10]

Although our animal natures do not save us from the dangers of the world, they do exist and they do perform a role in our lives. Thus, in *Watcher in the Shadows,* the unaccountable resources of the human body protect Dennim:

> I have the impression that my unconsciousness was not total; if it was, then there is some primitive savior in the damaged animal watching on its behalf until the higher nervous centers regain control.[11]

We have animals inside us, Household says, and the sooner the hero recognizes this and comes to terms with it, the better off he will be.

Along with the identification of man's physical nature with that of animals, Household includes the utility of bestial or primitive human rage. The beginning of the change from prey to hunter in *Rogue Male* comes when anger floods the civilized conventions of the hero's life and thought:

> Yet I was mad with grief and hatred. I describe myself as then mad because I did not know it. The tepidity of my sorrow was not indifference; it was the blankness which descends upon me when I dare not know what I am thinking. I know that I was consumed by anger. I remember venmous thoughts. Yet at the time I was utterly unaware of them. I suppressed them as fast as they came up into my conscious mind. I would have nothing to do with grief or hatred or revenge.[12]

Anger here enables the hero to win—it molds introspection into effective force. In *Red Anger* and *Hostage London,* both written thirty years later, anger, surrendering the intellect to the emotions, kills both Rory and Despard, but it kills them in a way which satisfies the victim and gives a chance and an example to a naive and bumbling society.

The aristocrat succumbing to pure anger, though, does not complete Household's formula for the psychology of the hero—if it did we would be back to nasty, brutish and short as a way of life. Conscience justifies and shapes and atones for anger. Thus several of Household's novels bring specific spiritual direction to the action: most notably we can see this in Anton Tabas, the ecumenical religious seer in *The High Place.* Many of the novels are specifically and literally confessions. *Rogue Male, The High Place* and *Hostage*

London are all confessional diaries prepared by the heroes (as is, for that matter, *Dance of the Dwarfs*), and the other books (with the exception of *Arabesque, The Three Sentinels, The Lives and Times* and *The Last Two Weeks*) are first person narratives with confessional passages.

The confession, of course, is the traditional means of delineating one's spiritual desires, one's human derelictions, and one's drive toward conversion. We can look at *A Time to Kill* as a representative example. The confessional form lies at the core of the difference between the two Roger Taine books. *A Rough Shoot* is an adventure romp, while *A Time to Kill* includes "the cry of human suffering" which Household missed in Buchan. At the end of the action, after an orgasm of rage, murder and mayhem, Taine likens his own consciousness to that in tragedy:

...I myself, when I watched the revival of some tragedy, have often wondered how the last man left upon the stage could bear his life thereafter.

***

Well, I suppose the dramatist merely assumed that the last man upon the stage went to his priest, and that was that. We, less simple and fortunate, have to put up with more secular authority. But in fact a man who has such a wife as I has little need of a psychologist. She saw what was wrong and persuaded me to tell it, and these pages are for her.[13]

Taine's confession may not have the complexity of that in *Rogue Male* or the spiritual orientation of *The High Place*, but it does show clearly the central place of self-awareness and love orientation in Household's world. These things keep us out of the jungle, they are basic properties of our human estate, and they, like substantial grace or honor, cannot be taught or acquired: if one needs to be schooled in these things he will never possess them.

For Household, love does not exclusively mean emotional or spiritual attachment to another human being or transcendent god. Naturally, women prompt the heroes' action in most of the novels from the executed lover in *Rogue Male* (a pattern repeated in *The Three Sentinels*) to the family in the Taine books, to Olura, to Nadja in *The Lives and Times,* to Zia in *The Last Two Weeks*. Household, however, has difficulty portraying real women, and he tends to exclude them (using the dead lover), to minimize them in the action (Cecily Taine), to make them objects of pathos (Nadya's freak show physique), or to mythologize them. This last category becomes the most significant for Household, the woman as the symbolic embodiment of the land, for, increasingly, the land itself represents the most important object of love.

For Household, the land forms part of the complex web which links modern man with both his preevolutionary animal past and with his first human ancestors. In *Watcher in the Shadows* he ties modern man to nature: "I believe that for the animal always, and for man sometimes, fear is only a vivid awareness of one's unity with nature."[14] If this connection to nature occasionally occurs to men, so also do reminders of the ties between his primitive ancestors and the land. *Red Anger* contains the fullest account of these influences, with Gurney and Rory both acknowledging the presence of King Arthur and his farmer soldiers seeping into their consciousness as they hide among prehistoric barrows and stone circles. The land and its past create part of modern man's instinct, as they do for Taine in *Rough Shoot* when he says: ". . . one somehow knows, in a countryside that forms part of one's blood, what the sweep of the land is likely to be."[15] Indeed, symbolically, Household's heroes, like Antaeus, draw strength from contact with, immersion in the earth. Thus, rather than being a descent into hell, as suggested by the presence of a cat named Asmodeus in *Rogue Male*, going into the earth prepares and strengthens Household's heroes. The hero of *Rogue Male* emerges from his burrow purified and able to act, Taine meets the crisis in *A Time to Kill* in a smugglers' cave, Yarrow in *The Courtesy of Death* comes into contact with self in the myth-filled caverns of his ancestors, and Rivac goes into an ice cave before he untangles the action in *The Last Two Weeks*. Land gives strength with its connection with man's past, but it also provides the peace for one to look into himself. As Amberson says in *The High Place:* "If a man is to become psychiatrist at the bedside of his own sick soul, then the fee that he must pay is absolute inaction."[116] It is on and in the land that one can best examine one's soul.

More than simple strength to compete in adventure action or a place to meditate, the land is the end of that meditation. Nature in Household comes to give man a Wordsworthian feeling of being. In *Hostage London* Despard has a nature epiphany on a Greek island at the beginning of the novel. Later it falls into place, much as it does in the poetic experience of Shelley:

But the health of society is not of universal value. What is? As I try to answer that, the switchboard of the brain at once connects me to Paxos. From youth on I have experienced similar unforgettable communications when I have a passing ecstasy which has nothing to do with human society and which is, I think, common to all animals. I am only able to describe it as surrender to a purpose, though I do not know what purpose there can be except to force me to surrender. What I receive from the switchboard is only a vivid memory of shape and color, containing neither prohibition nor encouragement nor any undertone of morality. All it conveys is: *you are a part of this.*[17]

The land giving spiritual meaning to the individual is the final answer in Household's search for the proper relationship between the individual and the state. It is an answer which grew out of a prolonged struggle over the subject which we can follow. In his first novel, the Brothers of the Third Hour choose to withdraw from society to try to influence it by positive examples. By the time of *The High Place*, Household proposes spiritually oriented passive resistance to disable the blind and greedy state and to convince it to wither away. *Thing to Love* suggests that states or political ideals have no real value and that the only thing to love and sacrifice for is another human being. Beginning with *The Three Sentinels,* Household uses the land as the answer to the perceived ills of the twentieth century: consumerism and bureaucratic government. In a definite sense he sympathizes with what others might consider the crack-pot, revolutionary antics of the young and displaced (see the commune in *The High Place,* Olura's fervent organizing, the demonic religionists in *The Courtesy of Death*, and Magma and the Christian anarchist in *Hostage London*) who see the symptoms of the century's illness but not the cure. As Garay in *The Three Sentinels* revolts against the state and the company and for a limited agrarian existence, Household increasingly focuses on a return to the land as man's only hope. If Greene's characters can believe in nothing larger than a home, Household's people can believe in nothing larger than a farm. Thus, Tessa, in *Red Anger,* makes Household's point:

The only way out Voltaire could see was to cultivate one's garden. So I'm going to. There's no means of giving all this [the countryside] to millions of townsmen who wouldn't be content with it anyway. So I might as well enjoy peace and keep a patch of sanity in the world.[18]

The farm includes and transcends Household's other political statements. It connects man to the soil, to his physical nature, and to the spirit in the earth. Farms tie man to his ancestors and they mock human government, controlled as they are by sunlight and rainfall. They test the individual's strength and resolve as well as rewarding proper community effort. They provide also the solitude necessary for an individual to come in touch with the depth and breadth of his being.

Developing a hero who knows, feels and acts upon this

information is the first and most important hero pattern in Household's books. Thus, the Class X man, the aristocratic rebel who commits himself to proper values and examines his conscience dominates the fiction until the seventies. In two novels of the seventies, though, Household does try to show the other side of the picture. *Doom's Caravan* and *The Three Sentinels* contrast the hero who has examined himself and his world and found knowledge which he converts to rebellion, with the humane and reasonable administrator who tries to maintain not only order but decency in the conduct of social business. *Doom's Caravan*, drawing on Household's war-time experience, juxtaposes a compassionate Field Security officer with Oliver Enwin, who embodies the characteristics of most of Household's earlier heroes. We see the difference between the two men best in the officer/narrator's attempts to compass Enwin's attitude toward the war:

I hesitate to call him a pacifist. There is no clear-cut name for the man who refuses to kill his fellow human beings just because he is ordered to do so by his government and is willing to use unlimited violence when ordered by himself.[19]

The bureaucrat forces Enwin to aid in the war against the Nazis, but only temporarily, for he then skips out and creates an isolated paradise for himself and his wife. Household gives the same story a tragic twist in *The Three Sentinels* where he reintroduces the same character types: the man who upholds the romantic ideal despite its impracticality, and the man who tries to combine reason with compassion. In the long run, though, Household does not hold readers with these polar characters, because he does not effectively examine the psychology of conviction in them and because he creates them in novel structures instead of in adventure romance plots which he handles most effectively.

In all his books, Household's main strength is his narrative ability: the capacity to tell a story of a complex hero facing multiple threats and eluding them. Although his picaresque heroes, Howard-Wolferstan and Bernardo Brown, have an Ambleresque quality of innocents being caught in the grinders of intrigue and adventure, his heroes who order themselves to act do so out of motives which are uniquely Household's. In terms of villains, however, Household plays down doctine in favor of standardized evil which the readers assume and which draws its identification from the structural necessity for an antagonist. Of course, Household does give his villains appropriate doctrinal coloring—there are Nazis in *Rogue Male* and *Doom's Caravan*, neo-Nazis in *Rough Shoot,* communists in *A Time to Kill, Fellow Passenger, Red Anger* and *The Last Two Weeks,* the OSA in *Olura* and international anarchists in *The High Place* and *Hostage London*—but this identification, in most cases, has only minor significance. Evil exists in many of the books only insofar as the hero defines the villain in order to clarify his own motive and doctrine. Further, Household almost always gives a double perspective on his villains. First, for the villains he uses the pattern of the group with the representative figure to provide the requisite threat to fuel the adventure plot and still keep the possibility of showing at least one human being on the wrong side. He almost always tries to show the human side of the antagonists. This may have come from Household's experience in the Middle East where Arab, Jew and Briton alternately murdered and respected one another. At any rate, in the books we find antagonists like Elisa Cantenmir in *The High Place* who are not evil at all, as well as antagonists like Pink in *Rough Shoot* and *A Time to Kill* who, before our eyes, change from bogies into frail human beings once prejudice and doctrine disappear.

Partly because of the human face of villainy, Household's espionage plots frequently concentrate on the after effects of spying rather than the conniving and execution of international dirty tricks. Thus, *Rogue Male* starts after the hero has lined Hitler up in his sights, *Watcher in the Shadows* wraps up events which are fifteen years old, *Red Anger* begins after Rory's trial, and *The Last Two Weeks* commences after Kren has encoded information about Warsaw Pact troops. This sharpens the focus, on one level, upon the hunt and chase action, but it also shows, on the character level, people who have in some way failed at their intelligence jobs and who are, consequently, more human. Instead of well-ordered intelligence work, on the organizational level we see the effect of foul-ups. In *Fellow Passenger*, in fact, Household gives us a paean on muddle: "O eloquent, unjust and mighty Muddle! As I look back to that moment in my ignominious but distinguished present, I cannot resist a digression in praise of Muddle."[20] The good soldier Svejk lives. One man, using his brains and intuition, can twist authority into knots. He can be here or there—a chimney sweep or a farm laborer. Muddle works for the good guys. Now, granted, Household often does resort to the *deus ex machina* to snatch his heroes out of the muddles which they have created—seen most blatantly in the anonymous narrator in *Olura*, but present, really,in most of the novels. Most often, however, by stirring up chaos, Household's heroes do win small victories which give spiritual fulfillment, capsules of peace in a violent world, and, occasionally, as in *Rogue Male, Red Anger* and *Hostage London* (the books in which the heroes die at the end), they win another chance for the people whom they love (*Red Anger*) or another chance for all of society—given that Hitler's death would have changed history.

Although he fought against it, Household, in essence, carries the techniques and attitudes of Buchan into the Post-War world. The love of land, the leavening of adventure, the concern for human beings, and the distrust of organizations exist in both men. Household is more forthcoming about his total consciousness than Buchan, but in many ways he transmits Buchan's insights modified by the knowledge of gentleness which part of society has gained in our era, and modified by grief for what is done to us and what we have been forced to do. He is, perhaps, more like Mountbatten who dismantled the Empire because it needed to be done and was humanly right, but still longed for adventure on his destroyer flotilla, than he is like Churchill, who stood on the ramparts defending, for good or bad, the old way of life. Household is a forerunner of the small is beautiful movement, finding that small is beautiful not because it is mean but because it is human.

NOTES

[1] *Rough Shoot* (114 pages) and *A Time to Kill* (104 pages) are really novellas. The former appeared in *The Saturday Evening Post*. According to Household, "*A Time to Kill* was meant to appear in one volume with *A Rough Shoot* [as it does]—a story of attack followed by one of defense." *Against the Wind* (Boston: Atlantic-Little Brown, 1958), 221.

[2] *Watcher in the Shadows* (Boston: Atlantic-Little Brown, 1960), pp. 212-3.

[3] *Against the Wind*, p. 233.

[4] *The Lives and Times of Bernardo Brown* (London: Joseph, 1973), p. 287.

[5] *Against the Wind*, p. 209.

[6] *Rogue Male* (Harmondsworth: Penguin, 1977), p. 41.

[7] *The High Place* (Boston: Atlantic-Little Brown, 1950), p. 45.

[8] *Rogue Male*, p. 9.

[9] *Rogue Male*, p. 10.

[10] *Rogue Male*, p. 135.

[11] *Watcher in the Shadows*, p. 227.

[12] *Rogue Male* p. 152.

[13] *A Time to Kill* (Boston: Atlantic-Little Brown, 1951), pp. 220-21.

[14] *Watcher in the Shadows*, p. 174.

[15] *A Rough Shoot* (Boston: Atlantic-Little Brown, 1951), p. 87.

[16] *The High Place*, p. 70.

[17] *Hostage London* (Harmondsworth: Penguin, 1977), pp. 65-6.

[18] *Red Anger* (Harmondsworth: Penguin, 1977), p. 146.

[19] *Doom's Caravan*, (Boston: Atlantic-Little Brown, 1971), p. 142.

[20] *Fellow Passenger* (Boston: Atlantic-Little Brown, 1955), p. 111.

Chapter 11
Peter Cheyney
(1896-1951)

Before World War II Peter Cheyney made himself famous by introducing two heroes who were fairly new to British detective fiction: Lemmie Caution and Slim Callaghan. Lemmie Caution, appearing first in *This Man is Dangerous* (1936), is an agent of the American FBI and brings the characteristics of the hard-boiled detective hero to British fiction. He drinks hard, fights hard, loves hard and talks like a character out of Damon Runyan, for example in this passage from *I'll Say She Does* (1945):

> Figure it out for yourself that I am one of these poetic guys who is always lookin' around for beauty. I have got that sort of eye. Maybe you mugs also know that this palooka Confucius who is a smart boyo who is always ready with a wise spiel, and who has himself a good time tellin' the rest of the world where it gets off the ridin' rods, has summed up all this business when he said: "The beauty of women is like the alligator waitin' in the bulrushes." Just when the sapient bozo thinks he is all set for a big time with some allurin' *femme* he is only on the threshold of havin' the pants kicked off him an' bein' hit for a home run.[1]

The Lemmie Caution detective novels, much in the same vein as Sapper, combine comedy with hard-hitting action and a bit of detection. Slim Callaghan, Cheyney's second hero, naturalizes the hard-boiled American detective. Slim is a limey counterpart of Philip Marlow, Sam Spade and the rest. As a private detective he recognizes the wholesale corruption of society:

> That sort of thing happened in America. It didn't happen in London!
> He grinned at the thought. Didn't it![2]

And he faces this with weary courage and a modicum of wit.

Now that we have met Mr. Caution and Mr. Callaghan, we can dismiss them for a while since we are not interested in detective stories here. Early in his career Cheyney also became involved with espionage. Cheyney's first literary job involved helping Harold Brust rewrite autobiographical material for inclusion in "Tinker's Note-book," an off-shoot of Sexton Blake's adventures, printed in the *Union Jack*. Brust, one of the first members of Scotland Yard's Special Branch, was involved with most of the politically sensitive events in the first quarter of the century. He saw the assassination of Carlos of Portugal, arrested Lenin, guarded Edward VII, Balfour, Churchill, Kitchener and Ian MacPherson, moved on the fringes of the siege of Sidney Street, arrested Horst von der Doltz, the German spy, and also arrested Emily Davidson (who later threw herself in front of the horses at the Derby). As evidenced by his autobiography, *I Guarded Kings: The Memoirs of a Political Police Officer* (1935), Brust was a garrulous name-dropper; nevertheless, he had experienced, first hand, the world which Oppenheim and LeQueux described in fiction, and he could have been a gold mine for a writer interested in espionage. Cheyney, though, was not interested.

When Cheyney began writing spy novels in earnest with *Dark Duet* (1942), he gave us some perspective on how he fits into the tradition of spy fiction:

"But yes," said Guelvada. "Why not? This is the best hotel in Lisbon. It has everything. It even has fat blonde German spies all dressed in black velvet gowns hiding behind the palms in the lounges. It only needs William LeQueux here to write a book about it. It's a scream, *n'est-ce pas?*"[3]

He also put himself at variance with the traditions of the so-called "puzzle" detective story in his spy novels, for example in *Sinister Errand* (1945):

I came to the conclusion that the difference between what is usually called a detective story and the things that happen in real life is that in the novel there is some sort of pattern of events predestined to fit into each other. A jigsaw which must have a certain solution because the pieces will only fit into certain sections. But life isn't like that. Anything can happen, and it does. But it happens without any sort of cohesion, and it is more by luck than by cleverness that one stumbles on a fact that matters.[4]

We need to ask, if he is not in the romantic tradition of LeQueux or the ordered tradition of the detective novel, where can we place Cheyney? And then it is also convenient to ask, so what? What does he do for the development of the spy story?

The answer to the first question is fairly easy: in the passages I quoted above, Cheyney lies. He does belong to both the romantic tradition as well as to the "puzzle" tradition of the British detective novel as it existed between the wars. In the thirties, however, the fashion began to shift, and many writers made a show of abjuring romance and logic for realism. With Cheyney, that is all that it is, a show. Exotic scenery featuring lush nights in Portugal and the Bahamas, inscrutable and beautiful women with secrets, schoolboy romantic leads, unalloyed villains, and unquestioning patriotism drive Cheyney's spy novels as surely as they drive those of Oppenheim or LeQueux. Cheyney's heroes just dance sambas or tangos rather than waltzes. His novels end happily, his heroes get the girls, and evil gets flushed down the drain in the good old romantic tradition. Likewise, even though he bad mouths it, Cheyney builds on and uses specific mental conventions of the detective novel. In his detective novels and his spy novels, which turn on the solution to a problem, someone invariably compares the problem to be solved to a jigsaw puzzle. His novels do, in fact, run on puzzles. Further, Cheyney returns again and again to the old detective writer's device of refusing to show the readers a significant piece of information: thus in *Dark Bahama* (1950) we get an ellipsis where Cheyney omits Ernie's discovery about the real location of the Steyning Formula in order to make the end of the novel work.

Cheyney, then, is in the mainstream of the traditional spy novel, so that answers the first question. To answer the second question—why is he important—we need to look at some of Cheyney's window dressing. First of all, in Cheyney's spy novels as in his detective novels we get the introduction of various American elements, drawn mostly from the hard-boiled detective story and the gangster film, which he blends with the traditions of the British detective novel and spy novel. Secondly, Cheyney combines in his omelet a dash of realism in the form of sex and violence in order to bring the romantic tradition up to date. Finally, he introduces what are essentially new attitudes toward Secret Service organizations.

The espionage organization as an organization does not go back terribly far in spy fiction. The British predilection for the amateur dominates the form through the thirties. Oppenheim's heroes, exempting people like Miss Brown of X.Y.O., do pretty much without organizations; Buchan cares more for private enterprise as does, on another level, Sapper; Horler, Beeding and Coles introduce government agents but care little for their organizational connections beyond the fact that they legitimize the hero's status; and Ambler and Greene (until *Our Man in Havana*, 1958) focus more on people than organizations. Cheyney is really the first spy writer to stress the role of a particular and (to use his typical adjective for it) peculiar organization which dominates the lives of the agents in his books. Probably because he started writing spy novels amidst the layered bureaucracy of wartime, Cheyney begins the essential action of his spy novels in the corporate offices of an espionage establishment. In these offices there works a dedicated, nubile secretary, and there are piles of folders and flimsies. As we find in the first paragraph of *Dark Duet*, "A suggestion of efficiency was provided [for the office] by a steel filing-cabinet."[5] In offices like this one Cheyney shows espionage and counter espionage reduced to business propositions. Thus, again in *Dark Duet*, we get this telephone conversation:

> Well, what are you going to do, sir? You can't move through the Department of Home Security, can you? There is nothing official on the woman.... You can't prove anything...." Fenton shrugged his shoulders. His smile became more incisive. "Well ... if you think the case merits it you could always use Process 4 or 5...." He paused. "In this case, sir, I would suggest Process 5...."[6] (Cheyney's ellipses)

Here Cheyney shows his readers an intra-government (presumably) transaction to murder a German agent. The organization reduces it to cold, hard, efficient, scientific terms.

Cheyney's spy bureaucracy includes, on the lowest levels, factotums to tail people, dispose of bodies, carry messages and do other semi-skilled labor. They appear in the books simply as names, like Vane the ambulance driver in *The Stars are Dark* (1943), or Stott the watcher in *Dark Street* (1944). On the next level we have the ostensible heroes of the novels, the agents and the killers, the skilled help: agents like Kane, Fells, Kerr and others, and killers like Guelvada, Greeley and Salvatini. Most important to the corporate entity, however, we have the chief executive. Increasingly, during the war years, Cheney's novels dwell upon the acumen, knowledge and burden of the chief executive who runs the espionage organization. Cheyney, although he does introduce some one-shot espionage executives like Fenton in *Dark Duet* and Ransom in *Dark Hero* (1946), develops two main authority figures throughout a number of novels: there is, first, Quale (who appears in *The Stars are Dark, Dark Street, Dark Interlude* [1947] and *Dark Bahama*) and, less importantly, there is the Old Man (who appears in *Sinister Errand* and *Ladies Won't Wait* [1951]). These leaders hold all the answers, know what everyone is doing and select who will live and who will die; they are aloof, machiavellian and callous. But underneath... well, I want to deal with that later. It is enough to say that Cheyney gives us more than a shadow organization. Perhaps his "peculiar" organization is not fully articulated, hung as it is only on bits of realistic detail, but it forms part of the accelerating obsession with the spy establishment which we can find in mid-century novels.

Cheyney's agents, in addition to their organizational background, introduce direct and impolite methods. All his spy novels show murder as the main tool of counter espionage, and in many cases he draws his heroes as hired killers who bump off German or Soviet agents who have been too pesky or successful. Further, Cheyney, in at least one case (*Ladies Won't Wait*), shows individuals being blackmailed into acting as agents, and he is almost frank about the use of sexual lures in order to obtain information. Thus we hear the following interchange between Quale and his female agent, Zilla, in *The Stars are Dark:*

> "I hope you're not going to ask me to sleep with this paragon?"
> "I never have yet, have I?" he said. "Although you know perfectly well if it were necessary I should."[7]

If murder and sex form part of the spy's arsenal, violence forms another. During the course of Cheyney's detective novels, he invariably introduces a scene in which the hero either beats someone up or gets beaten up himself. Unlike the stylized clip on the point of the jaw which we find in Sapper and other novelists of the twenties, Cheyney takes some pains to draw more accurate violence. In *Dark Interlude*, for instance, O'Mara gets kicked in the stomach, is pistol whipped and has his fingers burned with a cigarette lighter when the Nazis try to make him reveal the location of Quayle's headquarters. The violence almost always shades into torture: Cheyney uses that old stand-by the Chinese water torture in both *Spinster Errand* and *Ladies Won't Wait*. But, of course, torture has a purpose. It, like much of the violence in Cheyney, comes out of good, healthy (or unhealthy, depending on one's allegiance) sadism. Every novel contains at least one shooting in the stomach, which Cheyney associates with a particularly gruesome way to go. His killers get a real kick out of murdering people. Ernie Guelvada, Cheyney's main assassin character, hums and sings before, during and after carving up someone's guts (he is a knife man), and Horace Greeley grins a toothy grin as he machine guns the Germans at the close of *The Stars are Dark*. Cheyney is careful to repeat in every book the maxim imputed to Robespierre, that you can't make an omelet without breaking eggs. Spying is a violent business, and it takes tough men to succeed in it.

In this doctrine of toughness Cheyney differs in a number of ways from earlier spy novels. Sure he is more frank in portraying violence, but the important point is that on a superficial level Cheyney espouses a sort of existentialism. This accounts for the fact that the motivating action in Cheyney's novels is so weak. Typically we do not hear about the political motivation of the plot (the stolen papers, the captured agent, the verification of V1 strikes) until we move well into the book, and at the end of the novel the political motivation really makes little difference. Cheyney, with his meager abilities, tries to show us a violent, cruel world in which action and courage sometime make a difference and sometimes do not. The novels all tell us, at one point or another, like a superficial reading of Sartre, that it makes no difference:

Life was damned funny and there was nothing you could do about it. Either you played it along or it played you along.[8]

Well, if I'm right about you Janey, I'll fix you one day. By God, I will ...! Because— not that it mattered—I was rather fond of Olly.[9] (Cheyney's elipsis)

I hope for very little and expect nothing. I'm damned glad of what I get.[10]

Life is going to screw people. For Cheyney this is the only logic:

Being logical to me means being tough, because in any truly logical situation somebody has to get hurt.[11]

Love is interesting, but so is life, with the exception that one may seduce countless women, but one cannot seduce life—not often—because life, unlike a woman, strikes back at one logically.[12]

It is a cruel world and there is nothing you can do about it. Further, it is a cruel world and there is nothing you can do about your own character. Cheyney shows people whom the past has created. Thus Ernie gets fulfillment in knifing Nazis because as a boy he witnessed Germans raping his mother and killing her and his father. The cruder Freudian implications, naturally, are there just as they are present in some of Cheyney's other characters. Many of his people run along certain grooves which arbitrary circumstance has made for them. Rene Berg, for instance, falls among bootleggers and murderers in Chicago and this dictates his character as shown in *Dark Hero*. All this seems to demand that Cheyney depict an indifferent, mechanically arbitrary world in his books where chances for transcendence or traditional heroism are nil. But this is manifestly not the case. His novels are, in fact, romances in most senses of the word, and there exists no real pain, no real despair, no real people. There is an exit, and it is through the door of the American hard-boiled story.

Numerous forces produced the hard-boiled detective story in the U.S.: the Depression, prohibition, the tale of the American West, dime novel fiction and the genius of Hammett, Chandler and Joseph

Shaw. Beginning with Carroll J. Dailey's story "The False Burton Combs" in 1922, the hard-boiled detective story became the most important form of popular expression in America, spreading, as it did, into other genres like science fiction and the western. Hard-boiled stories began in pulp magazines like *The Black Mask*, but they quickly appeared as books and then films—Hollywood rapidly gathered both Chandler and Hammett to its bosom. Partly the hard-boiled story came from American literary antecedents and reflected social conditions in the United States. Partly, however, it was a revolt against the mannered artificiality of the British, Edwardian detective story which appeared on both sides of the Atlantic with writers like R. Austin Freeman and Arthur B. Reeve. It rejects the heavy stress put on logic and minutiae in these stories (what came to be known as the "crossword" element) and in its stead puts a bumptious anti-intellectualism, and a stress on action and character. Thus Captain Shaw, the editor of *The Black Mask*, wrote to Horace McCoy that "My impression is that you agreed that it would have a stronger punch to a character to have his strength brought out by his acts rather than by the writer's statement."[13] As it evolved in the hands of writers like Hammett, Chandler, Whitfield, Gardner and the like, the hard-boiled story had certain clearly-marked characteristics: 1) it dealt with sordid crime and slimy people; 2) it tended to elevate the detective not only above the criminal but above ordinary citizens as well; 3) it dealt with violence, but violence which was choreographed and unrealistic in its impact; 4) it stressed the work ethic, personal integrity, as well as other romantic motives; 5) it brought popular fiction closer to a real picture of human sexuality but nonetheless skirted explicitness or complete frankness; 6) it stressed action over thought; 7) it evolved a hero notable for his courage, stamina and persistence; 8) it developed a dialogue filled with colorful slang and witty retorts; 9) it communicated through a writing style which was terse and understated; 10) it stressed stoic resignation to the harshness and inbecility of people and events. Ultimately the hard-boiled story contains no more substantial realism than any other popular form, and it brims with fuzzy thinking and thematic contradiction. But it is striking, especially to a culture which is unlike that of the United States.

Hard-boiled stories and their celluloid progeny, hard-boiled gangster films, made a considerable impact on Britain. The British accorded literary status to Chandler and Hammett long before they gained it in the States. As early as 1927 Dorothy Sayers could allude to *The Black Mask* (in *Unnatural Death*,) with some confidence that her readers would know what she was talking about. During the late twenties and early thirties the American gangster joined the American millionaire as a stock character in British popular fiction.

Enter Peter Cheyney. Cheyney had never visited the U.S. and knew very little about the country, its laws, people, institutions or language. His fiction contains, for Americans, lots of real groaners: in *Dark Bahama,* for instance, he has an American private detective refer to "Red Indians," which is equivalent to having a Britisher mention "French fries," and in the same novel he uses the "State Line of Miami" as the jurisdictional limit of the State Police. Come, on, though. Let's be fair. Rather than these niceties, Cheyney is really interested in tommy guns, prohibition, gangsters, the FBI and hard-boiled detectives. Starting with his first Lemmie Caution novel through *G. Men at the Yard* (1953), Cheyney brought American characters, ambience and language (as he created them) to British readers, showing how American detectives and gangsters think, work and talk.

American connections also form a substantive part of Cheyney's spy novels. Michael Kells, the hero of *Sinister Errand* and *Ladies Won't Wait,* is half-American; Rene Berg, the hero of *Dark Hero,* goes from the Ozarks to gangland Chicago to British Naval Intelligence; *Dark Bahama* takes place, in part, in Miami; and Ernie Guelvada's diction (as Cheyney points out every time he introduces him) is an odd concatenation which includes dollops of American slang interjections like "You're telling me!" and "baby," "hey" and "goddamn."

The imitation of the hard-boiled detective story and its transfer to the spy novel gives Cheyney his historical signifcance. Without this gimmick he would simply be another third-rate, no-talent hack. Thus it is important that we look at the particular ways in which Cheyney uses conventions from the hard-boiled tradition in his spy books.

1. *Clearly Cheyney's spy novels deal with sordid events and slimy people.* His villains, Nazis and Communists all, do bad things. They kidnap, torture and kill people. Cheyney, though, shows their moral perversion largely by labelling them as Nazis and Communists. During and directly after the war this technique was sufficient to establish evil in the popular mind, and Cheyney justifies his heroes' use of the same methods (kidnapping, etc.) on the grounds that these animals deserve a dose of their own medicine, and also to counter the idea that the war was being ineptly prosecuted because of a traditional British sense of law, decency and fair play. Quite the same sort of logic turns up a bit later in Spillane's

detective novels like *I, the Jury* (1947).

2. *Cheyney shows his agents to be superior to ordinary citizens.* Cheyney's spies know things which ordinary people do not know and which, if they did know them, would scare their pants off. The population of the average novel resembles what one finds under a rock: the cocktail parties in *Dark Duet* and *Dark Wanton*, for instance, crawl with loathsome, empty people. Even the folks who are supposed to be normal pale in significance when compared to the spy. Thus in *The Stars are Dark* Greeley considers that "...three quarters of the people in England didn't even realize the lengths that the Germans would go to in order to win the war—or the length to which people like Quale and the ones above him *had* to go in order to stop 'em from winning it."[14] Theirs is a heroic service. It requires self-sacrifice, unheralded and unrewarded, for if agents get caught doing illegal things they must answer to the law made for ordinary people. This is the case in Cheyney's books before, during and after the war.

3. *Cheyney's novels depict violence but minimize its impact.* Erle Stanley Gardner, in "The Case of the Early Beginnings," relates a conversation which he had had with a man who was actually beaten up by thugs: he could not do anything for the three months he spent in the hospital. In *Dark Interlude*, which I cited above, Nazis work over O'Mara who, additionally, has debilitated himself physically in order to fit the role he is playing. Yet after the torture he gallivants around the countryside, gets a few bandages and then traipses off again. Either he received a pretty sissy beating or the whole thing is moonshine. The same is true of gun play. Here, for example, is one of the murders from *Dark Hero*: "He fired once. The glass made an odd sound as it smashed on the cement floor. Berg looked at the man as he lay on the floor. There was a surprised expression on his face."[15] Real violence, phooie! Truncated passages like this one portray very little of the real scene of violent death. And Cheyney describes most deaths this way, although he does sometimes mention blood and allows the victim a brief death-rattle. Violence does not appear in Cheyney's novels to tell us anything about real violence; it appears in order to show the heroes' nonchalance and toughness.

4. *Cheyney's heroes do their jobs.* Their jobs, in fact, define these people and they worry that without them they would be rootless, aimless and useless. We can see explicitly in *Dark Interlude*:

Actually, his reaction to the events since the arrival of the woman Tanga in the afternoon was one of relief. In effect, the things that had happened were good for

O'Mara, inasmuch as he had ceased to think about himself, the effects of alcohol, the general depressions of the last months. He was concerned with more important things. He was working. He was in effect once more O'Mara.[16]

Work makes the man. No hewers of informational wood or drawers of political water, Cheyney's agents need real international hostilities, war hot or cold, to survive. Greeley makes this point to Quale in *The Stars Are Dark:*

" 'You wait till this bleedin' war's over, Mister Quayle. It'll be so peaceful that a lot of us won't even know what we're doing. We shall feel lost.' "[17]

They will be lost without the opportunity for excitement, and for Cheyney (he admits it in most of the books) excitement exists only when a man hazards his life.

5. *Cheyney does bring in a particular view of sexuality, but one which is neither real nor explicit.* Being the son of a successful corset maker, Cheyney gave his male heroes an eye for the female form, but I've got to add, not its content. Without exposing their sexual fantasies or compiling detailed anatomical descriptions, Cheyney makes his heroes appreciate the female body. In pubs, for instance, Ernie Guelvada invariably asks for a drink from a bottle on a top shelf so that the barmaid will have to reach to get it and thereby show off her figure. Although on the level of pure plot women often serve as conscientious agents, in general Cheyney does not acknowledge this until the end of the book—as with Janey in *Sinister Errand* or Aurora in *Dark Wanton.* Look at the titles of some of Cheyney's detective books: *Dames Don't Care* (1937), *You Can't Hit a Woman* (1937), *Can Ladies Kill?* (1938), *Dangerous Curves* (1939), *I'll Say She Does.* Women's chief use in the detective novels and the spy books derives from being betrayers or potential betrayers. He cannot, therefore, tell us who the good ones are until the end of the book. Female villains, though, appear often in Cheyney's books. He fits them into his general use of realism (which, in effect, boils down to introducing unpleasant things) and in a number of places he introduces women with zestfully unhealthy drives: for instance in *Dark Wanton* he shows the sexual thrill which a woman gets while watching men pommel one another, and in *Ladies Won't Wait* two women separately confess to Kells that women in general love to be beaten by their lovers. On one level, therefore, Cheyney writes more frankly than do previous writers about sexual matters in that he does bring sex into the books, but on another level he is neither as pruriently descriptive of sexuality as, say, Spillane, nor as sensitive to women's natures as, well, almost anyone else. With Cheyney it is safe to say that a little learning of

Freud is a dangerous thing.

6. *Cheyney consistently stresses action over thought.* When it comes to delineating characters' minds, Cheyney is actively anti-intellectual. In *The Stars are Dark* we get these two representative examples: " 'Greeley was right. The great thing was not to think. Thinking, said Greeley, got you nowhere',"[18] and " 'You're beginning to indulge in self-analysis—the first sign of an inferiority complex'."[19] In the institutional framework of espionage, Cheyney's agents do their jobs without thinking because thought would be a detriment to action as well as a sign of mushy-headedness. The same holds true on the level of action of plot. Although, as I have noted, Cheyney does include remnants of the detective tradition in his novels, as in *Sinister Errand* where the hero repeatedly mulls over the facts of the situation, his plots stress movement. As Kells points out in the same novel—" '...just go right ahead and take a smash at everything that got in the way. The process can be damned interesting—especialy if somebody takes a smash at you first'."[20] Consequently Cheyney's spy novels move from the clump of murders at the beginning to the clump of murders in the middle to the clump of murders at the end. Within this framework, Cheyney equates locomotion with ratiocination, and his heroes either pace and think or they agree with Kells, this time in *Ladies Won't Wait:* "If I have to think—and I don't profess to be very fond of the process—I'd rather think...in the Jaguar than anyplace else."[21]

7. *Cheyney bases his characterization on courage, stamina and persistence.* Yes. To go on to belabor this would be repetitious and obvious. Suffice it to say that Cheyney's favorite word is "tough" and he repeats it with wearisome persistence.

8. *Slang and witty repartee form the basis of the dialogue in Cheyney's books.* Wit, of course, is relative. We've already seen Cheyney's use of slang and wit in the passage from *I'll Say She Does.* In the spy books, slang, as I've already suggested, comes in most often with Ernie Guelvada: "He would think in pedantic—or what is considered correct—English, or in English interlarded with slang and Americanisms that he had learned from the moving pictures."[22] We get O'Mara's speech spiced with "boyo's," Kells identifies himself in one instance as Santa Claus, Ernie pops in a few "babies" and "heys." Cheyney tries to rise to the occasion, but ultimately he cannot write snappy dialogue in the manner of Beeding or Coles.

9. *Cheyney tries to write terse, elliptical prose.* Reviewing the passages which I have quoted so far, readers can see the lavish use of ellipses, dashes, short sentences and repeated sentence structure.

Rather than being craftsmanlike imitation of Hammett, however, this probably resulted from Cheyney dictating his novels. Harrison, in *Peter Cheyney, Prince of Hokum* (1954), quotes the following remarks from Allan Sinclair: "And over the fire, I said, 'Peter, you can't write for nuts; but you are the best story-teller I've ever listened to. Why don't you get yourself a Dictaphone and tell your stories straight to it?' "[23] If this is what Cheyney did we cannot impute stylistic matters to Cheyney but to the typist who transcribed the Dictaphone cylinders. Suffice it to say that one does not look for sophisticated, subtle or interesting style in Cheyney's books.

I have already dealt with stoic resignation, so we will leave out number ten. There is, however, one other possible influence of the hard-boiled story which makes all the difference in Cheyney's spy world. In Hammett's Continental Op stories and novels (*The Red Harvest* [1929] and *The Dain Curse* [1929]), the Op does not act as an independent agent. The Old Man, the manager of the Continental Detective Agency, orders the Op to investigate messes and he expects results and not whining excuses. He sits in the background, stays at the office and sends agents out into a cruel world. Now, in Hammett the Old Man acts only in the framework of the stories, illustrating perhaps a minor point about authority or anti-authority. With Cheyney it is different. The authority figure, Quayle, Fenton or (get this) the Old Man, is the real hero of the novels and most of the character and thematic impulses point to him. He does not act himself but acts through his agents; he plans and thinks.

Cheney devotes practically half of *The Stars are Dark* to Quayle silently suffering for his agents, for their risks and their deaths. He, however, does not have to stoically accept harsh reality because he can marshal people and create events so as to change situations for the good of the whole. He uses violence and violent people to remake the world. Christlike and benign—okay, he does get a bit grumpy at times—the authority figure provides justification for the fact that the agents of good use the same means as the agents of evil. It is a case of my boss is right and yours is not. It is also, perhaps, an extension into his fiction of Cheyney's political beliefs. Before the war, Cheyney was a member of Oswald Mosley's British Union of Fascists, and this manifests itself in Cheyney's high valuation on discipline and order.

Cheyney's literal Fascism may also be the cause behind the sexism and racism consciously or unconsciously displayed in the books. Cheyney almost always introduces pairs of heroes in his spy books: one is the agent and romantic lead and the other is the killer.

The killers in most cases are foreigners. Ernie, Cheyney's chief assassin, is Belgian, and Salvatini, in *Ladies Won't Wait*, is Italian. Kane, Fells, Kerr, Frewin, Iles and, to a lesser extent, Kells and O'Mara, function as or are upper-class Englishmen who are capable of leadership and have a touch of finer sensibilities. Kane, for example, in *Dark Duet*, wants to take the chief Nazi agent back to England for trial, but Ernie steps in and insists on murdering him. I do not, however, want to suggest that Cheyney's killers appear as social outcasts like Fawn in LeCarré's books. Cheyney presents them as happy, contented, likeable people. Indeed, Ernie Guelvada is the most likable and memorable of Cheyney's spy characters.

Cheyney imbues all his characters, the agents and the killers, with heavy doses of romance, and if they are outcasts from society, they are Byronic or better yet, Shelleyean outcasts who serve society which would revile them but which would be crushed under the jackboot of tyranny without them. In spite of the superficial and naive stabs at violence, sexuality and realism, Cheyney is at root a romantic writer who always opts for the successful hero and the happy ending. His real importance comes from the conventions which he borrowed and half-naturalized—the elements of the hard-boiled story. Ultimately his novels are worth very little, but without Cheyney and his broad popularity in the forties and fifties, Ian Fleming's novels would have only part of their content, Deighton would have lost much of his nameless hero, and LeCarré would have had less to react against.

NOTES

[1]*I'll Say She Does* (New York: Dodd, Mead, 1946), p. 10.
[2]*The Urgent Hangman* (New York: Dodd, Mead, 1952), p. 75.
[3]*Dark Duet* (New York: Beagle, 1971), p. 62.
[4]*Sinister Errand* (London: Collins, 1945), p. 38.
[5]*Dark Duet*, p. 7.
[6]*Dark Duet*, p. 9.
[7]*The Stars are Dark* (New York: Dodd, Mead, 1943), p. 107.
[8]*The Stars are Dark*, p. 121.
[9]*Ladies Won't Wait* (New York: Dodd, Mead, 1951), p. 21.
[10]*Dark Duet*, p. 15.
[11]*The Stars are Dark*, p. 32.
[12]*Dark Bahama* (New York: Beagle, 1971), p. 140.
[13]As quoted in Donald K. Adams, *The Mystery and Detection Annual—1972* (Beverly Hills: Adams, 1972), p. 146.
[14]*The Stars are Dark*, p. 74.

[15]*Dark Hero* (London: Collins, 1946), p. 124.
[16]*Dark Interlude* (London: Collins, 1947), p. 50.
[17]*The Stars are Dark,* p. 178.
[18]*The Stars are Dark,* p. 118.
[19]*The Stars are Dark,* p. 126.
[20]*Sinister Errand,* p. 23.
[21]*Ladies Won't Wait* p. 25.
[22]*Dark Duet* , p. 19.
[23]Michael Harrison, *Peter Cheyney, Prince of Hokum* (London: Spearman, 1954), p. 265.

Chapter 12
Manning Coles
(1899-1965; 1891-1959)

ADELAIDE FRANCIS OKE MANNING and Cyril Henry Coles together wrote twenty six novels using the pseudonym Manning Coles and five novels which first appeared under the pseudonym of Francis Gaite.[1] The Gaite books, beginning with *Brief Candles* (1954), are what passed as comic novels in the early fifties and need not overly concern us here. The Manning Coles novels, however, are all, roughly speaking, spy books, and we need to look at them to see both the promise and the failure of the form during and directly after World War II. Coles' novels promise to provide a popular yet realistic brand of the spy book which would knife through some of the sillier conventions which had attached to it, and they promise to carry on the buoyant fictional tone of the twenties and thirties into the post war world. Yet in both areas Coles fails to deliver the goods. As one novel follows another, rousing action grinds into repetition and cliches, and real wit disappears leaving only a light tone in its stead. Coles, likewise, leaves behind any attempt at realism after 1942. Perhaps to his credit, Manning Coles never adopts the violence and stridency of Cheyney or Spillane, but what remains is an eviscerated form hobbling along because it still provides steady income for the writer, because he could not breathe originality into his favorite techniques, and because no one else had shown how to write a spy story in the world of post-war Britain.

Coles' first novel, *Drink to Yesterday* (1940), is not auspicious as a fictional structure. It tells a story of espionage during the First World War, mainly by means of separable episodes: the spies steal papers, murder a German scientist reputed to be breeding cholera germs, and burn down some important zeppelin hangars. The book holds together because it contains an intermittently introduced threat of the spies' exposure by a big-wig in German intelligence, and because its main action is framed by a murder trial in the thirties which asks and then covers up questions about a contemporary death, but, most importantly, the book holds readers' attention because it says some important things about the impact of espionage upon individuals' lives. *Drink to Yesterday* tells the story of Michael Kingston, who is snatched out of the front lines to serve in British Intelligence. Here he becomes the partner and student of the jocular Tommy Hambledon, who takes Kingston into Germany to spy on the enemy's heartland. These two play dirty tricks on the Germans, but they quickly find out that they are no fun. Their ethical dilemma comes when they murder Amtenbrink, a gentle, retired scientist whom they believe to be experimenting on cholera germs to be dropped on London. Antenbrink, however, specifically refused to do this inhuman work, and Kingston and Hambledon learn later that they have murdered a likeable, courageous, and innocent man. This starts to bore into Kingston's conscience. The continuing struggle for Kingston, however, is the harrowing secrecy and isolation of his job. Although he secretly married early in the novel, he cannot tell his wife the nature of his war work and this, inevitably, leads to bitterness, estrangement and loneliness. Coles contends that an intelligence agent sells his soul, and even after the war anonymity is imposed upon him because of his past as a spy. Kingston finds some peace after the war, running a garage in the English provinces, but in the thirties an enemy from his past hunts him down and murders him. Now, much of this is nonsensical and melodramatic, positing a world which, to our minds, never existed. But the vague urge toward realism is there too. We can see some of this in the objectivity and sympathy directed toward German soldiers and civilians. Coles also tackles the cliches of the popular spy story. Tommy teaches Kingston that neither physical disguise nor secret codes not fastidious planning has any place in the field agent's life. *Bull-Dog Drummond*, as usual for this sort of attack, comes in for its share of abuse. Thus, just before his death Kingston sits down for a spot of light reading:

He carried his tray into his sitting-room and read, while he was eating, a book the doctor had lent him called *Bulldog Drummond*. How delightfully easy the career of an Intelligence agent would be if only life were a little more like that!
One went about upon entirely unlawful occasions armed with automatics and never, never met a policeman at the wrong moment.[2]

This is not Kingston's world—although it would become Tommy Hambledon's world in the later novels. The hero's death receives only an official cover-up from an ungrateful government. He does not even receive a letter from the General—Haig, not Washington—as Cooper's spy did.

Coles made only one attempt to follow-up this fictional blend of realism and sentiment. Although *This Fortress* (1942) contains espionage elements, its focus lies elsewhere. The book describes the impact of Nazi bombing raids on Westerly, a small village in Hampshire, and its inhabitants. Its frame story, the tale of Tom Langrish's love affair with a German woman shortly after the First World War, exists largely to display Nazi-German arrogance. We do, though, find some limited spy business in the novel, which turns mostly on irony and sentiment. In the course of an accidental bombing raid on Westerly, George Matthews sacrifices his life to rescue two children from a bombed house. Matthews is, however, a German spy who oriented the bombing raid by directional radio. Ignorant of this fact, the townspeople subscribe enough money to pay for the construction of a Spitfire which they insist the Air Corps christen "George Matthews." *This Fortress*, however, has little but historical interest and it was the last attempt which Coles made at realism or sober themes. In all the subsequent books he turned to adventure and comedy.

By and large, Coles' novels teeter on the edge of the spy genre and some of them tip into the area of the simple adventure story or the gangster yarn. With the exception of *This Fortress*, first of all, Coles puts very little political orientation or dogma into his books. Of course he gives his villains the appropriate political labels for the times: Nazis in *Toast to Tomorrow* (1940), *They Tell No Tales* (1941), *Without Lawful Authority* (1943), *Green Hazard* (1945) and *The Fifth Man* (1946); Neo-Nazis in *Let the Tiger Die* (1948) and *Now or Never* (1952); and Communists in a whole raft of novels such as *Dangerous by Nature* (1950), *Alias Uncle Hugo* (1953) and *No Entry* (1958). We can, however, pretty much interchange the bad guys in the books since Coles makes absolutely no attempt to describe or delineate the political tags of the villains. The counterpart to this is Coles' indifference to describing national political or economic conditions. *Alias Uncle Hugo* and *No Entry* both take place in communist countries, but beyond a few *pro forma* descriptions, particularly in the later novel, of the hard life under the totalitarian jack boot, these books could have been set anywhere. The same holds true for the experience in Franco's Spain in *A Knife for the Juggler* (1953); there is no political comment.

Coles' setting provides geographical obstacles as well as some universal human institutions, like police forces, which he needs to work the adventure plot. In large measure, the political or economic ideologies of the host countries make no difference at all. On the level of basic plot motivation, too, Coles has only the most superficial interest in political or ideological tiffs between or within states. Thus, Coles' plots vary from those having no discernible espionage interest, like *Diamonds to Amsterdam* (1950) which involves manufacturing artificial diamonds and murder, to those having an espionage interest tacked on, like *Crime in Concrete* (1960) where Tommy Hambledon tracks down a gang of crooks which, in the past, has dealt in international secrets, to those plots in which espionage issues dominate and color characters and incidents, like *Now or Never* which deals with a neo-Nazi cell, Martin Borman, and an attempt to revive the bad old guys through Hitler's son. Totting them up, I find that most of Coles' plots belong in category two; that is, these are novels which should have and would have been written and classed as thriller detective stories thirty years earlier, but Coles makes them spy novels because he perceived that the spy hero was displacing the detective hero as the popular center of adventure interest.

Coles wrote only a limited number of plots and then reproduced them again and again. These are: the behind the lines plot, the capture/escape plot and the Black Gang plot. From *Drink to Yesterday*, Coles wrote a number of novels about English agents working behind enemy lines. The early behind the lines novels—*Drink to Yesterday, Toast to Tomorrow, Green Hazard*—break down into separable episodes in which the hero (Tommy Hambledon, exclusively, after the first novel) does sundry acts of sabotage to irk and annoy the Nazis. In the later books of this type—*Alias Uncle Hugo* and *No Entry*—Coles eliminates the structural weakness of episodic plotting by having the hero travel for almost half the novel, and he gives him one definite mission to fulfill: in both cases Hambledon must rescue a young man who is trapped in communist territory. Even though the late books of this type show a more reasoned construction, Coles uses the same source to suppy the power for all the behind the lines plots. The secret service hero in all these books impersonates some well-known individual. His disguise is one of identity which rests on psychology and false papers rather than a disguise of appearance built of fake hair, false stomach and the cosmetician's pharmocopoeia. Coles works the plot around suspense in that lurking somewhere just off stage is someone who can identify the hero or who is intent on demonstrating that he is a spy. Thus, in *Toast for Tomorrow* Tommy Hambledon's fingerprints are on file from the First World War and all that Dr. Goebbels needs to do is to ring up the record office in order to pin the hero in his specimen case. The hero is, in every case, too nimble to let this happen.

Coles' second stock plot is the traditional adventure fiction gambit of capture and escape which is motivated and framed by a criminal investigation. *Not Negotiable* (1949) is a typical example. Here Tommy looks into the distribution of banknotes forged during the war by the Nazis. Letord of the *Surete* occasionally assists him, just as Bagshott of the Yard helps out in the books set in England. Tommy beards the villains in their hide-out, but they capture him. With Letord's help he escapes and collars one of the crooks, but he, shortly, escapes. The Belgian police arrest Hambledon and then release him. At this juncture, the crooks take to kidnapping one another and they bag Tommy and toss him into a cellar. The police arrive, catch the cooks and, in the space of one paragraph, the hero solves, explains and concludes the complex international plot, now taken over by the communists, to destroy the West by flooding it with funny money. Change the details and this is the plot of many of Coles' books: *The Man in the Green Hat* (1955), *The Basle Express* (1956), *Crime in Concrete* (1960) or *Search for a Sultan* (1961). In each case, movement and the character of the hero, real and alleged, are the chief elements in these novels. Coles' books are peculiar in their construction: none of the novels cited above, or indeed any of Coles' books, has much of a denouement. When the action stops, the book stops. Coles refuses to taper things off before the end: he does not elaborate on or tie up the grains of motive which he gives to individuals or groups, he does not have to marry off subsidiary heroes or heroines, since, with the exception of Forgan and Campbell, none appears, and he does not have to round off the hero's character because the hero's character never needs explanation. Coles believes that his readers want only action and he amputates his books so that they do not whimper off dealing with human concerns at the end.

The last important plotting pattern in Coles' novels we can, after Sapper's book with the same title, call the Black Gang plot. In spite of the dig at Sapper's *Bull-Dog Drummond* cited above, a good deal of Sapper works its way into Coles' novels. Take, for instance, *A Knife for the Juggler*. Here the nominal villain (nominal in that he is really a good and sympathetic character in spite of the fact that he disrupts East-West relations) goes about kidnapping communists and sending them off to an island off the coast of South America where they will be forced to live a literal and harsh version of their utopian fantasy. This comes directly from Sapper's *The Black Gang*. Sapper bases *The Black Gang* on the premise that vigilante action works much better than the official machinery of law enforcement in dealing with real criminals, so Hugh and his chums round up nasty people and either send them to the police or ship them off to their island to work in the "workers' paradise." Coles repeats the essentials of Sapper's plot first in *Without Lawful Authority* where Warnford and Marden phone in tips to the police and deliver spies to Whitehall or Scotland Yard. Quite the same thing happens in *With Intent to Deceive* (1947) where Hyde, Selkirk, Forgan and Campbell send packets of villains to Scotland Yard. *Night Train to Paris* virtually repeats this book, and the plot gets its final run-through in *Death of an Ambassador* (1957). Coles works this sort of plot rather better than the capture and escape plot in that, except for *Death of an Ambassador*, he does not have to keep up the pretense of a mystery. Coles' mysteries are puerile, intentionally so, in that he wishes to do nothing to offend or befuddle his readers. *Without Lawful Authority*, *With Intent to Deceive* and *Night Train to Paris* all have split narratives so that the readers more or less simultaneously watch the vigilantes and the police. This rids us of the mystery and it speeds up the pace of the action.

Dealing as he does with traditional plots, Coles' most conspicuous failure comes in not meeting the first criterion of most adventure plots—the villain. None of Coles' novels has a real villain. The novels are supposed to have villains, but in every respect that counts, they do not. The single element which enables Buchan, Sapper, Beeding and the rest to run their capture and escape plots is the Master Criminal, the King Spy, the Nemesis to all right-thinking-and-living folks. This antagonist plots the evil, dispatches his troglodytes, suavely argues with the hero, and does lots of other things. These writers do not always believe in him, but they use the Master Crook to make their plots work. Now, Coles does bring Master Criminals and their gangster toadies into his books, regularly. A mysterious individual named "The Boss" figures in *They Tell No Tales*, and, at the other end of the chronology, a wicked emir stands behind the shenanigans in *Search for a Sultan*. The problem is, though, that Coles holds these people offstage until the last extremity of the plot, and we do not see them striving with the hero, or, indeed, doing much of anything. They whirl past in Coles' haste to snap the action of the plot shut. The villains' petty agents, gangsters, supplant the real villain in the readers' minds. This all indicates two possibilities: either Coles did not have much apprehension or appreciation of nightmare fantasy and thus could not detail it in the figure of a villain, or he recognized the absurdity of dusting off a creaky old cliche in the forties and the fifties. Whatever the reason, though, this illustrates Coles' timidity in that he could neither eliminate the Master Crook entirely nor present him as a fully developed character.

In all of Coles' most successful novels there exists more than a touch of the picaresque. This even holds true of the Francis Gaite books where we find, in the Latimer brothers, a pair of picaresque ghosts. The picaresque not only had real impact on Coles' characterization (which I will take up a bit later) but it also has a discernible impact upon plot. At mid-century we find several spy writers consciously turning to the picaresque in drawing their characters and plots, and bringing this element, which has always lingered in the background of the traditional adventure story, into its own. Household, for instance, deliberately introduces the picaresque into *Fellow Passenger,* Ambler uses it in the Arthur Simpson novels, and Coles returns to it again and again. To some extent, historical and artistic necessity forced this choice. After the war, spy writers, as we have seen with Coles, hesitated to return to the Master Crook fiction which so dominates spy fiction between the wars. Some writers, of course, could and did continue to organize their fictions around the conflict of the traditional hero and the Napoleon of Crime. Fleming, for instance, does it over and over again. Also, some British writers, tired of war-engendered violence, needed a formula which would give them movement and excitement, but which would minimize violence, which would avoid sententiousness and tough talk, and which would give scope to urbanity and comedy. The picaresque story seemed to provide these things. The picaresque story, traditionally, follows the actions of a rogue who travels about viewing different aspects of society, and who engages in escapes from situations which are, at once, dangerous and comic. Although, as I noted above, he could never quite relinquish the Master Criminal, Coles uses many elements of the picaresque to power his books. Most contain the *picaro*, the rogue, in the character of the hero, or in one of the subsidiary characters, and many parts of Coles' plots point to picaresque inspiration. Since Coles has nothing to say about social conditions or organization, we do not see much of them in the hero's travels. We do, however, see multitudinous travels, and the organization of episodes of capture and escape to fuse tension with comic absurdity. First of all, there is a great deal of travel in Coles' books: *Let the Tiger Die*, for instance, chases all over Europe from Scandinavia to Spain, and *Search for a Sultan* runs us from London to rural and urban France to Switzerland to North Africa. While bouncing around Europe, Coles' con-men heroes plan to outwit their enemies through farce or the author uses fate to arrange appropriate high jinks for them. Their captures and escapes as well as the ends which they arrange for the villains often have a boffo strain. In *Let the Tiger Die* British agents enter the scene disguised as fishmongers and save their chief by producing a fish filled with sneezing powder. *Knife for the Juggler* shows the same agents loosing a bus load of communist agitators on a riled up crowd of Spanish townspeople engaged in heated debate about fire engines. Two of the novels, *Without Lawful Authority* and *The Basle Express,* include scenes in lunatic asylums where the agents wander among comically bewildered inmates. *Search for a Sultan* shows Tommy being saved by a zany elephant trainer and his animal (probably drawn from Buchan's *The House of the Four Winds*) and in *The Basle Express* Tommy is repeatedly debagged by the villains and he is in the buff when he corners them at the end of the plot. Coles's comic incidents depend on physical embarrassment or introducing unexpected elements. They occur in series and in semi-detachable episodes. In short, they bring the picaresque to the spy novel as a method of plotting, governing tone and reducing tension. If Coles had been able to break with the thirties, this would have enabled him to write a new kind of spy novel; if he had been able to closely identify with the thirties it would have enabled him to produce books in the older vein. As it is the picaresque allowed Coles to write some reasonably amusing scenes and it helped him, a bit, to shape his characters.

Thomas "Tommy" Elphinstone Hambledon is the hero of all of Coles' spy novels, with the exception of *Drink to Yesterday* where he appears as a secondary character. He does not come into *This Fortress*, but this book is hardly a spy novel, even by Coles' loose definition. Tommy first enters as a schoolmaster turned spy in *Drink to Yesterday*. At the close of this novel he is missing, presumed drowned in the North Sea. In *Toast for Tomorrow,* however, he washes ashore in Germany, with a case of amnesia. Believing himself to be a German, Tommy lives and works in Germany between the wars. He joins the Nazi party and becomes Hitler's Chief of Police. Regaining his memory at the *Reichstag* fire, Tommy recommences spying on Germany. After escaping to England at the end of *Toast for Tomorrow,* he becomes a Secret Service ace, dashing off to help Scotland Yard with vaguely political cases, and scooting about the world to help the Foreign Secretary when he perceives cracks in the mortar of international relations. He ought to be reasonably feeble by the time of the last novel, 1961, but he never ages, never marries, never has a fixed household, never has an inner life, never, in fact, does anything other than be a spy hero.

Coles, pretty clearly, copied Hambledon from Beeding's Colonel Alistair "Toby" Granby. There are a number of similarities between the two: both men are short, active, devoted to a particular kind of comic diction, conscious of the absurd roles and conditions into which action thrusts them, and occasionally aware of their natures as fictional characters. Tommy Hambledon is the less vital of the two characters, and he grows more anemic in the books of the late fifites, but, then, Beeding's hero might have faded too if he were forced to deal with the nineteen fifties, and his creator might have altered his style if he had to write for the postwar reading public. Nevertheless, the hero's obscurantism (he frequently asserts his ignorance of the arts), the merely occasional nature of his wit, and Coles' conscious refusal to develop, however briefly, a circle of friends for the hero, show how the writer is incapable of reproducing the urbanity of the thirties, yet is incapable of giving it up to break new ground with character.

Coles does briefly develop two facets of Tommy's nature—his school teaching and his past in Germany between the wars. In *Drink to Yesterday, They Tell No Tales, Green Hazard, The Fifth Man* and *Among Those Absent* Coles provides Tommy with characters who function as assistants and students who learn from and admire the more experienced man. This is especially pronounced in the Bellair-Hambledon relationship in *They Tell No Tales,* probably created in order to compensate for Tommy's failure to convince Kingston about the spy's proper role in *Drink to Yesterday.* After *Among Those Absent,* in 1948, Coles does not substantially use the master-student pattern because he had decided to develop a wry sorcerer's apprentice relationship between Tommy and his new assistants, Forgan and Campbell. The later allusions to Tommy's past as a teacher, like those in *Alias Uncle Hugo,* have no real bearing on his character or on the plot. Just as Coles uses and then drops Tommy's past as a teacher, so does he develop and then forget the hero's German connection. In two novels, *Toast for Tomorrow* and *Green Hazard,* Tommy, in an assumed role, lives in Nazi Germany. There he forms relationships with two groups of Germans: he pals around with the piggishly jovial Goering and bumps into Goebbels and other Nazi officials, and he also forms real ties with average, anti-Nazi Germans—Reck, Fraulein Rademeyer and the Webbers. Coles' propagandistic purpose is pretty clear. He does, however, take Tommy's real German friends out of this framework and develop them as Tommy's family. The hero takes Reck back to England and his adopted mother, Fraulein Rademeyer, also escapes to England at the end of *Toast for Tomorrow.* It sounds very much as if Coles is going to develop them as Tommy's circle in the subsequent books: most writers who use series characters do this. Sayers develops the

Wimseys, Beeding develops the Granbys, Buchan develops the Hannays, etc. Reck appears in *They Tell No Tales* and Coles mentions Fraulein Rademeyer in the same novel, but then they disappear. Charles Denton, Tommy's fellow agent in the early novels, also passes into nonentity after a handful of novels. Quite the same thing happens with the hero's past in Germany. One would think that years of amnesia followed by years of playing a role on Hitler's staff would have considerable psychic impact. But it does not. In *Alias Uncle Hugo*, when Tommy chases around Berlin, the narrator leaves out the fact that at one time Tommy was the Chief of Police in this city. These refusals to engage any level of the hero's past point to a drastic about-face in Coles from *Drink to Yesterday*. Once Coles attempted to deal with people's psychic stress, felt when doing the job of the secret agent, but once was enough. In all the subsequent novels Coles wants to exclude from Tommy's character all elements from the past, events and people, which might interfere with his role as a picaresque adventure hero.

As he functions in Coles' novels, Hambledon plays both active and passive roles. He is, of course, the regular adventure hero in many of the books, being captured by and then escaping from the villains, or gavotting around behind the enemy's lines, throwing assorted monkey wrenches into his unsavory plans. In *Toast for Tomorrow* or *The Basle Express* or *Crime in Concrete* we see Tommy playing his active role. He is the secret service ace, and Denton describes him in this mode in *Toast for Tomorrow*:

He is certainly a star.... If I'd organized a mansized revolution in a foreign capital city and it had 'gone wrong a little' as he puts it, I should bolt at once. Not he. He opens the door to callers, with a gun in each of his pockets, and waits 'till the storm subsides.[3]

Hambledon is a tough proposition, and his mental attitudes go along with his demeanor. Whenever he justifies his role as an agent, which he does more frquently in the early novels, he does so in terms of vengeance. *Toast for Tomorrow*, for instance, runs as much on finding and killing Kingston's murderer as it does on undermining Nazi rule. Tommy's concern for vengeance, moreover, is never cool and detached. He says this to the happily conniving Ulseth in *Green Hazard*: "The time will come when you will regret this. Look at this room again a moment, look at me, and remember this scene when you die screaming."[4] Ulseth, indeed, provokes Tommy by trying to blow him to bits, but Coles, much later, shows the hero, after the heat of the moment has passed, planning and executing a plan to smash and kill Ulseth who shows himself to be jovial and almost pathetically human. This is a hard man. As the adventure hero, though, Tommy only plans small episodes. In general he drifts along with events, relying not only upon his own skills but also, clearly, depending upon fate. One of his catch phrases is "some situation will doubtless present itself," and it always does. This attitude, moreover, not only places Tommy in a line with heroes like Buchan's Hannay who get continual legs up from Providence, but it also relieves the author of the burden of scrupulously planning sequences of events and chains of motivation. The hero's role as adventure hero appears in both Coles' early and late novels, but it is not the only role which Tommy fills.

In about half the novels Tommy functions as a passive observer, participating in the substantial spy action at the end of the action if at all. *Without Lawful Authority, With Intent to Deceive, Diamonds to Amsterdam* and *Night Train to Paris*, to cite only a few examples, show the nominal hero, Tommy Hambledon, doing little beyond commenting on the actions and antics of other characters who do the spy work and make the plots run. Coles turns to this side of Tommy, the passive side, for a couple of reasons. First, although Tommy is not overtly fastidious about the law, police rules, the sanctity of private property, and so on, Coles does make him a government official who cannot engage in the sort of mayhem, allegedly necessary for justice and security, which occurs in most of the novels, so this gets shifted to surrogates pretty quickly, and its delegation to others corresponds with a damping down of the hero's thirst for vengeance. Secondly, Coles does not wish to turn Tommy into a plain detective character, and, consequently, in the books which focus largely upon crime, the hero simply follows the police around. Finally, Coles wished to produce broader comic effects in his spy novels, and eventually decided that, in spite of his leaning in this direction, it would be better to shift much of the funny business from Tommy to Forgan and Campbell.

Running through both Tommy's active and passive incarnations, Coles frquently reminds readers that Tommy is part con-man, part rogue, part picaro. This enters most concertedly for the first time in *Green Hazard* where Coles introduces an abundance of confidence tricks. Here Tommy peddles snake oil to the Nazis in the form of a non-existent explosive, playing the role of Ulseth, while the real Ulseth, himself a con man, works his own scam in another part of Berlin using Tommy's assumed name. Coles makes the connection between the con-man and the spy in any number of places. In *The Fifth Man* Tommy himself makes the point: "I always say that confidence tricksters are good Intelligence agents gone wrong. I should have made a passable con man myself, but the career has its drawbacks."[5] Indeed, Cobden, who is a professional con man working in tandem with Tommy in *Among those Absent* (which has no spy connection), tells the hero that "you ought to be the con man, not me."[6] This linking of the spy hero to the confidence man opens up several lines of exploration. The con man deals in illusions just as the agent does: one sells shares in nonexistent corporations and the other sells plans for nonexistent weapons or strategies. Coles largely ignores this role except for a superficial treatment in *All that Glitters* (1954), and, of course, *Green Hazard*, since he has no real interest in the nuts and bolts of espionage. But there are other connections between the con man and the spy. The confidence trickster's wares, just like secret agent's, have a short life-span: the pigeon quickly discovers that he has been had, and the spy's bogus information is unstable and volatile. Both professions, therefore, depend upon the quick sale and the first train out of town. This motive underlies the movement in *Alias Uncle Hugo* where Tommy pretends to be Commissar Peskoff, speeds off the next day, sells Ordzinov's corpse to a bewildered platoon of Russian soldiers, and then drops into the role of Hugo Blitz. It all depends on wit, timing, bluff, daring and fast reflexes—qualifications for the shell game or for Coles' brand of secret agent.

Tommy finds that he can talk, think or bluster his way around most hayseed Continental officials. Because Coles does not deal with character, we do not find any cunning assessments of people's weaknesses, something else which ties the con man with the picaresque spy. Instead he occasionally fixes on the spiel: the con man-spy's ability to talk persuasively and at length on any given topic. To this Coles adds the sentimental myth that the con man realizes the comic potential of his profession and his relationships with people. From this and from the con man's patter come Tommy's diction.

Tommy Hambledon is no Bertie Wooster or Peter Wimsey or Toby Granby. For any number of reasons, including the level of his intended audience, Coles does not, and perhaps cannot, consistently build up a self-consciously comic diction for his hero. But he does try to do it intermittently. When he tries to give Tommy comic speech, Coles, like Wodehouse or Sayers or Beeding, usually starts with some sort of literary allusion, as in this passage from *The Fifth Man*:

"...the end of the interview would open the door of a concentration camp, or more likely"—Hambledon levelled an imaginary rifle—"bang, bang! Bury me this carrion. Is that a quotation from Shakespeare?"

"I don't know," said Bagshott, "But—"

"I can't account for it," said Hambledon, "but I often say things that sound to me like Shakespeare. You know—"

"What you mean," interrupted the chief inspector, "is that these Nazis are so untrustworthy themselves that they can't trust anybody else."

"Precisely. Untrust begets untrust, and liars lies. There I go again; it even scans."[7]

Over the long haul, however, Coles does not put many comic literary references into Tommy's speech. He tries to create the illusion that his hero quotes literature, as in the mention of Tommy's quoting in *Dangerous by Nature* (1950), but this has no basis in the rest of the novels. Instead of carrying out the comic potential of the quoting hero, Coles more often works on the comic potential of the mixed metaphor, as in these two examples from *Without Lawful Authority*. In the first Tommy reads a letter from *The Times*:

" 'What ... is England coming to? Once the door-ever-open to the by-inordinately-despotic-governments-oppressed stranger, now the loathsome trail of a more-than-Nazi tyranny bars the entry of a—' "

"Can a trail bar an entry?"[8]

and a bit later he whimsically indulges in the same sort of thing:

"They are beginning to explore stones and turn avenues and all that, to see if we can find a ground for mutual agreement to start talks on."[9]

This sort of reference stays with Tommy's speech through a number of books. In addition to the literary allusions and the mixed metaphors, Coles gives Tommy other standard tricks of comic speech. In *The Fifth Man* we can witness an example of the comic series:

"Those two escaped prisoners ... have fairly roused the country, believe me. Home Guards called out, fire watchers, Farmer Giles with a double-barrelled gun, old Uncle Tom Cobley and the Wurzel-Under-Slug Town Band."[10]

Here we speed from the believable to Uncle Tom Cobley from the folk song "Widdecombe Fair" to the patently absurd place name. In *Diamonds to Amsterdam* we get a passage of absurd invention:

"Such as visiting cards or a silver cigarette case presented to Mr. Albert Jenkins by the Red Lion branch of the Sons of Suction to commemorate the occasion when he balanced a pint pot on his nose for a record period of five minutes, twenty and one fifth seconds."[11]

Coles, as these excerpts witness, can write competent comic diction and he knows most of the tricks of the trade. In many ways he brings to mind Chandler's remark about Milne's *The Red House Mystery:* "It is an agreeable book, light, amusing in the *Punch* style, written with deceptive smoothness that is not as easy as it looks."[12] This style has an impact on the character of the hero. It makes him seem witty, ingenious, detached from life's follies and tragedies, and very much alert to his environment: after all, one cannot comment on the minutiae and intricacies of speech without being aware of the rest of the environment—ideally. The problem is that Coles lacks consistency and purpose here as elsewhere. Some of the books have more comic diction than others which have only a light tone. Especially in the later books Coles forgets that Tommy ever had a peculiar diction and even in the early novels Tommy's diction is not unique. Other characters speak precisely the same way, down to identical allusions. The Wurzel-Under-Slug passage quoted above comes, not from Tommy, but from a Nazi spy operating in England, a character whom Coles does not in other respects develop. It would be kindest to suggest that Coles was trying to move Tommy out of the witty insouciance of the detective and spy heroes of the twenties. Perhaps, though, it would be truer to suggest that Coles simply did not care about development or consistency.

When Coles wrote *With Intent to Deceive* (1947) he intended to focus on the old initiation story and center on an innocuous bungler named, heavy-handedly, James Hyde. He developed for this story two minor characters who help Hyde to evade the police and visit vengeance on the gangsters. In these two characters, William Forgan and Alexander Campbell, Coles realized that he had new characters possessed of comic potential and adventure utility, so he developed them and used them in a number of novels (*Let the Tiger Die, Now or Never, A Knife for the Juggler, The Man in the Green Hat, Crime in Concrete* and *Search for a Sultan*). Whenever Forgan and Campbell appear, Tommy's role changes: he becomes the witness to comic absurdity instead of a participant in it. Forgan and Campbell are wise innocents. Coles connects them to childhood in that their usual job is running a model shop in Clerkenwell Road. They have a penchant for practical jokes—they are the ones who introduce the fish filled with sneezing powder in *Let the Tiger Die*. Often they introduce the discordant element which sets off the comic fracas, as in *A Knife for the Juggler* where they lecture a meeting of Stalinists on the virtues of Yugoslavian communism. They do all this with such innocence that the readers are convinced that there is a high order of cunning behind it. In the English tradition of amateurism and within Coles' framework of the picaresque, they are consummate con men. Coles makes this clear in the following passage from *Now or Never:*

Monsieur Albert Baptiste was a prosperous-looking little gentleman in very good clothes with an expensive watch-chain across his semi-lunar front. He had charming and friendly manners, trustful brown eyes and an air of unworldly inexperience. He was a confidence trickster by profession; on a previous visit to Paris, Campbell and Forgan had met him in a cafe where he practiced his art upon them. They had cheerfully allowed themselves to be led along to the point where the climax was imminent and then engaged in an animated discussion with each other, Baptiste being present, about the various ways in which he could arrange the finish....

"Messieurs," he gasped, "have pity. It is quite evident that I, a poor minnow, have challenged a pair of tritons."[13]

As part of their flim-flam and as part of their identities, Coles makes Forgan and Campbell speak in the manner of a vaudeville cross-talk act. In terms of plot, Coles uses them to minimize seriousness of threats and violence: they never take people or events seriously, although they are very tender about each other. Coles uses them as the *deus ex machina* in the plots. They drag Hambledon out of danger, effortlessly gain information, and they tidy up details which the hero cannot. Coles, through them, shifts Hambledon's character to the slightly amused but slightly embarrassed official who still has some of the boy left in him but must deal with other adults. Coles, however, suffers from the same weariness with Forgan and Campbell that he does with Tommy. They are engaging and funny in the novels through *A Knife for the Juggler*, but afterward they only go through the motions.

The normal range of characters in Coles' books runs to: Tommy, police officials, gangsters, con men and Forgan and Campbell. No significant female character appears, in spite of Adelaide Manning. Other than Forgan and Campbell's affection for each other, no real human contact develops: no love, no male cameraderie. The books exist for their plots which depend on their pace and on an occasional echo of traditional stories—Robin Hood in *Among those Absent*, Jekyll and Hyde in *With Intent to Deceive.* Insofar as his novels communicte anything beyond plot, they return to Sapperish points about the uses of law, authority and force. Coles, though, does not obtrude this on us as does Sapper, and he dilutes it with stabs at urbane comedy.

In all, Coles shows the anemic end of the spy tradition begun before the First World War by Buchan. Coles has lost the Master Crook, the verve of muscular Conservatism, the sophisticated audience, and many other things which drove the spy novel before the Second World War. Coles could have included these things, but did not. Instead his novels prove what scarcely needs proof: that fiction without people or issues cannot survive. Coles tries to make bricks without straw, with splashes of comedy and daubs of character, but it simply will not work, especially since he will not pay attention to the things which he can do well. Over the past two years I have read all of Buchan, all of Sapper, all of Beeding, and all of the works of any number of spy writers. Without reference to notes I can recall a few details about most of their plots. But not with Coles. His plots refuse to stay separate and distinct. Here, again, Raymond Chandler's essay "The Simple Art of Murder" seems to be more appropriate to Coles than it is to Milne when he says, "The English may not always be the best writers in the world, but they are incomparably the best dull writers."[14]

NOTES

[1]Coles' Francis Gaite novels are: *Brief Candles* (1954), *Happy Returns* (1955), *The Far Traveller* (1956), *Come and Go* (1958) and *Duty Free* (1959).

[2]*Drink to Yesterday* (New York: Knopf, 1941), p. 259.

[3]*Toast to Tomorrow* (Garden City: Doubleday, 1941), p. 120.

[4]*Green Hazard* (London: Hodder and Stoughton, 1947), p. 35.

[5]*The Fifth Man* (Garden City: Doubleday, 1947), p. 179.

[6]*Among those Absent* (Garden City: Doubleday, 1948), p. 50.

[7]*The Fifth Man*, p. 29.

[8]*Without Lawful Authority* (Garden City: Doubleday, 1943), p. 35.

[9]*Without Lawful Authority*, p. 95.

[10]*The Fifth Man*, p. 136.

[11]*Diamonds to Amsterdam* (Garden City: Crime Club, 1949), p. 65.

[12]*The Simple Art of Murder* (New York: Ballantine, 1972), p. 6.

[13]*Now or Never* (Garden City: Doubleday, 1951), pp. 33-4.

[14]*The Simple Art of Murder* , p. 12.

Chapter 13

Ian Fleming
(1908-1964)

THE PERSPECTIVE given by eighty-odd years of spy novels shows Ian Fleming to be a minor writer who, himself, did little to advance the form. Fleming possessed only meager talents as a maker of plots, and he fails absolutely when compared with the men who are popularly assumed to have been his teachers—Buchan and Sapper. He fails to render more than cartoon reality in his characters, either major or minor. With setting Fleming does do a bit better, as he needs to create settings to cover the lacunae in these other areas and to pad out his books in order to make them novels, and short novels at that. Finally, he has little to say in the way of theme: his conservatism is inarticulate and muzzy-headed when compared to, say, Buchan's or even Cheyney's. Yet James Bond is still synonymous with one type of spy, as witnessed by the allusions to him in Greene's *The Human Factor* (1979), and Fleming was the most popular spy writer of the 1950s and 1960s.

This, though, had little to do with either Bond's character as created by Fleming or the plots which he created. It came, rather, from the immense publicity boost provided by the revelation that President Kennedy enjoyed the Bond books. Also it came from the films made from the Bond stories. Neither of these things reflects the true quality of Fleming's novels: the films (there have been eleven to date),[1] for instance, reconstruct Fleming's plots, add the gadgets absent in the novels, rewrite the dialogue and provide a stable image of the hero unavailable in the books. More than anything, Fleming as a writer brings to mind *Our Man in Havana* (1958), where an author's fantasies, sometimes innocent, sometimes playful, grow out of the writer's grasp and become reshaped by the world. Fleming's creations certainly live lives of their own and plenty of people believe in them, but Fleming himself was hard-pressed to continue creating them out of Edwardian materials, padding from his travels, and from half-serious, half-fake fragments from his own fantasy life.

There are any number of traps for anyone trying to deal with Fleming's novels as novels. He eggs us on to play along with his psychological foolery; he encourages us to slip on the biographical fallacy; he pushes us to wind ourselves up in highlighted detail so that we will overlook the paucity of his books.

In addition to two collections of short stories (*For Your Eyes Only [1960]* and *Octopussy [1966]*, Fleming wrote eleven spy novels: *Casino Royale* (1953), *Live and Let Die* (1954), *Moonraker* (1955), *Diamonds are Forever* (1956),, *From Russia, With Love* (1957), *Dr. No* (1958), *Goldfinger* (1959), *Thunderball* (1961), *On Her Majesty's Secret Service* (1963), *You Only Live Twice* (1964) and *The Man With the Golden Gun* (1965)—the twelfth Bond book, *The Spy Who Loved Me* (1962), cannot really be called a spy book even by Fleming's loose standards. Until the 1950s Fleming whiled away his time as a soft-news journalist among the old-boy network of Fleet Street. According to Pearson in *The Life of Ian Fleming* (1966), Fleming found the spur to thriller writing in his contact with the tradition (albeit adulterated) of the American hard-boiled detective:

> In March, 1950, on his return from Goldeneye [Fleming's retreat in Jamaica] via New York, he described himself in the *Sunday Times* as "fortifying" himself "for the strato-cruiser flight home with *My Gun is Quick* [1950] by Mickey Spillane, which the *New York Times* had just reviewed with horrified awe." But Spillane he found was a great disappointment, and he went on to lament the softening up and sentimentalizing of the American thriller.
>
> As he wrote, Fleming was undoubtedly reflecting on how much better he could do this sort of thing himself.[2]

The link with the hard-boiled detective is as good a place as any to begin an assessment of Fleming's spy novels, for not only Pearson ties him to this tradition, but other writers put him in line with Peter Cheyney—the English agent of the Hammett-Chandler school.[3]

Going back to Cheyney and his importation of tough-guy fiction, the hard-boiled story has a number of characteristics which separate it from other kinds of crime writing: 1) it deals with sordid crime and slimy people; 2) it elevates the detective/agent above both criminals and ordinary citizens; 3) it portrays violence, but this writers often minimize through choreography or stylization; 4) it stresses the work ethic, personal integrity, and other romantic motives; 5) it deals with sexuality but again in a less than real convention; 6) it stresses action over thought; 7) it employs a hero notable for his stamina, courage and persistence; 8) it uses dialogue compounded from colorful slang and witty retorts; 9) it communicates through a terse, understated style; 10) it stresses stoic resignation toward events and people. All this, of course, began in the United States in the twenties with Hammett and the *Black Mask* school. Spillane, Fleming's companion on the airplane, represents the bastardizing of this tradition and emphasizes sex and violence, influenced by the post-war morality of massive strength and the ethic of hitting the bad guy before he gets a chance to hit you—or swallow up defenseless Czechoslovakia.

Fleming fits some of these criteria, but not all of them. His books all deal with disagreeable people—although after *From Russia, With Love* he colors his villains a bit more with the tradition of the "gentleman crook" which comes from the English thriller—but Fleming does not show us very much of them beyond mouthing a psychological label. Likewise, moving out of the manicured detective story, Fleming may narrate us to the edge of some sordid events (rape and castration usually) but they, too, belong to the game of quack psychiatry which he plays rather than a realistic urge. The big crimes in Fleming's books do not belong to the hardboiled tradition of grubbiness, but rather to the international morality of the spy novel. Fleming does, though, raise his hero not only above criminals but also above ordinary citizens. In *On Her Majesty's Secret Service*, for instance, Bond reflects on declining taste caused by international vulgarians scuttering about the continent. Also, in *The Spy Who Loved Me*, Fleming uses Bond's job as an agent to lift him beyond the pale of ordinary folks:

"The top gangsters, the top FBI operatives, the top spies are coldhearted, coldblooded, ruthless, tough killers, Miss Michel. Yes, even the 'friends' as opposed to the 'enemies.' They have to be. They wouldn't survive if they weren't."[4]

In spite of his lone-wolf existence, though, Fleming frequently makes Bond fidget over morality and fight with the idea of his chosen profession as a gun-man. Like Spillane and other hardboiled writers Fleming wished to quicken the sensations of violence in the popular novel. Thus he introduces a chapter entitled "Strong Sensations" in *From Russia, With Love*, and he occasionally brings in sensational violence like the agent being shredded by the train's snow fan in *On Her Majesty's Secret Service*. Nevertheless, Fleming does not on the whole use a great deal of violence, and what violence enters comes in confined pockets like the torture scene in *Casino Royale*. Some of the sexuality in the Bond books, further, comes from Spillane. Bond, like Mike Hammer, constantly notices women's bodies—usually animate bosoms, always straining and pointing. The sexual symbolism in Fleming and Spillane also connects: Spillane's hero's name, Mike Hammer, and the travesty intercourse in *I, the Jury*, look toward the myriad attempts to castrate Bond, and the women's names like Pussy Galore. Other than establishing certain, playful frameworks for characterization, though, and demonstrating that Bond is exuberantly heterosexual, much of Fleming's use of sexuality draws on the love-romance rather than the hard-boiled tradition. In terms of action, almost all of Fleming's novels suffer from comparison with the hard-boiled story: they do not stress action but use it as a cap for a series of placement scenes of big gulps of padding—in *You Only Live Twice,* for instance, Bond receives no threats from and does not even encounter Blofeld until the last thirty pages of the book. What fills up the remainder may not be thought (actually it is semi-exotic travelogue about Japan) but it certainly is not action. Bond, like Sam Spade or Mike Hammer, certainly has courage, stamina and persistence, but, once more, this draws on the schoolboy story (as seen at the end of *The Man with the Golden Gun* where Bond cannot finish off Scaramanga unless it is a fair fight) as well as Fleming's half-hearted attempt to probe how far the physical and psychic fiber of a man can be strained. Later I will say something about Bond's string of errors and ineptness, but here all we need to know is that his personal energy does not come from the hard-boiled school. Finally, in terms of style, Fleming learned little from hard-boiled writers. His pseudo-shocking openings and short sentences come from journalism as Vivienne's remarks on style in *The Spy Who Loved Me* make clear.[5] Neither is Bond's dialogue particularly witty or tart. If people believe that, they have been duped by the American-made and American-rewritten Bond films which give the hero non-canonical utterances—in the film of *Thunderball,* for instance, Bond shoots one of Largo's agents with a spear gun and then comments, "get the point," something (perhaps blessedly) which never occurs in the novel.

On the whole, Fleming qualifies as a hard-boiled writer, but only by a slim margin. Some of his similarities can be found in much mid-century crime fiction—the increase in sex and violence for instance. Some of his similarities to hard-boiled writers merge with native traditions like the schoolboy story. Fleming learned little about narration or action from the hard-boiled tradition, and the source of his morality lies elsewhere. Perhaps most importantly, Fleming drew a few details and one of his continuing obsessions from American tough-guy fiction. The most apparent of these details, of course, are Bond's secretaries (Loelia Ponsonby and Mary Goodnight). Actually Bond has little use for a secretary: how much correspondence does he have? Misses Ponsonby and Goodnight come rather directly from the private eye's secretary in Hammett or

Spillane who is luscious, slightly stand-offish, motherly and wildly in love with her boss. Bond, however, like his private-eye forebears, passes over this available, lovely girl-next-door in favor of foreign and exotic women who involve him in adventure (this is especially notable after *Moonraker* in that all the subsequent heroines, except Goodnight in *The Man with the Golden Gun,* are non-English). Another superficial detail from the hard-boiled story is the attention paid to guns in the Bond books. This is particularly Spillanesque: Bond absolutely feels that his pistol is an extension of himself. The gun lore with its details of calibre, stopping power, etc. is only one facet. Spillane gleefully uses the gun as the penis figure and Fleming follows along, making this explicit in the materials about Scaramanga's fascination with his golden gun.

Although there is some gun fascination in the books, Bond does not use his gun much; the hard-boiled/western motif of gun-play comes into only a few books. Only three conclude in gun-play (*Diamonds are Forever, The Spy Who Loved Me* and *The Man with the Golden Gun*); Bond dispatches the villains by other means or they are dispatched by a *deus ex machina.*

Guns, ultimately, form only part of that section of the hard-boiled tradition which holds most importance in shaping Fleming's world. The gangster is that section which holds Fleming's fascination. Fleming, like many British writers going back to Edgar Wallace, was absolutely taken in life and art by the idea of massive organized crime and corruption in the U.S.

In his series of journalistic pieces, *Thrilling Cities* (1959), for example, Fleming says nothing about Los Angeles beyond quoting Police Captain Hamilton's crime statistics; likewise in Chicago, he spends most of his time visiting and describing the shrines of gangsterdom. In *Diamonds are Forever, Goldfinger* and *The Man with the Golden Gun* Fleming chants the litany of gangs over and over—the Purple Gang, the Spangled Mob, the Machine; Cleveland, Detroit, Chicago, Los Angeles. Three of the novels (*Live and Let Die, Diamonds are Forever* and *The Man with the Golden Gun*) deal almost exclusively with gangsters as antagonists. Indeed, in almost all the novels the villains are more gangster than political antagonist. Thus, for example, LeChiffre in *Casino Royale* is less a Red agent than a gangster union official who has invested money in a string of cat houses and who travels around with his team of torpedoes. *Goldfinger* and *Thunderball* are nothing more than stories of the utlimate heist, the Brinks job, the Big Knockover with a tiny bit of international garnish thrown in. In 1961, when Fleming gave up the Cold War in his books and dropped the gloss that the

Soviets cause all the nastiness in the world, he created S.P.E.C.T.R.E., which is nothing more than the mob's mob, bringing together all the best and brightest hoods in the world.

Within this framework of gangsters running through the novels, Fleming is pretty snooty. From *Live and Let Die* and *Diamonds are Forever* he shows American gangsters to be merely incompetent gunsels when compared with a British gentleman-secret agent. Thus Bond effortlessly infiltrates and then knocks over the Spangled Mob on its own turf in Las Vegas, just as in *The Spy Who Loved Me* he makes short work of two creepy hoods who threaten Vivienne Michel and plan to defraud an insurance company. Indeed, Fleming's exposure of Bond to American hoodlums turns him into an active hero/avenger rather than the passive agent hero who appears in *Casino Royale* and *Moonraker*. European hoods (there are no real British gangsters in Fleming), though, are another matter, as are those from the Orient. During his account of Hong Kong in *Thrilling Cities* Fleming pays some attention to Chinese Tong organizations, and *Dr. No*, too, deals with these gangs with awe and respect. Marc-Ange Draco, the Mafia *capo* in *On Her Majesty's Secret Service*, is remarkably efficient and, in fact, part hero of the book. The really big gangsters use American hoods as their flunkies and patsies in both *Goldfinger* and *The Man with the Golden Gun*—in the latter the American crooks seem paunchy, white-belted tourists compared to the Spanish and Russian big shots. Europeans, Fleming shows, think big and have a ruthlessness absent in their decadent cousins. Fleming illustrates this in his repeated use of the summit meeting of gangsters. In *Goldfinger, Thunderball* and *The Man with the Golden Gun* we find that the chief hoodlum calls his agents together and then executes one of them just to show his omniscience and omnipotence.

Nonetheless, Fleming's novels are not gangster stories in the hard-boiled mode where Spade or Marlowe share some of the filth of their environment. Bond has nothing in common with Drax or Scaramanga or any of the others. Richard Usborne and O.F. Snelling[6] make a good deal of Fleming's development from Buchan and Sapper. Contemplating this position, though, does not move us far toward understanding Fleming: certainly Fleming draws a few scraps from these writers—a boy maturing in Britain in the twenties and thirties could scarcely avoid it—but he lacks the plotting ability of the former and the crude but boisterous humor of the latter. Fleming certainly owes more to Edgar Wallace's gangster fiction, but especially he owes a debt to the Victorian spy novels of LeQueux and Oppenheim, and he also draws huge chunks of inspiration from the popular love romance.

Usborne's title, *Clubland Heroes* (1953), suggests that Buchan and Sapper wrote books about men steeped not only in the values but also the atmosphere of the English club: Bertie Wooster and the Drones Club from the serious point of view, if you will. In terms of atmosphere, though, Buchan deals very little with the hero's immersion in his club. Dick Hannay, in fact, rejects the world of clubs in *The Thirty-Nine Steps* (1915) and exists principally out of doors in the other books. Likewise, Hugh Drummond spends most of his time out on the tiles or swilling beer at home. Granted, both heroes have their circle of chums and public school morality upon which clubs lived, but they both live their lives out of doors, out of the clubs, and many of their attitudes, for good or ill, are those of the outdoorsman, the hunter. Stepping backward, Oppenheim and LeQueux represent a more enthusiastic acceptance of the club and the clubman's world. They thrive on life within the confines of the club. Oppy, particularly, starts his novels and plots their action through the rooms and corridors of expensive and opulent settings. His heroes and heroines dress impeccably and eat and adventure (if we can call it that) in fancy Victorian/Edwardian hotels, clubs, embassies and country houses. They, rather than Hannay or Sandy or Peter or Hugh or Tiny or Tiger, are the real clubland heroes and from them Fleming got considerable material.

Meticulous attention to details of dress and other social rituals, as Wodehouse knew so well, along with appreciation of a specific cuisine and cellar and a standard of comfort which runs to traditional furniture and decoration, lies at the heart of the clubman's life. We find this in Oppenheim and we also find it with a vengeance in Fleming. One of the most remarked upon features of Bond's characterization is his fastidious adherence to personal custom and etiquette. He always smokes Morelands, he always drinks vodka martinis, he always wears a black knit tie, and he particularly loves his aged Bentley roadster—even it if gives way in later books and if Felix's Studilac is more brutally muscular. Likewise Bond, although he insists that he is no gourmet in *On Her Majesty's Secret Service*, likes good food and champagne. The place where Bond feels most himself is M's club, Blades. We get a big dose of Blades in *Moonraker*, and Fleming introduces it in a number of later books. What I suggest is that Bond is the essential clubman, intent on comforting rituals of dress and consumption, and that the books' occasional carping about the degeneration of modern life (Bond's reflection in *Goldfinger* that women become lesbians because so many men today are "pansies," for instance) comes from the clubman's affection for his safe Edwardian hidey-hole and his grumblings about how the world outside the club is going to hell. One of the significant indicators of all this in Fleming's early novels, where his style and diction reveal most, is his use of the word "Victorian" as a key for the things Bond most desires. Thus it reflects in the following passage on Blades from *Moonraker:*

"In short, membership of Blades, in return for the £50 a year subscription, provides the standard of luxury of the Victorian age together with the opportunity to win or lose, in great comfort, anything up to £20,000 a year."[7]

The same term crops up in *Diamonds are Forever* when Bond sees Spang's reconditioned vintage train:

For the first time in his life he saw the point of being a millionaire, and suddenly also for the first time, he thought that there might be more to this man Spang than he had reckoned on.
    The interior of the Pullman glittered with Victorian luxury. The light from small crystal chandeliers in the roof gleamed on the polished mahogany walls and winked off silver fittings and cut-glass vases and lampstands.[8]

The Victorian luxury of things combined with risk forms Bond's ideal. It is an ideal,though, which Fleming knows is on its way out. In *Dr. No* he reflects on the fate of Jamaica's incarnation of Blades, the Queen's Club:

Such stubborn retreats will not long survive in modern Jamaica. One day the Queen's Club will have its windows smashed and perhaps be burned to the ground, but for the time being it is a useful place to find on a sub-tropical island—well run, well staffed and with the finest cuisine and cellar in the Caribbean.[9]

Bond is, in part then, a throwback to the richer and more "manly" days of Oppy and LeQueux, even if he knows that they are running out. He does, though, do his best to combat those who set out to destroy the society of peace and rich comfort. One look at Bond's antagonists shows this. Except for *From Russia, With Love,* Soviets come into Fleming very little. He, of course, puts them in the backgrounds of the books as ultimate motivators but their doctrinal stance, though anathema to Fleming, has almost nothing to do with the real villains in the books. Fleming's villains draw their menace from being exhibits from his half-playful psychological zoo (I will touch on this later), but much of their threat comes from the fact that they represent offenses to the clubman's world. All have crashed their ways into the Gentleman's Club, but they do not belong—they are as common as linoleum. Thus Drax, with all his millions, and

Goldfinger, his later incarnation, act the part of *nouveau riche* slobs who buy their ways into the gentleman's sanctum. Both not only conspicuously consume but also have not lost their peasant greediness and low cunning, for they both cheat at cards—the traditional worst sin going back to the days when jolly Edward was only a prince. In *Moonraker* and *Goldfinger* Bond acts as the special agent of clubland to expose their essential gaucherie. Bond, in all, lives a parable of Fleming's view of post-war Britain. He lives in comfort, sure enough, but it is modest comfort, for Fleming repeatedly mentions Bond's austere salary. His adversaries possess the big bucks and with them have been able to buy a few of the outward signs of old respectability (Spang's toy train or Goldfinger's classic Rolls, for instance), but they put these to foul uses and, carrying their immorality even further, they want to possess the whole world: they want everything for themselves. The books show how they lose (often ironically destroyed by their own devices, as Drax's rocket and Dr. No's guano) and how Bond wins, but Bond's victories are only temporary. He may get a night of love out of it, but victory usually leaves the hero bloody, wounded and exhausted. Worse still, Bond's task never ends because there are more of "them" than there are "us," and if the comfort of the club and its civilized excitement are to survive, Bond has to continue working.

If these particular facets of the clubman's world activate some of Fleming's creations, the love romance also plays a large role in the Bond books. Here again we return to the world of Oppenheim and LeQueux, for these inventors of the spy novel not only wrote love romances but also, invariably, mixed elements of the love romance into their spy plots. Now, most spy writers, whether from natural bent or desire to broaden their audience, shoehorn love stories into their plots. Indeed one way of separating realistic from fantastic spy stories is to look for the presence or absence of a love plot.

Most often in the twenties and thirties we get a breezy and subordinate boy-meets-girl, girl-gets-kidnapped action in with the spy adventure. But this is not what I mean in regard to the love romance in Fleming. I am talking about the *cliched* but immensely popular kind of love story: stories like *The Sheik* (1921) or those by Barbara Cartland, which have their own sets of conventions of plot and character paying careful attention to defining love. Among these conventions we find motifs like the woman with the secret, defrosting the standoffish man or woman, the initiation to love, and examining the "exciting" relationship between violence and sex.

Fleming, in spite of his reputation as being a soft-core pornographer of strictly male fantasies, fills his books with ideas taken from the realm of the female-directed love romance.

If novices in Fleming wish to test this statement, all they need to do is to start their reading with *The Spy Who Loved Me*. This book, the only novel in the canon narrated in the first person, clearly defines itself as a love romance. Vivienne Michel narrates her life story, beginning with her two unpleasant introductions to sex. During the main action of the novel, two grotesque goons hold her prisoner in an isolated motel in the forests of upstate New York, but, fortunately, James Bond drops into the narrative, saves Vivienne's life and virtue, and then gives her a night of love which will fuel her fantasies for a long time. Beyond a doubt, *The Spy Who Loved Me* is a love romance and not a spy novel. Rather than being an anomaly to Fleming's works, though, it simply codifies a number of tendencies present in all his fiction. His first novel, *Casino Royale*, for example, has a large gobbet of romance in it: the last third of the story brings in the woman with a secret motif with Bond trying to break through Vesper's hard shell so that she can admit and enjoy the love which is truly within her. At the end of the book Bond succeeds, but Vesper commits suicide holding Bond's image in her mind because her secret is too tragic to coexist with the love she has for Bond. In *Diamonds are Forever* Fleming uses two other romance themes—the woman reconstituted by purpose and love, and the blighting effects of unfortunate early sexual encounters. Thus Tiffany is a hollow-eyed hanger-on in the world of gangsters until Bond appears, whereupon she chooses to cast her lot with him and strike a blow at her real enemies by helping him. This theme becomes that of the reconstituted prostitute in several later books. Thus Pussy Galore gives up her bullish ways partly because of prolonged contact with Bond in *Goldfinger* and, even more clearly, Domino leaves her loose life as Largo's mistress when she learns of her brother's death and acquires the soothing company of a good man, Bond, in *Thunderball*. In terms of examining women's first, unfortunate sexual encounters, Fleming creates Tiffany Chase's character out of the fact that gangsters gang-raped her during her adolescence. Most of the first quarter of *The Spy Who Loved Me* details Vivienne's early grubby affairs. In *Dr. No* Honeychild Rider was raped in adolescence by a Jamaican planter. This motif even carries over to Kissy Suzuki in *You Only Live Twice*, where Kissy cloisters herself far from modern civilization after being the object of indecent advances in Hollywood. Further, in the line of the romance, Fleming not only stamps the mental lives of many of his heroines with rape in childhood, but he also builds his plots on the threat of rape. Paradoxically, Fleming's heroines face the threat of rape in the action of the novels, but this threat comes from impotent villains. Now, Fleming, following *The Sheik*, holds that

"All women love semi-rape. They love to be taken. It was his sweet brutality against my bruised body that made his act of love so piercingly wonderful."[10]

The problem is that the villains lack sexuality: Blofeld, Goldfinger and Dr. No are clearly neuters. They cannot provide rape, so they invent travesties of it, as in Dr. No's spread-eagling of the naked heroine in the path of migrating crabs. The hero, of course, can provide the real thing. Fleming makes his female characters long for honest-to-goodness rape by a handsome, half-tender, half-brutal expert named Bond, and in this he merely develops love romance themes begun in 1921 by E.M. Hull.

Fleming fills Bond's sexual fantasies and some of his actions with a combination of moderate violence and sexual fulfillment. He holds up his hero as the ice man, cold, hard and unyielding toward women. This stance, however, as in the romance, is only a veneer. Bond, underneath, is really a sentimental softie, melting and vulnerable once the first violent onslaught of love expires. He, like the romance hero, constantly carries a torch for lost love; and he constantly loses love once he finds it. In *Casino Royale* he loves and loses Vesper and in *Moonraker* Gala stands him up for a real detective; Tiffany goes back to America in *Diamonds are Forever*, Honeychild has her nose fixed and marries another in *Dr. No,* and Blofeld murders Bond's bride at the end of *On Her Majesty's Secret Service*. Bond forever moons about headquarters and M has to tactfully assess his latest heartbreak and prescribe a course of adventure as a cure. Fleming's hero is no flower-hopping bumblebee, but, in the terms of the love romance, a tragically unlucky lover thwarted most often by circumstances but occasionally, as in *You Only Live Twice,* by the iron demands instilled into him by his career.

In addition to the informing qualities of the hard-boiled story, the Oppenheim clubland tradition, and the love romance, Fleming also used some of the techniques of the classic, clue-oriented detective story in his early novels. Thus he includes in *Casino Royale* problems to be solved (how does the opposition know about Bond's identity?) and uses at least one word-clue to string the problem and solution together (Bond calls Vesper a "bitch" upon first meeting her and uses the word again when he knows the truth). We can see Flemming's use of detective technique more clearly,

212 The Special Branch

though, in *Moonraker*. Here he implants clues of the story of the werewolves, the murderer's "Heil Hitler," and the inscribed lines on the chart which Bond finds; he also keeps off the revelation of Drax's plot to incinerate London until late in the book. Fleming also puts a tiny bit of the detective in Bond: in the early books Bond combines the logical and the intuitive detective as shown in Fleming's repeated use of "he reflected" and "he felt"—especially in *Casino Royale*. Bond, though, is no detective: he does not solve problems with his head or his inspiration. Neither is any of Fleming's novels a detective plot in any meaningful way. Most readers can guess what Drax is up to in *Moonraker* long before the operatives in the book do. Fleming, though, used some detective structure in his early books because he knew of no other ways to unify his plots. He left it as quickly as he could find another way of doing things.

Structurally Fleming essentially worked with the episode. He makes *Casino Royale*, for instance, out of three separate incidents (the card game, the kidnapping and the love story), and though he tries to unify them with character and crumbs of detective structure, the episodes fall apart, making the last third of the novel a detachable love romance short story. Throughout Fleming's novels, in fact, we find that the chief unifying elements, the threats provided by the villains, rest on the nonsensical premises like the Soviet blue movie in *From Russia, With Love* and Dr. Shatterhand's suicide park in *You Only Live Twice*. His imagination almost always works in episodes. Thus he repeats his favorite episode, the card game, in *Casino Royale*, *Moonraker* and *Goldfinger*. Here Fleming is at the height of his powers. He sees gambling as the symbol (albeit hackneyed) of risk and, as seen earlier, he also uses it to represent the high life. Additionally, for the thriller writer, these card games provide a long series of capture and escape involving luck and skill and they compact these things into a limited capsule of space and time. Fleming handles these episodes with some facility. With other kinds of episodes he is less sure. At his worst Fleming builds up a few episodes into a short novel (and all his novels are quite short) by adding padding. Sometimes this padding, like the fight of the two gypsy women in *From Russia, With Love* adds a spot of sensationalism and lightly brushes on character. At its worst, though, Fleming's padding degenerates into incompetent travelogue: in *You Only Live Twice*, for instance, Bond visits a Kobe beef farm and massages a "cow," but Fleming neither makes this relevant to the story nor does a good job of journalism in that he fails to explain the peculiarities or the quality of Kobe beef.

Finding that detective structure had no place in Bond's world, Fleming came up with a new way of tying disparate episodes together in *Diamonds are Forever*. He binds up this pointless episodic novel with a framing story about diamond smugglers on the South African veldt. He used the same device with more elaboration and success in *From Russia, With Love*. Here he gives us an extended opening picture of Grant, Klebb and SMERSH (some seventy pages worth), drops this and follows Bond to Turkey and on the Orient Express, and then pops Grant into the action in an unexpected guise. Here Fleming combines the frame story with the old romance technique of making important characters disappear only to zip them in when least expected. Further, Fleming here makes his plot serve his characters as he actually sets up a point-by-point comparison of Grant and the Soviets and Bond and the Secret Service. Although after this novel Fleming dropped the articulated frame story, he did in *Thunderball* evolve it into split narration which switches from the bad guys to the good guys. In leaving this technique, though, he lost his most effective method of binding incidents together and stumbled into structural messes like *You Only Live Twice*.

With *Dr. No* Fleming focused some of his earlier material by returning to the pattern established in *Live and Let Die* and learned from the thriller writers of early in the century. All his early books, save *Diamonds are Forever*, depend on large, grotesque villains. Returning for inspiration to Fu Manchu, however, moves Fleming toward the villain who is not only enormously powerful and grotesque, but who is also part intellectual and part "gentleman crook." *Dr. No* uses some of the furniture of Sax Rohmer's novels (the secret lair, the mad scientist, biology gone berserk) but more importantly it shows a shift toward emphasizing the intellect and organizing power of the villain, which is shown earlier in Mr. Big of *Live and Let Die*. This tradition fuels *Goldfinger* and all the Blofeld books (*Thunderball, On Her Majesty's Secret Service* and *You Only Live Twice*), but it runs out of steam, especially in the Blofeld books, after Fleming has exhausted the original exploration of the gentleman crook; thus Blofeld is a paper figure after his initial appearance in *Thunderball* in spite of the megalomaniac speeches in *You Only Live Twice*.

At the end of his career, Fleming opened up about the essential substance of his plots. In *On Her Majesty's Secret Service* Bond muses, early in the novel that

"It would be amusing to reverse the old fable—first to rescue the girl, then to slay the monster."[11]

The same sort of allusion comes into *You Only Live Twice* with Tiger forecasting Bond's action:

"But, Bondo-san, does it not amuse you to think of that foolish dragon dozing all unsuspecting in his castle while St. George comes silently riding towards his lair across the waves?"[12]

Writing fables was Fleming's plotting object from the very beginning. Here lies the reason that all of Fleming's villains carry tags like ogre (Le Chiffre), giant (Mr. Big), dragon (Drax), toad (Klebb, etc.), and why Fleming puts damsels in distress in all the books—most notably Titiana Romanova in *From Russia, With Love*, named after the extinguished Russian ruling house. In addition to the dragon story Fleming also employs the nineteenth-century American myth of the western gunfight which reaches full fruition in *The Man with the Golden Gun* (which appeared first in the American magazine *Playboy*). Fleming's underlying fable is the simplest, and perhaps therefore the most powerful, myth on which he layers, often incompetently, other plot and character motifs as well as his own, self-conscious psychological games.

On the skeletal level Fleming constructs most of his plots the same way. First there are opening scenes at Headquarters to give necessary background and to legitimize the hero with his institutional allegiance. The hero then travels and Fleming incorporates passages of local color. Arriving at the main scene of the action, the hero explores the ground and meets the villain. Then there are physical and/or psychological tests for the hero to undergo. Finally the hero eliminates or aids in the elimination of the villain. In working on his endings, Fleming frequently has recourse to the *deus ex machina*: the SMERSH killer eliminates Le Chiffre, the rocket destroys Drax, Pussy saves Bond, Domino kills Largo, Terry rescues Bond from Blofeld's minions, and Felix saves Bond's bacon. Part of this reliance upon outside agencies may have been due to Fleming's amateur plotting, and part may have come from his sense of the traditions of the romance, but it inevitably has an impact on the character of the hero—one which many people overlook.

In lots of ways Bond is a bungler. Look, for instance, at *Casino Royale*. By rank accident he avoids being atomized by bombs. He misses the microphone which has been planted in his room. At the casino he loses the stake given him by London and would have lost the card game and the mission but Felix Leiter slips him a packet of

C.I.A. cash. Next he not only fails to save Vesper from the kidnappers, but he also gets himself irrevocably in the soup and must be saved by the SMERSH trigger man. Finally he fails to detect Vesper's true role and needs to be told of it in her suicide note. We can multiply incidents like this in many of the early books: in *Moonraker* Bond's only plan is to light a cigarette on the launch pad until Gala suggests resetting the rocket's gyros; in *Diamonds are Forever* he watches a jockey being tortured and then needs to be saved, in turn, by Tiffany and Felix. It goes on and on: Klebb stabs him in *From Russia, With Love*, and Draco leads the raid on Blofeld's eyrie in *On Her Majesty's Secret Service*. Couple this with Bond's continual bad luck with women and we have a pretty sorry sort of superspy; we almost have a *Trent's Last Case* (1914) of spydom. But why does Fleming do this? One of his motives lies in his desire to make Bond a realistic figure instead of a cartoon.

If, indeed, Bond's general ineffectiveness in the worlds of action and love comes from Fleming's desire to draw a realistic picture, we can be absolutely sure that this is the motive in his delineation of another side of Bond's character. Strung throughout the novels we find Fleming introducing passages which reflect Bond's revulsion with his role as spy and assassin. This forms the heart of Bond's quasi-philosophical talk with Mathias in *Casino Royale*. In *From Russia, With Love* Bond shrinks from Darko's coldblooded assassinations: "But Bond had never killed in cold blood, and he hadn't liked watching, and helping, someone else do it."[13] In the opening of *Goldfinger* Bond mopes about killing a Mexican torpedo in the case which he has just finished. Part of Fleming's hero clearly retreats from violence and killing and longs for the sort of island idyl which the amnesiac Bond enjoys in *You Only Live Twice*.

Much of this, though, is baloney. Bond does, after all, act as an assassin. In the books we see him personally killing the antagonists in *Diamonds are Forever, From Russia, With Love, Dr. No, Goldfinger, The Spy Who Loved Me, You Only Live Twice* and *The Man with the Golden Gun*. Further, in *Diamonds are Forever* and *Dr. No*, the killings can only be termed assassinations since the victims have no chance. In spite of Fleming's assertion that Bond has never killed in cold blood, in *Casino Royale* Bond tells Mathias of two assassinations which he has carried out—one on a Japanese spy in New York and one on a Norwegian double agent. What is the double-O number for, slicing cheese? The license to kill was, after all, Fleming's invention.

Part of Bond undeniably goes back to the traditions of the adventure hero. Plenty of adventure heroes, Hannay for example, begin their experiences starting from the bog of ennui. Fleming follows right along. At the start of many of the novels he consciously sinks Bond into the torpor of routine life. Thus in *From Russia, With Love* he gives us this picture:

> At 7:30 on the morning of Thursday, August 12th, Bond awoke in his comfortable flat in the plane-tree'd Square off the King's Road and was disgusted to find that he was thoroughly bored with the prospect of the day ahead. Just as in at least one religion, *accidie* is the first of the cardinal sins, so boredom, and particularly the incredible circumstances of waking up bored, was the only vice Bond utterly condemned.[14]

Bond needs to be out doing things; he needs adventure. Fleming shows this in *Goldfinger*: "But, in Bond's case, Goldfinger could not have known that high tension was Bond's natural way of life and that pressure and danger relaxed him."[15] Hence Bond the gambler presides in Fleming's card games, Bond the race car driver presides in Fleming's car chases, and Bond the killer presides over the final clashes with the villains. Here is no super-conscious intellectual who winnows motive and meaning. Bond really likes the killer's life. Fleming says so in *Dr. No*: "The license to kill for the Secret Service, the double-O prefix, was a great honour. It had been earned hardly. It brought Bond the only assignments he enjoyed, the dangerous ones."[16] He makes it clear to Tracy Draco, in *On Her Majesty's Secret Service*, that even after they have settled down in the rose-covered cottage, he will continue his profession which takes him into the snares of the world—no Gauginean cop-out for him.

What gives here? How can Fleming tell us about Bond's victims and then deny them four books later? How can he give Bond a sensitive conscience and then show him intent on adventure? Is he trying to show us a schizoid hero? Of course not: Bond is no schizophrenic. Fleming, if confronted with Bond's irregularities, would probably give us the "foolish consistency" answer which many readers take. We can always concentrate on the manic regularities of the externals of dress and ritual (which exist, perhaps, to give focus to an otherwise shifting character) and forget about personalities. Or we can say that Fleming was a lazy and inexperienced maker of characters. Even after reading all twelve of the Bond novels we know very little of Fleming's hero aside from the externals. In *From Russia, With Love* Fleming may try a bit harder and give us a few glimpses into Bond's inner world (during his flight to Turkey, for example), but we see very little of this elsewhere. Perhaps the main reason for this, aside from general unconcern, is Fleming's narrative manner. First person narration is the staple of action spy fiction; it has some clear advantages (speed of identification, efficiency and credibility in story telling) for this sort of story. All of Fleming's immediate forebears used it: Buchan, Sapper, Beeding, Cheyney, etc. But Fleming, conceivably because of his ties to Oppenheim, opts for third person narration and because of this choice coupled with limited talent, he gives us a picture of the world which occasionally approaches vividness—but he also gives us a muddled picture of his characters.

But, ultimately, it is not the narrative. Manning Coles as well as other writers can do perfectly consistent spy stories in the third person. It is Fleming. Give him a continuing character and, chances are, he will blur it and muddle it up by shifting his sources and aims. Take the head of the Secret Service, M. Fleming based M. on the cold-hearted, super-brainy, omniscient head spy created by Cheyney and traceable to the head of the detective agency in the hard-boiled story. Thus Fleming shows M. as aloof from petty human concerns when he is ready to throw Bond on the trash heap at the start of *You Only Live Twice*. On the other hand, Fleming wants to humanize M., so he gives him a tasteful tolerance of Bond's love life and he pushes in a few innocent quirks, like the health-food kick in *Thunderball*. In fact, he tries to make M. into the headmaster to Bond's schoolboy hero. Thus Bond wants to show the old boy that he is still top boy in the house in *Dr. No*. The problem is that Fleming accidentally allows the old Buffer to be incompetent—especially in the later books. In *You Only Live Twice*, for instance, he sends Bond on a putative suicide mission to Japan, but he clearly does not have a glimmer that Blofeld is stirring up a strictly private Japanese cesspool. Worse yet, in *On Her Majesty's Secret Service*, M. is disgusted with Bond's energy and incapable of figuring out a plan even when he knows that Blofeld menaces Britain with aerosol anthrax. M.'s problem, actually, is that Fleming has a hard time creating the infallible brain at the beginning of the book when he has no clear idea of the details of the end.

Fleming's stable of characters includes the hero, the head of the Secret Service, the villain and the girl. He carries them from book to book keeping the same general outlines but changing details when it suits him. The one other character-type which Fleming employs is the man who fully enjoys life. In *From Russia, With Love* and *You Only Live Twice* Bond meets Darko and Dikko whose robust enjoyment of life—enjoyment of food, drink and women—serves as an inspiration for Bond. Fleming also introduces subsidiary agents, Mathias and Leiter, who largely serve to pull Bond out of the soup, but who are also Bond's friends since they, presumably, share his experience with danger. Leiter also serves as the character who

provides most of the verbal comedy in Fleming's books—see
Thunderball, for example.

Fleming, though, has little interest in people *qua* people; he uses
the characters as psychological counters in a game of simplified
psychology. I have already mentioned Fleming's penchant for
building female characters on the basis of their first sexual
encounter. He is even more simplistic when it comes to villains. Most
of the bad folks derive their evil from a psychological or social quirk
which Fleming points out decisively in the narrative, for example
this passage on Hugo Drax from *Moonraker*:

"Yes," said Bond.... "It's a remarkable case history. Galloping paranoia. Delusions
of jealousy and persecution. Megalomaniac hatred and desire for revenge. Curiously
enough," he went on conversationally, "it may have something to do with your teeth.
Diastema, they call it. Comes from sucking your thumb when you're a child. Yes, I
expect that's what the psychologists will say when they get you into the lunatic
asylum. 'Ogre's teeth.' Being bullied at school and so on. Extraordinary the effect it
has on a child."[17]

Drax is a villain because he sucked his thumb as a child: this is
either aimed at four-year-olds or it is supposed to be funny. We do,
though, find other villains whose evil stems from a physical
aberration: Tree, the humpback in *Diamonds are Forever*, Red
Grant the werewolf, Goldfinger the shrimp, and the hairless
gangster (from Maugham's hairless Mexican?) in *The Spy Who
Loved Me*. Fleming even includes a physio-psychological level to
Bond which Adam Hall would later take up in the Quiller books. In a
number of novels he talks about just how much physical and
psychic stress a man can endure with Bond as the subject of the
experiment and with M. and the staff psychiatrist as observers. This
gloss of psychology, of course, gives a modern motive to the knight-
dragon fairy tale upon which Fleming builds his novels. But lurking
underneath is the suggestion of spoof. This peeps through in *The
Man with the Golden Gun* where Fleming paints with broad strokes
Scaramanga's background as an elephant boy and an account of
the pistol-penis symbolism. This could be Fleming's psychological
primer for pre-adolescents, but I think it is spoof. Fleming enjoyed
constructing vignettes of abnormal psychology for his villains and
put them into the books as a lark. Dr. No shows this best of all. How
can we take seriously a man who makes his pseudonym, Julius No,
out of a conscious rejection of his father so that it reads No Julius?

Indeed, rather than being exercises in craftmanship, Fleming's
novels are exercises in self-indulgence. Bond's habits are Fleming's
habits, the filler in the books comes from material picked up on

journalistic jaunts (like those paid for by *The Sunday Times* and included in *Thrilling Cities*), and the villains emerge from fiddling with popular psychology. With these Fleming raked together material from the love romance and the Victorian spy story, and added a modicum of construction learned from Buchan or Sapper. Occasionally he worked on structuring a novel, like *From Russia, With Love, Dr. No,* or *Thunderball,* and these are his best efforts. Nevertheless, his best are poor stuff when compared to his predecessors or successors in the spy novel. No publisher today would even consider printing *Casino Royale*, and if it were not for the films, James Bond would mean as little to the contemporary consciousness as, say, Okewood of the Secret Service. It is, then, historical accident which has made a public figure of a muddled hero created by a third-rate hack.

NOTES

[1]Films have been made from *Dr. No* (1963), *From Russia, With Love* (1964), *Goldfinger* (1964), *Thunderball* (1965), *Casino Royale* (1967), *You Only Live Twice* (1967), *On Her Majesty's Secret Service* (1970), *Diamonds are Forever* (1971), *Live and Let Die* (1973), *The Man With the Golden Gun* (1974) and *Moonraker* (1979).

[2]John Pearson, *The Life of Ian Fleming* (New York: Bantam, 1967), p. 161.

[3]Pearson, p. 205.

[4]*The Spy Who Loved Me* (New York: Signet, 1964), p. 141.

[5]*The Spy Who Loved Me*, pp. 45-6.

[6]*Clubland Heroes*, and O.F. Snelling, *007 James Bond: A Report* (New York:Signet, 1965).

[7]*Moonraker* (New York: Signet, n.d.), p. 26.

[8]*Diamonds are Forever* (New York: Signet, n.d.), 116.

[9]*Dr. No* in *Gilt Edged Bonds* (New York: Macmillan, 1961), p. 10.

[10]*The Spy Who Loved Me, p. 128.*

[11]*On Her Majesty's Secret Service* (New York: Signet, 1964), p. 27.

[12]*You Only Live Twice* (New York: Signet, 1965), p. 100.

[13]*From Russia, With Love* (New York: Signet, n.d.) p. 129.

[14]*From Russia, With Love*, p. 72.

[15]*Goldfinger* (New York: Signet, n.d.), p. 81.

[16]*Dr. No*, p. 25.

[17]*Moonraker*, pp. 151-2.

Chapter 14
Len Deighton
(1929—)

THE GOLDEN AGE of the spy novel began in the early nineteen sixties, and it has lasted for twenty years—or, at least a good case can be made for this historical generalization. During the period the spy novel separated itself decisively from the thriller. Both Greene and Household began to call their spy books novels instead of entertainments or romances. The spy novel began to attempt to portray espionage realistically. Many of the new writers had worked in Intelligence (LeCarré and Ted Allebeury, for instance), and they attempted to realistically portray the espionage organization from the Circus, to Deighton's W.O.O.C.(P), to Haggard's Security Directorate. They also examined the ethical and moral impact of spying on individuals who do it. Partly, this new trend resulted simply from a generational shift: many of the new writers were born in the thirties (Deighton and LeCarré) and missed World War II. Also the new trend came from a revolt against Ian Fleming's gross oversimplification of the form, and new writers leap over Fleming to older writers like LeQueux and Buchan who can be useful if reevaluated and brought into line with a more honest view of men and institutions. Much of the motive for the spy novel of the sixties, however, came from the attraction-revulsion felt by Britons about the defections of Pontecorvo, Burgess, Maclean and Philby, and by the spy trials of the fifties, like that of Fuchs. Especially in the case of Philby, libel laws prevented writers from using this material until Kim defected to the Soviet Union. During the sixties and seventies, the spy novel edged closer to main-stream literature and out of the paperback ranks of popular fiction. We can see this in the fact that established writers like Anthony Burgess used the spy form for their own books (see Burgess' *Tremor of Intent*, 1966). One of the most important of this new generation of spy writers is Len Deighton.

To date, Deighton has written a war novel (*Bomber,* 1970), a novel about cinema personalities (*Close-Up*, 1972) several cookbooks, some non-fiction about World War II *(Fighter, 1977* and *Blitzkrieg*, 1980) and nine spy novels: *The Ipcress File* (1962), *Horse Under Water* (1963), *Funeral in Berlin* (1964), *The Billion Dollar Brain* (1966), *An Expensive Place to Die* (1967), *Spy Story* (1974),

Yesterday's Spy (1975), *Catch a Falling Spy* (1976) and *S.S.—G.B.* (1979).

In these novels Deighton attempts to give readers a taste of the real world of espionage in its institutional and personal relationships. Doing this, he turns at critical points to traditions of the spy story in order to focus his plots or to evaluate or reevaluate the conventions themselves. He represents a recent movement toward making the spy novel into a carefully wrought artifact: in spite of the hectic pace of his plots, Deighton tries to give us tough, poetic description and image structure for his fiction. This is a world apart from the spy novel factories, like Manning Coles or Victor Canning, of the fifties who turned out the same rough product over and over, making only superficial changes in the package and paying little attention to structure or style. Deighton, within limits, works at evolving his spy fiction and we can see, so far, three separate trends in his spy novels (one in the pre-1967 books, another between 1967 and 1977 and finally the 1979 novel). Lastly, he created a hard-boiled hero who is genuinely English and defiantly hard-boiled as opposed to the awkward American transplants introduced by earlier writers.

At first glance, Deighton looks like a writer devoted to giving his readers a realistic peep through the veil into the hidden world of spying and spies. There is a pronounced strain of the iconoclastic historian in Deighton which we can see clearly in his non-fiction work, *Blitzkrieg*, which undercuts the popular conception of the Fall of France. In his first four spy novels Deighton seems intent on providing this same sort of thing for the spy business. He gives us footnotes and appendices in order to detail the secret world, translate its jargon, and explain its peculiar customs. *Funeral in Berlin*, for example, has forty two footnotes: some explain foreign words or customs, some refer us to the appendix for fuller information, but most flesh out the myriad details of the closed world of spying. Here are three representative samples of the footnotes in *Funeral in Berlin:*

*To catch people with stolen passports, or people who spend nights in the East, the passports are often marked with a tiny pencil spot on some prearranged page.[1]

*Our radio procedure is designed to make an eaves-dropper think we are a taxi service. For this same reason our car pool uses radio equipped taxi cabs with the flags always set at "hired."[2]

*MECO: Mechanical Corporation, 155 Birmendorferstrasse, Zurich. An agency which buys jet planes missiles and talent on behalf of the Egyptian government.[3]

The appendices in the first four books do the same thing, only at greater length. The appendix in *Horse Under Water*, which at nine pages is the longest, gives readers, among other things, material on telephone tapping, details on Nazi counterfeiting of banknotes, and excerpts from the court martial of H. Peterson (one of the characters in the novel). As the last item suggests, Deighton both invents this material and gets it from genuine research. Now, he could easily have included all this material in the narrative without resorting to notes or appendices. The scholarly apparatus, though, gives the material weight and an air of importance. It stands witness to the books' verisimilitude. Along the same lines, the early novels use graphics to argue for the fact that we are entering the real world of spies, even if it exists in the parallel universe of fiction. Thus, *The Ipcress File* begins with a reproduction of an official flimsy, *Horse Under Water* starts with a facsimilie letter from Smith's secret file and the endpapers of *Billion Dollar Brain* reproduce a Honeywell data processing sheet. All this, however, merely represents Deighton's point of fictional attack. He runs no risks of D. Notices, and state secrets, substantial or otherwise, remain safe. Essentially Deighton has little wish to delve deeply into the complex and narratively tedious real world of the spy. The detail is important, though, if readers are going to accept the organizations and, through them, the themes which he develops.

In the first four novels, Deighton expends a good bit of energy developing one, particular intelligence organization: the W.O.O.C.(P). Physically, his descriptions of this spy bureau do not go much beyond Fleming's portrait of the Secret Service. W.O.O.C.(P) headquarters is disguised as a commercial building and its staff boils down to a boss, a couple of secretaries (one ascerbic, omniscient and middle-aged, and one sympathetic and nubile), and two or three agents. Deighton gives them an I.B.M. computer—something which he would develop thematically, especially in *Yesterday's Spy*—and some motion picture apparatus, but the physical layout seems more like the headquarters of a private detective agency than the center of a government bureau. But there are other layers to his imagination. First of all, Deighton works at showing the realities of inter-organization jealousy, and the necessity for organizations to play politics before they can spend any time on their mandated business. The (P) in W.O.O.C.(P) stands for "provisional," and thus it becomes especially important for this particular branch of government to engage in the political game in order to survive. In *The Ipcress File*, Dalby, the head of W.O.O.C.(P), puts finding the vanished scientist, Raven, in this organizational perspective:

> But if we found the Raven I think the Home Secretary would virtually disband his confused little intelligence department. Then we could add their files to ours.[4]

RULE ONE: the relationship between different departments of the same government rests on the drive for power. RULE TWO: Budget is the outward sign of success. Again, we have Dalby reading the corporate scriptures in *The Ipcress File*:

> " 'It's January. If we could do this in January,' he said. January was the month that the Government estimates were prepared. I began to see what he meant."[5]

The Ipcress File is a special case, since it presents an intelligence agency with a double agent at its head. Deighton does, however, carry the same motif over into the other early novels. When Dawlish first takes over W.O.O.C.(P), the narrator admires (as he will later despise) the fact that he knows all the moves in the corporate game:

> He [Dawlish] had done well that year. The January estimates had been submitted to Treasury and Dawlish had about doubled our appropriation at a time when many people were predicting our close-down. I'd spent long enough in both the Army and the Civil Service to know that I didn't like working in either; but working with Dawlish was an education, perhaps the only part of my education that I ever enjoyed.[6]

Dawlish unobtrusively knows how to use the system without ever being as crass as Dalby: he quietly loads committees with his people and gently slips his budget into paperwork backwashes where no one will see them. In spite of this, and in spite of his idiosyncratic cultivation of weeds in his actual garden at home (mirrored in his cultivation of the narrator at the office), Dawlish is no philanthropist. No one in power can be in this sort of world. Deighton's first spy book, *The Ipcress File*, begins with an epigraph from *Henry IV, Part I* in which the machiavellian Worcester broaches the topic of rebellion to his brother and nephew. Throughout, all the way to *S.S.—G.B.*, Deighton's administrator-bureaucrats seek power, and their means lie in machiavellian cunning, craft and self-protection. His hero recognizes the fundamental truth about this in *Funeral in Berlin*:

> On the other hand, this is a government department like all other government departments; without money it could not exist. There is the danger that people who allocate the money are going to feel that they should be immune from spying. That is why, every time someone is after my blood, Dawlish protects me. Dawlish and I have a perfect system. It is a well-known fact that I am an insolent, intractable hooligan over whom Dawlish has only a modicum of control. Dawlish encourages this illusion.

One day it will fail. Dawlish will throw me to the wolves.[7]

If we accept the fact that the same agent narrates all the novels except *S.S.—G.B.*, the hero does quit before Dawlish can make him wolf-bait, but Dawlish's appearances in *Spy Story* and *Yesterday's Spy* as a repulsive arachnidan character drive home the fact that he, and his ilk, are capable of cynically sacrificing the hero—or anyone else.

The organizations in Deighton's novels care little about practical effectiveness in the international arena or about ultimate good and evil. The most extreme case of this comes into *S.S.—G.B.*, where Nazi officialdom feels relief when the United States takes from them the costly burden of arcane atomic research. The bad people in most of Deighton's novels remain as they began, are pensioned off, or get bought off with sinecures: Jay in *The Ipcress File*, Smith in *Horse Under Water*, Hallam in *Funeral in Berlin*. To the hero's question in *Horse Under Water* about whether Smith, the villain, will be arrested, Dawlish replies, "What an extraordinary question; why would he be arrested?" This indifference to justice or values extends into the international sphere as well. Thus, *Funeral in Berlin* starts by quoting a conversation between Kruschchev and Allen Dulles which ends with: "Yes. We should buy our intelligence data together and save money. We'd have to pay the people only once."[9] This attitude, indeed, forms the basis for most of Deighton's plots. The major powers wish only to be quiescent: they do not wish to spread or to defend the faith. Individuals, being unpredictable or corrupt or idealistic or unbalanced, muck up the *status quo* through private enterprise, and governments quietly collude to quash this. The best example of this is in *Billion Dollar Brain*, where a wealthy American takes it upon himself to export Western ideals, and free Latvia from Soviet domination, but both British and Soviet governments combine to squash him as a freak. The same thing happens to an M.P. in *Spy Story*, where plans to assist a defecting Soviet admiral threaten polite agreements and games played by both sides. Deighton's hero, put in perspective by the title of *Yesterday's Spy*, receives the unenviable job of defeating the renegades and maintaining the gentlemen's agreements of the world, unenviable because he himself is a renegade and defiantly no gentleman.

In all the spy novels, except *S.S.—G.B.*, Deighton uses an unnamed narrator as his hero. He makes this hero a spokesman for the spy as a type, and, as such, he not only illustrates bits and pieces of tradecraft but also draws his character from the realm of the hard-boiled detective hero. Deighton's hero, moreover, possesses certain marked British attributes which contribute to the presentation of the anti-organization theme in the novels. The hero also changes over the course of the books, and his growing weariness points to Deighton's shifts in the focuses of his spy stories.

Deighton's unnamed hero is, first of all, a spy. As a spy he sprinkles the first four novels with what amount to maxims for spies, for example:

"A spy has no friends," people say; but its more complex than that. A spy has to have many friends, in fact many sets of friends. Friends he's made by doing things and by not doing other things. Every agent has his own "old boy network," it cuts across frontiers, jobs and every other loyalty—it's a sort of spy's insurance policy.[10]

There is no room for heroics, vendettas and associated melodrama in an efficient shop. You stand up, get shot at, then carry on quietly.[11]

The greatest tribute you can pay to a secret agent is to take him for a moron. All he has to do is to make sure he doesn't act like one.[12]

"Stok [the KGB big-wig] is a bloodthirsty bastard." "So are we all," I said. "Ruthless and doomed."[13]

In *The Honorable Schoolboy* LeCarré speaks of "the hard men" and hard is precisely Deighton's point. His hero is no desk jockey or systems analyst, but a practicing agent—actually he becomes more of a foot soldier after *An Expensive Place to Die*, for, before this he is something of a pet, albeit a vicious one, at headquarters, to be kicked and used by bureaucrats. In spite of the maxims for spies and the scholarly apparatus, Deighton actually shows us little of the agent's role as information gatherer. His agent goes through various bizarre and baffling experiences and he unravels them at the end of the novels, but it has little to do with real espionage. What it does have to do with is Deighton's use of spying as a metaphor for personal integrity, persistence, mental toughness, as well as machiavellian cunning. We need to note that if Dalby and Jay, the bureacratic villains, are the crafty rebels from Deighton's Shakespearean quotation, then the hero is Prince Hal. The hero stands for values and he has plenty of enviable personal qualities, but, as Shakespeare shows Hal freeing the Douglas, Deighton shows his hero sneaking two Czech agents out of Britain to serve as his own insurance policy.

But to return to personal integrity, persistence and mental toughness, Deighton absorbed these qualities from the hard-boiled detective tradition. Of course the American hard-boiled tradition exerts main force on the British spy novel from Cheyney to Fleming.

Both these writers rely, to a large extent, on reproducing mechanical, external elements of the hard-boiled hero without understanding the deeper significance of the figure. Deighton is different. For one thing he does not derive his inspiration from degenerate heirs of the hard-boiled story, like Spillane, as Fleming does. Instead he was lucky enough to start writing late enough to take in Raymond Chandler—a later-comer to the form, writing well into the fifties. Deighton learned much from Chandler. He alludes to him—through Philip Marlowe—in *Spy Story*, and it is evident that some of Deighton's habits of description were learned from Chandler, as a passage from *An Expensive Place to Die* can illustrate:

Summer rain is cleaner than winter rain. Winter rain strikes hard upon the granite, but summer rain is sibilant soft upon the leaves. The rainstorm pounced hastily like an inexperienced lover, and then as suddenly was gone. The leaves drooped wistfully and the air gleamed with green reflections. It's easy to forgive a summer rain; like first love, white lies or blarney, there's no malignity in it.[14]

Short sentences, similes, personifications, alliterations: this is figurative prose like so many passages in Chandler. In *An Expensive Place to Die* Deighton also makes a pretty clear comment on the other side of the hard-boiled tradition. Here a windy English writer holds forth in a bar on the subject of James Bond:

" 'But I have always immensely adored violence. His [Bond's] violence is his humanity. Unless you understand that, you understand nothing'."[15]

Whereupon someone punches the speaker into insensibility with great technique and precision. Only an imbecile or an anthropoid would, this incident says, love violence. Sam Spade does not love it; Marlowe does not love it. Even if deviants like Mike Hammer love violence, Deighton's hero does not. What counts in the original hard-boiled writers is style, and here Deighton understands Hammett and Chandler better than shoals of smaller fish have. The essence of the hard-boiled story lies in placing a man in a perverse relationship with authority and circumstances. That man's responses in word, thought and deed mark him off as a hero—as someone from whom readers can learn important things.

Deighton's hero has some of the popular marks of the hard-boiled detective. The writer, for one thing, undercuts the traditional image of the adventure hero by giving his character specific, normal details. Thus, in Deighton the hero mutters about the back pay due him throughout *The Ipcress File*, and he fights a diet battle to combat his imminent bloating into the shape of the Michelin tire man in *Horse Under Water*. At the office he sits around making up paper-clip chains (*Ipcress File*) and paper eucalyptus trees (*Billion Dollar Brain*). Deighton sets this man with whom we can identify, and places him in a depressingly realistic atmosphere. He uses detail in the same way here to draw this atmosphere:

"The long lavatory-like passages were dark and dirty, and the small white cards with precise military writing labelled each green-painted door."[16]

This is where the hero works. Like Deighton's hero, most of us are domineered or bored; we are mostly over-weight, and most of us work in places which seem shambles or sterile to the unattached observer. To give us further, realistic detail about the hero, Deighton, like Hammett with the Continental Op, makes his hero a "big, ugly man." As common as he is, though, hard-boiled writers like Deighton make their heroes special by showing them defying their surroundings and surmounting their normal, inert, boorish, lazy selves.

In the twenties Hammett introduced one method which hard-boiled chararacters may use to defy their surroundings: the wise-crack. Deighton is very good at creating wise-cracks and they set his hero off. Here, Stok, the Russian, in on the receiving end:

"I wish you would try to understand" said Stock. "I am really sincere about giving you my allegiance."

"Go on," I said. "I bet you say that to all the great powers."[17]

A short time later the hero dishes it out to Hallam:

Hallam looked up and raised a bony finger. " 'War is a continuation of politics....' You know what Clausewitz tells us."

"Yes," I said. "I'll have to have a word with Clausewitz. He keeps on saying that same thing over and over."[18]

Numerous characters in the novels describe the hero as a man who is constantly impertinent and purposely irritating. This is another facet of the hard-boiled hero. Lots of us would like to be impertinent or irascible, but we know that if we did it once, a pink slip would be franked over to us pretty quickly. This may be true today, but it was staggeringly felt in the depression of the thirties when the hard-boiled story grew up. If we cannot get away with telling people off, the hard-boiled hero can. Deighton's hero sums this up in *The Ipcress File*:

It doesn't take much to make the daily round with one's employer work smoothly. A couple of "yessirs" when you know that "not on your life" is the thing to say. A few expressions of doubt about things you've spent your life perfecting. Forgetting to make use of the information that negates his hastily formed but deliciously convenient theories. It doesn't take much, but it takes about 98.5 per cent more than I've ever considered giving.[19]

The hard-boiled hero has a license to sneer at his employers, because of his integrity and devotion to the ideal, but, practically, his liberty comes from the fact that he does a dirty job which no one else will do. The hero's comeback to Smith in *Horse Under Water* says "spy," but we could insert the term "private eye" and believe that Hammett or Chandler wrote it:

"No one owns a spy, mister," I told him, "They just pay his salary. I work for the government because I think this is a good place to live, but that doesn't mean that I'll be used as a serf by a self-centered millionaire. What's more," I said, "don't give me that 'fatal' stuff because I've taken a post graduate course in fatality."[20]

This sense of absolute independence while working for someone else is the sort of thing which, perhaps, only physicians indulge in in the real world, but private eyes and spies possess in the hard-boiled story.

If the hard-boiled character need not take anyone's abuse, his nature and his job alienate him from almost everyone. With tongue in cheek, the hero in *An Expensive Place to Die*, says: "I'm a professional. I wouldn't tell my mother where I keep the fuse wire."[21] Deighton's hero begins and ends alone—after *Billion Dollar Brain* his loneliness increases because of the author's introduction of lovers and friends who all disappear. His alienation comes from his job as a spy, and from his peculiar position as an Englishman in a very English establishment. Deighton shows all these things in the first novel by linking the hero with Barney, the Black CIA man who is the only person caring enough to warn him about the nets being spread for him. As the hero puts it in *The Ipcress File*, "What chance did I stand between the Communists on the one side and the Establishment on the other."[22] Rather than whining about it, though, the hero accepts his aloneness as simply part of the general human condition:

"Look," I said, "everyone *is* alone, born alone, live alone, get sick alone, die alone, everything alone. Making love is a way for people to pretend they aren't alone. But they are. And everyone in this business is even more so, alone and aching with a lot of untellable truths in his brain-box.

The hero takes alienation magnifed by persecution as part of his own identity: it is all that anyone will ever find out about himself. To spend time and energy searching for this evident fact is a waste of resources. In *An Expensive Place to Die* Deighton has at some of the vague, romantic mumbo jumbo which surrounds the individual thrashing around trying to find himself. First, we get

"True to what?" I asked. "True to scientists, true to history, true to fate, true to what?"
   "True to itself," said Datt.
   "The most elusive truth of all," I said.[24]

and then

"You are cynical as well as ignorant," said Datt as though making a discovery. "Get to know yourself, that's my advice. Get to know yourself."
   "I know enough awful people already," I said.[25]

The important thing is not becoming, but being. Thus Maria, in the same novel, sees the hero as irreducible identity—"He was a man, and that said everything there was to be said about him."[26]

Going back to the genesis of Deighton's hero, as American as he is—coming out of the hard-boiled story, having served an apprenticeship with the CIA, and having been accused in *Funeral in Berlin* of American dress and syntax—the hero's character revolves on some essential English facts. For Britons, one of the most disturbing facts of the whole Burgess, Maclean, Philby, Blount affair was that these men who turned traitor were products of the upper class English system: the Oxbridge route. From a doctrinal point of view, they failed as Britons and they failed the precepts of classical education which should have developed them as British leaders—the playing fields of Eton and all that. This is precisely where Deighton starts with his hero. He is not an old boy. From provincial Burnley, Lancashire, the hero's dad was a railroad worker, and Deighton opposes the Oxbridge education with his hero's degree in math and economics from a red brick university. The first four novels contain lots of passages which reflect on old boy establishment prejudice toward him as well as his animus toward them. Here we have the hero and Dalby, the public school man, in *The Ipcress File*:

Dalby tightened a shoelace. "Think you can handle a tricky little special assignment?"
   "If it doesn't demand a classical education, I might be able to grope around it."[27]

This is a bit of light-hearted persiflage, but the subject comes up again and again, often with serious tone. Thus Hallam, in *Funeral in Berlin*, reacts to the hero as an

"Upstart," said Hallam.
He put a finger against the cat's ear. The cat purred. An upstart from Burnley—a supercilious, anti-public school technician who thought he was an administrator.[28]

As if to move the hero's prejudices against public school types into the realm of reasoned judgment, Deighton introduced two secondary characters in *The Ipcress File* and *Horse Under Water*. The first is Chico:

Chico always looked glad to see me; it made my day. It was his training, I suppose. He'd been to one of those good schools where you meet kids with influential uncles. I imagine that's how he got into the Horse Guards and now into W.O.O.C.(P) too; it must have been like being at school again. His profusion of lank-yellow hair hung heavily across his head.... He had the advantage of both a good brain and a family rich enough to have him using it.[29]

In spite of his reputed brain, Chico screws up everything that he touches and needs the anti-public school technician to save his bacon. Bernhard, in *Horse Under Water*, is the same sort of nincompoop. Here, the novel virtually ends with this comment on classy British education: " 'The only thing I learned at Cambridge,' said Bernhard, 'was how to put on a pair of fifteen-inch trousers without first removing my chukka boots'."[30] In the first few books, Deighton reverses situations so that the teddy boys come out of the prestigious universities while the knowledgeable, sensitive, competent men work their way out of the lower classes. The hero, far from being aggressively ignorant, displays fairly wide erudition. He can quote Loyola, Xenophon, Milton and Lao-tse; he knows Kierkegaard and Cezanne, and appreciates Ives, Berg and Schonberg. He has acquired all this, but not the "weedy accent" of the elite. Deighton focuses much of his hero's character in a brief incident in *Billion Dollar Brain*:

I wondered if they passed that Trade Union (positive vetting) file over to someone else or whether they were keeping it for my return. None of those public school boys would be able to do that job with the instinct that I would be able to bring to it. Yet some of the people concerned would be people I was at school with; and in any case it would call upon allegiances that I had continuously pushed into the rear recesses of my mind.[31]

The significance here does not lie with the government poking around into union leaders' lives; it lies with the hero's recognition that he can best do the job and yet his consciousness that he is reluctant to do it. This we need to set against the self-assured pomposity of the public school old-boy network—the folks who brought Britain Burgess and Maclean.

In the long run, Deighton does concede that people from the upper middle class and even from public schools can be human. Ferdy Foxwell in *Spy Story* is human in spite of his wealth and education; indeed he is more human because of his connection with traditional things, including coal fires, rather than computers and international conniving—a motif also apparent in *Yesterday's Spy*. In *Catch a Falling Spy*, the hero finds something repulsive but also something awesome about Mann's and Dempsey's honesty and devotion to duty which comes from their parallel public school backgrounds. Indeed, Deighton's latest hero, Archer in *S.S.—G.B.*, is an Oxford-educated rich kid.

Now then Deighton's development as a writer, which I have been referring to all along, really grows out of the three stage development of his hero. In the early novels—say up to half way through *Billion Dollar Brain*—Deighton develops his hero as the hard man. He has romantic interludes, but they are brief and unsentimental. Most of his energy he directs toward keeping himself from being used by people in power. In these books there are no hard and fast ideological prejudices, and Stok of the KGB is a spokesman for humane concerns in *Funeral in Berlin* and *Billion Dollar Brain*

With *Billion Dollar Brain* the hero starts to change. At the end of this book he violates orders and this brings him to the dilemma of whether to assassinate his friend, Harvey Newbegin. With *An Expensive Place to Die* Deighton moves him out of the headquarters of W.O.O.C.(P) and isolates him in the field. His love affairs in *Catch a Falling Spy* and *Spy Story* are more detailed and they turn out unfortunately—one lover leaves him and the other turns lesbian. In these middle novels the hero opens up more fully to compassion, as with Champion's son in *Yesterday's Spy*, and his friendship with Mann and Foxwell. Here he feels the straight-jacket of British reserve: "He deserved some warmer reassurance, something that reflected the times we'd had together. Something that told him I'd stake my life upon his judgment—be it good or bad. But I was too English for such extravagances."[32] These books are more ideologically simple, seen in the Israel-Egypt background of *Yesterday's Spy*, and especially seen in the change of Colonel Stok from an avuncular figure to the mechanical KGB thug who appears in *Spy Story*. In these books Deighton drops the scholarly apparatus of spy realism and turns the hero's cynicism on itself, making clear that cynicism is really idealism:

> "You were too cynical," said Byrd. "I should have expected you to crack." He stared at me. "Cynics are disappointed romantics, they keep looking for someone to admire and can never fine anyone. You'll grow out of it."
> "I don't want to grow out of it," I said.[33]

By the time of *SS.—G.B.* Deighton changes or develops his hero in a third way. Here, of course, the hero has a name, Archer, and he comes from and exists in a world far different from that in the early novels. Archer, in fact, seems much like a hero out of classic British detective fiction, once it was toned down by the realism of the thirties. In *S.S.—G.B.* Archer undergoes a conversion, even though Deighton does not detail it very much, when he commits himself to the resistance fighters. He is, further, a loser. Unlike the early hero who knows all the facts and acts properly upon them, Archer is led up the garden path by Mayhew, and he never senses the truth until the condemned Hugh fills him in at the end of the book. Here the issues of duplicity and power are much more complex than in the earlier books because Deighton, like Ferdy Foxwell in *Spy Story*, finds far more challenge and fruit in reprogramming old battles than in piddling around with abstract speculations about future wars.

In a sense, Deighton's writing, in spite of its contemporary reference and relevance, grows out of historical conventions of the spy novel, and the author's reconstruction of them using new variables. In *The Ipcress File* and *An Expensive Place to Die* he goes back to the Master Criminal plot so popular in the twenties and the thirties. Both novels rely on the machinations of one perverted genius who has government officials in his pocket and who does nasty things in order to swell both his purse and his ego. Like their earlier counterparts, both villains are worldly wise and pretend to hold themselves aloof from society's foibles. Datt and Jay both offer analysis and advice to the hero in the tone of the weary pedagogue who knows that his student is too thick-headed to learn. Jay is even an epicure. All this is conventional and we can find it in the villains of Sapper and Beeding. What Deighton adds is the unconventional ending. At the end of *The Ipcress File* we find Jay yanked out of the kidnapping business and given a nice job as a civil servant, while his tool, Dalby, gets killed. Datt, in *An Expensive Place to Die,* dribbles down from a heroic enemy of the West into a prissy social scientist scampering around trying to preserve his dubious data. On the whole, though, the Master Crook scheme is a relatively minor element in Deighton's books. Where the conventions of the spy novel really inform Deighton's writing is in *S.S.—G.B.* The novel updates *The Battle of Dorking* and LeQueux's replays of its scenario in his imaginary war books. Like LeQueux's war prophecy books, *S.S.— G.B.* recounts the invasion of Britain by picturing popular landmarks destroyed by the fighting (like Buckingham Palace), recounting the fighting through London's suburbs, focusing on the development of a secret weapon, and picturing Britain's eventual salvation coming from across the sea. Deighton, however, sets the imaginary war in the past rather than in the future, but the conventions of the spy novel help his best structured spy novel.

That *S.S.—G.B.* is Deighton's most structured novel does not mean that he did not try to structure his earlier books. *S.S.—G.B.*, though, does not rely, like the earlier novels, on movement, fast and frequent movement. *Funeral in Berlin*, for instance, goes from London to Germany to France to Czechoslovakia, and back and forth between these places. The same thing happens in all the pre-1979 novels, and often the globe-trotting becomes dizzying. We follow the hero to the Soviet Union, the United States, Africa, Finland, Spain, Portugal, France, the Arctic Circle, Belgium, Bikini Atoll, and so on. All this travelling serves as more than a chance for Deighton to draw exotic scenery. It functions in the mystery organization of the novels. Deighton hops his hero and his readers about so quickly that they have little time to consider the questions or to observe the clues which the author places in the text. He is able, in this way, to give readers a surprise ending, much like those in the hard-boiled detective story where the hero knows but does not have time to unravel the mystery until the very end of the action. But Deighton does try to hold his hectic action together by other means. He structures by repeating small motifs, like the hero's back pay in *The Ipcress File*, or his adipose tissue in *Horse Under Water* and *Funeral in Berlin*. This technique culminates in the repeated bird images in *An Expensive Place to Die* which tie the novel together. These things do not make the plots any easier to follow—and part of Deighton's point is that spy action is often so convoluted that we cannot follow it—but they provide familiar landmarks so that the readers have an illusion of structure. Deighton does, though, sometimes use images to point to theme. There are Scrabble references in *Billion Dollar Brain* which frame the hero in his American interlude, and which coincide with the simile:

" 'Computers are like Scrabble games,' I told her. 'Unless you know how to use them they're just a boxful of junk'."[34]

More important than this reference are Deighton's references to crossword puzzles in his first few novels. The crossword, of course, is a favorite detective story metaphor from the twenties onward. It implied then the powers of a superior mind snapping in the crossword answers from an encyclopedic store of knowledge. Deighton, however, does not use crosswords this way. His hero carries a crossword puzzle around with him, but he has a devil of a time with it, as with these two passages from *The Ipcress File:* "I crossed out 'rondoletto' and wrote in 'dithyrambs,' which made twenty one down 'awe' instead of 'ewe.' It was beginning to shape up."[35] Fifteen pages later we get: "Walking back to the house, I decided to try 'dithryrambe' without the final 'e.' This would make ten down 'eat' and not 'sat' or 'oat.' I was really getting on now."[36] In the middle of the novel, Alice, the secretary, completes the puzzle, but the hero pretends not to notice it, just as he pretends not to notice the solution to the crime-spy puzzle which he arrives at as Alice finishes the crossword. In normal experience, crossword puzzles have this effect on most of us: we bumble around trying this word or that word. Deighton reflects this and he uses the puzzle as a structural member and as a clue, manifestly obscured, to the whole perplexing business.

In any number of ways, then, Deighton represents the Golden Age of the spy novel. He deals with serious, contemporary issues within the tested conventions of the detective novel and the spy story. He has interest in narrative craft, beyond simply repeating elements of the adventure story. His principal character is more than a stooge, and he grows to reflect the writer's own development. While Deighton still remains a spy novelist instead of simply a novelist, he brings a good deal of repute to the form.

NOTES

[1]*Funeral in Berlin* (New York: Dell, 1966), p. 25.
[2]*Funeral in Berlin*, p. 52.
[3]*Funeral in Berlin*, p. 62.
[4]*The Ipcress File* (New York: Fawcett, 1965), p. 15.
[5]*The Ipcress File*, p. 16.
[6]*Billion Dollar Brain* (London: Cape, 1966), p. 39.

[7]*Funeral in Berlin*, p. 137.

[8]*Horse Under Water* (Harmondsworth: Penguin, 1965), p. 227.

[9]*Funeral in Berlin*, endpapers.

[10]*The Ipcress File*, pp. 127-8.

[11]*Horse Under Water*, p. 93.

[12]*Funeral in Berlin*, pp. 100-1.

[13]*Billion Dollar Brain*, p. 156.

[14]*An Expensive Place to Die* (New York: Putnams, 1967), p. 67.

[15]*An Expensive Place to Die*, p. 67.

[16]*The Ipcress File*, p. 10.

[17]*Funeral in Berlin*, p. 28.

[18]*Funeral in Berlin*, pp. 77-8.

[19]*The Ipcress File*, p. 105.

[20]*Horse Under Water*, p. 140.

[21]*An Expensive Place to Die*, p. 14.

[22]*The Ipcress File*, p. 70.

[23]*Horse Under Water*, p. 158.

[24]*An Expensive Place to Die*, p. 89.

[25]*An Expensive Place to Die*, p. 236.

[26]*An Expensive Place to Die*, p. 79.

[27]*The Ipcress File*, p. 14.

[28]*Funeral in Berlin*, p. 16.

[29]*The Ipcress File*, p. 12.

[30]*Horse Under Water*, p. 228.

[31]*Billion Dollar Brain*, p. 162.

[32]*Catch a Falling Spy* (New York: Harcourt, Brace, Jovanovitch, 1976), p. 62.

[33]*An Expensive Place to Die*, p. 209.

[34]*Billion Dollar Brain*, p. 222.

[35]*The Ipcress File*, p. 29.

[36]*The Ipcress File*, p. 44.

Chapter 15
John LeCarré
(1931—)

David John Moore Cornwell chose a pen name without regard for people who have to write it as a possessive. The name LeCarré, though, does bring to mind a number of important associations. It echoes the name of one of the inventors of the spy novel, William LeQueux, and it demonstrates the tensions so important to Cornwell's own spy novels. With its French meaning, the square, LeCarré stands for the finished geometrical figure opposed to LeQueux, the line, limping along to infinity. The figure of the square also represents the antithesis to the circle, the Circus, the name of the spy organization which LeCarré invents and chronicles in his novels. To date, Cornwell has used the name LeCarré for seven espionage books: *Call for the Dead* (1961), *The Spy Who Came in from the Cold* (1963), *The Looking Glass War* (1965), *A Small Town in Germany* (1968), and the Karla trilogy—*Tinker, Tailor, Soldier, Spy* (1974), *The Honourable Schoolboy* (1977), and *Smiley's People* (1980). LeCarré is also the pseudonym for Cornwell's two non-espionage novels, *A Murder of Quality* (1962), a detective novel featuring George Smiley, and *The Naive and Sentimental Lover* (1972), a regular novel contrasting the worlds of the bourgeois and the artist.

LeCarré connects himself with the established traditions of the English spy novel. He does this through the associations of the pseudonym of LeCarré, and he also acknowledges John Buchan in choosing Mr. Standfast for his hero's workname, and in borrowing the name of Craw in *The Honourable Schoolboy* from Buchan's newspaper proprietor in *Castle Gay* (1930). Nevertheless, LeCarré represents those things which are most contemporary in the spy novel. Unlike the fantasies of Fleming or Hall, Le Carré portrays an enervated Britian reeling from its fall from international power and its own internal problems. He uses the spy organization to examine not necessarily spies, but the way in which men serve institutions and institutions serve men. Chiefly, though, he uses the spy novel as a vehicle to explore human identity and the actions and reactions which contribute meaning to otherwise empty lives. Finally, LeCarré has concentrated upon the literary craftsmanship of the spy book. None of his fictions comes out overnight following the same pat literary formula. His first novel, *Call for the Dead,* shows all of the tightness and consciousness of a first-class literary maker, and he has continued to develop his skills in the complex point of view and the intricate plots of his recent novels. In his most recent novels, *The Honourable Schoolboy* and *Smiley's People,* LeCarré tends to turn inward and backward, developing the past of his own fictional world. Rather than narcissism, though, this represents a general trend in literature, from Updike's *Rabbit Redux* to Barth's *Letters,* to return and augment early material, to contrast the past with the present, or to acknowledge the creation of a world and its people as the most important facet of literary imagination. All of these elements move LeCarré out of the category of popular fiction into the class of regular literature. With *The Honourable Schoolboy,* particularly, average readers begin reading with the notion that they will enjoy this best-seller; they proceed with the idea that they ought to appreciate the novel which reviewers have praised, but they then give it up whining that it is too confusing, too hard. This is, of course, absurd: try Pyncheon, try Barth, try Burgess. LeCarré does not really challenge us as readers. If he is difficult, it is because his world and ours is difficult; his manner of presentation is not simply that of beginning, middle, and end, but then real stories do not develop simply. After Conrad, LeCarré gives us the most thorough, the most realistic, the most thoughtful, and therefore the most disturbing, portrait of the secret world found in spy fiction.

LeCarré began writing about spies because of the security crisis in post-war Britain. Literally, George Smiley, the principal spy in the LeCarré novels, enters, or reenters, the secret world in the first novel instead of staying at Oxford because of

...the revelations of a young Russian cypher-clerk in Ottawa [who] had created a new demand for men of Smiley's experience.[1]

This refers to the actual defection of Igor Gouzenko on September 5, 1945; Gouzenko's defection led to the falling dominoes of arrests, trials, and defections in the fifties: the arrests of Alan Nunn May and Klaus Fuchs for passing on nuclear secrets, and the defections of Bruno Pontecorvo, Guy Burgess, Donald Maclean and, finally, Kim Philby. In *Call for the Dead,* LeCarré twice alludes to Maclean and Fuchs (he avoids mentioning Burgess, perhaps because of his insignificance as a security danger or perhaps because of the complexities raised by the fact that both Burgess and LeCarré were old Eton boys—although in *The Naive and Sentimental Lover,* the heroes adopt the pseudonyms of Burgess and Maclean for a night on the town in Paris). Throughout most of his books LeCarré centers his plots on double agents, moles, and defections. *Call for the Dead* concerns the security clearance of Fennan, a Foreign Office official controlled by the East Germans. *The Spy Who Came in from the Cold* reverses things and deals with a British agent in the woodwork of East German security. *Tinker, Tailor* is a Philby novel, tracing the discovery of a Soviet mole in the garden of British security. A Soviet mole in the People's Republic of China lies at the heart of *The Honourable Schoolboy. Smiley's People* concludes a motif begun in *Tinker, Tailor,* showing the successful intimidation of a Soviet official in order to force him to defect. The double agent opens up all sorts of fictional possibilities for the spy writer. LeCarré could have treated this material on a simple game level (you hide them, we find them), or he could have played it as an international game (Soviets 4; British 4), but he does not. Double agents and defectors are more than plot material. LeCarré views defection in somewhat the same light as Greene does in *The Human Factor:* it is a test of consciousness, not so much for the individual who leaves, mentally or physically, but for those who remain behind and must deal with themselves.

For LeCarré man is essentially an isolated, undefined entity, existing in a world which is terribly difficult but one in which identity is possible on a number of levels. To find the essential LeCarré, we need first to consider the phrases which he repeats in one novel after another. The first is a quotation from Hesse, here taken from *Call for the Dead:*

But who could tell? What did Hesse write? "Strange to wander in the mist, each is alone." We know nothing of one another, nothing. Smiley mused. However closely we live together, at whatever time of day or night we sound the deepest thoughts in one another, we know nothing.[2]

Like this statement on human isolation, LeCarré repeats in several novels an anecdote illustrating the emptiness of existence. Here Smiley recites it to a murder suspect in *A Murder of Quality:*

"You know, Fielding," he said at last, "we just don't know what people are like, we can never tell; there isn't any truth about human beings, no formula that meets each one of us. And there are some of us—aren't there?—who are nothing, who are so labile that we astound ourselves; we're the chameleons. I read a story once about a poet who bathed himself in cold fountains so that he could recognize his own existence in the contrast. He had to reassure himself, you see, like a child being hateful to its parents. You might say he had to make the sun shine on him so that he could see his shadow and feel alive."[3]

If bathing in fountains is an effete method of demonstrating one's existence, LeCarré introduces a sterner, more authoritative passage in several of the novels. Here, Jerry Westerby solves his crisis of motivation by recalling it and later acting upon it:

Even now, he needed that long to bring himself to the point, because Jerry at heart was a soldier and voted with his feet. *In the beginning was the deed,* Smiley liked to say to him, in his failed-priest mood, quoting from Goethe. For Jerry that simple statement had become a pillar of his uncomplicated philosophy. What a man thinks is his own business. What matters is what he does.[4] [LeCarré's italics]

This is a definitive statement for the heroes in LeCarré, but he uses other motifs to shape the hero's consciousness. First comes a point about the proper shaping of doubt. This runs through *The Looking Glass War,* but Alan Turner in *A Small Town in Germany* gives it its fullest formulation:

He looked once more at the diary and thought: Question fundamentals. Madam, show this tired schoolboy your fundamentals, learn the parts, read the book from scratch— that was your tutor's advice, and who are you to ignore the advice of your tutor? Do not ask *why* Christ was born on Christmas Day—ask whether he was born at all.[5]

Even if one knows the proper question, people in LeCarré face situations in which all solutions are equally true or equally false. To establish this situation in his books, from the last chapter in *Call for the Dead* ("Between Two Worlds") to *Smiley's People,* LeCarré implies these lines from Arnold's "Stanzas from the Grand Chartreuse":

> Wandering between two worlds, one dead
> The other powerless to be born
> With nowhere yet to rest my head,
> Like these, on earth, I wait forlorn

People do not, though, have to moulder among monkish crypts for LeCarré has another alternative, again contained in a quotation, which he occasionally brings in. In *Tinker, Tailor* Roy Bland gives us this solution:

An artist is a bloke who can hold two fundamentally oppoisng views and still function.[6]

So says F. Scott Fitzgerald and so says LeCarré. The formula, then, goes: isolation, questioning, knowledge of relativity, synthesis, action. Out of these literary fragments LeCarré builds a path of behavior, a body of characters, nine plots, and his world.

LeCarré bases his world on the fact, stated by Hesse, that we know very little about other people. Just as importantly, his characters know very little about themselves. In the novels LeCarré puts his people into circumstances in which they have opportunities to find out about themselves or, failing this, to absorb identity from their surroundings. On the easiest level, the institution—whether the Department of *Looking Glass War* or the Circus—provides roles, goals and identities for its employees. We can see this with characters like Connie Sachs, "Mother Russia," in the Karla trilogy. In spite of her eccentricities, without her archives and the direction given by research, Connie, as seen in *Smiley's People,* is a gin-sodden wreck, facing the horror of death without props or resources. The Circus, too, gives focus to the lives of bureaucrats and wheeler-dealers in LeCarré. Saul Enderby and Sam Collins act as chameleons in *The Honourable Schoolboy* and *Smiley's People,* coloring themselves to fit the current requisites of their jobs or the temporary hue of international affairs. Thus Collins, in the first book, is a sinister figure clawing his way up to a permanent job on the fifth floor, but, having achieved this, in *Smiley's People,* he becomes a grinning, brow-beaten toady because his situation demands it. All of this culminates in *The Looking Glass War,* where LeCarré presents a full-scale demonstration of institutions making people's lives. Here Taylor, Avery, LeClerc, Haldane, Leiser, and even the janitors draw their moods, their very beings from the Department. Thus LeCarré opens up Avery's mind and shows that:

He thanked LeClerc, thanked him warmly, for the privilege of knowing these men, for the excitement of the mission; for the opportunity to advance from the uncertainty of the past toward experience and maturity, to become a man shoulder to shoulder with others, tempered in the fire of war; he thanked him for the precision of command, which made order out of anarchy of his heart.[7]

For all of the agents in the field, Leamas, Leiser, Westerby, the institution provides a pre-packaged identity not only with the false papers and cover story, but, more importantly, in the prescribed rules of behavior drummed into them at training school and in the goal of the mission itself. Therefore, at the end of *The Spy Who Came in from the Cold,* when Leamas has lost his illusions about almost everything else, he still believes in his mission:

"There's only one law in this game," Leamas retorted. 'Mundt is their man; he gives them what they need. That's easy enough to understand, isn't it? Leninism—the expediency of temporary alliances. What do you think spies are: priests, saints and martyrs? They're a squalid procession of vain fools, traitors, too, yes; pansies, sadists, and drunkards, people who play cowboys and Indians to brighten their rotten lives. Do you think they sit like monks in London, balancing rights and wrongs? I'd have killed Mundt if I could, I hate his guts; but not now. It so happens that they need him. They need him so that the great moronic mass you admire can sleep soundly in their beds at night. They need him for the safety of ordinary, crummy people like you and me."[8]

If we know nothing of ourselves, LeCarré says, spying and its institutions can give us identities—identities which can be base or which can be noble.

The problem with this sort of identity resides in the fact that "there isn't any formula that meets each one of us." The agent is a human being and consequently imponderable. In *The Looking Glass War,* Haldane, the old spy, answers Avery's query about agents' motives only with questions:

"Why do agents ever do anything? Why do any of us...
Why do they consent or refuse, why do they lie or tell the truth? Why do any of us?"[9]

During the course of each of the LeCarré novels, the hero steps out of line, breaks the pattern, sees other goals and identities and commits himself to them. In *The Spy Who Came in from the Cold,* Leamas commits himself to love; Leiser, in *The Looking Glass War,* on a lesser scale, does the same thing; Leo, in *A Small Town in Germany,* commits himself to justice; Jerry, in *The Honourable Schoolboy,* commits himself to love; and George Smiley does a similar thing by refusing the victor's spoils at the close of *Call for the Dead, Tinker, Tailor, The Honourable Schoolboy* and *Smiley's People.* These acts define these particular characters; these are the plunges into cold fountains; these are the proofs, not of December 25, but of Christ's existence. Fixing identity, committing oneself, in *The Spy Who Came in from the Cold, The Looking Glass War, A Small Town in Germany,* and *The Honourable Schoolboy* comes only with the hero's death. Only then can his identity remain fixed and stable in a world whose only constant is change.

On a personal level, LeCarré gives his characters worlds in which little remains stable: wives betray husbands, husbands destroy wives, friends betray friends, students reject teachers, individuals deceive themselves. Smiley's marriage, Avery's marriage, Lacon's marriage, Lizzie Worthington's marriage, even Karla's marriage all split apart, leaving characters between love and isolation, commitment and isolation. The world in LeCarré is not, however, chaotic: from the very first novel, LeCarré builds his fictional world on polar issues, and he continues to portray a world of opposites in each novel. The mind versus the body, the past versus the present, contemplation versus action, secrecy versus intimacy, the institution versus the individual, aloofness versus consciousness, the Cousins (the CIA) versus the Circus, the state versus the individual, absolutism versus relativity: these are some of the alternatives upon which LeCarre strings his novels. A certain type of person (for LeCarré, the bureaucrat) thrives in this world of ambiguities, like an amphibian living on both land and water but never wedded to either. For his heroes, however, it is an unbearable strain to live an uncommitted, undefined existence. They cannot tolerate the position of being "between two worlds," and they act, they engage themselves to one of the alternatives and pass out of the world of flux. They all do it except George Smiley, the continuing hero of the LeCarré novels, who, like Fitzgerald's artist, repeatedly attempts to find a human path between clashing extremes.

LeCarré brings George Smiley into all of his spy novels except *A Small Town in Germany,* which is an experiment with the hard-boiled hero. In *The Spy Who Came in from the Cold* and *The Looking Glass War* Smiley plays minor roles, but even in these books his appearance is important to the message of the plot. In fact, the author's desire to include his continuing character in his plots causes LeCarré to make Smiley a menacing character in *The Spy Who Came in from the Cold* because he wants to include Smiley but cannot invent a role for his humanistic nature in this plot. Despite this one breach of artistic judgment, LeCarré has spent a good deal of his creative energy since 1961 in delineating Smiley and comparing other characters to him in order to make points about the human condition.

Physically, George Smiley is a made-to-measure anti-hero. He is, in the term which LeCarré applies to several other characters, "one of life's losers." In the context of the schoolboy novel, Smiley would be the non-athletic fat boy. In the context of the adult espionage novel, he remains the fat boy, the outsider. At the beginning of *Call for the Dead,* LeCarré introduces him to us as

Short, fat, and of a quiet disposition, he appeared to spend a lot of money on really bad clothes, which hung about his squat frame like skin on a shrunken toad.[10]

Especially in the early novels LeCarré keeps the image of the toad attached to Smiley: his wife, in remembered conversations, calls him "toad" and "toad lover." LeCarré makes Smiley a largely passive character. He wants to be left alone, and other people (Frey, Control, Haydon, Karla) initiate the action in the novels while another group of characters (Mendel, Prideaux, Westerby, Gulliam, Fawn, Toby) performs the important deeds in the books. As we can see in *A Murder of Quality,* Smiley comes from the tradition of the cerebral detective and not from the tradition of the spy hero. Especially in *Call for the Dead* LeCarré emphasizes not his physical acts but Smiley's intellectual travels, which are those of the intellectual detective: he finds clues, makes lists, and suddenly synthesizes this information. Thus, *Call for the Dead* turns on the following passage:

> As he stood gazing at the little shepherdess, poised eternally between her two admirers, he realized dispassionately that there was another quite different solution..., a solution which matched every detail of circumstance, reconciled the nagging inconsistencies...the realization began as an academic exercise without reference to personalities; Smiley maneuvered the characters like pieces in a puzzle, twisting them this way and that to fit the complex framework of established facts— and then, in a moment, the pattern had suddenly re-formed with such assurance that it was a game no more.[11]

The detective element remains with Smiley through all of his adventures. He must detect the mole at the Circus in *Tinker, Tailor,* he must discover why Moscow pays Drake Ko such large sums of money in *The Honourable Schoolboy,* and in *Smiley's People* he must unravel the reason that Soviet hoods have been bothering Maria Ostrakova. He does solve all of the problems, but like most fictional British detectives since the late 1920s (Sayers' Peter Wimsey, for example), Smiley always finds, to his grief, that the hunt must end in the kill and that the kill can be bloody, senseless and obscene. But this gets too far ahead of the argument.

The introduction of the term academic, as in the passage above, holds much for LeCarré, and in his novels he uses it not only as a general description of people and behavior, but he also explores its real application to the intelligence community. George Smiley belongs to the older generation of intelligence workers from a time when the spy establishment was founded and run by true academics. LeCarré frequently goes through the litany of the founders' names. There was Jebedee, Smiley's tutor at Oxford.

There was Fielding, the French medievalist from Cambridge, Sparke from the school of Oriental languages, and Steed-Asprey who had been dining at High Table the night Smiley had been Jebedee's guest.[12]

During the war, LeCarré tells us, spying grew out of the academy, it was an amateur enterprise, it has traditional associations, it was upper class and unorthodox, and it died when the war ended:

> Gone for ever were the days of Steed-Asprey, when like as not you took your orders over a glass of port in his rooms at Magdalen; the inspired amateurism of a handful of highly qualified, under-paid men had given way to the efficiency, bureaucracy and intrigue of a large government department.[13]

This passage gets us to the institutional theme which I will take up later, but it also cements Smiley in with the older generation of academic humanists who temporarily became spies to serve their country and their ideals. From the start LeCarré feels that the academic side of Smiley, not just the quality of his mind, needs to be emphasized. In introducing us to his hero, the narrator of *Call for the Dead* says that he

> ...dreamed of fellowships and a life devoted to the literary obscurities of seventeenth-century Germany. But his own tutor, who knew Smiley better, guided him wisely away from the honours that would undoubtedly have been his.[14]

The word "wisely" here suggests that Smiley will be able to achieve selfhood in the conflict and spiritual tensions of espionage, whereas the purely academic life will give him only static non-entity. Smiley, however, never goes far from the academe in his new profession as a spy. In the history which LeCarré builds for him we learn that, after Oxford, Smiley taught in Germany and that directly after the war he, like the other dons turned spy, left the Circus and returned to Oxford to teach and do research. Throughout the novels Smiley continues his involvement with German baroque literature, and characters frequently mistake him for a schoolmaster. The school, as we will see later, assumes a vital metaphoric role in these novels. On the character level, though, it affects Smiley because an essential part of him is a teacher. Particularly in *Call for the Dead* and *The Honourable Schoolboy*, LeCarré includes Smiley's students, Frey and Westerby, in the plots in order to bring out the intellectual and emotional complexities and paradoxes implicit in the teacher-student relationship.

Smiley also lives with the complexities and paradoxes of his marriage to Lady Ann Sercombe. This is a match of Beauty and the Beast, the Princess and the Toad. Smiley's Ann, aristocratic and painfully beautiful, takes up a life of philandering from the second sentence of *Call for the Dead.* She runs off with a Cuban race car driver, and, as the books proceed, fills her dance card with myriad names—including that of Bill Haydon, Moscow's spy at Circus. Yet, from the end of the first novel to the scene in the middle of *Smiley's People* (the only place in the canon where she actually appears), she always returns to Smiley seeking reconciliation. From an objective viewpoint, Ann is a tart and Smiley is a besotted cuckold for indulging her in her infidelities. Yet in the novels she represents more than this. She stands for Smiley's unwilling and masochistic relationship with conventional, upper-class life. The question of "How's Ann?" reminds readers of Smiley's separation from people like Saul Enderby or Roddy Martindale. Ann, moreover, stands for a variety of human contacts which Smiley wants and needs but cannot achieve. This stands out when LeCarré describes Smiley's relationship with Mendel in *Call for the Dead:*

> It was four o'clock. They sat for a while talking in a rather desultory way about bees and housekeeping, Mendel quite at ease and Smiley still bothered and awkward, trying to find a way of talking, trying not to be clever. He could guess what Ann would have said about Mendel. She would have loved him, made a person of him, had a special voice and face for imitating him, would have made a story of him until he fitted into their lives and wasn't a mystery any more... "Toad, do ask him to dinner. You must. Not to giggle at but to *like.*"[15]

This part of Ann, Smiley realizes, is half artificial—he realizes that she would soon dismiss Mendel from her consciousness—but he craves her easy sociability. He also needs Ann's perceptive and definite analyses of his own pesonal dilemmas—

> Only Ann, though she could not read his workings, refused to accept his findings. She was quite passionate, in fact, as only women can be on matters of business, really driving him to go back, take up where he had left off, never to veer aside in favour of the easy arguments.[16]

Finally, Ann's continued presence represents for Smiley the goal of love. LeCarré never makes this point mawkishly; indeed, in *Call for the Dead,* he belittles it at the end of the novel referring to Smiley's return to Ann as "the pathetic quest for love." Yet this Sisyphean quest, which lasts through the middle of *Smiley's People,* is superior to the quest for the "black grail," one's enemies, Karla.

That Smiley possesses the sensitivity to realize his equivocal positions is another main point in his character. Coming, as I have said, from the Golden Age detective hero, Smiley combines acumen with human sympathy. In *A Murder of Quality,* the narrator tells us that

...once in the war he had been described by his superiors as possessing the cunning of Satan and the conscience of a virgin...[17]

Just as Karla provides a contrast to evoke Smiley's humanity in the later novels, Mendel provides one in *Call for the Dead.* As a policeman, Mendel accepts that his job requires him to deal with "the squalor" of criminals and the criminal mind, and he ignores the causes of deviant behavior because his role requires him to expunge the effects of human wickedness. Smiley, on the other hand, also deals with the effects of wickedness, but he always acknowledges and grieves for the causes. He steps out of the role of George Smiley and tries to see what others see and feel what others feel. Interviewing a woman who later turns out to be a communist agent, Smiley goes beyond the hunt and analyzes himself as the hunter:

Smiley felt suddenly sick and cheap. Loyalty to whom, to what? She didn't sound resentful. He was the oppressor.[18]

Very early LeCarré attaches the term "toad" to Smiley. This works as an anti-heroic physical description, but it has a mental referent too. Smiley is Mr. Toad from *Wind in the Willows,* constantly becoming other people, and refusing the domestic comforts of Toad Hall for the arduous life of the road. He has the unique capacity for being not only himself but also being everybody. LeCarré makes this fact clear with the self-consciously over-blown rhetoric in *Smiley's People,* when the Superintendent reflects upon his encounter with Smiley:

Not one face at all actually, the Superintendent reflected...more your whole range of faces. More your patchwork of different ages, people, and endeavors. Even—though the Superintendent—of different faiths.

...

An Abbey, the Superintendent decided. That's what he was, an abbey.... An abbey, made up of all sorts of conflicting ages and styles and convictions.[19]

Smiley can be everybody and be himself—indeed he needs to be everyone to be himself, just as Fitzgerald needs to be himself and Gatsby. If Smiley is not quite Shakespeare's "heavenly mingle" of Rome and Alexandria, or Arnold's wished-for synthesis of old and new, he is the only character in LeCarré who can stand between two worlds and, if not reconcile them, live with the opposites thrust upon him by life.

In the last two novels, however, LeCarré shows the dissolution of Smiley's abbey. Unlike the eternally youthful adventure hero of the conventional spy book, Smiley, never young, grows older in the novels. With age he loses his ability to respond to life in a private and flexible manner. At the end of *The Honourable Schoolboy* he admits as much in a letter to Ann:

Today, all I know is that I have learned to interpret the whole of life in terms of conspiracy. That is the sword I have lived by, and as I look round me now I see it is the sword I shall die by as well. These people terrify me, but I am one of them.[20]

In *Smiley's People,* George moves from the multifaceted human being to the single-minded one. Whereas in his first encounter with Karla, the Russian spy-master (described in *Tinker, Tailor),* Smiley projected himself onto Karla, in the last novel quite the opposite happens and Smiley, as a logical but depressing consequence of their competition, becomes the remorseless gamester just when Karla proves that he *is* like Smiley. In doing this Smiley cuts himself off from Ann, refusing the invitation she offers in the middle of the novel. He wins Karla's defection, but loses himself; he, like Antony, goes over to Rome and betrays his heart. Smiley, in *Smiley's People,* moves from between two worlds, but in so doing he loses the humanity which he possessed. All he has left is his painful consciousness—as in the Hardy poem "I Look into My Glass":

> I look into my glass
> And view my wasting skin,
> And say, "Would God it came to pass
> My heart had shrunk as thin."
>
> (1-4)

But Smiley is just one man. As old Craw says in *The Honourable Schoolboy:*

"The old order changes not, let it run on. You won't stop the wheel—not together, not divided—you snivelling, arse-licking novices! You're a bunch of suicidal tits to try."[21]

The wheel represents the fundamental change of human exitence, but it also stands for the force of humans acting in concert through the institution. The people in LeCarré live and work in institutions which give them roles and often subsume their uniqueness. Drawing the institution, therefore, becomes of utmost importance to LeCarré and his fictions, not only in order to present his spies' worlds fully and realistically, but also to delineate problems of human behavior. In a 1977 interview LeCarré described the world of Circus as:

>...a microcosm of all institutional behavior, and the ever-repeated dilemma which overcomes individuals when they submit their talent for institutional exploitation.[22]

To a far greater extent than Cheyney or Fleming or Deighton or Hall or Haggard, LeCarré brings the institution of the Circus across to his readers. First, he gives it local habitation and a name. His spy organization is not a series of initials (M.I.6; WOOCP; etc.) but a nickname, bringing it more intimately to our attention. It resides in an Edwardian building on Cambridge Circus in London. Especially in *The Honourable Schoolboy* LeCarré renders a sense of place, describing the torn-up walls, the piles of plaster, and the litter, of papers. Although he does not describe them in detail, LeCarré gives readers the impression that the Circus is, really, the headquarters of an extensive institution. Once again he does this by giving name, or nickname, and location—

>...the Sarratt Nursery...the experimental audio laboratories in Harlow; the stinks-and-bangs school in Argyll; the water school in the Helford Estuary...the long-arm radio-transmission base at Canterbury...[and] the wranglers' headquarters in Bath, where the code-breaking went on.[23]

Once LeCarré hooks readers by the places, he dips them into a world of professional jargon. We find LeCarré speaking of lamplighters, babysitters, scalp-hunters, yellow-perils, sound-thieves, ferrets, honey traps, bugger-all, cousins, etc. These draw us further into the secret world and through them LeCarré also shows how people within institutions invent their own jargon, not to communicate more effectively but to cut themselves off from the outside world (in *Smiley's People,* George, retired for some months, has to ask the meaning of "bugger-all), and also to humanize their own inhuman realm through inventing nicknames. LeCarré knew his Orwell. For the same purposes he shows the jargon extended to a special, insiders' language when Jerry speaks Red Indian to Smiley in *Tinker, Tailor,* and with Craw's Vaticanese in *The Honourable Schoolboy.*

Unlike other spy writers, who concern themselves only with the present moment of their secret bureaus, LeCarré weaves the history of Circus through his novels. He, of course, ties this history to changing internal and international climates in Britain, but most of his attention goes to the personalities of the administrators who reflect the changes on a personal level. During the war, Circus was run by academics, Fielding, Jebedee, Sparke, Steed-Asprey, and Landsburg (added in *A Murder of Quality*). During this era, LeCarré suggests, Circus thrived because of the heroic state of the nation and the genuine class, brains, wit, and amateur status of its leaders. In *Call for the Dead* we meet the first post-war chief of Circus, one Maston. Maston dithers over issues, fawns on Ministers and M.P.'s, and lets his own people down:

It comforted the Great to deal with a man they knew, a man who could reduce any colour to grey, who knew his masters and could walk among them. And he did it so well. They liked his diffidence when he apologized for the company he kept, his insincerity when he defended the vagaries of his subordinates, his flexibilities when formulating new commitments. Nor did he let go the advantages of a cloak and dagger man *malgre lui,* wearing the cloak for his masters and preserving the dagger for his servants.[24]

Not only is Maston the complete bureaucrat, he lacks class: Smiley brands him as "a barmaid's dream of a real gentleman." With *The Spy Who Came in from the Cold* LeCarré cans Maston and brings in Control as the head of the Circus. Control has a bit of the old school about him: he is upper-class, dreadfully efficient, and a former don. Unlike the old academics who were brilliant, jovial and open, Control is the irascible scholar who works in secret and bitterly attacks what he perceives to be folly. Control is the spy's spy, the fictional cliché, holding all of the threads, coolly analyzing human motives, playing the Great Game successfully with his nation's enemies. He may get things done, but he is at first a sinister figure (in *The Spy Who Came in from the Cold*) and then, in *Tinker, Tailor,* he becomes a pathetic individual, cut off from his fellows, alone in a world of paranoia. After Control's death in *Tinker, Tailor,* the mantle passes to shallow, middle-class Percy Alleline. According to the Circus rumor mill, Alleline had been Control's student at Cambridge, "and a bad one." Maston recruited him to the Circus—thereby linking him to the bureaucratic type—where he achieved some success through his "faculty of bullish persuasion." Alleline possessed a "fatal reverence for the Americans" which caused him to flub a job in Egypt and landed him in a desk job. From there he used his political influence to promote himself to a more influential job, and from this job, Moscow Center gave him the material to oust Control and take his job—because he was a nincompoop. After the fall of Alleline and his Svengali, Bill Haydon, Smiley becomes the head of Circus in *The Honourable Schoolboy,* and he proves to be a master of intelligence technique. In the same novel, however,

Smiley as a leader and administrator loses to Saul Enderby and Sam Collins. These two, who take over the Circus in *Smiley's People,* are politicians in later-day Britian who believe that the path to strength lies in falling in with the Americans, as opposed to Control who "despised them and all their works...." This is also the sword by which they perish, for in *Smiley's People* Parliament has caught the fever for open government from the United States, has axed many of Circus' functions, and is considering alteration of the Official Secrets Act on the pattern of the Freedom of Information Act in the U.S.. Although he is not part of Circus, Oliver Lacon shows the contemporary decline of the service. Acting as liaison with the Cabinet, Lacon helps, albeit fussily, to unmask the mole in *Tinker, Tailor.* In *The Honourable Schoolboy* he sits on the fence, neutrally observing events, unsure of which way power will move. By *Smiley's People,* though, he has become a eunuch.

Although there are variations within them, from this organizational history emerge two types. The first type, which encompasses Lacon, Maston, Alleline, Enderby, and Control, plays the game and will do anything to win. Granted, for Control, winning may have some international or doctrinal significance, but winning counts more than anything. For the others, and especially for LeClerc in *The Looking Glass War,* winning means perpetuating one's place and one's institution, and staying in power regardless of the cost in life or the damage done to one's personality by pandering. The second type is different; Smiley is different. Power means little to Smiley, enacted in his repeated retirements and resignations. When Michael Maccoby describes "the craftsman" in his book, *The Gamesman: The New Corporate Leaders,* he also gives a fairly accurate picture of Smiley's executive character:

The craftsman holds the traditional values of the productive-hoarding character—the work ethic, respect for people, concern for quality and thrift. When he talks about his work his interest is in the *process* of making something; he enjoys building. He sees others, co-workers as well as superiors, in terms of whether they help or hinder him in doing a craftsmanlike job. Most of the craftsmen whom we intereviewed are quiet, sincere, modest, and practical.... Although his virtues are admired by everyone, his self-containment and perfectionism do not allow him to lead a complex and changing organization. Rather than engaging and trying to master the system with the cooperation of others who share his values, he tends to do his own thing and go along, sometimes reluctantly, toward goals he does not share, enjoying whatever opportunities he finds for interesting work.[25]

All of this describes Smiley with fair accuracy, except, perhaps, the last sentence. George does try to convince others of his values—especially Jerry in *The Honourable Schoolboy*—and he only goes along so far with those who do not share his values. Thus he quits the Circus after the war, after the action of *Call for the Dead* and after the action of *The Honourable Schoolboy;* in *Tinker, Tailor* and *Smiley's People,* in fact, Smiley is not a member of Circus but an outsider. So far, however, the organization has always drawn Smiley back to it, because for Smiley it is more than a limited company peddling whalebone or jute. These products are as temporary as are presidents, controls, ministers, and agents. For Smiley the Circus is both a mundane organization and a transcendent one: it is a church and a school.

Whenever he introduces the subject of organizations in the novels, the metaphors of the church and the school abound. These are the transcendent institutions, in their ideal state, to which all other institutions aspire. In the novels the idea of the school plays a more important role, but LeCarré does pointedly use the idea of the church to describe espionage institutions. From an organizational point of view, the church is a perfect corporate institution—not democratic sects but episcopal ones. It has a clear purpose, a desirable, even unique, product, a rigorous and clear organizational structure, and highly efficient means of motivating employee and consumer alike. Particularly in *The Looking Glass War,* LeCarré uses the image of the church to enrich his portrayal of an organization. Here, the Department induces its members to view their employer in religious terms:

For its servants, the Department had a religious quality. Like monks, they endowed it with a mystical identity far away from the hesitant, a sinful band which made up its ranks.[26]

In this novel the members of a seedy espionage department boost their sense of purpose by consistently drawing parallels between their misdirected and fumbling business, and the church. The director becomes a primate elected by his fading connection with the glamor of World War II, and his priests lead Leiser through a purposely mysterious set of novitiate vows. To their confusion, the people in *The Looking Glass War* discover that their prelate is only a powerless cleric or even an unordained clerk (LeClerc) and that their faith rests on a past which is absolutely dead and the illusion of the nonexistent Soviet missiles. This novel dwells upon the irony of forcing the mundane and temporal into the exalted and spiritual realm of the church. But this does not mean that it cannot be done: *The Spy Who Came in from the Cold* shows this. LeCarré builds this novel on the contrast of Fiedler and Leamas: of British democracy and communist totalitarianism. Fiedler does his job for East German security because he believes in the reality of utopian Marxism. He is shocked by Leamas' lack of philosophy, and at the start of the novel Leamas has little knowledge of his own motives, beyond hatred. By the end of the book, though, he does, and we ought to see this in a religious framework. He realizes that London means something:

They don't proselytize; they don't stand in pulpits or on party platforms and tell us to fight for Peace or for God or whatever it is. They're the poor sods who try to keep the preachers from blowing each other sky high.[27]

This is pure LeCarré: an anti-church devoted to keeping other faiths from destroying the world. This church takes "pansies, sadists and drunkards, people who play cowboy and Indians" and ennobles them by giving them a role in a transcendent institution. Many of its adherents leave it for other faiths, for it promises no victory, but unremitting toil. Only George Smiley tries to live up to the destructive discipline, and even he, as Jerry Westerby puts it, is a "failed cleric."

At one time in his life, the biographical notes tell us, John LeCarré taught school at Eton College. Perhaps as a consequence of this (it *is*, after all, also a standard locale in the detective story), two of his books use public schools as locales: *A Murder of Quality* takes place at a major public school, and the Jim Prideaux sections of *Tinker, Tailor* occur at Thursgood's school. Both of these novels portray teachers and students and develop two of the countless variety of relationships which can develop between teacher and student. As we have seen, LeCarré mirrors reality by making dons the founders of Circus, and he makes his major character, George Smiley, an academic and former teacher. Further, just as the church as a metaphor illuminates the world of espionage organizations, the school as an idea has a great deal to do with the secret world in LeCarré.

Behind the use of the school metaphor lies the assumption that Circus as an institution performs the same function that the school does. Behind Smiley's predicaments in all of the novels rests the fact that Circus and the school serve two sets of goals which can become contradictory and mutually destructive, given sets of perverse circumstances and the errant nature of human beings. As institutions, cultures create schools for a number of practical reasons. Schools train people for jobs, they insure cultural continuity and a smoothly running society, and they produce theoretical knowledge needed for practical things—from divorce counselling sessions to lasers. But they play another role as well. Schools aim at preparing people for life, at passing on the accumulated wisdom of mankind, and at seeking out knowledge regardless of its impact on society. Schools try to awaken individuals to their own and others' humanity, they try to harbor and protect the true and beautiful, and they strive to teach people how to become their own teachers.

As LeCarré depicts the Circus in his novels, it fulfills some of the same functions as the school. First, it serves the specific culture that created it, servile to the culture's wishes and objectives. It also, like any other intelligence agency, collates, interprets, and publishes information. LeClerc in *The Looking Glass War,* Connie and DiSallis in *The Honourable Schoolboy,* and Smiley in all of his novels, engage in pursuits identical to one kind of scholarship which collects and analyzes information. If LeClerc is deluded as an individual it is, in large measure, because he is a bad scholar and handles information dishonestly. If the academic historian needs to be careful in his interpretation of facts, so does the intelligence officer: LeCarré insists on the spy-historian analogy through the point of view which he adopts in the novels. Not only do schools and spies gather information, they both train individuals in useful skills. In *The Looking Glass War* we see an ironic contrast between the real academe and the spy school when Haldane and Avery set up their one-horse training school in a house near Oxford. Circus' training school for agents comes in to most of the novels, but it plays a vital role in *The Honourable Schoolboy* where Jerry, cut loose in Hong Kong, thinks again and again of the material at Sarratt. There agents learn how to shadow, how to rendezvous, how to kill. Following through on the education analogy, Circus' function is to serve its society. It may proselytize for budget but it does not develop policy: it has no ideas. Obviously, what LeCarré presents us with here is a sterile machine dealing in dead or deadly information and devoted to death and not life. Countless schools do this, too: they enslave and neuter the human spirit rather than liberating it.

Schools, though, can develop in another direction. In *The Honourable Schoolboy,* LeCarré exploits the ideals of the school to a greater degree than in any of the other novels: part of its structure and much of its characterization depends upon the academic comparison. What LeCarré suggested all along about Smiley becomes apparent here—he was and will always be a schoolmaster. The other characters in *The Honourable Schoolboy* grow from their relationship with Smiley as the schoolmaster. Connie and Disallis are his staff and the other men are his students. Smiley administers, educates, plans courses of study, and attempts discipline. LeCarré includes in the novel two interview scenes with Westerby and Colins which feel very much like the boy's interview with the headmaster in the schoolboy novel. He also portrays his major characters as clearly defined schoolboy types. Gulliam is the upperclassman who dependably does routine chores for the headmaster. Fawn is the fawning brown-noser whose viciousness is subdued only by the sense of authority which he gains from dogging the master's steps. Sam Colins is the dishonorable schoolboy who, rumor has it, cheated rather than worked his way through Oxford. During the course of *The Honourable Schoolboy,* Colins prefers maneuvering and scheming to forthrightness and hard work, adopting the manners and the ethics of the casino which he runs during his rustication. Jerry Westerby is, on the other hand, the honorable schoolboy. No genius, Jerry seems to be loud-mouthed athlete turned mediocre reporter in *Tinker, Tailor.* In the next novel, however, LeCarré shows that Westerby learned something from Smiley beyond tradecraft. He puts into action the ideals which George only teaches. LeCarré, in *Honourable Schoolboy,* brings Smiley and Westerby close together. He does this particularly through the descriptions of Ann Smiley and Lizzie Worth. Both Smiley and Jerry have failed marriages and they love the same sort of women. Both Ann and Lizzie are irresponsible, and both have affairs with brainless Latin he-men (Ann's first infidelity is with a Cuban race car driver and Lizzie's is with the Mexican, Tiny Ricardo, ace aviator). However worthless these women seem, the pursuit of them represents the heroes' striving for the spontaneous, human side of life. This is the parallel between Smiley and Jerry and it operates through the metaphor of the school. Education, when it works, should liberate people and make them their own teachers: thinkers as diverse as Nietzsche and Leonardo have insisted that the student who cannot surpass his master has failed him. In *Call for the Dead* Smiley comes close to despair because one of his former students, Dieter Frey, has betrayed his education:

Everyting he [Smiley] admired or loved had been the product of intense individualism. That was why he hated Dieter now, hated what he stood for more strongly than before: it was the fabulous impertinence of renouncing the individual in favour of the mass. When had mass philosophies ever brought benefit or wisdom? Dieter cared nothing for human life: dreamed only of armies of faceless men bound by their lowest common denominator.[28]

With Jerry Westerby, though, Smiley wins. Jerry's quixotic love for Lizzie and his attempt to protect the Ko brothers define him. He weighs the opposites (Lizzie is a whore and Drake Ko is a thug; he loves Lizzie and the Kos' love is admirable) and acts to protect the ideal. This enables Smiley and the reader to honor him. George cannot give himself to Ann, and, as *Smiley's People* shows, he cannot protect the human side of a wicked person even if he values this humanness. He may not be able to make the leap of faith, but he can and does prepare Jerry for it, and Smiley succeeds because Jerry surpasses him.

In terms of plot, LeCarré began and, in a sense, remains a detective story writer instead of an adventure writer. His *A Murder of Quality* reminds us that LeCarré was interested in the detective story form, and this is evident when we examine his spy plots— particularly the early ones. *Call for the Dead* may deal with international intrigue but it is a detective novel. In it LeCarré introduces clues, shows the detective compiling lists, and shows the detective's moment of insight but withholds the name of the guilty party until the action climax. Here, too, he uses a detective writer's device as old as Christie's first novel, *The Mysterious Affair at Styles* (1919), the device of raising suspicion, then dismissing it, and then demonstrating guilt. *The Spy Who Came in from the Cold,* likewise, grows out of detective plotting. Here, in the flip-flops on Mundt's allegiance, LeCarré only modifies the guilty-innocent-guilty technique of the first novel. In this novel LeCarré also provides clues to the readers for the solution of the plot: Smiley's brief but ominous appearance in the early part of the narrative. LeCarré, in *The Spy Who Came in from the Cold,* does more than write a detective plot with espionage trappings. Through his creation of atmosphere, character, and dialogue LeCarré takes us out of the make-belive world of detective fiction and thrusts us into the grubby world of the cellars of internatonal politics. We can more easily believe in the double-cross—the accusation of Mundt in order to clear him—when it occurs in the grimy realm of political jockeying than we can believe in the double-cross in the pastoral setting of the traditional detective novel. Further, LeCarré in this novel ties the plot not to the intellectual game, but to the inversion of values which we find in all of his novels: if Mundt is evil to the East Germans he is good to the West regardless of his moral worth.

After *The Spy Who Came in from the Cold,* LeCarré stopped trying to plot his novels as writer-reader detective stories with clues planted for us to see and a trick at the end. In *A Small Town in Germany* he switched types of hero, and made Alan Turner the hard-boiled detecive who uncovers facts because he crashes into events and people. He does, granted, give us a Prologue showing Leo tracking Karfeld, but *A Small Town in Germany* does not have the clue orientation or the trick-ending of the previous novels: LeCarré does not invite us to guess about guilt or the solution. After *A Small Town in Germany* the only remnant of detective technique in the plotting of his novels lies in the fact that LeCarré constructs his books by hoarding information and dribbling it out to the readers. He knows all of the facts which create the ending and could give them to the readers early on, but instead he doles the facts out one at a time in order to unfold the plot through gained knowledge rather than, say, adventure. In the early novels, when tied to other plot devices, this creates detective stories, while in the later books, when coupled with the narrator's voice, it contributes to the aura of history which LeCarré intentionally weaves into his books.

From the very first chapter that he wrote, LeCarré slanted his espionage novels toward history: the opening chapter of *Call for the Dead* is "A Brief History of Mr. George Smiley." As we have seen, as one of his main objects LeCarré writes the history of his imaginary spy organization from World War II to the present. More than anything else, the point of view in the novels pushes us toward a historical perspective. The narrator in LeCarré is a detached observer who tries to piece together reality out of certain, known fragments. He follows leads into the distant past, into disparate locales, and into known fragments of people's lives. He deals with rumors and gossip—especially when concerned with Smiley's marriage. At the start of *The Honourable Schoolboy,* the narrator runs through a number of theories about the historical origins of the Dolphin case, and then proceeds to report a truer history. Like a responsible historian the narrator refuses to draw conclusions where there are no facts. Thus at the end of *The Honourable Schoolboy* he gives us the following statement:

Was there really a conspiracy against Smiley of the scale that Gulliam supposed? If so, how was it affected by Westerby's own maverick intervention? No information is available and even those who trust each other well are not disposed to discuss the queston.[29]

This ties in with the root assumption in LeCarré: we cannot really know other people who are forever locked in themselves. All we can know is the external history, but we, as individuals, ought to have the insight not to ask about December 25, but to ask the essential but factually unanswerable question about whether Christ, or love, or truth existed at all. In asking that question we move toward making them exist.

Like Conrad or like Greene, LeCarré uses the espionage form for wider human purposes than those present in the adventure story. The world of espionage, for him, intensifies the human condition and highlights questions of identity and existence. In the novels about Circus we glimpse a perplexing and frightening world, but still a world in which choice operates and in which individuals can find themselves and touch other people. LeCarré possesses considerable narrative talents which we can see when comparing his Cambodia in *The Honourable Schoolboy* to Adam Hall's Cambodia in *The Kobra Manifesto* (1976). With him we can observe a trivial genre like the spy novel used to enrich mainstream literature.

NOTES

[1] *Call for the Dead* (New York: Pocket Books, 1970), p. 7.
[2] *Call for the Dead,* p. 38.
[3] *A Murder of Quality* (New York: Signet, 1964), p. 124.
[4] *The Honorable Schoolboy* (New York: Knopf, 1977), pp. 445-6.
[5] *A Small Town in Germany* (New York: Coward-McCann, 1968), p. 200.
[6] *Tinker, Tailor, Soldier, Spy* (New York: Knopf, 1974), p. 247.
[7] *The Looking Glass War* (New York: Dell, 1974), p. 73.
[8] *The Spy Who Came in from the Cold* (New York: Dell, 1974), pp. 214-5.
[9] *The Looking Glass War,* p. 127.
[10] *Call for the Dead,* p. 1.
[11] *Call for the Dead,* pp. 128-9.
[12] *Call for the Dead,* p. 3.
[13] *Call for the Dead,* p. 7.
[14] *Call for the Dead,* p. 3.
[15] *Call for the Dead,* pp. 51-2.
[16] *Tinker, Tailor, Soldier, Spy,* p. 73.
[17] *A Murder of Quality,* p. 65.
[18] *Call for the Dead,* p. 21.
[19] *Smiley's People* (New York: Knopf, 1980), p. 40.
[20] *The Honorable Schoolboy,* p. 533.
[21] *The Honorable Schoolboy,* p. 532.
[22] *The Washington Post,* 9 October 1977, p. E1, col. 5.
[23] *The Honorable Schoolboy,* p. 51.
[24] *Call for the Dead,* p. 8.
[25] M. Maccoby, *The Gamesman: The New Corporate Leaders* (New York: Simon & Schuster, 1976), p. 42.
[26] *The Looking Glass War,* p. 73.
[27] *The Spy Who Came in From the Cold,* p. 215.
[28] *Call for the Dead,* p. 147.
[29] *The Honorable Schoolboy,* p. 532.

Chapter 16

Adam Hall
(1920—)

EVER SINCE 1943 Adam Hall has written a novel on the average of once a year. Through the fifties his output was so high that he used six other names: Mansell Black, Simon Rattray, Warwick Scott, Trevor Dudley Smith (his original name), and Elleston Trevor (his legally adopted name). Some of his novels portray pieces of history, like *The Big Pick Up* (1955) which describes Dunkirk, some follow detective heroes, like the Hugo Bishop novels appearing under the name Simon Rattray, and some fall into the broad category of adventure books. Trevor, to use his correct name, has, however, achieved most of his success writing as Adam Hall. As Hall he has completed eight spy novels: *The Quiller Memorandum* (1965), *The Ninth Directive* (1966), *The Striker Portfolio* (1969), *The Warsaw Document* (1971), *The Tango Briefing* (1973), *The Mandarin Cypher* (1975), *The Kobra Manifesto* (1976) and *The Sinkiang Executive* (1978). In these books Hall takes up the mantle of Ian Fleming, but he far surpasses Fleming in craftmanship and intelligence, he copies Len Deighton in up-dating the hard-boiled hero to fit the role of a British spy in the sixties, he, like other writers after mid-century, hurls a few brickbats at the concept of the institution, and, out of the best of motives, he gives his readers a surfeit of psychology.

For consistency and ease, since I have already discussed the hard-boiled hero, I will simply trot back out the criteria which I have applied to others in this school. Hall's spy hero, Quiller (this, Hall tells us, is not his real name, but a work name), like all his hard-boiled kin, acts separately from others and tends to view himself as different from and often superior to other people. In all the novels Quiller insists that he will only play the game if it is a one-man show; he will have no part of operations which involve other agents (usually of a type which Hall calls a shield, or secondary agent dispatched to protect the principal spy), because he believes that they only increase his risks and that the helpers may be downright incompetent. Quiller is a friendless individual, indulging in quick sexual liaisons between missions (Hall, though, provides him with a steady partner, Moria, in the later books), suspicious of his equals, contemptuous of those below him, at odds with his superiors, and abusive toward most people. He uses the concept of "the professional" as a standard of judgment. Thus, much as Forsyth will later ennoble the Jackal, Quiller admires the murderer Kuo in *The Ninth Directive* as well as the terrorists in *The Kobra Manifesto* while he despairs of the amateur Polish patriots in *The Warsaw Document*. This separateness and superiority manifests itself in overt racism in several places: in *The Quiller Memorandum* the hero sees all Germans as secret Nazis, and in *The Ninth Directive*, the only flaw in the aforementioned professional, Kuo, is his suspicious Chinese nature:

...I knew who they were because I'd seen them before, hundreds of them, Russian and Czechoslovakian and Polish and French and Italian and Turkish, average and undistinguished men in respectable suits and worn shoes.... Of course they vary in their temperaments: the subtlest are the French and they'll hang on whatever you do; the Italians will do well until they see a girl and then they'll go off with her and leave you flat.... [1]

Forgetting this sort of rubbish, Quiller does stand apart from ordinary folks because the job which Hall gives him demands it. Further, the books prove out the value of Quiller's insistent isolation, because he always wins in spite of the odds, so he must have more on the ball than other professionals, especially those that do not happen to be English. Isolation from others, though, is not difficult for Quiller. Hall makes it clear that isolation satisfies his nature:

There was something disgusting about the way I had to put my feet precisely where he put his, turning my head exactly as he did: it was just deep in my nature to resent being dependent on people, even people as good as Ferris, and now I was dependent on this gross creature, my life linked intimately with his. [2]

Follow this formula: literary convention, plus espionage coloring, plus psychological background. Hall uses it with the hero's isolation and he will come back to it again and again.

If violence makes the hard-boiled hero, then Quiller fills the bill. Hall makes Quiller a hard man who frequently engages in violence. He assassinates a villain in *The Ninth Directive*, forces another into a fatal car crash in *The Tango Briefing*, and kills people with his hands in *The Mandarin Cypher, The Kobra Manifesto, The Warsaw Document* and *The Sinkiang Executive*. These encounters with death do not merely flit past the reader's attention as unimportant parts of the books. Hall gives them extended coverage and fulsome detail: the fight in the lavatory in *The Warsaw Document*, for instance, covers six pages, as opposed to fights in other writers which take, at most, a paragraph or two. These are no stylized pugilistic encounters either, but passages in which Hall wants to bring violence home to his readers, as in this passage from *The Sinkiang Executive*:

> He moved very fast and pain flared in my arm as the pressure came on—he was going to break it and I curved a thumb-shot for the eye and missed and struck again and missed and went on striking until his head rolled back and I felt the softness of the eye and struck and dragged my arm free and went for the throat....[3]

As Hall goes to some pains to point out in the first novel, Quiller's business lacks nice rules of etiquette. For Hall, this ties together Quiller's separate superiority and his violence:

> We are alone. We are committed to the tenets of individual combat and there is no help for him who fails. Save a life and we save a man who will later watch us through the cross-hairs and squeeze the trigger if he gets the orders or the chance. It's no go.
> The car burned and the man screamed and I sat watching.
> We are not gentlemen.[4]

Quiller has witnessed the depth of human depravity—in the first novel we learn that he worked as an agent in a concentration camp during the Second World War—and he works at a job in which paranoia is not a mental disorder, so he remains aloof from others and turns to real violence when he is threatened.

Hall also programs into his agent a variety of hard-boiled sexuality. Quiller is sexually active in most of the novels from his bedding of Inga in *The Quiller Memorandum* to his pseudo-rape of Liova in *The Sinkiang Executive*. Hall, determined to be liberated, includes *soissant neuf* and cunilingus in several books. Thus, in the manner of the hard-boiled writer, Hall attempts frankness about sexuality. Quiller's encounters with sex, however, appear in brief passages, narrated without much prurience but also without much enthusiasm. They fit into a Flemingesque pattern of the hero as the complete lover and women defined by their psychological quirks: warped minds, that is, produce warped sex. Sexuality also represents one constituent part of the complete male hero for Hall, but in Quiller sexual performance is only a mechanical part of the technical specifications of the type. He receives no pleasure from his contact with women, and most of the women with whom he has contact are either Secret Service groupies or enemy agents or lesbians or bi-sexuals or miscellaneous deviants like the Hitler-fixated Inga. In the later books, Hall alludes to Quiller's long-term attachment to Moria, an affair reminiscent of that in Cheyney's *Dark Duet*. We, however, never see her, and we hear of her only in connection with the hero's will with the clause "roses for Moria," and Quiller's own ruminations on the symbolism of her name. His job and his world deny Quiller any sort of normal sexuality, and Hall uses sex in order to define the hero's potence within the boundaries of his demanding and irregular work. Hall does not, however, delve into this as he does with the other parts of Quiller's psyche, for to do so would bring in abstractions like love, and this would clash with his other purposes which are concrete in the extreme.

Like his hard-boiled private eye predecessors, Quiller's primary definition of himself comes from his fanatical devotion to his work. He is no child of the welfare state, swaddled from cradle to grave in security and within these limits enjoying the pursuit of happiness. He has attached himself to a job, and, more importantly, to an employer, which makes his life extremely arduous. Hall keeps coming back to indirectly characterizing Quiller through repeating the following description of his employer:

> If you work for the Bureau you've got to work to the rules and they're strict. The Bureau doesn't officially exist. If it existed it couldn't do the things it's been designed to do: things that could never be countenanced even at Cabinet level. So if you get into a jam in the course of a mission you can count on London to help you but only up to a point: the point where they see there's a risk of exposing the Bureau, of letting it seem to exist. Then they'll cut you off and you'll know it because the set's gone dead or the contact doesn't show up and then God help you because London never will.[5]

One of the principal rules by which the Bureau works is 'never let the agent know what he is doing.' In every novel, Quiller falls into a trap and accepts a tough assignment, he dashes around and then discovers by himself what he is really supposed to be doing: in *The Warsaw Document*, for instance, he goes abroad to watch a probationary agent and to gather material on the Polish underground, but ends up with evidence that Moscow is about to invade Poland and give Warsaw a dose of Prague Spring. London, Quiller says at some point in each book, sees its agents as ferrets: "An agent is sent like a ferret into a hole and he is not told if there is a dog at the other end."[6] Further, Quiller's bosses are no jovial ex-schoolmasters or brilliant fatherly types, or conscience-ridden intellectuals—most are mean, nasty, insufferable people. And the agent must deal with lots of them. Working in the field, Hall's agent becomes subject to two levels of authority. First, the Local Control does the liaison work, passing information along to London as well as acquiring equipment, and second, London Control makes all the big decisions. In the early novels Hall creates as chief of London Control one Parkis, a prissy, inhuman genius who treats his agents like robots and gives them as little consideration as cold meat. Parkis and Quiller, predictably, develop a real antipathy for each other. In the later books, where Hall, like Len Deighton, adds more common humanity to his agent, he changes the organization of the Bureau, giving it an executive board including the more humane Eggerton, but Hall is reasonably vague about this.

Even with a few nice people at the top making policy, the Bureau is no philanthropic organization: in *The Sinkiang Executive* its officials trap Quiller into committing a murder in order to induce him to take on a highly dangerous assignment. If most of the people in London Control are nasty, so can be the directors in the field: in *The Tango Briefing* and *The Ninth Directive* Loman controls Quiller, for whom he represents all the priggishness, inhuman authority and false rectitude of Parkis. Hall does, however, usually give Quiller better bosses away from London, allowing him to operate entirely alone or with the sympathetic Ferris as Local Control. Not only does Hall give Quiller difficult, conniving people to work for, he also denies him decent working conditions. With a stab at realism, there are no Aston Martins out of the public purse for this hero. Instead, as Quiller constantly complains, there is a tight-fisted harridan in charge of accounts who goes over his car hire chits and hotel bills, ready to take exception to the smallest extravagance.

A person could put up with high-handed bosses, petty bureaucrats, and a lonely life if the job were a really good one. But Quiller's is not. The Bureau uses Quiller, and all its other agents, as human targets. Thus, Quiller, and the other hypothetical agents of whom he speaks, not only has no inkling of the purposes of his missions, but London's main objective is to place him in mortal danger so as to shake things loose: "Because we don't *know* anything. We don't know who they are or how many or where they are or what they're doing or why. We have to find them by letting them find us first, and they can be anywhere....[7]" London makes Quiller a kamikaze. They launch him into Nazi headquarters, onto a Chinese missile platform, into the enemy's clutches in Warsaw, and into Soviet airspace in a stolen jet; they even ask him to explode himself with an atomic device in one of the novels. Why would anyone choose to do these things? Hall provides a number of answers for this poser. First off, Quiller suggests that ideology plays a very small part, if any, in motivating the agent: "Ideology isn't enough. It seems enough; it's blinding and belongs to the heart. But it won't save you from being found one fine day on the floor with a cheese-wire mark on your throat."[8] Hall bolsters Quiller's motivation with the idea of professionalism. The men in London are the highly competent professionals, and Quiller admires them for this even if he bridles under their control. He almost always comes up with the notion that "they are good at their jobs and I am very good at mine, otherwise they would not have chosen me, so I will live up to that standard." This leads, if not to patriotism, to a rough but working loyalty to the Bureau. In *The Tango Briefing* Quiller puts it this way: "...he wasn't a professional spook and he didn't possess the bruised lopsided sense of loyalty to the Bureau that's always there like a scarecrow wherever we go."[9] These, however, are abstractions and Hall is more interested in the concrete. This he provides for Quiller in the contrast between the life of the spy and the middle class suburbanite:

You do it to scratch an itch, that's all. I'm not talking about the ones who do it for the money—they're just whores. Most of us do it because we don't get a kick out of watching the telly and pushing a pen and washing the Mini on Sunday mornings; we want to get outside of all that, be on our own so we can work off our scabby neuroses without getting arrested for it.[10]

This quote is from *The Warsaw Document*, but by the next novel, *The Tango Briefing*, Hall makes Quiller's motives even simpler: "...if he picked a man like me it meant ... he'd wanted someone who was in this game for the kicks with nothing to lose."[11] Finally, in *The Sinkiang Executive*, Hall reduced Quiller's motives to their most essential form, when Quiller says, "I am what I am and I do what I do and ... it's too late to make any changes."[12] This sounds very much like one of the pronouncements of Race Williams, the first of the hard-boiled detectives. Why do they do their jobs? Because of abstract qualities, because of their societies, but mostly because they are themselves. Quiller, therefore, suffers the physical and psychic hardships of his job because they define him and because Hall wants to find an occupation which will put the human organism under maximum strain.

In the original hard-boiled stories from America, the hero gets shot, stabbed, drugged, coshed and generally ill-treated, and then he bounces right back and completes his job. This is, of course, to the highest degree, unreal, but it reflects the hero's fanatical—or religious—devotion to the work ethic (they would never think of calling in sick) and it also delineates another specification for the hero: he must be a physically tough man. Whereas most of us would be ready for intensive care, the hard-boiled hero can take a beating and keep on fighting. Hall portrays Quiller this way. His hero forever gets himself well and truly mangled, but continues to function as if nothing had happened. Torn and bleeding, he still engages in strenuous activity and wins the day because of his physical endurance. *The Ninth Directive* shows this pretty well. Toward the end Quiller is 1) shot with a dart gun, 2) concussed with a grenade, 3) exposed to cyanide fumes at close range, and 4) involved in a serious crash. Immediately after the car crash he engages in a karate match with a tough, healthy professional killer, and after winning this he devises and executes a complex plan to rescue a kidnapped British diplomat from the Chinese. Could you or I do this? Could Quiller do it? The question is irrelevant since this is one of the conventions of the hard-boiled story.

As Chandler suggests in "The Simple Art of Murder," the hard-boiled hero needs to speak the language of the mean streets which he inhabits. This point of view and the diction of the hard-boiled story separate it from more hoity-toity kinds of fiction. Like many other hard-boiled writers, Hall narrates all the Quiller books from the first person point of view. Quiller tells us his story. He consistently breaks up normal time by lurching ahead of the action and then filling in lacunae. More to the point, he makes frequent generalizations about spies (thus tying himself to the rhetorical centers found in hard-boiled detective stories), and he records his own internal dialogues. Moving away from the overly descriptive, purple passages in his earlier works, Hall makes most of Quiller's observations to the point and dressed down in normal syntax and vocabulary. Since Quiller has little lyric sensitivity or poetic apprehension, we do not find the quantity or the quality of the poetic language which appears in Chandler or Deighton (whom Hall follows in any number of ways). Quiller, though, does occasionally use bits of American slang, and rattles off a few raw, wise-cracking comparisons which mark the wit, cultural level and stance toward authority of the traditional hard-boiled hero, as in this observation on the Bureau in *The Tango Briefing*: "...it's a weak point and we think it's dangerous and we're always asking the Bureau to do something about it but you might just as well try selling a jockstrap to a eunuch."[13] Tough talk from a tough man. There is, if you will, an inconsistency here if we force it: Quiller, the books tell us, is an accomplished linguist, speaking French, German, Portuguese, Russian, Cantonese, Thai, Italian, Arabic and Radinda-Tanath (an Indian dialect). Here Hall is in the spy writer's bind. One needs to place his agents in foreign countries, but how does one handle the language problem? There is a show-off factor in Hall, too, with pages of German dialogue to impress the readers. Here Hall finds that the street origins of the hard-boiled story and the diplomatic origins of the spy story at least rub if they do not clash: is it credible for the hard man to be such an accomplished linguist?

Finally, the virtue and potential weakness of the hard-boiled story rests with its action orientation. From one external perspective, the Quiller stories possess lots of action. In the early novels, especially *The Quiller Memorandum* and *The Striker Portfolio*, Hall plots by repeating instances of threat, capture and escape. From *The Ninth Directive* onward, he took up the cause of the chase, and we get car chases in *The Ninth Directive, The Striker Portfolio, The Tango Briefing* and *The Warsaw Document*, we get the airplane business in *The Korba Manifesto* and *The Sinkiang Executive*, and, as a variation, we get a scuba adventure in *The Mandarin Cypher*. If it is not outright capture or escape or chase, Hall spends a lot of time in all the novels detailing how someone follows Quiller or how Quiller follows someone, combining some tradecraft with low-level suspense. At the end of his novels, Hall tries to build up to the big action and then slam the door on the intruding foot of the denouement in order to leave the readers with the conviction that his novels are brim-full of action. Overall, though, Hall fails as an action or suspense writer. One main cause is his propensity to telescope time. In *The Ninth Directive*, for instance, we receive three and one half pages of text between cause (the thrown hand grenade) and effect (the blast of the grenade). Witness also Quiller's monstrous hyperbole in *The Warsaw Document:*

For a long time, for two or three seconds, I let myself relax, bringing the strikes closer to give him confidence.[14]

If you are extremely fast, you can read this quotation in two or three seconds, but is that a "long time"? From the perspective of the action, therefore, Hall's world seems to exist under water where everything happens in slow motion and without much effect in terms of excitement or suspense. Quiller's absorption in analysis particularly hobbles the movement of the action-adventure elements which Hall includes in his plots. On the surface, Quiller is an action character who does not mull things over, or fantasize, or philosophize, or do much analysis in spite of the lists which he makes up in the novels. Right out of the Skinner Box, he reacts to his surroundings without troubling his higher mental centers. The trouble is that while he tells us about his spontaneous actions in the face of danger, he also describes the whole text book on why people react spontaneously. This shows us that Hall really feels a stronger pull in directions other than toward that of the hard-boiled story.

In all, Quiller possesses many of the characteristics of the hard-boiled hero. He convinces readers of his essential toughness much better than James Bond does—even if Hall cannot transmit this as well as Deighton and others do. Hall gives us the hero's bias against organizations, his sharp tongue, his stamina and his sexuality. The cover art on the Quiller novels, in fact, advertizes that with Quiller we will find the conventional hard-boiled hero, portraying, as it does, the figure of a man in a trench coat with a Spillanesque, pork-pie hat. The silhouette version would serve as well for Harry Palmer, while the fully articulated figure on the later novels (U.S. editions, at least) would serve for Marlowe or Spade. Half of Hall truly wants to make Quiller the hard-boiled hero, but the other half wants something altogether different—this half wants to write about psychology.

Once a writer, in composing, decides what will happen and to whom it will happen, a lot of work still remains before the concept becomes a drafted novel. Setting, atmosphere, ancillary characters and dialogue, interior and exterior, need to be added. If a writer does these things inexpertly we are apt to call them padding—as with Fleming's *You Only Live Twice*. If he executes them competently, we call them setting, atmosphere, etc. Now, Hall is an old horse, schooled in the standard detective story. The detective story, however, can be a very bad school for writers of other kinds of fiction, for it depends on the writer providing a welter of accurate information out of which only one tiny fragment will eventually matter to the plot. Readers of detective stories accept this as part of the game. Very good detective writers make all the information interesting and we do not mind its irrelevance; mediocre ones merely bore us with it. Hall, in this connection, does have a good deal of specialized information on tap in the spy novels: he knows about a lot of things. The problem is that he tells it to us, as in this example from *The Ninth Directive*:

All the Husquaranas are beautiful but the finest they make is the 561. It is a .358 Magnum center-fire, with a three-shot magazine, 25 1/2 inch barrel, hand checkered walnut stock, corrugated butt-plate and sling swivels. The fore-end and the pistol grip are tipped with rosewood. The total weight is 7 3/4 pounds and the breech pressure is in the region of 20 tons p.s.i., giving a high muzzle velocity and an almost flat trajectory with a 150-grain bullet.[15]

Average readers simply do not need or want this sort of detail—they want something like Forsyth's description of Jackal's weapon in *The Day of the Jackal*. The point is that this particular rifle and the murder which Quiller commits with it in *The Ninth Directive* have only secondary importance to the plot. Quiller forever tells us the mechanical specs of the gadgets which he uses. When he uses a camera we learn about type, film, shutter speed, f-stops, etc. Hall, moreover, does this simply to do it—because he knows about these things. Readers receive no emotional impression and consequently the details quickly vanish from the consciousness. We could ascribe this to an attempt to gild the realistic atmosphere, but then Zola would have never made it as a spy writer. Instead, readers come away with the impression that there is some padding at work.

If Hall misjudges the amount of detail needed to describe mechanical objects—something which he tends to get away from in the later novels—he seems to do the same sort of thing when he describes the hero's psychological condition. I have already mentioned the grenade attack in *The Ninth Directive* which takes three and a half pages to finish; Hall fills this space with psychological material like the following:

Reaction time covers three phases: time required to sense the signal, to decide on the correct response, and to respond. Affective factors: age, state of health, fatigue, alcohol, caffeine, so forth. Greatest artificial influential factor: training (i.e. habit formation).

The typical reaction time of a jet pilot receiving a visual signal (unexpected approach of another aircraft) is 1.7 seconds, this total comprising: 0.9 seconds to sight, focus and evaluate visual signal, 0.5 seconds to reach decision (evasive action), and 0.3 seconds to respond (move controls). A period of intensive training by ground simulation (bombardment of spasmodic signals) will reduce the reaction time to less than half, and such training—even after a lapse of years—will continue to effect reduction to a smaller extent.[16]

This is no isolated example. Every novel details Quiller's psychological and physiological condition at specific junctures— adrenelin out-put, blood-flow to the muscles, conditioned responses, everthing short of the condition of his bladder and bowels. Either this material represents gross self-indulgence and lack of judgment or Hall tries to tell us something with it beyond the range of the adventure story, or both.

It is not that hard to fathom Hall's inclusion of mounds of psycho-biological information. Even if it vitiates the virtues of the adventure plot, Hall genuinely wants to explore the nature of action from a semi-scientific perspective. Although he does dabble in psychological caricature *a la* Ian Fleming, he is serious about psychology. He wants readers to understand the psychic states of the secret agent and he gives his readers common referents so that they can understand them—the airline pilot, for instance. He also wants to get across the point that physical training for the active life does little good without psychological training. No doubt Hall came to this because of the publicity of "brain washing" (see Condon's *The Manchurian Candidate*, 1959, and Deighton's *The Ipcress File*) and he presents torture sessions in *The Quiller Memorandum* and *The Striker Portfolio*. But to counteract this, Quiller constantly brings up the Bureau's training establishment in Norfolk where agents learn psychological fitness as well as the physical kind. Hall wants Quiller to have defenses in the newest vogue in international intrigue. Because he is so well prepared, Quiller dwells on psychobiological subjects; as the strong man glories in his strength, so Quiller glories in the employment of his whole person.

Hall, however, wants to do more than emotional temperature taking, like that which we find in Ambler's *Journey into Fear*. In *The Ninth Directive*, Quiller refers several times to "the Maltz system of psycho-cybernetics." This is our clue: Quiller is the cybernetic man, a fictional experiment in cybernetics. Cybernetics is a recent discipline which attempts scientifically to understand and describe systems of communication and control. On the mechanical level it considers decision-making applied to artificial intelligence (i.e. computers), but it also considers the decision-making process in humans from, among others, the bio-chemical point of view, and thus extends into the field of psychology. It asks why and how particular organisms do this instead of infinite thats. Now, as Hall sees it, the secret agent provides a complex and fascinating model of human decision making. If, like Quiller, the spy acts alone, we eliminate direct social pressure from his decisions, and if, like Quiller again, the spy must take action in the face of danger, we see how organisms react under stress when prolonged rational thought is impossible. So, the Quiller novels present us with cybernetic experiments, and the detailed physio-psychological information recorded in the text forms a laboratory report. Quiller tells us that certain observable factors cause his decisions. First, Quiller reports that people make decisions because of inherited features. Thus he records this passage on nervous or olfactory information which our brains receive:

It's not only dogs that have a sense of smell, the ability to sense alien presence in the environment, or its recent presence. All animals have it, but in varying degrees of refinement. In humans it has been atrophying over decades since they began living with machines... but in creatures of the wild it remains highly developed. In creatures of the wild and in those few of us who express and incur mortal enmity in pursuit of our complex purposes.[17]

Our inherited, primitive nervous systems send us stimuli to prod our decision-making. The agent feels these and can reevolve the senses to their original sharpness. Quiller also reports that in combat, when we need fast responses, we switch back to the automatic killer instincts of our distant forebears:

There is nothing new about the primordial components of speed and surprise: they are essential to any attack.... Two further psychological components come into play when life is actually threatened: the instinct to survive and the ability to relax and allow the primitive animal to perform in its own right.[18]

But humans are more than instinctual. For Hall, and for Household too, we simultaneously get information from our animal brains and from the advanced centers of our evolved human brains. Thus, in *The Ninth Directive*, Quiller tells us that, "The animal is easily satisfied; the encephalon is more demanding."[19] Hall never specifies the exact nature of human intelligence, but he makes it pretty clear that at least parts of it are computer-like. Quiller's simile in *The Sinkiang Executive* illustrates: "Total memory came back like shoving a cassette in the slot."[20] If Hall falls short of a detailed explanation of exactly how the complex human organism makes decisions (and who can blame him), he does make clear who the boss is. In *The Mandarin Cypher*, just before he slips out into the water in his frogman gear, Quiller considers his status: "It brought more sweat out and I was duly warned: with only three and a half hours to go I'd better start shutting down the spleen."[21] The mind is the boss. Thus we see Hall developing in Quiller a prounounced mind-body dichotomy. The mind gives the orders and the machine—body— follows them. In *The Tango Briefing* this shows when Quiller explains that the only way to deal with pain is "to remove the mind from the body and to look at the situation objectively—the pain is expressed in the nerves and is perfectly natural but it doesn't have any significance: it's totally physical and there's no message...."[22] It is simple enough for the brain to command anything that it wants to, but if there is a dichotomy, then we need to consider the body's point of view. Bodies, or at least mine, take violent exception to mutilation or abuse or sundry unpleasant things. Not just mine or yours, though. Quiller's body does have something to say about being pummelled or pulped. What we find, from *The Tango Briefing* onward, is that Quiller holds brief but spirited dialogues with his body:

I don't like this one.
It was too big, and going too fast

I think we ought to go back.
Bloody little organism rearing its
head; all it could think about was
survival.
SHUDDUP.[23]

In most of the novels Quiller codifies the mind-body dichotomy as "mind think," and "stomach think," and the agent ultimately needs both: the body does, after all, have the final say in the argument, for it can kill the brain by dying. Thus the total organism needs to sort out whether the body or the intellect provides the proper decision for each given situation—as at the end of *The Tango Briefing* where the brain does give way to the body and invents a safe way of exploding an atomic device.

The adventure story and humanistic psychology can co-exist without problems, but combining the adventure story with scientific examination presents hurdles which either cannot be overcome or which Hall cannot overcome. Quiller cannot simultaneously be a psycho-cybernetic model and an adventure hero. This shows acutely at the end of the plots: the adventure story demands a fast pace but the scientific study must linger to analyze. Hall opts for the adventure answer. Thus the thriller takes over in the description of Quiller's final acts and psychology goes by the boards. Suspense and aloof analysis do not mix, and apparently in his most recent novels Hall may be coming to realize this.

In spite of his attempts to cover new material, Hall's writing fits easily into known traditions. First, Quiller takes over elements from James Bond which Fleming highlights but bungles. Bond is not the superman spy—Quiller is. Hall also moves Fleming's farcical psychologizing to a more dignified and complete, if popular, level. He also takes over Fleming's numbering technique: Bond's 007 indicates his qualifications as an assassin while Quiller's 9 indicates his reliability under torture. Household also flits into Quiller's background, for Hall and Household both consider man's primitive and animal inheritance as lying behind his roles in action; Hall tries to show this in the city while Household, wisely, plays it against the background of nature. Finally, Hall owes most to Deighton. Their tough guy heroes have real similarities, but this could be due to the conventions of the hard-boiled story. Hall, however, seems to take over the record concept from *The Ipcress File* in the documentary titles of his novels, and he may have also been inspired by the torture session in Deighton's first novel. Although he far surpasses Fleming as a writer, Hall does not measure up in talent or popularity to Household or Deighton because, although he knows the tricks of the trade, he has not yet found the perspective or the inspiration to write top notch spy fiction.

NOTES

[1] *The Sinkiang Executive* (Garden City: Doubleday, 1978), pp. 194-5.

[2] *The Striker Portfolio* (New York: Simon & Schuster, 1968), p. 142.

[3] *The Sinkiang Executive*, p. 221.

[4] *The Quiller Memorandum* (New York: Simon & Schuster, 1965), p. 75.

[5] *The Tango Briefing* (New York: Dell, 1974), p. 22.

[6] *The Ninth Directive* (New York: Simon & Schuster, 1966), pp. 95-6.

[7] *The Striker Portfolio*, p. 28.

[8] *The Striker Portfolio*, p. 81.

[9] *The Tango Briefing*, p. 77.

[10] *The Warsaw Document (Garden City: Doubleday, 1971), pp. 21-2.*

[11] *The Tango Briefing*, p. 33.

[12] *The Sinkiang Executive*, p. 19.

[13] *The Tango Briefing*, p. 71.

[14] *The Warsaw Document*, p. 232.

[15] *The Ninth Directive*, p. 99.

[16] *The Ninth Directive*, p. 206.

[17] *The Mandarin Cypher* (Garden City: Doubleday, 1975), p. 55.

[18] *The Kobra Manifesto* (Garden City: Doubleday, 1976), p. 163.

[19] *The Ninth Directive*, p. 175.

[20] *The Sinkiang Executive*, p. 130.

[21] *The Mandarin Cypher*, p. 142.

[22] *The Tango Briefing*, p. 175.

[23] *The Kobra Manifesto*, p. 69.

Chapter 17
Frederick Forsyth
(1938—)

IN THE NINETEEN SEVENTIES an immense market for the novel of international intrigue existed in both America and Britain. Older writers like Ambler and Household supplied part of the demand, as did the writers of the sixties: Hall, Deighton and LeCarré. But the market would absorb many more spy novels, particularly if they met certain requirements not always fulfilled by writers like Ambler and LeCarré. In the seventies the middle class reading public, educated but not sophisticated, wanted a return to the thriller, but the thriller with more literary polish and surface realism than those, say, of Fleming. It wanted novels showing realistic and complex international action with an informed grasp of facts and events, but without moral ambiguities, depressing personal histories, and real intellectual challenges. Frederick Forsyth met this need with his four hugely successful novels: *The Day of the Jackal* (1971), *The Odessa File* (1972), *The Dogs of War* (1974) and *The Devil's Alternative* (1980). In these novels Forsyth takes the traditional techniques of the thriller, of which he has a high level of mastery, and combines them with the principle of that other popular genre, the historical novel, creating the perfect entertainment for the seventies.

From the 1960s major British spy writers moved concertedly toward verisimilitude. Writers suggested, more and more, that their fictions came out of the real world of espionage. Thus we get a bunch of novels about Burgess, Maclean and other defectors, and Deighton summons up the notion that his fiction is really a government document with the title of *The Ipcress File*, and Hall does the same thing by labeling his books as memorandums, documents and portfolios. In the seventies, this trend produced novels which move from current attempts at realism to historical reconstructions which are more demonstrably real. In *S.S.—G.B.* Deighton recreates World War Two with a Nazi victory in Britain and in *The Eye of the Needle* (1979) Ken Follett posits a spy threat to the Allied invasion of Normandy. In a way, this movement reflects a self-conscious maturity with the spy novel returning to its origins in the war prophecy book, but it also applies new twists to the treatment of hypothetical history. Actually, Frederick Forsyth led the way to the historical fictions of the seventies, for he is the first major contemporary spy writer to mine history for his material. Of his four novels, only *The Dogs of War* takes place in the present. *The Day of the Jackal* and *The Odessa File* both take place in the recent past (1963), while *The Devil's Alternative* jumps into the future of 1982. Not only does he usually displace us in time, but Forsyth also repeatedly returns to certain historical events in order to focus his fiction. The two most important of these are the assassination of President John F. Kennedy, and the civil war in Zaire over Katanga Province. The former, of course, covers the core of *The Day of the Jackal*, but Kennedy-style assassinations also occur in *The Odessa File* and *The Devil's Alternative*. The Katanga civil war gives Forsyth the figure of the mercenary soldier which he brings into the Jackal's background and then expands to fill the whole of *The Dogs of War*. In addition to starting from historical facts, Forsyth does in his novels what the war prophecy writers of the 1880s and 1890s did. He takes certain tendencies in politics and culture and hypothetically projects them. All his novels rest upon *what-if*s: what if the OAS hired a professional killer to murder Charles deGaulle? what if platinum were discovered in a rinky-dink African state? what if the head of the KGB were assassinated by Ukrainian nationalists? what if ex-Nazis provided technical assistance to Egypt to make missiles? Indeed, as Forsyth continues to write, the number and complexities of his hypotheses increase from the single projections in *The Day of the Jackal* and *The Odessa File* to the more numerous projections in *The Dogs of War* and *The Devil's Alternative*. Moreover, Forsyth has one important advantage over nineteenth century futurists like LeQueux: he is not huckstering for any particular political program like army reform, and can consequently present events from a more detached position.

Forsyth possesses another advantage. He treats his material in the manner of the historical novel rather than in the journalistic fashion of LeQueux or the memoir style of Erskine Childers. The techniques of the popular historical novel help to shape his fictions. For one thing, Forsyth writes big books. With the exception of *The Odessa File*, they all extend to over four hundred pages: these are no one-evening thrillers. Within these bounds he paints a large picture. In every novel, Forsyth fills the readers' passports by taking them all over the world: to England, Holland, France, Italy, Spain, Yugoslavia, Germany, Africa, the Soviet Union, the United States, Israel and a few other places as well. Part of this, admittedly, grows out of the crook's tour of the thriller writer, but part also grows out of Forsyth's drive toward the historical novel, for the historical novel moves to cover the antecedents and progress of historical events. Take, for instance, all the geographical moves in *Vanity Fair*. The historical novel nature of Forsyth's diverse settings becomes clear when we read them along with his characters. As he deals with immense space, he also introduces very large casts of characters: he deals with seemingly innumerable people and one wonders how he even invents names for them. In *The Devil's Alternative*, for instance, I counted ninety-odd named characters, along with a score or so of nameless people. It almost sounds like Tolstoy with his vast space and crowds of people. This sort of practice surely lies outside the necessities of thriller plotting. It points to the historical novel. Now, writing historical fiction is not a one alternative game: there are all sorts of historical novels. The most recent metamorphosis has been the journalistically inclined, historical expose book. This, clearly, is the category of *The Odessa File*, for Forsyth declares his purpose in dedicating the book "To All Press Reporters," and in the Author's Note averring the truthfulness of his sources and information. In this novel, Forsyth, like many Britons, has an anti-Nazi and anti-German axe to grind. The other novels, however, fall into a more traditional pattern of historical fiction. In Scott or in Cooper, the first step in the historical romance is to develop the novel's milieu through drawing detail—Ivanhoe's armor, for instance. Since Forsyth deals with recent history, that of the nineteen sixties, he cannot achieve atmosphere through depicting strange cultural artifacts, so instead he renders the sixties for us by portraying public figures. In *The Day of the Jackal* we get, of course, deGaulle, in *The Dogs of War* we read a dossier on Black Jack Schramme, in *The Devil's Alternative* Forsyth brings in thinly disguised versions of Margaret Thatcher, Jimmy Carter and Zbigniew Brzezinski, while in *The Odessa File* we see Simon Wiesenthal and the assembled leaders of Israel. We attend meetings at the Elysee Palace, the White House, 10 Downing Street, and the Kremlin. On top of specific people and important places, Forsyth renders details about some institutions and things in order to complete the historical scene. Thus we learn about the OAS, the stock market, the super tanker and the spy satellite. He describes these things briefly but clearly as they form important background for his historical fictions. We can appreciate the importance of historical background for Forsyth when we consider that, except in *The Devil's Alternative*, in his novels the important action does not begin until well past the three-quarter post in the story: the Jackal does not enter France until page 391 and he does not enter Paris until page 439; the mercenaries in *The Dogs of War* do not land in Zangaro until page 391. This is not to suggest that Forsyth loads down the bodies of the novels with background detail unrelieved by suspense; quite the reverse. But the background detail plays an important role in the readers' appreciation of the novels.

In the historical novel, although real figures make cameo appearances—Richard in *Ivanhoe* or George Washington in *The Spy*—the main focus covers an invented individual who becomes caught in the conflicts of his culture and the conflicts between different cultures. This, at least, is Walter Scott's formula which we can see in Ivanhoe's position relative to the Normans and the Saxons in medieval England. Understanding this helps to explain the positions of Forsyth's characters. Lebel, in *The Day of the Jackal*, stands between all sorts of conflicting forces (his job and his wife, for instance), but the most important extremes are the accurately drawn historical influences of the anarchic brutality of the OAS on the one hand and the equally cruel tactics of the French Secret Police, the SDECE, on the other. Quite the same pattern occurs in the other books. Peter Miller, in *The Odessa File*, exists in the crease between German bureaucratic corruption, Nazi perverseness and Jewish revengers. In *The Dogs of War*, Cat Shannon steers between capitalist imperialism, African corruption and *bona fide* African patriotism. The entire world in *The Devil's Alternative* quivers between the active forces for the self-determination of the Ukraine, Soviet expansionism, and those seeking world peace. Although placing his heroes between clashing opposites has an Ambleresque ring, especially in *The Dogs of War* which resembles Ambler's *Dirty Story,* Forsyth does not deal with the alternatives of the philosopher or the individual in search of peace or identity.

There are demonstrably real issues and real institutions from Forsyth's chosen historical periods with which the heroes must deal, not intellectually, but in practical terms, and Forsyth has less interest in whether his heroes win or lose than in drawing the historical picture. His heroes simply deal with the collision of cultural forces in ways which reflect their status and age. Thus Lebel, the civil servant, shrugs off the gruesome methods of the SDECE and does his job of catching the Jackal, while Miller, Shannon and Munro, because they are younger, less attached men, rebel against the establishment's choices and act according to their own morals and motives.

Wired into the uses of history in Forsyth is the fact that he was once a reporter. All the novels witness this with the compact descriptions and the encapsulated, paragraph biographies. The journalistic aura also contributes to the purposely non-judgmental tone found in all the novels except *The Odessa File*. This neutral stance, too, accords with Forsyth's historical pretense. He does not write to present moral tirades, but to describe direct causes and direct events. Other factors contribute to this, but Forsyth's journalistic tack is partly responsible for the amoral portrait of the Jackal, who never seems a slavering villain, as well as the mixed sympathies evoked by James Manson in *The Dogs of War* and by Andrew Drake in *The Devil's Alternative*.

We need to recognize the presence of historical material and motives in Forsyth's novels not only because these things attract readers' attentions and interest, and broaden the appeal of his books, but also because they allow him to make the more important part of his fiction work—the thriller part. The trouble with the thriller writers of the teens and twenties is that with the exception of World War I stories, they based their plots on untenable hypotheses. No one can really believe that Carl Peterson is about to asphyxiate us with poison gas, or that Fu Manchu's zombies will thwart Scotland Yard. We need to make a gigantic effort to suspend our disbelief from page one. Forsyth, though, by using the material and techniques of the historical novel as a fulcrum, levers readers into a quasi-real world in which they experience excitement and tension more directly because everything seems probable. We can believe in assassinations of public figures after the Kennedy brothers, and we can also believe in *coups d'etat* in Africa, dirty weapons in the hands of the United Arab Republic, and the pollution of the North Sea with oil from a ruptured super tanker. The historical atmosphere makes readers accept Forsyth's premises and once they do this, they become easy prey to his orchestration of conventional thriller technology.

In a sense the thriller in the hands of Buchan or Sapper has a set of conventional techniques as structured as those of the epic—the thriller, in fact, can be considered a modern variety of the epic. The most binding of these conventions is that in the thriller something big must be at stake: Britain, the British Empire, the world. Thrillers' issues need to be much more grave than, say, the limited scope of the regular detective novel which only involves one death and questions about guilt or innocence of a handful of people. Forsyth knows all about this, and, in fact, he increases the weight of the threat to the world in each succeeding novel. In the first book President de Gaulle's life and the prospect of political change in

France are at stake. *The Odessa File* ups the ante, and summons up the destruction of Israel and genocide. These threats, hardly negligible, seem small when compared to the next two novels. *The Dogs of War* goes far beyond the threat to the sovereignty of pest-ridden Zangaro by introducing the figure of the General as well as the fact of Shannon's secret plans, and places the independence and dignity of the whole continent of Africa in the balance. In his most recent novel, Forsyth goes still further, raising not only the possibilities of an ecological holocaust, but also ringing in the spectre of a Soviet invasion of Europe and a nuclear shootout between the USA and the USSR. Here Forsyth shows his firm grasp of the first rule of thrilling writing: the bigger the stakes, the bigger the risks, and the greater the readers' involvement.

The thriller works very much on Marvell's principle of were there world enough and time, no problem would be pressing, for we would have the leisure and scope to work it out. Lacking these things, problems do present real difficulties, and to concentrate them, thriller writers work with clock, calendar and atlas to manipulate time and space to make problems more aggravating than they really are. Normally the thriller uses time and space in conjunction, again, in order to make problems more acute. Forsyth's novels cover a lot of ground. In every case, arriving at the principal, critical locale involves difficulties. The principal locale is not only distant from the place that the book starts, but getting there necessitates a whole series of geographically oriented preparation moves. Thus the Jackal starts in London, goes to Rome, Brussels, Paris, London, and then back and forth before he sets out on his last run to Paris: Lebel and the police need to make these moves, too. Quite the same thing happens in *The Odessa File* and *The Dogs of War*, and, with a different perspective (the moves of the narrator and not the hero) in *The Devil's Alternative*. Forsyth plots so that each of these geographically linked preparation moves forms a vital part in the whole action, and, therefore, along with the overall risk of failure or success in the main action, the characters risk failure at every stop along the road. Not only does Forsyth use failure due to circumstance (like Grossens' difficulties in manufacturing the Jackal's gun), he also adds the dangers of customs posts and other routine dangers which face the person who must travel. Traveling in Forsyth does present lots of dangers, from the bomb in the front suspension of Peter Miller's Jaguar to the MIG interceptors sent up to shoot down the *Blackbird* in *The Devil's Alternative*. Within the scope of Forsyth's novels, getting there is three quarters of the tension—and fun. Paying a lot of attention to geographical movement has the ultimate advantage of holding off the climax until the last moment. We do not arrive at the Jackal's blind, or Roschman's hideout, or Zangaro until the very end of the respective novels. Once we do arrive, Forsyth narrates a burst of action and lingers only long enough to provide a condensed, journalistic post mortem, and to close with a mystery kicker to send the readers off bemused by the undercurrent of complexity in the plot which they never imagined.

As far as human beings are concerned, though, space may as well be infinite, for just considering the size of the Earth, no one can really imagine having been everywhere and thus having exhausted space. Space, by itself, therefore, does not provide the ultimate tension for the thriller. Time, on the other hand, we all understand; we will all exhaust our time, and we get little examples of this every day. In the Western tradition, various secular and religious forces urge us to use our time wisely because salvation may ride on it. Time, therefore, gives a much more useful tool to the thriller writer than space. Forsyth, like the thriller writers of the teens and twenties, knows all about this: that the terminal date is one of the essentials of the thriller. He gives us terminal dates in every single book. In *The Day of the Jackal* and *The Dogs of War* the national holidays of France and Zangaro stand at the crux of the action: the Jackal and the mercenaries must do their respective jobs on that one particular day or not at all. On all other days the respective Presidents will not be available for assassination, and, further, the schemes in both novels will be thwarted by outside forces unless they are executed on that given day. The terminal date in *The Odessa File* occurs when Nasser has fireable rockets, and, in *The Devil's Alternative*, two end dates coincide—that for the release of the oil into the North Sea, and the date after which there will be an irrevocable political shift in the Politburo. Thus the terminal dates make the big issues work and they reciprocally act upon another: the time limit makes the issue more vital, and the issue makes the time more important.

As vital as the terminal date is to the thriller, it can work by itself only in short novels. If the writer wants to produce long books, something must be done to keep up the pressure in the middle of the plot, between setting the terminal date and its advent. To fill this need, Forsyth, first, invents sets of intermediate dates within the frame of the terminal date. The action of Forsyth's novels depends upon intricate preparations which he attaches to geographical movement. He also connects time pressure to these preparations. Thus, the Jackal needs his rifle by a certain date, Shannon needs a ship before the invasion, etc. Here we get small scale doses of tension and release within the overall tension and release tied to the big issue and the terminal date. The second technique is simultaneous action. Forsyth often switches the focus of the narration to give readers an engrossing pattern of meanwhiles. Thus he goes back and forth from the Jackal to Lebel to the Special Branch to Kowalski in order to multiply the readers' commitments and, at the same time, to keep them unfulfilled. This technique, which Forsyth uses in all his novels, comes from old-fashioned serial writing practice where the writer knew and played with the fact of the difference of the time in the story and the time lapse between monthly episodes. Forsyth, however, turns to simultaneous action for more than simply the entertainment value of a narrative technique. Look back at the historical novel. In historical novels, time presents not only the background but becomes the principal issue, and the novelists show us characters who triumph or fail because of their use of time. For Forsyth, too, time tests the mettle of his characters and it redeems events from the somewhat dubious moral nature of his heroes. Time connects, for him, disparate things, like Israel's victory in the Seven Day War and Peter Miller's dead father, and although it may produce both the *Titanic* and the iceberg, as in Hardy's poem, the author shows it redeeming the world: thwarting the Jackal, exposing the Odessa organization, providing a real chance for Zangaro, and promising a real chance for peace between the West and the Soviet Union. As in *The Devil's Alternative*, Lazarell and Mishkin may be done to death by a nasty system, but after the transient characters disappear, the world gets better. It seems almost Shakespearean.

Forsyth's use of split time narration to induce suspense into the middle of his plots extends into and influences his characterization. Here he moves away from traditional thriller practice which centers on a single, moral hero who wins against all odds. Instead, he shows the action, not of the hero or villain, but protagonist and antagonist. Because of his historical bent, and because it can intensify the emotional impact of his plots, Forsyth eases up on the conventional good and bad identifications and causes his readers to make an investment in both parties. The natures of the Jackal and Lebel, of Shannon and Manson, of Munro and Drake, show precisely what Forsyth is about. In *The Day of the Jackal*, in the normal course of things, Lebel would be the single hero working against great odds to save his country from disaster. He is, in fact, the traditional thriller hero, which Forsyth suggests when he labels him "the best detective in France." As it works out, though, he is not quite alone as the focus

of our sympathies. Forsyth, first, tones down our identification with
him by linking him indirectly to the horrible and graphically
described torture of Viktor by the French Secret Police, which, by the
way, British and American readers are ready enough to believe.
Then Forsyth involves the readers with the Jackal. He does this by
describing him as the traditional English hero—tall, suave and
efficient. More than this, he attaches the term "professional" to him,
mirroring the cult of the professional which we have found in Hall.
He also catches readers' interest by involving them in the unfolding
of the technical process of preparing for an assassination. In this
way he divides the audience's sympathies, much as they are divided
at a professional sports match: the crowd may have an emotional
attachment to one side or player but it is really concerned with
watching an exciting contest. With *The Odessa File* Forsyth
switches back to the hero-villain pattern with Miller versus the
Nazis, because he can hardly make the Butcher of Riga into a
sympathetic character, but he returns to the semi-neutral pattern
with *The Dogs of War*. Here Forsyth presents three competing
factions to collide in the struggle for domination of platinum-rich
Zangaro: Manson and the interests of Big Capital, Shannon with
his secret allegiance to the General, and the Soviets who hope to
influence the platinum market. Each group and each individual has
its own plusses and minuses. Manson is a grasping and
unscrupulous capitalist, but Forsyth hooks the readers over to his
side by catching them up in watching the process of manipulating
the stock market. With the Soviets, Forsyth defuses Western anti-
Soviet bias by letting readers see Soviet scientists frustrated by the
inefficiency of centralized planning. With Shannon Forsyth needs
to counteract the moral disadvantage of his hero being a mercenary
soldier. Instead of using Shannon's plan to install the General in
Zangaro as a method of saving our estimation of his hero (he wants
to keep this for the surprise at the end of the novel) Forsyth gives
Shannon Ambleresque speeches about fighting against all sides
which want to crush the little man. Sensing that even this will not
work, Forsyth gives Shannon a hero's suicide in the face of cancer
which is supposed to redeem him through pathos and remove him
from the scene. *The Devil's Alternative* goes even further in
spreading out the readers' sympathy, interest and identification.
This novel really has no protagonist or antagonist, other than,
perhaps, Western civilization. The leaders of the U.S. and the
U.S.S.R. seem admirable in their struggles with warmongers in
their respective governments, but they also agree to the repulsive
murder of the two Ukrainians. Likewise, Adam Munro turns from

the typical, romantic, rebellious secret service hero into a murderer, and Andrew Drake, whatever his quixotic attractions for readers, is ready to loose a million gallons of oil into the North Sea. In every case, Forsyth introduces potential heroes and villains in whom the readers invest sympathy and establish other attachments, only to unseat this, and then he reestablishes the moral alignment through the final scenes—the Jackal is a murderer and Drake is a fanatic. Doing this, Forsyth certainly intends to magnify the thriller element in his novels, but he also reinforces a historical point, that the culture survives, forgetting individuals who helped or hindered it.

In writing this chapter I have not used one quotation from Forsyth's novels, and this indicates something about the nature of the books. They are fundamentally composed of background material and plot. The people in them may do earth-shaking things, but they do not say much which arrests the readers. Forsyth's action certainly implies things, but his characters, with few exceptions, do not put meaning into words. This, too, may be one of the attractions of Forsyth for readers of the seventies, who, tired of rhetoric without action and action without effect, wanted to see definite things done which they, for the space and time of a novel, could believe in. This Forsyth supplies.

Chapter 18

Summary

SOME ISOLATED EXAMPLES of spy literature appear early in the nineteenth century. We can, if we want to, trace the spy story back to one of Cooper's sillier novels, *The Spy* (1821), or to Poe's detective tale, "The Purloined Letter" (1845). We do not gain much information about the British spy novel from these works, and, although both writers were widely known in Britain, neither *The Spy* nor "The Purloined Letter" has much to do with evolution of the spy story in Britain. To find the beginning of the spy story, indeed to find the real beginnings of most popular forms, we need to look at the end of the nineteenth century. During this period the conditions of the culture virtually demanded the creation of popular literature. The 1880s and 1890s saw the spread of literacy, the increase in leisure, and the introduction of new technology in the home and in industry which would make popular literature inevitable. Individual writers and publishers ranged widely to find plots, characters and themes which would attract the new mass audience. In the 1880s we see the heyday of the schoolboy Imperial adventure story directed or redirected at an adult audience with Stevenson's *Treasure Island* (1883) and Haggard's *King Solomon's Mines* (1886). We see Doyle really starting the detective story band wagon with *A Study in Scarlet* (1887) and we also note Anthony Hope's political fantasies beginning with *The Prisoner of Zenda* (1894). Now, it seems as if I am leading up to a pat formula for the genesis of the spy novel: Imperial adventure story, plus detective story, plus Ruritanian fantasy equals the spy novel. This formula certainly accounts for John Buchan's novels, especially the later ones about Dickson McCunn, but Buchan did not start the spy novel. He got much of his inspiration to start writing thrillers from E. Phillips Oppenheim, and Oppy comes from altogether different traditions.

The first spy novels in Britain were products of William LeQueux and E. Phillips Oppenheim. LeQueux and Oppy drew their fictional materials from the Sensation Novel, from the love romance and from the war prophecy novel. All these forms blossomed in the 1880s. They crystalized into the spy novel when the Dreyfus Case rocketed espionage and its sentimental potential into the public eye.

282

Joining Dreyfus material with war prophecy themes and with characters and settings from the love romance and the Sensation Novel, Oppenheim and LeQueux created the spy novel in the late 1890s. Their novels are, however, so trite, contrived, bloated and badly written that what we see in the next decade is several other writers trying to modify or destroy their sentimental and inept fictions and trying to direct interest in spies along other lines, to other classes of readers than the largely female audience aimed at by LeQueux and Oppenheim. Conrad, with *The Secret Agent* (1907) and *Under Western Eyes* (1911), slashes away at the Byronic pomposity of LeQueux and Oppy. He tries to give spying back to the pathetic, grubby people who do the dirty work, and he directs the attention of highly literate readers to the issues of espionage. On a more mundane level, Erskine Childers, in *The Riddle of the Sands* (1903), directs spy fiction toward a male audience instead of the lady typists of LeQueux and Oppenheim, and he began the process of adapting spy material to the adventure story.

During its first decade and a half, British novels of international intrigue repeated certain popular themes. First of all, many did not deal with spies and spying in Britain but intended to show readers the rotten state of European governments and their slimy approach to international relations. LeQueux, in *The Day of Temptation* (1899) and *Behind the Throne* (1905) shows readers the dreadful state of affairs in Italy, just as Oppenheim in *The Mysterious Mr. Sabin* (1898) actually deals with the internal affairs of France. When the early spy writers touch on Britain, they always work on or try to work up the nation's paranoia. LeQueux, Oppenheim and Childers tell British readers that just about everybody in the world wants a piece of England's Empire, and that most nations are not above invading England itself to glut their own colonial appetites. Going as far back as 1898 Germany is the chief potential gobbler, but Russia in Kipling's *Kim* (1901) and Buchan's *The Half Hearted (1900)* is also out there slavering over Afghanistan. In most of the spy novels of this beginning period, defense plans or papers of some sort provide the principal espionage interest. This, of course, reflects old-fashioned, fortress-oriented military thinking, but, more importantly for the writers, it ties in with the palpitating and agonizing dilemmas of blackmail. Thus instead of chasing papers around as secret agents will do in the twenties and thirties, people in the novels of the nineties simply moan over them. With the exception of Conrad, though, most writers used espionage as a container into which to pump other material from the sentimental effluent of Oppy and LeQueux, to the spiritual concerns of Kipling.

Shortly before the First World War the spy novel went through its second birth—this time with the detective story, the adventure tale and the political fantasy standing as god-parents. What the anemic traditions of the spy novel needed was a spy writer like Buchan who would inject new life into the form and bend it more significantly toward a male audience, or at least away from the hypothetical audience fashioned around LeQueux's and Oppenheim's conceptions of what shop girls wanted to read. Buchan brought to the form a good dose of Stevenson's adventure writing, as well as the moral significance of Bunyan and the love for wood-craft found in Baden-Powell's military works and later in the Boy Scout movement. Richard Hannay moves out of the ritzy, perfume-scented saloons of Oppy and LeQueux, and he shows, in the traditions of the schoolboy novel, the virtues of the healthy, responsible, active man.

During the First World War there was a general move away from the rococo fripperies of the nineties and toward realism—toward it versus to it. Oppenheim takes up the putative spies behind the actual zeppelin raids on London and the Battle of Jutland's impact on public morale. In *Greenmantle* (1916) and *Mr. Standfast* (1919), Buchan deals with actual battles. Valentine Williams uses Mara Hari in *Okewood of the Secret Service* (1919). In these books, too, action and suspense take over from the sentiment of the spy novels of the first wave. Even these, though, contain an awful lot of heroic moonshine in their modifications of real espionage to fit the plotting and character patterns of the adventure yarn.

After the war we can follow the spy novel developing in what is essentially the school of Buchan, for Buchan had established a vogue for the adventure story in which an international political objective stands at the end of the adventure road instead of the traditional objects of treasure, or self, or family. George Valentine Williams falls into this school, but the best known of Buchan's followers was H.C. McNeile, or "Sapper." With the Bulldog Drummond novels, Sapper adopted Buchan's adventure formula to the uses of blatant militarism, overt national paranoia and vigilante justice, but he also heightened the humor potential of the spy novel. Sapper's novels seem like college rags perpetrated by boisterous, dunderheaded and sadistic undergraduates. Francis Beeding follows the Buchan formula, too, but he adds Wodehousean humor instead of Sapperian brainlessness.

Directly after the war many writers were at a loss for antagonists for their spy books. For a time the Red Menace reared its head, especially in books written about the time of the General Strike. Agatha Christie's *The Secret Adversary* (1922), Sapper's *The Black Gang* (1922) and Oppenheim's *Miss Brown of The XYO* (1927) all reflect fears of anarchy and bolshevism. By and large, though, Soviet communism appears in relatively few books of the twenties and thirties. Instead writers opted for the Master Crook, the megalomaniac intent on taking over the world, or at least part of it. Thus there were the villain in Buchan's *The Three Hostages* (1924), Sapper's Carl Peterson, Williams' Clubfoot, Beeding's long line of power-made geniuses, as well as other writers' gangster kings intent on world domination. As we move into the thirties, there is a tendency to fuse the Master Criminal with the armaments manufacturer, witnessed not only by Williams' *The Fox Prowls* (1939) and Sapper's *Bulldog Drummond at Bay* (1935), but also by the villains of more sophisticated writers like Ambler and Greene.

From the late twenties, there began a small but powerful move away from the jocular, action-fixated spy novel. First there was Somerset Maugham's collection of short stories, *Ashenden, The British Agent* (1927), which reflects on the author's low-keyed intelligence work during the First World War. Buchan himself wrote *The Prince of the Captivity* (1933) in the early thirties, a novel largely devoted to social and political ideas rather than perilous deeds. Early in the thirties, too, Greene began to use the spy novel as a means of examining man's spiritual condition, and at the end of the decade Household combined Greene's exploration of the conscience with Buchan's early adventure orientation. Also, late in the thirties Ambler, in *Epitaph for a Spy* (1938), reintroduced Conrad's stress on the little people who are the labor force of the espionage corporation.

World War Two was not really a boom time for spy novels. We find Beeding turning to the *roman a clef* with his books on the Fall of France. Greene's *The Ministry of Fear* (1943) and Coles' *Drink to Yesterday* (1940) attempt different varieties of objectivity toward Germans and German agents. The most significant movement in the spy novel during the war was Cheyney's introduction of the hard-boiled hero and his praise of the morality of violence. Gone, or almost gone, is the sportsman spy, and very present is the tough guy spy who is as violent as the enemy, but smarter and right because he is an Englishman and on the correct side. Since all these wartime motifs intimately involve people, we also see a shift in the objects of spy books. Between the wars spy writers gravitated toward the game of "who's got the papers," or the chase plot involving a secret weapon. During the war, though, writers began to look more closely at the human personality—whether from the political, moral or psychological point of view. Sometimes this produced bubble-brained concoctions like Cheyney's Dark books, but it also produced *The Ministry of Fear*.

After the war there occurred the inevitable mop-up of Nazi stragglers, but in the fifties British spy writers again found themselves without purpose since they had lost their villains. Just as after the First World War the Soviet Union serves as a bogey in some novels, but these seem half-hearted and anemic. Fleming's villains are not really communists, and, in spite of an attempt or two, the Soviet Union passes out of the works of Ambler, Household and Coles. To fill the void left by the lack of an antagonist, writers turned to other plot patterns. Fleming, in his own bizarre and incompetent way, combined the old Master Crook with the gangster in a new variety of hard-boiled story. Coles, Household and later Ambler adopted the organizing pattern of the picaresque novel as a means of dealing with the new world. Even though the picaresque motive lies under many spy novels of the adventure tradition, few writers really exploited it until after the war when it could serve both as an entertaining medium and as a vehicle for saying serious things, and then passing over them.

The fifites also generated the material which was to form the core of the British espionage novel of the sixties. During the early fifties several spy trials and several defections to the Soviet Union exposed what seemed to be serious weaknesses in the British systems of education and government. Allan Nunn May and Claus Fuchs were tried and convicted of passing atomic secrets to the Soviets, and Bruno Pontecorvo, Guy Burgess, Maclean, and, later, Kim Philby skipped out on their government jobs and went into exile in the Soviet Union. These things had little impact on the spy writing of the fifties, partly because of many writers' inability to handle them, partly because public sensitivity was still too raw to want to have its nose rubbed in what some viewed as national failure, and partly because of the lingering threat of libel suits while Kim Philby lived, unconvicted, in England. Writers of the sixties, however, took up the subject of the defectors. LeCarré, Deighton, Hall, Anthony Burgess and Greene all eventually came to the subject of the home grown spies. Most of these writers, however, did not use it as an occasion for witch hunting or class bickering, but turned to introspective analysis of what Britain had made of herself in the twentieth century. Thus the theme of bureaucratic incompetence burgeons in LeCarré, Deighton and Greene. Americans change from bumptious younger brothers into aloof and sometimes malign cousins. Computers and systems analysts replace the common room and the gathering of dons. In response to this new world, some writers posit a return to the small is beautiful ethic of a limited, quasi-pastoral existence: Greene seems to do this and Household certainly does.

Average readers, however, can absorb only so much gloom and doom. Popular literature can only come close to reality for short spurts, for if it continues to be too "significant" the public will desert it. In the seventies, therefore, spy novels returned to the simpler world of the thriller. To make the thriller suitable for the literate middle class audience, writers turned first to combining it with the principles and practices of the historical novel, as Forsyth does in *The Day of the Jackal* (1971). Writers like Deighton returned to the war prophecy novel, but turned the prophecy backward to World War II instead of forward to wars with imagined enemies like Surinam or Pitcairn Island. Thus books like *S.S.—G.B.* (1979), and Ken Follett's *The Eye of the Needle* (1978) allow the writer and the reader to enjoy manipulating events without the risk that these things may come true.

For ninety years now the spy novel has been the most popular kind of fiction in both Britain and America. From the literary point of view this has happened because the form is loose enough to adapt to many sorts of plots and characters, and unselfconscious enough to be able to borrow elements from other kinds of popular fiction from the detective story to the love romance. Where else could one find writers as different as Conrad and Sidney Horler or characters as diverse as George Smiley and James Bond? From the practical point of view, the spy novel has hit upon the ideal popular hero, for even if readers realize that there are real spies, they have little information about them. To date spies have not suffered the same comparison to reality that other popular heroes have—although the rash of CIA exposes in the US may have some impact on this. In 1915 Baden Powell described spies as ghosts and a form of this remains in the contemporary description of spies as spooks. Like science fiction, spy novels are largely useless in projecting the future or in influencing much current social or political thinking. Since the teens, however, the spy book has stopped trying to predict the next war and has shifted to more modest, more concrete fictional aims. From its very beginning the spy novel has sought to give lessons in deportment, from Oppenheim's and LeQueux's ginky aristocrats, to the heroes of the sixties, keel-hauled by events and institutional bullies. This makes the spy novel run, and so does the fact that the spy book, after a decorous and necessary time lag, mirrors the nation's view of itself. Thus, in the past ninety years spy novels graph Britain's change from a stately Empire to a nation of plucky sportsmen, to a society dependent on a few morally right tough guys, to a people living on a small island who need to fit their lives to existence in a limited world, but a limited world rich with history, pastoral beauty and fruitful human relationships. Here we have the useful element of spy fiction which is also its *dulce*. *Dulce*, too, are the cheap thrills, the temporary constriction and release of the readers' emotions, and the simple pleasures of seeing enemies confounded and friends married off. These parts are as temporary as governments, but when the spy novel gives way to or is subsumed by another form of popular entertainment, it will leave some enduring books: *The Secret Agent, The Ministry of Fear, Rogue Male, Tinker, Tailor, Soldier, Spy* and perhaps *The Intercom Conspiracy, Funeral in Berlin* and a few others. It will also leave behind a record of craftmanship which other kinds of popular literature will wonder at and admire.